The Briti

The short story remains a crucial – if neglected – part of the British literary heritage. This up-to-date critical overview maps the main strands and figures that shaped the British short story and novella from the 1850s to the present.

The British Short Story:

- offers new readings of both classic and forgotten texts in a clear, jargon-free way
- locates the short story within its original contexts – from the mid-Victorian period, through the fin de siècle and First World War, the 1920s and 1930s and on to the present day
- combines discussion of different modes of publication and a range of literary contexts (e.g. 'Modernism', 'Gothic', 'the New Woman')
- considers key themes (e.g. class, women's roles and ambitions, crime, the city and empire)
- leads the way to further reading and research on individual authors and genres, their output and contexts, and the short story more broadly.

Emma Liggins is Lecturer in Literature at Manchester Metropolitan University. She is the author of *George Gissing, the Working Woman and Urban Culture*.

Andrew Maunder is Principal Lecturer in Literature at the University of Hertfordshire. His publications include *The Facts on File Companion to the British Short Story*, and he is the author of *Bram Stoker* in the *Writers and Their Work* series.

Ruth Robbins is Head of the School of Cultural Studies at Leeds Metropolitan University. Her publications include *Subjectivity, Pater to Forster, 1873–1924* and *Literary Feminisms*, all in Palgrave Macmillan's *Transitions* series.

Outlining Literature

Published

The British Short Story: Emma Liggins, Andrew Maunder and Ruth Robbins

Literature and Science: Charlotte Sleigh

Outlining Literature
Series Standing Order
ISBN 978–0–0230–28483–8 hardcover
ISBN 978–0–0230–24898–4 paperback

You can receive future titles in this series as they are published by placing a standing order. Please contact your bookseller or, in case of difficulty, write to us at the address below with your name and address, the title of the series and the ISBN quoted above.

Customer Services Department, Macmillan Distribution Ltd, Houndmills, Basingstoke, Hampshire RG21 6XS, England

The British Short Story

Emma Liggins

Andrew Maunder

Ruth Robbins

palgrave
macmillan

First published 2011 by
PALGRAVE MACMILLAN

Palgrave Macmillan in the UK is an imprint of Macmillan Publishers Limited,
registered in England, company number 785998, of Houndmills, Basingstoke,
Hampshire RG21 6XS.

Palgrave Macmillan in the US is a division of St Martin's Press LLC,
175 Fifth Avenue, New York, NY 10010.

Palgrave Macmillan is the global academic imprint of the above companies
and has companies and representatives throughout the world.

Palgrave® and Macmillan® are registered trademarks in the United States,
the United Kingdom, Europe and other countries.

ISBN 978–0–230–55170–1 hardback
ISBN 978–0–230–55171–8 paperback

This book is printed on paper suitable for recycling and made from fully
managed and sustained forest sources. Logging, pulping and manufacturing
processes are expected to conform to the environmental regulations of the
country of origin.

A catalogue record for this book is available from the British Library.

A catalog record for this book is available from the Library of Congress.

10 9 8 7 6 5 4 3 2 1
20 19 18 17 16 15 14 13 12 11

Printed and bound in Great Britain by
CPI Antony Rowe, Chippenham and Eastbourne

Contents

Acknowledgements

We would like to thank the following people for their help and support in completing this book: Lorna Shelley, Berthold Schoene and Robert Graham who offered invaluable advice and help with proofreading; Kenyetta Cohen for her secretarial assistance; and Kate Haines at Palgrave for her support and encouragement for this project. The students at our various institutions have been very important in the shaping of this book, and we're grateful for their engagement. At Edgehill, the students on the British and American Short Story module from 2001–3, which Emma Liggins taught with Robert Graham. At Leeds Metropolitan University, the students of the Reading Short Narratives module (2006–present), developed by Ruth Robbins with Andrew Lawson. And at Hertfordshire the students of the module Between the Acts: Late Victorian and Edwardian Literature (2008–present) taught by Andrew Maunder.

1
Introduction: What Is a Short Story?

This question has always exercised critics and commentators on the short story, and often involves them in extraordinary contortions to avoid the simplest and most circular answer: a short story is a story – a narrative sequence of events, episodes or connected emotions – which is short. Even if the term 'story' is reasonably uncontentious (and frankly it is not entirely agreed upon), shortness introduces an element of relativity which causes major problems for the short-story critic. A short story is short generally in contrast to the longer prose narrative the novel. Ian Reid goes so far as to say that 'in its current usage "short story" is generally applied to almost any kind of prose narrative briefer than a novel', and shortness can lead to accusations of 'slightness and slickness',[1] of lesser status and lesser seriousness than the larger work of prose fiction. Size, apparently, matters. Critics therefore often operate by analogy with other forms to describe the short story's special status. As Dominic Head has suggested, visual metaphors in particular are frequently used,[2] although these have the disadvantage of presuming a specific patterning in short fiction, forgetting that all narrative is essentially temporal, understood through time, rather than primarily spatial as visual art is. Thus, Valerie Shaw suggests that the volume of short stories can be usefully likened to an art exhibition,[3] and William Boyd, in a 2004 *Guardian* article, writes that the short story is comparable to an exquisite miniature painting, 'art in highly concentrated form', whose effects are akin to those of the multivitamin pill: 'a compressed blast of discerning, intellectual pleasure'.[4] Or the critic turns to metaphors derived from poetry: the short story is to the novel what the lyric is to the epic – the first is personal, compressed, fragmented and emotional, and the second is universal, expansive, totalising and objective. This is fine as far as it goes, but it has the risk attendant on any binary definition: that one side of the opposition is more highly valued than the other, which has indeed been the tendency – the personal and compressed elements of short fiction are less 'important' somehow than the objective, universal, expanded story of the epic.

This is a book which seeks to consider the British short story. It is therefore ironic and potentially dangerous for us to turn first of all for our definition to the American short-story writer, poet and critic Edgar Allan Poe (1809–49). As Harold Orel has argued, the British tradition in short fiction is very different from that of the Americans, for whom the short story is a kind of national genre: 'the English short story', he writes, 'developed independently of Poe's philosophy of composition'.[5] We should therefore be wary of assuming that Poe's strictures on the development of the genre are strictly applicable to a different national context. Yet Poe certainly is – perhaps reasonably, given the uncanny nature of his fictions – the ghost who haunts the feast of critical accounts of the short story, and despite cautions and caveats about his influence we cannot ignore his presence. In North American magazines (*Burton's Gentleman's Magazine, Graham's Magazine, The Pioneer*) Poe was writing for and about a specifically American version of the short story, which he named the 'tale'. American literature is absolutely not just British or English literature with a different accent; it has a particular history and set of contexts. Although the two countries, as Oscar Wilde (1854–1900) once put it, are divided by a common language, their founding myths and central stories are very different. Nevertheless, in defining the nature of the short story, we could do considerably worse than turn to Poe's comments on it.

In a series of essays and reviews from the 1840s in which he repeats and refines his ideas, Poe describes the short prose tale as his ideal form of fiction for the modern world. He was seeking to develop a new genre that would speak specifically to and for the 'new' country America, contrasting the modernity of the United States with the dusty, moribund traditions of fiction in Europe, particularly Britain. In a letter to his friend Charles Anthon, he wrote: 'I perceived that the whole … energetic, busy spirit of the age tended wholly … to the Magazine literature – to the curt, the terse, the well-timed, and the readily-diffused, in preference to the old forms of the verbose and ponderous & the inaccessible.'[6] Curtness and terseness – the virtues of brevity – are extolled above the European traditions of verbosity and ponderousness. We should not, however, assume that this was an entirely disinterested or utterly aesthetic choice. Poe was extremely aware of the marketplace for which he sought to write. At least as much as he is making a plea for shortness, he is also telling his reader what will sell. And although he is discussing the America of the 1830s and 1840s, much of the commentary about magazine literature and the *zeitgeist* of modernity was also true for Britain during the same period.

In a review of *Twice-Told Tales* (1837) by Nathaniel Hawthorne (1804–64), Poe laid out his aesthetic and practical stall for the advantages of the shorter form. He began with the practical consideration of length to define what he meant by the prose tale which was his ideal form of reading. Such a tale would require 'from a half-hour to one or two hours in its perusal'. This is better than reading a novel because '[w]orldly interests intervening during the pauses of perusal, modify, annul, or counteract [its effects]'.[7] His aim was that the reader's 'soul' should be entirely at the disposal of the author's whim during the period of reading. This pragmatic consideration – that readers can sit and read only for relatively limited periods – leads to Poe's second key intervention in defining the genre, the question of skilful plotting which combines with timing to make the reader utterly focused on the text. When it comes to plot, he dismissed mere complexity as the key issue and defined the proper plot via an architectural (a spatial) metaphor: 'The greatest involution of incident will not result in plot; which, properly defined, is *that which no part can be displaced without ruin to the whole.* It may be described as a building so dependently constructed, that to change the position of a single brick is to overthrow the entire fabric.'[8] This means for Poe that the story must be constructed in such a way that its weight is distributed largely towards the ending. He advises would-be writers, for instance, to begin with the denouement and work backwards from there. The twist in the tale/tail, the shock or surprise of a short story, is fundamental to his discussion.

Not unnaturally, therefore, Poe's short stories tend towards the sensational, the shocking, the ghostly, weird and uncanny. Indeed, in a piece published in 1838, 'How to Write a *Blackwood's* Article', he wrote: 'Sensations are the great things after all. Should you ever be drowned or hung, be sure and make a record of your sensations – they will be worth to you ten guineas a sheet.'[9] His stories also show – as this quotation would suggest – a lively eye to the financial main chance. Thus, although there are problems with adopting Poe as a founding father for the British short story – not least that most Victorian short stories, as Orel points out, were considerably longer than Poe prescribed[10] – he did identify two key ways in which the short story might be understood. The first is that the short story has its origins in magazine fiction: it is commercial fiction, made for the marketplace, often as filler material to pad out the editorial matter and occupy the space between advertise-ments. That economic fact has a major impact on its aesthetic shaping. It is part of the argument of this book that the contexts of production, including economic contexts, often have an determining effect on the aesthetics of what is produced: romance and finance come together in the short story, perhaps even more acutely than they do in the novel, because the short story's ephemeral life in periodical publication makes that relationship much more immediate.

A second point to draw from Poe is his emphasis on 'perusal' – on *reading*. Short stories have probably existed, in the sense of short nar-ratives being told, since the dawn of time. Dean Baldwin's impres-sive anthology *The Riverside Anthology of Short Fiction: Convention and Innovation*, for example, begins with an Aesop fable and includes works such as a parable from the Gospel of St Luke, a story from the medieval author Boccaccio's (1313–75) *Decameron*, and a fairy tale rewritten by Charles Perrault (1628–1703) in the seventeenth century.[11] Our defini-tion of the British short story, however, depends crucially on the short form as *a written form that is meant to be read*. Almost all examples of the shorter forms before the beginning of the nineteenth century, even if they were written down, are actually stories that inhabit an oral tradi-tion. They are considerably more formulaic (set once upon a time in a land far away, with structures such as the three wishes and easily leg-ible morals) than those that were published in the periodical press of Victorian England. And although some genre forms, such as the ghost story, bear the traces of an oral tradition (a striking number of Victorian ghost stories begin with a narrator telling his or her experiences to a domestic audience around a winter hearth, dramatising the oral even as they leave it behind), they are literary rather than oral forms, presuming a single audience member at a time rather than a collective audience. The unity of impression that Poe strove for in his fictions concerns the impression made on a single reader. The emphasis for us, therefore, is on *texts*, their production by writers and their reception by readers.

A third element of definition for us is the question of what we mean by 'British'. A number of the writers to whom we pay attention are not strictly British. Katherine Mansfield (1888–1923) was born in New Zealand, Henry James (1843–1916) in the United States, James Joyce (1882–1941) in Ireland – and there are other examples. In these specific cases, Mansfield was a colonial subject, but one who deliberately (wil-fully even) made the journey to Europe, and her first audiences were British because her works were published in British organs and by British publishers. Henry James is more easily explained: in 1915, during the

First World War, he naturalised as a British subject in solidarity with the country in which he spent a considerable portion of his life and writing career. More controversially, Joyce, the Irishman, was for all his early life a British subject, since at that point in history Ireland was part of the empire. He was utterly resistant to the British, but eschewed learning the Irish language and wrote always in the alien mother tongue of the hegemonic power. We have been pragmatic about our definitions of Britishness. Geographical boundaries are not everything, and history changes them.

As we have already suggested, then, compared with writers and critics in the United States, where the short story has for a long time been recognisably a form with its own moral, social and aesthetic dimensions, British writers and critics have been far less willing to write or theorise about it. Certainly it is the case that when we look at mid-nineteenth-century Britain, there is no exact starting-point; it is impossible to find an Edgar Allen Poe-like figure who advocates the kind of unified effect championed by early American critics. And a great deal of the influence on the British short story has come from elsewhere, from figures such as the French realist writer Guy de Maupassant (1850–93) and the expatriate American Henry James. The appearance in 1871 of James's 'The Passionate Pilgrim', a story about (among other things) the clash between American and European cultures, seemed to show how the short story or novella could offer 'a surface really much larger than the mere offered face of the work', as James later put it.[12] The fiction of the prolific Russian dramatist and short-story writer Anton Chekhov (1860–1904), which included more than fifty stories, also influenced the development of the form, particularly in its modernist incarnations. Translated into English in the early years of the twentieth century, his tales of frustrated love affairs, economic worries and the dullness of middle-class marriage, which admirably condensed the subject matter of the nineteenth-century novel into key episodes in a character's life, offered a blueprint for the realist short story in Britain during the twentieth century. His interest in character and psychology, and his skill at dialogue gained from his success as a dramatist, were copied by important modernist writers of the 1920s, including Katherine Mansfield, who cited his work as a key influence on her own. The British short story is thus a complex, multiform creature. It is made up of relationships between the material world of the demands of publishing and the marketplace, specific aesthetic schemas and programmes, the conventions of genre and the influence of the writers of other nations. It is a mongrel or, perhaps more kindly, a hybrid, and its names and forms are legion.

Histories of the form

In terms of its history, the general consensus has been that in Britain it was not until late in the nineteenth century that the short story was born. The year 1884 has been seen as a key date in the history of the British short story. Roger Luckhurst records that this was the year the term 'short story' was used for the first time, and this dating reinforces the impression of the genre's relative modernity.[13] However, merely bestowing an official birth date on something does not mean that it did not exist before its apparent genesis. So, while it has been convenient to suggest that the short story did not flourish before the burst of activity during the 1880s, it is still possible to find a wide range of examples of the form from the earlier part of the nineteenth century – a point made in a recent study by Tim Killick.[14] He notes that there are a plethora of texts which have some kind of relationship to the modern short story – works by Maria Edgeworth (1767–1849), Walter Scott (1771–1832), John Galt (1779–1839) and Mary Russell Mitford (1787–1855) being notable examples. What we tend to see is that their shapes, together with the labels given them ('tale', 'sketch', 'fable', 'confessional'), are different. They are episodic and often connected by continuing characters and themes. Nor are these the only early examples. The 1820s saw the emergence of the street-wise, heroic detective as encapsulated in Thomas Gaspey's (1788–1871) *Richmond: Scenes in the Life of a Bow Street Runner* (1827), Samuel Warren's (1807–77) *Passages from the Diary of a Late Physician* (1832) and William Russell's (nd) 'Recollections of a Detective Police Officer' (*Chambers Edinburgh Journal*, 1849, published under the pseudonym Constable Waters). These writings – which often claimed to be based on 'real life', especially crime, and which were therefore frequently concerned with threats to property – began to exercise a strong fascination for the newly literate, newly moneyed nineteenth-century middle class. In the works of these writers we see the concise sketch or anecdote being turned into a story with a definite – often suspenseful – plot. These are deliberately 'realist' stories in that they use recognisable characters and carefully described settings and focus on the dangers and demands of modern society for the individual; they also reflect the widespread interest by mid-century in 'sensational' stories of crime and deviance, often taking place within the supposedly safe confines of the family home – something discussed in more detail in Chapter 3.

Explanations for the apparently late emergence of the short story in Britain, compared with the United States, have taken several forms. Wendell Harris, for instance, has argued that because of the dominance of the novel, 'the assumption that fiction should serve to reflect historical continuity and relationships posed a major obstacle to the writing of short fiction through much of the nineteenth century'.[15] The main reason, perhaps, was economic rather than aesthetic. Novels paid better, Brander Matthews noted in 1884, 'and therefore the man with a genius for story-telling takes to writing novels. In libraries and magazines there is a demand for long novels, and so we have serial novels and three-volume novels.'[16] And as Orel puts it: 'Novels were the central commodity, and short stories a by-product, filler material; the latter did not pay well ... books that collected short stories of a single author were chancy undertakings throughout the entire century.'[17] Yet, as we shall see in the early chapters of this book, it is outmoded to think of the Victorian reading public as existing purely on a diet of long novels, as demonstrated by recent research into nineteenth-century periodicals and the lesser-known fiction of canonical writers, as well as the huge output of popular writers now entering the canon such as Wilkie Collins (1824–99), Mary Elizabeth Braddon (1835–1915) and Sarah Grand (1854–1943). Almost all the major Victorian novelists wrote short stories at some point in their career, and many of these stories are now available online or in new editions.

Such research shows up the dangers in telling an evolutionary version of the history of any form. It is a tendency that can be seen in early histories of the novel, such as Ian Watt's magisterial *The Rise of the Novel* (1958), which traces the progression of the most popular form of fiction from the episodic, picaresque novels of Daniel Defoe (*c*.1660–1731), through the ironised and distanced quasi-epic novels of Henry Fielding (1707–54) and the much more personalised and intimate narratives of Samuel Richardson (1689–1761), in the service of an argument that the novel reached maturity and apotheosis in the works of Jane Austen (1775–1817), who combined the ironic distance of Fielding with the intimate concerns of Richardson. That evolutionary history has been repeatedly revised during the intervening half-century. Similarly, it would be all too easy to argue that the sensationalist tales of horror published in *Blackwood's Edinburgh Magazine* from the 1820s and 1830s onwards morphed into more sophisticated and domesticated narratives as the short story developed during the nineteenth century, reaching, in turn, the height of its development in the aesthetic blooms of modernist writers such as James Joyce, Katherine Mansfield and Virginia Woolf (1882–1941) in the early twentieth century. The most usual narrative trajectory argument is that the short story was distinguished from its short-fiction predecessors by an increasing realism, even paradoxically in stories such as ghost narratives, which went to considerable lengths to construct a version of authenticity to ensure a greater effect of horror when the monster entered. Realism in the smaller scale of the short story as opposed to the expansive scale of the novel, however, was problematic in that the short story could not provide a totalising narrative, which in many ways was the point of realism. Thus although there were notable experiments with social realist fiction (Arthur Morrison's [1863–1945] *Tales of Mean Streets*, 1896, for instance, or Rudyard Kipling's [1865–1936] brilliantly brutal 'The Record of Badalia Herodsfoot', 1890), the direction of travel of the short story at the end of the nineteenth century was towards increasing emphasis on psychology (internal events) as opposed to exterior happenings and their meanings. When modernist writers adopted the shorter form, they continued this trend, reducing external circumstances until – as in the stories of Jean Rhys (1890–1979) – there is almost no event at all. The consequence of this move from the carefully plotted fictions to the plotless story, as Clare Hanson has termed it,[18] is a greater emphasis on mood, psychology, emotion. The shift in interest is from *what happened* to *what is felt*, and from *what is told* to *how it is told*.

But quite early, in fact, the commentators and critics discerned the technical complexity of the short story. In a discussion of the short story in the mainstream journal *The Nineteenth Century* in March 1898, Frederick Wedmore emphasised the variety to be found in short fiction, which could take the form of an episode, a fairy tale, a tale of the uncanny, a dialogue or a comedy, but also, more in keeping with the fiction popular at the time, 'a vision of the sordid street, a record of heroism ... an analysis of an obscure calling, a glimpse at a forgotten quarter'. What it emphatically could never be was 'a novel in a nutshell', a definition found to be particularly unhelpful because serious readers were easily aware that 'it involves the exercise almost of a different art'. Rather, as late-Victorian examples were beginning to demonstrate, the story shares with drama 'the indispensableness of compression' and is often structured around 'omissions ... the brevity of its allusiveness'.[19] This is a comment on the Victorian short story, but it would not be out of place in a discussion of the modernist version of the form. And the concerns of late-Victorian women – especially the so-called New Woman writers, who, in championing greater opportunities for women, often made use of the relative freedoms of the compressed short narrative form – predict and pave the way for the psychologised fictions of the modernists. Thus, a little later, D. H. Lawrence (1885–1930) wrote in a letter of 1908, 'The great thing to do in a short story is to select the salient details – a few striking details to make a sudden swift impression',[20] gesturing towards the elisions and editorial decisions necessary in a shorter narrative which gives an 'impression' of an ultimately believable character, a glimpse or snapshot of ordinary life constructed as much from what is left out as from what appears on the pages.

For Lawrence and Wedmore, compression is an aesthetic choice, a resistance against the sprawling three-volume novel. For the New Woman writers, on the other hand, there were practical considerations in their choice. As Jane Eldridge Miller suggests, they were dissatisfied with the marriage plots of the Victorian three-volume novel and resisted the conventions of its narrative line by resisting its conventional plots.[21] As we shall see, short fiction offered an opportunity to explore new ways of being, sketches which both diagnosed the problems of femininity for their audiences and offered some alternatives to the marriage plot. Even more practical, however, was the consideration that their feminist agenda was not popular with the mainstream publishing presses and distributors such as W.H. Smith. Publication in organs such as suffrage journals and other little magazines was their only option in some cases. Yet again, the aesthetic and the practical, economic issues of publishing came together – a story that continued to be repeated, though less acutely, as the twentieth century went on.

By the 1890s, the decline in popularity of three-volume Victorian novels, many of which ran to 700 pages or more, enabled the rise of the short story in the literary marketplace. As Angelique Richardson has argued, 'in a speeded-up world, short stories offered immediate gratification; they did not necessarily bring closure, but neither did they leave their readers with the cliffhanger that had sold serialized novels'.[22] The form became an effective vehicle for explorations of the modernist technique of stream of consciousness perfected by James Joyce and Virginia Woolf in the 1910s and 1920s, in which the narration follows the arbitrary thought patterns of a character. Readers and consumers during the early decades of the twentieth century developed a taste for radical forms of creativity, for what has been referred to as 'the shock of the new', so the short story flourished in a culture which also enjoyed the work of Post-Impressionist and Cubist artists such as Vincent van Gogh (1853–90), Henri Matisse (1869–1954) and Pablo Picasso (1881–1973) and the experimental minimalist poetry of Ezra Pound (1885–1972), Mina Loy (1882–1966) and H.D. (Hilda Doolittle, 1886–1961). Literature generally, and the short story in particular, took lessons from the visual arts and from poetry, rejecting the organising device of plot, focusing on the interior rather than exterior lives of characters, disrupting chronology as a structuring order for narrative, shifting point of view and making increasing use of images and symbols to indicate moods (rather than narrate moral views), much as poetry is often supposed to do. But, as the various chapters on genre fiction and the sections on the twentieth-century story in the present volume indicate, the move into modernist modes of writing did not hold true for all short fiction. The evolutionary story of the move to sophistication and technical experiment belies the fact that the vast majority of short fiction published between 1900 and the present has continued to be written in broadly realist terms and often in obedience to the dictates of popular generic forms such as the romance, the adventure story and the detective story.

The decline in the number of periodicals being published in the mid-twentieth century, and the vogue for more conservative forms of fiction, might suggest something of a fallow period in terms of the development of short fiction in the aftermath of modernism[23] – another corrective to the view that the form has always renewed itself and moved towards ever greater complexity. In 1940, Woodrow Wyatt reported that the British short story had 'fallen on lean days'; he ascribed the decline to war-time paper shortages, together with the unwillingness of editors to take risks and the closure of several magazines. This was despite his championing of the short story as 'the poem of the modern world', amenable to being written by those who were employed in the armed services while they were between sentry duties or on leave.[24] In his discussion of post-war British short fiction, Dennis Vannatta considers the possible 'stagnation' of the form during the 1950s and 1960s, linking this to the 'uncertain market for the short story' and authors' decisions to lean towards the novel 'to project social concerns'.[25] Something – though not all – of this trajectory is evident in Malcolm Bradbury's classic anthology *The Penguin Book of Modern British Short Stories* (1988), which begins with stories by Malcolm Lowry (1909–57), Elizabeth Bowen (1899–1973) and Samuel Beckett (1906–89) – the latter about as experimental as it's possible to get – but moves to the harsher stance of two of the so-called angry young men, representatives of the 'social revolution' taking place in Britain during the 1950s: Kingsley Amis (1922–95) and Alan Sillitoe (1928–2010), who represent a return to the more traditional mode of realism. All this needs to be considered in relation to the vibrancy of the short form in the British Isles during the twentieth century, particularly in Wales, Scotland and Ireland, whose short-story writers often invoked political as well as literary alienation from the rest of Britain. Thus the Welsh twentieth-century story tradition encompassed such writers as Caradoc Evans (1878–1945), R. Hughes Williams (*c*.1878–1919), D. J. Williams (1885–1970), Kate Roberts (1891–1985), Rhys Davies (1901–78) and Glyn Jones (1905–95), some of whom wrote in Welsh rather than English. The Scottish tradition, which will be one focus of the present volume, encompassed Muriel Spark (1918–2006), Alasdair Gray (b.1934) and, more recently, Bernard MacLaverty (b.1942), James Kelman (b.1946), Margaret Elphinstone (b.1948), Janice Galloway (b.1955), Irvine Welsh (b.1958) and A. L. Kennedy (b.1965). Writing in the 1980s – a time when the economic (and literary) north–south divide which existed in Britain was becoming more acute – many Scottish writers, including Kelman and Welsh, began to use the language of the streets to give voice to the marginalised or unemployed working classes. Underlining the short story's tendency to find a position 'in the vanguard of experimental writing', Hanson has also noted that by the 1980s 'the contemporary interest in the short form [was] ... very much part of the postmodernist tendency',[26] as a diverse set of writers, including A. S. Byatt (b.1936), Angela Carter (1940–92), Ian McEwan (b.1948) and Toby Litt (b.1968), exploited the genre's capacity for fragmentation, obliquity and inconclusiveness, offering a style of writing which has maintained its popularity into the twenty-first century.

Critical approaches: the content and the form

In a story called 'The Story-Teller' (1914), Saki (pen name of Hector Hugh Munro, 1870–1916) tells what is, for him, a typically satirical tale. Saki's stories, drawing on the example of Oscar Wilde, are quietly subversive attacks on the stuffiness and conventions of Edwardian England. Recurrent characters such as Clovis and Reginald, or the host of unnamed bachelors who are the main protagonists of his stories, seek to prevent the other characters in their upper-class milieu from remaining comfortable with the habits and conventions of their privileged existence. 'The Story-Teller' narrates an uncomfortable train journey in which three very bored and therefore disruptive small children are travelling in a compartment with an accompanying aunt in the accidental presence of an anonymous bachelor. The aunt is an ineffectual guardian who is unable to keep the children in order, to the irritation of their fellow passenger. In desperation, after the bachelor has given her a pointed look and then glanced towards the communication cord, the aunt decides to tell her two nieces and her nephew a story. She begins an unenterprising and deplorably uninteresting story about a little girl who was good, made friends with everyone on account of her goodness, and was finally saved from a mad bull by a number of rescuers who admired her moral character. 'Wouldn't they have saved her if she hadn't been good?' demands the bigger of the small girls. It is exactly the question that the bachelor had wanted to ask (p. 350).[27]

Not surprisingly, the children reject this as being 'the stupidest story' they have ever heard, and one assumes that quite apart from its asininity and all-too-evident moral, the problem for them is that it is 'the same old story', a moral tale of the kind that maiden aunts always tell. It does precisely what stories for children are supposed to do – it instructs them in a moral lesson (be good) – while failing to live up to the other part of the literary bargain with its audience: it does not entertain them.

Not unnaturally, therefore, the children go back to being disruptive, until, in desperation, the bachelor decides to tell them a story of his own devising. His story, too, is about a little girl who is extremely good. Although this is quite unpromising and the children are not convinced, he holds their attention through the introduction of the unexpected: the little girl in this story is not merely good; she is 'horribly good'. 'There was a wave of reaction in favour of the story; the word horrible in connection with goodness...seemed to introduce a ring of truth that was absent from the aunt's tales of infant life' (p. 351). From the moment of this unexpected connection the bachelor has won over his audience. It is immediately clear that he is not going to tell the same old story. His little girl is given medals for goodness and, as a special privilege, is allowed to walk in the prince's gardens, playing with the pigs that are (incongruously) kept there. The bachelor embellishes his story with the kinds of detail that children like, such as the fact that one cannot keep pigs in a garden if one also wishes to grow flowers – and the prince preferred pigs to flowers: 'There was a murmur of approval at the excellence of the prince's decision; so many people would have decided the other way' (p. 352). To cut a short story even shorter, while the horribly good girl is in the prince's garden, a wolf arrives, hoping to catch a pig for supper. When the wolf spots a little girl instead, he decides that she would make a much tastier meal. She manages to hide from him, but the clanking of the medals she has won for her goodness gives away her position. The wolf eats her: 'All that was left of her were shoes, bits of clothing and the three medals for goodness' (p. 353). The pigs, incidentally, all escape unharmed.

The children love this story, commenting that it 'began badly, but it had a beautiful ending'. Predictably the aunt is less impressed: 'A most improper story to tell young children! You have undermined the effect of years of careful teaching' (p. 354). But what this story within a story demonstrates is that the aunt's careful teaching has been stultifying and ineffective. By taking the same basic ingredients – goodness, a small child, danger from a wild animal – and combining them differently, the bachelor has managed to do something new; he has twisted the tale/tail.

A critic might approach this story in a wide range of ways, many of which are broadly speaking 'contextual'; that is, they seek to place the story in a series of contexts for its production and reception, writing into the story a historical narrative that the story itself seeks to disguise. One could certainly read it as typical of Saki's oeuvre (it is very typical: maiden aunts are always stuffy and are always bested by either children or bachelors, and wild animals get to eat children, in fact or as a threat, in astounding numbers of his tales); thus one could use the relationship between the author and his various texts to provide some kind of unified view about Saki's particular interests. A biographical reading of the story would note that Saki, a child of empire, born in Burma, was sent home to England for schooling and lodged with an unsympathetic relative (an aunt, of course). The story could be seen as one of a series of acts of imaginative revenge for an unhappy childhood. And that would be quite interesting, though perhaps limited as an interpretive tool for thinking about the short story in general. One could also position the story in terms of a variety of literary histories, and our earlier comment that Wilde was an influence on Saki would certainly repay some investigation: the reversals of norms, the lightness of touch, the flouting of convention are all, perhaps, elements which Saki learned from his predecessor. Comparative studies within the author's work and beyond it, in the sub-genre of the satirical short story, are two approaches one might take. Similarly, one could use the story as evidence about a particular social class at a specific moment of British history. Why is this satire amusing? Because it speaks to a stereotype of stuffiness and conventionality that had some truth it in for the late-Victorian and Edwardian upper classes. And one could read it ideologically, for evidence about the relationship between the sexes: the responsible but dull spinster contrasted with the carefree and irresponsible bachelor tells us something about Saki's construction of gender and about the society out of which he grew. Finally, in terms of context, one might also look at how and where the story was published. In this particular case, it was first published in a collection of stories called *Beasts and Super-Beasts* in 1914, on the eve of the First World War (the varied literature of which is discussed in Chapter 7 of the present book). It consequently seems to speak to a lost world which was never quite the same again, as the phrase has it. It is unusual among the stories we consider in much of this book because it first appeared in volume form rather than in the more ephemeral periodical or magazine form, which tells us that there was a market for volumes of short fiction in the early years of the twentieth century (no publisher publishes except for money, to paraphrase Samuel Johnson [1709–84]). And, fascinatingly, it appeared in the same year as that far more famous and far more experimental volume of short fiction *Dubliners*, by James Joyce. The avant-garde and the conventional (even if it is a convention that has been somewhat subverted) co-existed in the same market and were perhaps read by some of the same audience.

Contextual approaches must always be supplemented with textual ones; indeed, the textual approach might be just as important for some kinds of critic. There is a formal symmetry to Saki's tale. Two stories are told, with the same ingredients in place; one falls flat, and the other, because of its unexpected juxtapositions and its refusal of moral teaching, is a triumphant soufflé of a fiction, at least for the internal audience. There is something to be said about the way in which the story is written, its manipulations of the conventions of oral story-telling, its insistence on the ways in which the internal audience interacts with the story (the children interrupt the bachelor, and he responds to their interruptions). And there is a metafictional element to Saki's story: it is a story about its own conception, a story about story-telling, which draws attention to the conventions in ways that stories more usually do not. It is slight and very short, but it is quite sophisticated in its manipulation of the rules of the game.

The point we are making here is that approaches to the short story can be varied indeed. In this book, we pursue a number of kinds of reading, some of which are largely contextual, some of which are more formal. It is often the case that the kind of story dictates the approach. When the plot is central, it is more likely that critics will focus on contextual issues. When technique and style are central, critics tend to be formalists in their approach. We have combined elements of the formal and the contextual in each chapter. Our argument is centrally concerned, as we stated above, with the relationships between the aesthetic choices a writer makes (the form) and the constraints on those choices (what an audience and/or publisher will accept, the market conditions, the political imperatives, the social contexts and so on).

Critical histories

Although it has enjoyed brief flourishes of critical interest, the British short story has tended to be neglected in recent years, pushed to the critical sidelines, something of a poor relation alongside other literary genres – especially since the 1980s. By this time, many commercial publishers disliked short-story collections, seeing them as unsaleable, and they pushed young authors towards the novel form. John Bayley has put forward the rather contradictory claim that 'to specialize too exclusively in short stories may result in writing that is too "essential", or too "poetic", too purely literary'.[28] The Irish writer William Trevor (b.1928), long recognised as one of the most important exponents of the genre thanks to such collections as *The Hill Bachelors* (2000) and *A Bit on the Side* (2004), has noted how for much of the 1980s and 1990s the short story was an incredibly 'unpopular' genre with British publishers, who got it into their heads that the reading public didn't like – or couldn't cope with – the form. In part this was to do with the sense, as Trevor explained, that the short story didn't sit easily in a publishing market which demanded light reading: 'You play a different game with the short story. You demand far more of the reader than you do with a novel, or television.'[29] In the first decade of the twenty-first century, however, there have been some small indications that this situation of critical and cultural neglect is starting to change. The year 2004 saw the launch of Small Wonder, Britain's first annual literary festival devoted to the short story. The launch in the following year of the BBC National Short Story Award and the Frank O'Connor International Short Story Award (named after the celebrated Irish short-story specialist [1903–66]) suggests that the short story is being taken more seriously – as it still is in the United States, where it is sometimes claimed as the country's 'national art form'.[30] The healthy, vibrant North American market for short fiction, which was said to be enjoying a 'golden age' as the millennium approached, is served by such short-story specialists as Alice Munro (b.1931), Ann Beattie (b.1947), Alejandro Murguia (b.1949), Lorrie Moore (b.1958) and Ana Menéndez (b.1970), who have helped to establish the collection as a valid alternative to the modern novel.

The history of the development of the form in Britain needs updating in the light of advances in critical theory, changes in the publishing market and the emergence of new writers in the past twenty years. Critical appreciation of the short story has tended to focus on its associations with the marginal, and a number of critics have linked it to alienation and the 'ex-centric' vision of the outsider. As Clare Hanson has usefully pointed out:

> The short story is a vehicle for different kinds of knowledge, knowledge which may be in some way at odds with the 'story' of dominant culture. The formal properties of the short story – disjunction, inconclusiveness, obliquity – connect with its ideological marginality and with the fact that the form may be used to express something

suppressed/repressed in mainstream literature ... the short story gives us the other side of the 'official story' or narrative ... [and] suggests that which cannot normally be said.[31]

For many writers, the short-story form has offered liberation from the formal restrictions of the novel, inviting experimentation and sub-version of the norms of the mainstream. The fluidity of the form has rendered it an effective outlet for the exploration and negotiation of gender, race, class and sexual identity, making it particularly popular with women writers and with others who feel in some ways marginal-ised or not fully secure within their communities: it has been signifi-cant in terms of representations of Irishness, colonialism and American national identity. The evolution of a more multicultural society has also affected the development of British fiction since the 1960s, with the greater attention paid to issues of immigration, hybridity and ethni-city in the short story mirroring, and also obliquely commenting on, a similar shift of emphasis in the novel. Writers such as Hanif Kureishi (b.1954), Jackie Kay (b.1961) and Zadie Smith (b.1975) have been active in this form. As Valerie Shaw reiterates, 'the short story has been free to cultivate diversity in an uninhibited way'.[32]

During the twentieth century, the short story began to be linked to more abstract visual and musical forms, with critics noting its similar-ity to visual art, photography and the development of film. It has also been interpreted in relation to the development of modernity, as the short story chimes with the aesthetics of modernism and its interest in psychology and the fleeting moment. Bored and restricted by the 'overpowering' constraints of the long novel, Virginia Woolf remarked in a letter of 1917, having just published her first story, 'The Mark on the Wall', 'I daresay one ought to invent a completely new form. Anyhow it's very amusing to try with these short things, and the greatest mercy to be able to do what one likes'.[33] Her stories and her later, more experi-mental fiction shared an interest in the 'unfinished', in 'the ordinary course of life',[34] as she sought to escape the outdated rules of fiction to embrace a 'new', more modern form. The prolific Anglo-Irish short-story writer Elizabeth Bowen, in her editorial introduction to *The Faber Book of Modern Stories* (1937), listed techniques, such as cutting and the unlikely placing of emphasis, which linked short fiction to film, and she argued that, compared with the 'forced continuity' of longer narratives, 'the new literature, whether written or visual, is an affair of reflexes, of immediate susceptibility, of associations not examined by reason: it does not attempt a synthesis'.[35] Bowen commented on the invalidity of using novels to express certain ideas, claiming that short stories were a more appropriate vehicle for examining the fragmentation and trauma of London during the Blitz. In an interview in 1980, the feminist novelist, editor and writer of short stories Angela Carter made a similar point about the liberation of departure from the grand narrative: 'The short story is not minimalist, it is rococo. I feel in absolute control. It is like writing chamber music rather than symphonies.'[36]

Although some critics have struggled to account for the fact that historically most writers have not dedicated themselves exclusively to this genre or form – John Bayley, for example, points out that 'the best short stories may have been written at odd moments by novelists or dramatists, or by a writer like D.H. Lawrence who was both novelist and poet'[37] – the phenomenon of authors writing across genres seems to offer a particularly fruitful area for enquiry. It is perhaps more helpful to follow Valerie Shaw, who urges us to reject 'the widespread notion that unless it can be seen as useful apprentice work for budding novelists, short-story writing must be a compromise of some sort'[38] and to consider short fiction as valuable and viable as the production of more critically acceptable novels.

Publishing the short story

The student reader of short fiction is most likely to come across stories in edited anthologies. This fact has some key effects which must not be ignored. Historically – certainly in the nineteenth century – most short fiction was published in periodicals and magazines, and magazine and even newspaper publication continues to this day to be a significant outlet for the form. The problems we encounter with anthologised short stories which had their origins elsewhere include the fact that it is extremely difficult to reconstruct the impact the story might have had when first read by its original audience among the adverts and serial fiction and editorial matter of a nineteenth- or twentieth-century periodical. Reading an anthology is also a different activity from reading a collection by a single author (where the organisation of the stories is in the writer's hands). There is no obligation on the reader, as Lynda Prescott has observed, to read anthologised stories in the 'right' order: 'A major virtue of anthologies is that they *can* be read selectively,' she writes in the preface to a recent collection of short stories from around the globe.[39] This is a form of freedom, but it has consequences for the impression that a given story makes: its juxtaposition with other stories, either through the reader's choice or because of the editor's ordering of the selection, can have unexpected (and possibly creative) outcomes. Moreover, anthologies have editors, and this fact also matters. The particular interests and preferences of a given editor can have a fascinating effect on what is perceived to be 'good' work, and there is often significant overlap among anthologies dealing with similar subject matter. As the writers of this book, we are not immune to this fact, by the way. Since we have sought to write a useful book, we have perforce had to spend a considerable portion of our time on works that are commonly taught on undergraduate programmes – and those programmes are often constructed, by necessity, in terms of the available anthologies. If the short story itself is affected by market conditions, so too is criticism about it.

The twentieth century saw the rise of the anthology of short stories, which often sought to collect together examples of particular types of story – in terms of genre (ghost stories and detective stories), in terms of authorship (anthologies by women writers) and in terms of national traditions (English, Irish, Welsh, Scottish short stories, for instance). These specially edited volumes began to appear regularly after the First World War, often with an emphasis on contemporaneity and modernity. Volumes such as Bradbury's *The Penguin Book of Modern British Short Stories* provided a selection of stories from a variety of authors (often, of course, predominantly male, English, heterosexual and middle class, though prominent women writers such as Woolf and Bowen usually featured). Only a quarter of the writers collected in *Modern English Short Stories* (1990) are female, though, as the editor suggests in the introduction, the anthology operates as a useful space for publicising the work of lesser-known writers alongside the ' "big guns" of literature'.[40] Developments in literary criticism meant that anthologies published towards the end of the century tended to collect narratives by authors with similar background, nationality, gender or sexual orientation.[41] Notable examples are A. S. Byatt's *Oxford Book of English Short Stories* (1998), Susan Hill's *Penguin Book of Modern Women's Short Stories* (1991) and David Marcus's *The Faber Book of Best New Irish Short Stories, 2006–7* (2007). Others deliberately encourage readers to reflect on cultural identities through the consideration of a wide range of authors and viewpoints. One example is the recently published *A World of Difference: An Anthology of Short Stories from Five Continents* (2008), which contains stories linked together by themes of cultural encounters and experiences of migration or uprooting, and produced by a 'diversity of writers', from established authors such as Nadine Gordimer (b.1923) and William Trevor to a younger generation of writers such as Rohinton

Mistry (b.1952) and Zadie Smith. The blurb on its back cover promises the variety which makes such collections appealing and marketable: 'in tone and mood the stories are as varied as in their geographical settings'. Its editor, Lynda Prescott, comments on the need for editorial organisation and the alternative ways in which a reader might approach such an anthology, likening the form to a music album: 'This particular sequence of stories aims to offer a reading dynamic enriched by shifts in tone, structure, narrative approach, pace and so on, that will work for anyone who approaches the stories in sequence, as well as for the reader who "dips in" more or less randomly.'[42] The chapters in this volume pay attention to the print spaces in which the stories under discussion first appeared, and indicate which stories have been most frequently anthologised and why.

One area in which the short story has seen a revival of interest involves the rediscovery of forgotten women writers by feminist critics since the late 1970s. This rediscovery has led to the production of a number of anthologies of short stories by women, helping to create a canon of female short-story writers from the nineteenth century to the present. Examples of these anthologies are Elaine Showalter's *Daughters of Decadence: Women Writers of the Fin de Siècle* (1993) and *Femmes de Siècle: Stories from the '90s: Women Writing at the End of Two Centuries* (1992), edited by Joan Smith, the latter comparing short fiction by late-Victorian writers with specially commissioned stories by prominent women writers of the 1990s. Editors of such anthologies have made some attempt to establish a tradition of women's short-story writing, though there is a tendency, as in other critical studies of the genre, to obscure the potential differences between British and American writers, or writers of other races, which might provide an alternative picture. In her revealing discussion of women's stories, Mary Eagleton expresses concern about the limitations of current critical approaches to women's short-story writing in terms of its highlighting of the female experience, asking 'is there ... a particular scope in relating gender to the short story? Can we create a criticism which is non-essentialist, non-reductive but subtly alive to the links between gender and genre?'[43] While it might obscure the meanings of a short story to ignore the gender of the author, it is surely productive to think beyond stereotypical conceptions of the 'woman's story' as limited in scope and necessarily 'different'. In this volume, we have attempted to position and examine women's short-story writing in relation to work in the same sub-genres by male writers (as in the chapters on ghost stories and adventure fiction) and to comment on the particular strategies of British women writers as they wrote about war, racism and urban experience as well as more traditionally feminine topics such as domesticity, motherhood and women's roles within the family. Chapter 11, on post-war women's stories, concentrates more exclusively on the development of women's fiction in relation to the rise of feminism in the later twentieth century, though the range and diversity of the selected stories, and the discussion of the different focuses of authors of different races and social backgrounds, are intended to offer a non-essentialist criticism.

The anthology is not, of course, the only means by which short stories make their way into the public domain. Many stories appeared originally in slightly different forms in magazines and newspapers rather than in collections. So the present volume also pays some attention to the changing market for short fiction in the nineteenth and twentieth centuries, with an indication of the nature and house style of the key journals and magazines in which many of the stories first appeared. The different reading dynamic offered by stories appearing in collections by individual authors, in contrast to those in anthologies arranged by genre or by the gender or nationality of the authors, can then subtly alter the reader's interpretations of the narrative.

Certain periodicals, such as *Household Words* (1850–59) and *All the Year Round* (1859–93), edited by Charles Dickens (1812–70) in the mid-nineteenth century, *The Yellow Book* (1894–97) and *The Strand* (1891–1950) in the 1890s, and the American journal *The New Yorker* (still running since its first issue in the 1925), dominated the fiction marketplace in particular periods, and thus were instrumental in crystallising desired thematic concerns and shaping future directions for the short-story form. Editors and publishers played a vital role in establishing the generic conventions of sub-genres such as the ghost story or the war story. In the 1940s the short story was encouraged in magazines such as *Horizon* (1940–50), which published works by Graham Greene (1904–91), Frank O'Connor, Evelyn Waugh (1903–66), Elizabeth Bowen and H. E. Bates (1905–74). Also influential was *Penguin New Writing* (1940–50), which published Rosamond Lehmann (1901–90) and Elizabeth Bowen alongside American writers such as Saul Bellow (1915–2005), Eudora Welty (1909–2001) and Tennessee Williams (1911–83). Other magazines were *Orion* (1945–47, 1959–), *New Writing and Daylight* (1942–46) and *The Windmill* (1948), as well as the more middle-brow *Penguin Parade* (1937–48).

According to Margaret Beetham, 'the magazine has developed in the two centuries of its history as a miscellany, that is a form marked by variety of tone and constituent parts', a space where the short story could be showcased alongside, and in dialogue with, articles on current affairs and domestic concerns. In our interpretations of the periodical form we need to pay attention to the shifting balance of power among editor, writer and readers.[44] It is therefore important to have an informed idea about the kind of journal in which some of these stories first appeared in order to assess them in relation to the possible generic conventions recommended (but not exclusively governed) by the editor and the demands of the market for which they were originally intended. Romance and finance never go away in the reading of texts.

Part I

The Victorian and Edwardian Short Story

2
Introducing the Victorian and Edwardian Short Story

The reputations of most Victorian writers of fiction rest on novels rather than short stories. Charles Dickens, arguably the most famous story-teller of the time, wrote many brief tales and sketches, but despite his friend Percy Fitzgerald's claim that he 'always seemed to hanker after the short story', Dickens's seemingly relaxed approach – his loose definition of the short story as 'anything told orally by a narrator within the story or as anything shorter than four serial instalments' – has helped ensure that this element of his writing has tended to be viewed as secondary to the novels.[1] A belief has sprung up that the great Victorian writers who are still read today – Wilkie Collins, Anthony Trollope (1815–82), Elizabeth Gaskell (1810–65), Mary Elizabeth Braddon, George Eliot (1819–80), Thomas Hardy (1840–1928) – had little sense of the short story's artistic potential. In fact, all these writers wrote short stories, though with mixed reasons for doing so. Both Elizabeth Gaskell and the *fin-de-siècle* naturalist writer George Gissing (1857–1903) wrote short stories unashamedly for money and discussed their reliance on swift payment for their stories in their letters. Gissing eased his struggle to support his dependants by writing stories and novellas despite his fear that he was compromising his artistic talents by pandering to the mar-ketplace; Gaskell increased her output of stories at certain times in her career to finance family holidays, notably getting £100 from Dickens for the novella *My Lady Ludlow* in 1858.[2] Another top earner was Anthony Trollope, who got £40 per story when he sold four of them to *Cassell's Illustrated Family Paper* in 1860 (roughly equivalent to £2,000 per story in today's values). In his autobiography Trollope claimed to have made £1,830 for three series of his *Tales of All Countries* (1861, 1863, 1870).[3] Thomas Hardy secured £125 for a Christmas story for *The Graphic* in 1889.[4] The majority of writers, of course, got nothing like these sums. In the 1850s, before she became a best-seller, Ellen Wood (1814–87), or so her family claimed, didn't get anything at all for her stories in the *New Monthly Magazine* (1814–84) and *Bentley's Miscellany* (1837–68).

Where and how these stories were published is an important part of their history. Generally speaking, anthologies of short stories as we know them today were unusual in the mid-nineteenth century (though they had flourished during the 1820s and 1830s). By 1850 the big publishing houses, which were notoriously reliant on Mudie's Circulating Library to buy large quantities of their titles, were not keen to commission them, preferring three-volume novels.[5] Those anthologies of stories which did make it to the bookshelves, such as Elizabeth Gaskell's *Round the Sofa* (1859), Anthony Trollope's *Tales of All Countries*, Dinah Craik's (1826–87) *Nothing New* (1861) and Wilkie Collins's *Little Novels* (1887), were the works of 'star' authors who had established readerships, but even then publishers did not expect to get much return beyond keeping the author happy – and thus loyal to their house.

Where the short story *was* popular with Victorian publishers was in magazines and newspapers, especially in special bumper issues for the summer holidays or the Christmas season. Thus the 1863 Christmas number of Dickens's magazine *All the Year Round* carried stories by its owner–editor featuring his popular character Mrs Lirriper, supported by tales from Edmund Yates (1831–94), Amelia B. Edwards (1831–92), Andrew Halliday (1830–77) and Elizabeth Gaskell. Editors and publishers recognised that a short story could act as 'bait', enticing readers with promises of new work by a popular writer. Something of this attitude is apparent in an 1859 letter to Anthony Trollope from William Makepeace Thackeray (1811–63), then editor of the popular *Cornhill Magazine* (1860–1975). Thackeray, aware of Trollope's modishness, and having already got him to write a serial novel (*Framley Parsonage*, 1860), tried to persuade him to contribute some short stories, which he likened to baking tarts: 'Don't understand me to disparage our craft, especially *your* wares. I often say I am like the pastrycook, and don't care for tarts, but prefer bread and cheese; but the public love the tarts (luckily for us), and we must bake and sell them.'[6]

Trollope cites this letter in his autobiography and evidently found it flattering; in the 1860s the *Cornhill* paid well, and for a writer as disciplined as Trollope it was no particular hardship to rush out 3,000 words. However, there is no sense that he disagreed with Thackeray's idea that the short story was nothing more than 'filler', a kind of cheap literary snack, quickly produced and consumed, with the potential to be re-sold at a later date by being gathered together with other previously published stories to form a collection.

It is thus possible to get some sense of the short story's commercial appeal at mid-century. A short story could be read – or 'eaten' – quickly. It could also, as Winnie Chan notes, be used to whet readers' appetites for a magazine's type of fiction. Finally, it offered instant – or almost instant – gratification. Unlike serial stories, which lasted for months, even years, the short story 'satisfied readers' need for plots complete with resolutions'.[7]

As well as *All the Year Round* and the *Cornhill*, popular magazines included *Bentley's Miscellany*, *Blackwood's Magazine* (1817–1980), the *Metropolitan Magazine* (1831–57), the *Family Herald* (1844–1940) and *Good Words* (1860–1906). And there were many, many more. Each had its own individual character – *Blackwood's* was conservative and intellectual, for example; *Good Words* addressed itself to a large evangelical readership – but what their editors shared was a belief that short stories were a way of drawing readers in.

What, then, did Victorian short-story writers write about? The basic answer to this question is, more than we might think. Take the example of the middle-brow, popular writer Anthony Trollope, a man who prided himself on his ability to work hard but remain a gentleman. Trollope, who had a bent for literary realism, was fond of announcing that his stories were prompted by 'the remembrance of some fact', that they were faithfully recording the bustling modern world around them.[8] And for readers this was part of their appeal. 'They are what they profess to be,' announced *The Times* in 1857 of Trollope's works, 'stories of modern life, told without any attempt at fine writing, without any striving after climaxes and points... They take English life as they find it.'[9] Trollope's careful observation of the people and places around him was deemed to be something that apprentice writers could do worse than imitate. Thus for the *Saturday Review*'s critic in 1870 Trollope's short story 'The Spotted Dog' 'exemplifies the legitimate use of a good realistic description' in the presentation 'of the tragedy of common life'.[10] 'The directness and verisimilitude of his [Trollope's] manner, and the absence of any attempt at fine writing, enable him to be far more really pathetic than the professed dealers in this kind of sentiment.' This last comment seems to be a swipe at Dickens, whose idiosyncratic descriptive style and favouring of grotesque characters encouraged a good many imitators, while Trollope's own style appeared more 'nondescript'.[11] The description under discussion in this review is of Julius Mackenzie, a writer down on his luck who arrives at the narrator's office seeking commissions: 'We well remember his appearance, which was one unutterably painful to behold. He was a tall man, very thin, – thin we might say as a whipping post... His big head seemed to lean forward over his miserably narrow chest. His back was bowed, and his legs were miserably crooked and tottering.'[12] This description continues for another four hundred words as the reader is given what Victorian reviewers sometimes termed a 'word-painting' – a description distinguished by its precision and thoroughness and by the apparent aim of wanting to make the reader 'see' the figure being described. The character is presented almost as a scientific specimen or anthropological object, the idea being that the successful storyteller is one who makes good use of his visual and aural senses. One critic of the time suggested that it was 'by the multitude of details of this minute kind that Mr Trollope makes one feel how great a social naturalist he is'.[13]

Trollope's stories are usually set in the present day. They tend to be of two sorts: one sort involving characters struggling with a moral dilemma over questions of career or courtship; the other sort comic and involving some form of social mishap or misunderstanding. Sometimes the outcomes are happy, as in the novella 'The Two Heroines of Plumplington' (1882), a courtship story set in Trollope's mythical Barsetshire. Elsewhere they are tragic, as in the macabre story 'Malachi's Cove' (1864), and downbeat, as in 'The Parson's Daughter of Oxney Colne' (1861). All three tales evince Trollope's famed interest in representing young (marriageable) female characters and the tough, life-changing decisions they have to take. As a writer Trollope was famously in tune with middle-class audiences, and his tales give a useful snapshot of mid-Victorian preoccupations and attitudes, including the idea that '[p]ure morals must be supplied', especially in magazines intended for a family audience.[14]

Trollope's realist tales, however, represent only a small part of the landscape of the Victorian short story. As we will see in Chapter 3, mid-century stories by George Eliot, Thomas Hardy, Ellen (Mrs Henry) Wood, Sheridan le Fanu (1814–73), Amelia Edwards, Mary Elizabeth Braddon, Rhoda Broughton (1840–1920), Wilkie Collins and Charlotte Riddell (1832–1906) covered a remarkably wide range of subjects: murder, adultery, degeneration, betrayal, and weird or 'uncanny' events – hauntings, the return of the dead, the experiences of 'second sight'. Such stories are a long way from the cosy, rose-tinted image we have of the mid-Victorians as a staid, earnest and rather dull bunch. As fictions they focus in uncomfortable and sensational ways on sexual passion, on marriage and on homes in which violence, or the possibility of violence, is always lurking.

Given this, it can be interesting to compare the subject matter and plot resolutions of shorter and longer pieces of fiction by a single author to assess whether short stories offered writers more freedom of expression or the opportunity to examine – or experiment with – topics felt to be unsuitable for the Victorian novel. While stories sometimes allowed novelists to experiment with ideas which they would explore at greater length in their novels or allowed them the pleasure of writing in an alternative medium, they could also reveal to the reader alternative areas of the author's interest. Elizabeth Gaskell's reputation as a rather maternal figure peddling domestic values, and as a campaigner for the rights of the working classes, does not fit easily with the interest in witchcraft and violence evident in her Gothic tales. At the end of the century, Henry James described his well-known tale of a governess haunted by the malign spirits of two previous servants, *The Turn of the Screw* (1899), to fellow-novelist H. G. Wells (1866–1946) as a 'shameless little pot-boiler', evidently taking satisfaction in 'squaring popular taste with his own highly demanding literary ideals'.[15] But the short story could also echo ideas developed in a writer's longer works. An interesting example is Robert Louis Stevenson (1850–94), whose Calvinist background and interest in the supernatural led to 'Thrawn Janet', one of his best-known works, published in the *Cornhill Magazine* in October 1881. It is the story of a small parish in olden days where a woman is believed to be in cahoots with the Devil, and it explores what Fred Warner has called a 'peculiarly Scottish sense of evil'.[16] In this sense the story has been seen as an important apprenticeship work in the lead-up to Stevenson's more famous novella *The Strange Case of Dr Jekyll and Mr Hyde* (1886). Yet 'Thrawn Janet' is important in its own right, not least for the ways in which its different elements – the interest in the uncanny and in feminine orality and utterance, its regionalism and use of Scots dialect as a form of resistance to English colonialism – suggest other facets of the short story as it was developing in the last third of the nineteenth century.[17]

Stevenson has been viewed as an important figure in the development of the Victorian – and Scottish – short story. For him, short stories were not simply a lucrative sideline but a recognisably separate form with their own rules. Equally influential was Rudyard Kipling (the focus of Chapter 5), who found enormous fame among readers of all classes with his collection *Plain Tales from the Hills* in 1888 and whose popularity began to suggest in new ways the short story's commercial and aesthetic possibilities. Kipling's skill has been universally acknowledged, but he was also fortunate in that the culture of the short story in Britain was beginning to expand by the time he started to write. Part of this expansion was due to improved printing technology, including the introduction of rotary presses, which improved the efficiency of typesetting.[18] But another part was due to the creation of a new mass of readers following the Education Acts introduced between 1870 and 1890. This legislation made elementary education compulsory for all and had the side-effect of prompting a flood of new cheap magazines and papers, many of which gave a central place to short fiction. Among the most popular were magazines such as *The Strand*, a sixpenny monthly featuring the first appearances of the famous detective Sherlock Holmes, and *Pearson's Weekly* (1896–1939), whose biggest draw was a long-running series of stories featuring Captain Kettle, a jingoistic merchant seaman who, like Holmes, always manages to save the day.

Many of those associated with *The Strand* claimed that it was this magazine, which sold 300,000 copies a month and carried no serialised novels, which was instrumental in changing the nineteenth-century attitude towards short stories. According to Reginald Stone, one of the magazine's editors, this exclusion of serialised novels was down to proprietor George Newnes's earlier success with snippet-filled *Tit-Bits* (1881), allied to a concern that readers would lose interest in a full-length serial. Short stories, he decided, would allow the magazine to offer readers their favourite authors but greater variety. They also allowed the magazine to ditch unreliable authors. Newnes's desire that the magazine should be organically complete each month, 'like a book', had major implications for what was published:

> It meant dropping the serial stories that were a feature of other magazines, including the American, and relying for fiction exclusively on short stories. They were a literary form in which few English writers then excelled. There was no English equivalent of [Guy de] Maupassant in France, or of Ambrose Bierce in America. English short story writers were in thrall to a convention of length, six thousand words minimum... Editors counted on stories to fill a given number of pages.[19]

The Strand was certainly an influential presence in the late-Victorian literary landscape. In addition to Conan Doyle, other best-selling authors regularly appeared in its pages: Grant Allen (1848–99), Walter Besant (1836–1901), Mary Braddon, Bret Harte (1836–1902), E. W. Hornung (1866–1921), L. T. Meade (1815–1914), Arthur Morrison (1863–1945) and E. Nesbit (1858–1924), alongside translations from the French of work by Maupassant. *The Strand's* legendary circulation figures helped ensure that the format became much imitated. Publishers realised that by advertising 'A Complete Short Story' they could pick up new readers each week, readers who did not have to have read the previous week's instalment of a serial story to understand the new issue's fictional offerings.[20]

Not everyone thought this a good thing for 'Literature', or for 'Art' generally. Indeed, it is in the discussions surrounding all the energetic readerly and writerly activities of the 1880s and 1890s that we begin to see the split into what would later be labelled 'high' and 'popular' literary culture. Something of this is apparent in an article entitled 'The Decay of the Short Story', which appeared in the highbrow *Fortnightly Review* in 1908. Here Edwin Pugh noted that the 'crop' of stories appearing in magazines had 'deteriorated' and that the magazines' pages were 'choked with all manner of vulgar weeds' (p. 635).[21] Even good writers – 'masters in the art of the short story' – were 'now, alas! boiling the pot with what ought to go to the waste-paper basket' because they had a ready market 'in the modern magazines that overload the bookstalls [and] affront the sensibilities with their loud, highly-coloured appeals to the eye of the casual passer-by' (p. 636). Picking up one (unnamed) magazine full of serial fictions, short stories and celebrity interviews with artists and actresses, Pugh suggested that 'there is not a word of any literary moment in it from beginning to end' (p. 636). 'The truth is', he announced, 'the stories chiefly sought after nowadays are those possessing qualities which we have had to coin new words and phrases to describe: such words as "vim," "snap," "go," "crispness," "breeziness"; they must "go with a swing," they must not "tail off," they must "grip the attention from the opening sentence"' (p.639). And all sorts of embargoes are laid upon the writers, he continued: their stories must not offend anyone's sensibilities; they must be adapted for reading aloud in the home circle; they must not be 'unpleasant' or 'painful'; they must conform to exigencies of space and lend themselves readily to illustration. Pugh went on to accuse well-regarded writers of the time such as Barry Pain (1864–1928), Henry Brereton Marriott Watson (1863–1921)and Lucy Clifford (1846–1929) – 'to select a mere handful' – of 'prostituting their genius to the level of what is commonly and erroneously held to be the prevalent taste' (p. 638). Would-be writers might, he suggested, do better to 'address themselves instead to securing the custom of a smaller class of more sophisticated and critical readers who would be sufficiently faithful and appreciative to ensure the permanent success of these more eclectic productions on a less ambitious scale' (p. 638). Better this than chasing after the popular middle-brow market in an undignified fashion.

Many short-story writers, however, recognised the power of the 'people', and some decided to tailor their work accordingly. Preparing his ghost story 'Owen Wingrave' (1892), Henry James (taking yet another shot at securing a popular readership) decided that it was 'a little subject for the *Graphic* – so I mustn't make it "psychological" – they understand that no more than a donkey understands a violin'.[22] James, whose agonised search for a wider audience is well documented, was quite prepared to compromise and to try to temper his difficult 'ground glass style'[23] if the occasion demanded it.

This sense of a shift in the market for, and value of, the short story was shared by James's Sussex neighbour H. G. Wells. Although Wells was a keen contributor to several of the new magazines, he accused their editors of dumbing down: 'deaden[ing] the conception of what a short story might be to the imagination of the common reader'.[24] Stories did not, it seemed, have to be much good to get published. There were so many magazines that, as Wells noted, works 'of the slightest distinction' tended to find an outlet. 'Short stories', Wells later recalled, 'broke out everywhere':

> Kipling was writing short stories, Barrie, Stevenson, Frank Harris; Max Beerbohm wrote at least one perfect one, 'The Happy Hypocrite'; Henry James pursued his wonderful and inimitable bent; and among other names that occur to me, like a mixed handful of jewels drawn from a bag, are George Street, Morley Roberts, George Gissing, Ella D'Arcy, Murray Gilchrist, E. Nesbit, Stephen Crane, Joseph Conrad, Edwin Pugh, Jerome K. Jerome, Kenneth Graham [sic], Arthur Morrison, Marriot Watson, George Moore, Grant Allen, George Egerton, Henry Harland...I dare say I could recall as many more names with a little effort.[25]

The fact that many of these late-Victorian and Edwardian 'jewels' are no longer remembered says much about the way the short-story form has tended to appear throwaway or 'of the moment', and also about the ways in which literary canons are formed. Wells's comments also point to other opportunities that existed for would-be writers. For example, the final name on Wells's list, Henry Harland, serves as a reminder that if a would-be story teller did not want to get published by *The Strand*, he – or she – could look instead to one of the more ostentatiously 'high-culture' magazines. The best-known and most commercial of these was *The Yellow Book*, founded in 1894 and edited by Harland. In contrast to the *Strand* (dismissed by some as a magazine for people who did not want to think), the *Yellow Book* published self-consciously difficult stories, the best of which, according to Harland, began with an 'impression'. 'That is to say you look about the universe, and you see something; and the thing you see produces within you a certain state of mind and a certain state of emotion.' The 'artist', as opposed to the 'normal man', is 'constantly possessed by a desire to give your impression expression in the particular form of art that it is your joy and your despair to cultivate ... But an impression is never a simple thing which can be conveyed in two minutes conversation. It is never an obvious thing. It is always a complex thing, it is always elusive. It is a thing of shades and niceties and fine distinctions.'[26] the *Yellow Book's* main rival was *Black and White*, which announced its arrival in 1889 with the statement 'there will be no serials'. In addition to its big-name authors, *Black and White's* other selling point was its lavish illustrations and artwork, which made it something of an *objet de luxe*, a symbol of good taste, designed to be displayed on the drawing-room table in houses of distinction. The same drawing room might also hold the *Pall Mall Magazine* (1893), the *Windsor* (1895) and the *Sketch*, which published a short story every week under the heading 'A Novel in a Nutshell'. Later *Chapman's* (1895), the *Royal* (1898), the *Grand* (1905) and *Nash's Magazine* (1909) also secured places at the centre of respectable popular British culture, as did a growing number of magazines for women, including *Woman at Home* (1893) and *The Lady's Realm* (1896).

Although magazines such as *The Yellow Book* and *Black and White* championed the short story as an elite aesthetic object – carefully crafted and polished – the economic possibilities of the form were now evident. Harold Orel has argued that 'once a short story had found its market in a [nineteenth-century] periodical, it was unlikely that a collection of short stories would find enough buyers to justify its publication',[27] but this does not seem to have been strictly true. By 1890 many authors and publishers appreciated the fact that the short story involved much less complex business arrangements. Noting this commercial element, the *Atlantic Monthly*, in explaining 'the present popularity of the short story with authors and public alike', suggested that 'here is a form of literature easy to read and write. The author is often paid as much for a story as he earns from the copyrights of a novel, and it costs him one tenth the labour. The multitude of magazines and other periodicals creates a constant market, with steadily rising prices ... The public pays its money and takes its choice'.[28] Capitalising on the increased demand for shorter fiction, well-established novelists such as Thomas Hardy and George Gissing published a number of collections of stories later in their careers, including stories some of their readers would already have read. Hardy's collections *Wessex Tales* (1888), *Life's Little Ironies* (1894) and *A Changed Man* (1913) were largely made up of work which had appeared before in magazines. In her research into Hardy as a short-story writer, Kristin Brady has noted 'the careful organization of [his] short-story volumes', which function as 'artistic wholes in their own right', with their own 'coherence and integrity',[29] suggesting the ordering principles at work when the writer of fiction became involved in the selection process. Contemporary reviewers tended not to pay much attention to Hardy's short-story collections, although some did recognise Hardy's efforts in grouping the stories. Edmund Gosse suggested that their highest 'merit consists, of course, in the tension of wild emotion, raising common scenes and common speakers...to the heights of tragedy'.[30] Writing in the *Bookman* in 1891, William Minto suggested that *A Group of Noble Dames* (1891) was 'a collection of strange cases in the relations between men and women', at the same time pointing out that all the heroines seemed ruthless and unscrupulous in their dealings.[31]

Given the fact that authorship itself was undergoing significant change and becoming more obviously professional, it is no surprise to find some writers using the short story to talk about what it was to be an author – as Henry James does in 'Greville Fane' (1892) and Vernon Lee (1856–1935) does in 'Lady Tal' (1892). James's story is about a popular female writer, Mrs Stormer (reputedly based on Margaret Oliphant [1828–97]), who has taken the view that writing is 'a profession like another'. She has supported her snobbish, grasping children by her 'imperturbable industry'[32] (p. 251), churning out saleable middle-brow fiction, her office 'a seat of trade' rather than art, her desk the 'battered and blotted accessory to innumerable literary lapses' (p. 251). As the story's narrator, who is tasked with writing Mrs Stormer's obituary, sees it, she did not produce 'literature', at least not according to his definition, but wrote instead 'stories by the yard' and 'went down to her grave without suspecting that though she had contributed volumes to the diversion of her contemporaries she had not contributed a sentence to the language' (p. 254). The phrase 'went down' perhaps suggests a moral to the story – one to do with selling one's soul and talents for the sake of a comfortable life. But the narrator nonetheless admires Mrs Stormer's hard work, her devotion to 'her daily stint' (p. 254). His sense of superiority towards her is tempered with affection, and also pity that artistically hers was a wasted life and that Leolin, the son and idol on whom she lavished so much attention (and money), was hardly worth the effort.

Vernon Lee's Lady Tal is another fiction writer. She is ambitious and wants advice from a famous novelist, Jervase Marion (this time supposedly based on Henry James). Marion believes that women and great art do not mix, but he finds 'the indications of a soul' when he reads the manuscript of Lady Tal's latest novel. Lady Tal is confident enough to assume a position of equality as a woman writer and disconcertingly suggests literary collaboration, rejecting the 'paternal' (i.e. patronising) tone with which Marion has attempted to control her. She insists that they 'ought to write ... together'.[33]

The emphasis in these 1890s stories on the ambitions – thwarted or otherwise – of women writers makes them very much of their time. Elaine Showalter has suggested that 'the best work of the decade [the 1890s] was in the short story rather than the novel' and that much of it came from female writers:

> The novel was a problematic genre for *fin de siècle* women writers, as many of them realised. Too often it tended to the didactic, episodic and stiff, whereas the short story was supple, impressionistic and intense. Women writers in the 1890s found in the short story a suitable form for the new feminist theories of the decade: the exploration of female sexuality and fantasy; the development of a woman's language, and the critique of male aestheticism.[34]

As Chapter 4 in the present volume will indicate, recent critics of the short story have followed Showalter in thinking about the feminine dimension to many short stories of the late nineteenth century. The *fin de siècle* has traditionally been seen as notable for stories by writers associated with the short-lived Decadent and Aesthetic movements, notably Ernest Dowson (1867–1900) and Oscar Wilde, whose texts were often associated in the public mind with 'outrageous' expressions of perversity and sensuality, full of ideas of *ennui* or moral exhaustion. However, it was the small-scale short stories by such 'New Woman' writers as George Egerton (1859–1945), Ella D'Arcy (1856?–1939), Vernon Lee and Ella Hepworth Dixon (1855–1932), among others, which seeped onto the literary market. Many of these writers can be seen to be dealing at least in part with the so-called Woman Question, taking in questions and viewpoints about female emancipation and about a woman's rights to education and to earning and keeping her own income and property.

As readers of the late-Victorian and Edwardian short story – by men as well as by women – we do not have to travel very far to realise just how much these texts can appear symbols of early feminist rebellion. Many writers of the time were preoccupied with the issue of 'woman': the independent woman, the unfulfilled woman, the 'monstrous' woman, the 'erotomaniac', the emancipated woman who committed the cardinal sin of 'unsexing' herself by personally rejecting marriage and motherhood altogether. Prior victimisation or neglect of women by men or by society more generally and the return from the dead of the victimised also provides the explanation for numerous ghost stories by late-Victorian writers. Stories such as Bram Stoker's (1847–1912) 'The Secret of the Growing Gold' (1892) and 'The Squaw' (1893) fit into this category, as do Lucy Clifford's 'Lost' (1883) and Vernon Lee's *Hauntings* (1890).[35] Overall, the increasing emphasis given to the women's short story by recent feminist critics can be seen as a rebuke to those twentieth-century critics who claimed the short story as a male preserve, even, as has been suggested, using phallic language to do so. Notable here is H. G. Wells's pronouncement that to produce its 'one single vivid effect', the short story must 'seize the attention at the outset, and never relaxing, gather it together more and more until the climax is reached... [It must] explode and finish before interruption occurs or fatigue sets in.'[36] The sexual thrust of Wells's account – an account which seems intended to privilege men's literary work – is unusual in its explicitness, but it does square with attempts by the literary intelligentsia of the 1890s to 'reclaim the kingdom of the English novel for male writers, male readers and men's stories', as Elaine Showalter puts it.[37] This was a mission which helped ensure that many fine short stories by women were brushed aside and ignored by those responsible for putting together anthologies and for teaching the short story – at least until recently.

For others at the end of the nineteenth century, the very shortness of the short story made it the obvious form for the breakneck speed of the new modern age with its trains, steamships, motorcars, omnibuses, telegrams and telephones. Bliss Perry believed the short story to be 'a kind of writing perfectly adapted to our over-driven generation, which rushes from one task of engagement to another and between times, or on the way, snatches up a story'.[38] This idea that the short story's brevity allows it to thrive in a fast-paced society has remained a popular one, as has the idea that it is a form particularly suited to conveying a peculiarly 'modern' sense of dislocation and uncertainty.

Given all this activity, how do we decide what to read? Where do we start? One of the things the following chapters do is to flag up types of short story which are proving to be of particular interest to critics today, including works by writers who have tended to languish outside the literary canon.

The years leading up to the outbreak of the First World War in 1914 saw the culture of the short story expanding to encompass detective fiction, including G. K. Chesterton's (1874–1936) Father Brown stories about a clergyman sleuth; colonial stories by Rudyard Kipling, Joseph Conrad (1857–1924) and Flora Annie Steel (1847–1929), with their examination of the so-called white man's burden in the far-flung reaches of the British empire; suffragette fiction, sympathetic to women seeking the vote; children's fiction, including the work of Beatrix Potter (1866–1943); plus the sharp, satirical observations of the Edwardian social scene by E. M. Forster (1879–1970) and the author known as Saki. Clearly, at any moment in the history of fiction a range of styles are likely to be in evidence as older writers continue to publish alongside members of a younger generation. However, in the next three chapters we will focus in depth on four kinds of short story spanning the middle and later part of the nineteenth century and the early twentieth century. Chapter 3 thus considers the sensational story and the supernatural story; Chapter 4, the New Woman story; and Chapter 5, the colonial story.

3
Victorian Sensations: Supernatural and Weird Tales

The development of the Victorian short story is inextricable from the nineteenth-century fascination with the supernatural, with its origins in the popularity of Gothic fiction at the end of the eighteenth century. As we saw in chapter 2, realist fiction from the pens of Anthony Trollope and others was popular during the period, but it is a misconception to categorise fiction of the period as wholly realist. The importance of Gothic paradigms and conventions to our understanding of cultural preoccupations, fantasies and modes of thinking also needs to be acknowledged. Recently Nicola Bown, Carolyn Burdett and Pamela Thurschwell have argued that for the Victorians, 'the supernatural was both fearful and terrible and ardently desired... an important aspect of [their] intellectual, spiritual, emotional and imaginative worlds'.[1] This chapter focuses on some of the ways in which writers of the day exploited this interest.

In his introduction to the uses of excess and transgression in the Gothic genre, Fred Botting has argued that 'uncertainties about the nature of power, law, society, family and sexuality dominate Gothic fiction',[2] and that these, coupled with Victorian obsessions with criminality and marital difficulties, threatened to expose the dark underside of respectable bourgeois culture. The 1860s saw the rise of the new genre of sensation fiction, popular novels about crime, violence, imprisonment and insanity, and the skeleton in the closet, which proved immensely appealing to a broad, cross-class readership. Lyn Pykett writes that 'gothic and its Victorian transformations might be said to be forms which are produced by fears and anxieties shared by late eighteenth- and nineteenth-century writers and their readers, and by common cultural anxieties: about sex and gender and relations between the sexes; about power (and its gendering); about the nature of the self'.[3] Victorian ghost stories featured many of the stock elements of eighteenth-century Gothic, particularly the 'spectres, monsters, demons, corpses, skeletons' listed by Botting,[4] but the standard, and stereotypical, characters of evil aristocratic villain and fainting vulnerable heroine became less conventional, replaced with vampiric *femmes fatales*, mysterious doctors and tortured professional men. According to Julia Briggs, the fear produced by ghost stories relies on the reader's recognition of a 'familiar world' which then becomes in some way uncanny: 'a tension between the known and the unknown, security and exposure, the familiar and the strange, scepticism and credulity, must always be maintained'.[5]

From the 1850s onwards supernatural stories increasingly engaged with scientific debates around mesmerism, clairvoyance, visions of the future and hauntings of various kinds, which were aired in the major periodicals of the day as part of a process which Elaine Ostry has identified as the 'popularising' of science.[6] The decline in religious faith, accelerated by the publication of Charles Darwin's *On the Origin of Species* (1859), meant that many Victorians were prepared to entertain the possibility of unknown realms after death and the existence of spirits, though those who reported sightings of apparitions or spectres were highly likely to be disbelieved and to be considered mad. Popular texts about the supernatural such as Catherine Crowe's (1803–76) *The Night Side of Nature* (1845) and *Spiritualism and the Age We Live In* (1859) set out to challenge this view and especially reinforced women's associations with the spirit world. The period from the 1860s to the 1880s has been classified as the golden age of spiritualism, when spiritualists and mediums, predominantly female, attested that they could communicate with the dead or temporarily take over the persona of dead people.[7] As the century progressed, advances in medical science and the growing interest in spiritualism resulted in the formation of the Society for Psychical Research in 1882, which set out to investigate 'all types of inexplicable phenomena' reported, primarily, by middle-class, educated 'people'.[8] Could a secular, sceptical age readily admit the possibility of unearthly phenomena which could not be easily explained by science?

Many women writers chose to express their dissatisfactions with the position of women in Victorian society through the medium of the ghost story. As Vanessa Dickerson has argued in her examination of Victorian women writers and the supernatural, 'the ghost corresponded particularly to the Victorian woman's visibility and invisibility, her power and powerlessness, the contradictions and extremes that shaped female culture' and therefore allowed for an exploration of the

'inbetween-ness' of feminine experience.[9] At a time when 'the spiritu-
alist conception of women as uniquely gifted in spiritual matters was
at once both liberating and restricting', according to Alex Owen,[10] tales
of the supernatural both reproduced and, in some cases, challenged the
cultural ambivalences about women's inferior position in society. The
fact that many ghost stories are narrated in the first person by a male
figure, whatever the gender of the author, has been linked to the generic
requirement that the story be framed as authentic or 'real'. This device
could also be used to direct attention away from women's traditional
association with the supernatural, an association which writers of ghost
stories might have felt to be limiting to the construction of their narratives. According to Diana Basham, this convention ensures that 'it is
the male consciousness which is made to encounter, puzzle over, interpret or be haunted by the mysterious "otherness" of the supernatural
agent, a feature which ... indicates that the challenge of the supernatural
is made directly to notions of masculinity itself'.[11] While many of the
stories considered in the following pages do seek to examine the effects
which the experiences of these phenomena have on rational, professional men, the emotional responses of women, sometimes bordering
on hysteria or linked to superstition, are also examined. Other stories
discussed here make use of alternative scenarios to break down these
stereotypically gendered reactions to the uncanny.

The haunted house motif was a favourite of both male and female
authors, not least because it allowed for an examination of the positions
and roles of men, women and servants within the household. As Julia
Briggs has pointed out, 'Ghosts, like detectives, commonly operated in
middle-class homes.'[12] This motif could also be used to raise questions
about the family, as ghosts of deceased family members often returned
to protest against their ill treatment or to remind survivors of the reason
for their untimely death. Short narratives about marriage, motherhood,
family relations and the fallen woman were given a supernatural twist,
often to correct double standards of gendered behaviour or to question gender roles. The haunted house motif was particularly appealing to women writers because it allowed an exploration of women's
position within the domestic space, their relationship to property and
their role within the family. In *Laws concerning Women* (1854), Barbara
Bodichon (1827–91) attacked the prevailing system whereby a married
woman 'ha[d] no legal right to any property', leaving her in the position of an infant, kept under *'reasonable restraint'*.[13] This system is confirmed by stories that show women restrained and infantile, denied the
freedoms available to men to roam beyond the private sphere. Suicide,

something of a taboo subject during the Victorian period, features regularly in tales of the supernatural, as it was beginning to do in the press, also raising questions about gender and the family. The appearance of ghosts of suicides or the ghost-seers' decisions to kill themselves out of fear point towards unacknowledged explanations for a crime usually attributed to temporary insanity and often associated with fallen women. Ghost stories could also function to highlight the professional or financial reasons behind male suicide by using the appearance of ghosts to unearth family disputes about inheritance, succession and the ownership of property.

Dreams, visions and spectral illusions: Charles Dickens, Wilkie Collins and Sheridan le Fanu

Many of the early ghost stories appeared in the two mid-Victorian weekly periodicals conceived and edited by the prolific popular novelist and journalist Charles Dickens, whose influence on the dissemination of the short story to Victorian readers has already been noted in Chapter 2. *Household Words*, which ran for nine years from March 1850, and its successor, *All the Year Round*, launched in April 1859, were both weekly family magazines aimed primarily at the middle classes. They included articles on science, technology, history and travel, as well as items of topical interest, such as homelessness, poor public health and working conditions.[14] In his role as editor, Dickens responded to a climate potentially receptive to supernaturalism by insisting that writers of ghost stories for his periodicals 'should consider difficult matters of evidence, authority and belief',[15] in addition to topical material and social problems, which helped to establish this as a prevalent generic convention up to the turn of the century and beyond. Ostry has argued that Dickens's periodicals, including these articles about the supernatural, were 'part of a large-scale effort to educate the Victorian public about scientific matters'.[16]

Building on the success of his Christmas books in the 1840s, the most famous of which remains *A Christmas Carol* (1843), in which the ghosts of Christmases past, present and future force the miserly Ebenezer Scrooge to change his ways, until 1868 Dickens edited and contributed to Christmas fiction supplements to *Household Words* and *All the Year Round* featuring supernatural tales by regular contributors. These remained, in both Britain and America, the most popular single issues of both periodicals, with the circulation growing throughout the 1860s.[17] As editor, Dickens sometimes constructed links among stories on a common theme.[18] His 'Haunted House' sequence for the 1859 extra Christmas edition of *All the Year Round* included tales from the viewpoints of the inhabitants of the house by Wilkie Collins and Elizabeth Gaskell, and a verse narrative by the poet Adelaide Anne Procter (1825–64) framed by Dickens's opening scene-setting.[19] The thematic concerns of the short narratives Dickens contributed were similar to those of his longer novels. From early sketches such as 'A Visit to Newgate', 'Criminal Courts' and 'The Prisoner's Van', collected in *Sketches by Boz* (1836), to the more mature realist novels, such as *Bleak House* (1853) and *Great Expectations* (serialised in *All the Year Round* in 1860), his work displays a continuing fascination with crime and punishment, particularly focusing on thieves, murderers and prostitutes, key figures in the urban landscape. His chilling story for the extra Christmas number of *All the Year Round* in 1865, 'To Be Taken with a Grain of Salt', which is organised around a murder trial in the Central Criminal Court (and which is now sometimes known as 'The Trial for Murder'), is narrated by the Foreman of the Jury, who has seen a vision of the murderer escaping from the murder scene after reading an account of the discovery of the victim in his morning paper.[20] The twist in the tale is that the murderer had realised that he was doomed on first sight of the Foreman, because he too had seen him previously in dreams: *'he somehow got to my bedside in the night, woke me, and put a rope round my neck'* (p. 143).[21] Typically, the rational male narrator finds himself unable to explain his vision, despite his knowledge of 'remarkable case[s] of Spectral Illusion' (p. 131).

Dickens's most famous story, 'The Signal-Man', published only a few years before his death, was part of a sequence of stories called *Mugby Junction*, about working and travelling on the new railways, for the 1866 Christmas number of *All the Year Round*. This issue also included stories by the popular writers Hesba Stretton (1832–1911) and Amelia Edwards. These two authors were named in the supplement and in the advertisements which preceded it in order to maintain circulation, as 'the house policy on anonymity' was partially relaxed in relation to more illustrious contributors.[22] Dickens's story picks up on the vogue for eerie tales which examined the uncertain state of mind of rational men forced to confront supernatural forces or visions of the future which intruded into everyday life. The narrative consists of two conversations between a 'troubled' signalman and an interested passer-by (the narrator) which take place late at night in a 'solitary' and 'dismal' place.[23] The conversations are about sightings of a terrified figure warning the signalman of the danger of an oncoming train. In its climactic ending, with the signalman's death on the line, the story suggests, but never confirms, that he has seen a vision of future events, as the engine-driver repeats the words and gestures of the warning figure, though it is also possible that the signalman wanders onto the tracks in pursuit of a spectre who is a manifestation of his unbalanced state of mind.

The idea that interpreting what are believed to be premonitions might alter the future course of events is also used to great dramatic effect in a later story by the very popular sensationalist writer Rhoda Broughton. In 'Behold, It Was a Dream', from Broughton's popular collection *Tales for Christmas Eve* (1873), the heroine sees the bloody bodies of her friend and her friend's husband, their throats slit, in a dream and is convinced that they have been murdered by one of their labourers, a man she later identifies working in the fields. The story ends with the heroine reading the ghoulish newspaper report of their deaths and the labourer's arrest, though it remains unclear whether the murder has actually been prompted by the couple dismissing the man from their employment.[24] This idea of dreaming the future can be seen as a reminder of 'the supernaturalness of the supernatural, the fact that it *is* otherworldly, inexplicable and strange'.[25] In Dickens's tale, the testimony of the person who has allegedly seen the ghost is treated with suspicion (in Broughton's, it is particularly ridiculed by the husband); it is seen by the rational passer-by as a product of the signalman's isolation. He points out that 'this figure must be a deception of his sense of sight; and how that figures, originating in disease of the delicate nerves that minister to the functions of the eye, were known to have often troubled patients' (p. 151), locating the signalman's vision in nervous disorder and classifying the signalman as a 'patient' who could be cured. Although he admits that he is himself unsettled by the signalman's narrative, he is more concerned about the state of mind of someone employed in such a responsible position: 'Would I (for instance) like to stake my own life on the chances of his continuing to execute [a most important trust] with precision?' (p. 157). Dreams or premonitions are used within the supernatural narrative to reveal fears about the future, about the dark side of progress.

The attempt to decode the warning offered by a ghost, which became a staple of supernatural fiction, is here linked to the topical issue of the new railways and the violent deaths they might cause or inspire. The undisguised interest of the passer-by, a kind of early train-spotter whose attention is 'riveted' by 'these great works' (p. 146) and the 'long and lonely hours' (p. 146) of the signalman's days, is perhaps corrected by the signalman's apprehensions of danger on the line, at a time when the railways, first fully operational in the 1840s, were hailed as a revolutionary development in public transport providing communication networks and facilitating travel across the country. By setting up the signalman, a former student seen to be 'educated above that station' (p. 148), as a man fallen on hard times condemned to serve in an isolated, 'unnatural' place, the story also evokes sympathy for the staff of the new railways. The passer-by sees his visions as 'the mental torture of a conscientious man, oppressed beyond endurance by an unintelligible responsibility involving life' (p. 156). The sighting of the spectre has prefigured an accident on the line and the death of a beautiful woman on the train, but at the time of the narrative the spectre has been appearing at the Danger-light, calling and ringing the signalman's bell. The repetition of the word 'danger' across the story, coupled with the signalman's anxiety that he is unable to prove impending calamities to his co-workers, reminds the reader of the risks of railway travel and of the powerlessness of railway staff to prevent accidents. The emphasis on telegraphy, a form of 'spatially distanced communication' essential to the expanding railways, serves to highlight the potential supernaturalism of new technology.[26] The unfortunate signalman, 'cut down by an engine' (p. 158), could alternatively be seen as a figure for one of the growing number of 'railway suicides' (often troubled professional men) discussed with alarm in the sensationalist press. It is also worth pointing out Dickens's own involvement in a traumatic railway accident in 1865, in which he witnessed first-hand the injuries the could be sustained by passengers in the event of a crash or derailment.[27] Less celebratory than many of the other stories in *Mugby Junction*, Dickens's narrative uses the supernatural form to register cultural anxieties about 'the new types of violence [the railway] has brought into being' and the casualties of new technology.[28]

The sensation fiction and stories of Wilkie Collins, at one time a protégé of Dickens, also reveal a fascination with violence, drawing on the conventions of criminal reporting in the press, which became much more graphic after the removal of Stamp Tax in the 1850s and helped to foster the public's taste for sensation. His best-selling sensation novel *The Woman in White* (1860), which examined issues of female insanity, incarceration, marriage, property and inheritance, was serialised in *All the Year Round*, as was his later novel *The Moonstone* (1868), which has been characterised by some critics as an early example of the new genre of detective fiction. His ghost stories, like his novels, are both sensational and topical, engaging with contemporary debates about the madness and violence of women, the law, psychology and medicine, as well as exploring anxieties about cross-class relationships. Alison Milbank has highlighted a darker side to his writing which has affinities with what critics now refer to as 'female Gothic', utilising motifs familiar from such writers as Ann Radcliffe (1764–1823) and the Brontë sisters (Charlotte [1816–55], Emily [1818–48] and Anne [1820–49]), including 'the entrapped heroine, the sinister house, ghosts, dreams, and a sense of a divine order'.[29] Collins's early stories tend to follow Dickens's house style in using male narrators to record their fascination with and horror at visions of the future or second sight. In his disturbing tale 'The Dream-Woman', first published in *Household Words* in 1855, Collins portrays the terrors of a struggling ostler, Isaac, who has a recurring dream that he is being knifed in his bed by an attractive flaxen-haired woman. He marries the woman, Rebecca, years later to prevent her from committing suicide as a result of her poverty. The story is framed by the narrative of Brother Morgan, who attempts to rationalise and medicalise the ostler's 'queer sleeping and dreaming' (p. 57).[30] Anticipating the focus in sensation fiction on the violent woman, often of lower-class origins, the story dwells on Isaac's troubled marital life with his drunken wife. 'The fearfully exact resemblance between the living, breathing woman, and the spectre-woman of Isaac's dream' (p. 72) suggests that the husband has had a premonition of his unhappy marriage and of the 'spectre-woman' who lies behind the respectable Victorian wife, so that 'fear of sleeping in the same room with her possessed him' (p. 75). Those unnatural women more interested in money and property than motherhood and domestic duties, who used marriage for their own ends and might use violence to protect their status, became objects of fascination in sensation fiction, spectre-women to their virtuous counterparts. The story's association of this fear with the bedroom, where the spectre originally appeared, might gesture towards male fears of female sexuality. The narrative leaves it open whether Isaac's dream will come true; despite keeping hold of the clasp-knife he saw in the dream, as if to prevent the spectacle of female violence, he cannot escape the fear that she will return to kill him. Yet, as the frame narrator remarks in the closing lines, 'Who can tell?' (p. 79). This ambiguity reflects unresolved discussions about dreaming, sleep-walking and states of consciousness.

The use of dreams as a key device for revealing the buried psyche runs throughout mid-century ghost stories – well before Sigmund Freud's *The Interpretation of Dreams* (1900) showed that dreams signify the workings of the unconscious mind. When linked to fear of sleeping in the bedroom, this device was often used to indicate unacknowledged or socially unacceptable sexual desires. In Collins's later novella *The Haunted Hotel*, serialised in *Belgravia* in 1878, those who sleep in room 14 of the newly modernised Venetian palazzo are oppressed by terrible dreams about a murder committed in the building. In one melodramatic scene the heroine, Agnes, wakes to find her erstwhile rival, the widowed *femme fatale* the Countess Narona, in a deep sleep next to her bed,

> possessed by a torpor like the torpor of death – insensible to sound, insensible to touch...her breathing was audible, rising and falling in deep heavy gasps. At intervals she ground her teeth savagely. Beads of perspiration stood thickly on her forehead. Her clenched hands rose and fell slowly from time to time on her lap. Was she in the agony of a dream? Or was she spiritually conscious of something hidden in the room? (pp. 201–2)[31]

What the Countess might be conscious of is the severed head of her murdered husband, which Agnes then sees floating towards them. What is interesting about the scene, however, is that the Countess, 'the dumbly-tortured figure in the chair', whose eyelids later open 'slowly like the eyelids of the dead' (p. 203) in response to the head's accusing stare, is much more disturbing than the figure of the ghost. She becomes an object of horror because of the 'agony' and torture of dreaming. Rather like the victims of vampires, she behaves as if possessed, and when her death is described towards the end of the novel, she is apparently still breathing in this unnatural way, 'like a person oppressed in sleeping' (p. 230), like one of the undead. Collins also refers to mesmerism as a possible explanation for Agnes's vision, having her accept that 'what I saw might be the result of magnetic influence communicated to me, as I lay between the remains of the murdered husband above me and the guilty wife suffering the tortures of remorse at my bedside' (p. 216). It is the guilty wife, hovering on the borders of insanity and haunted by the foreknowledge that Agnes will prove to be her nemesis in Venice, who operates as the supernatural figure here. Collins again draws the reader's attention to the spectacle of female violence, through the unnatural foreign figure with her 'corpse-like pallor' and 'the glittering metallic brightness in her large black eyes' (p. 90), who creates 'a sickening sense of horror' (p. 229) in the minds of those who know her story.

Another regular contributor to *All the Year Round* in the late 1860s and early 1870s was the Irish writer Joseph Sheridan le Fanu, who is also known for his sensationalist novels of the mid-Victorian period, such as *The House by the Church Yard* (1863) and *Uncle Silas* (1864), the latter based on an earlier short story, 'Passage in the Secret History of an Irish Countess', which was later revised as 'The Murdered Cousin'.

Often focusing on troubled professional men haunted by 'bestial companions' borrowed from folklore, such as menacing dogs, rats and monkeys,[32] his numerous ghost stories clearly influenced later Gothic writers, including Bram Stoker and Robert Louis Stephenson, and raised key questions about buried guilt, inheritance, the family, religion and sexuality. Alison Milbank has noted le Fanu's interest in the house as 'frontier post between private and public' and between 'the material and the spiritual', arguing that some of his haunted house narratives suggest that 'entry to the spiritual realm is possible'.[33] His most popular collection of stories, *In a Glass Darkly* (1872), borrowed Dickens's convention of framing a series of related tales: the mysterious figure of the physician Martin Hesselius leaves a number of 'cases' for the unnamed narrator who acts as his 'medical secretary' (p. 3) to edit and convey to the reader.[34]

The first story in this collection, 'Green Tea', previously published in *All the Year Round* in 1869, is a characteristic tale of an overworked clergyman, Mr Jennings, who finds it hard to complete 'the discharge of [his] duties' (p. 26). He is thought to be suffering from his nerves, but in his own testimony has been haunted for years by a monkey of 'unfathomable malignity' (p. 24), which appears on buses and in the street, as well as in the church and the vicarage. Thought to be less a 'spectral illusion' than a consequence of drinking too much green tea to keep his mind alert for nocturnal study, the monkey could be read as a symbol of the nervousness common to the male scholars who appear regularly in this kind of fiction, who invite such visions by working in remote houses during the dead of night. However, the monkey's 'intense and increasing fury' (p. 27) during prayers, and his significantly appearing in the pulpit, squatting on Jennings's Bible so he cannot read to his congregation, also suggest the crisis of faith thought to have been experienced by many Victorians around mid-century and accelerated by the publication of the evolutionary theories of Charles Darwin in 1859. Robert Louis Stevenson's later Gothic tale *Jekyll and Hyde* (1886) shows the respectable Doctor Jekyll horrified by the bestial Hyde's scribbling in his books, as another side of the self expresses the anarchic thoughts professional men are obliged to keep hidden. This sense of spiritual crisis is corroborated by the information that Jennings has had 'questions' to be 'settled' with the bishop, and has suffered from the despair and desperation which Hesselius believes can be alleviated by trusting in the power of God. What is interesting is that when Jennings finally bows to the monkey's urgings to kill himself and is discovered with his throat slit, covered in blood, his behaviour can be attributed by the narrating physician, after a medical explanation of his symptoms and similar cases he has treated, to the 'complaint' of 'hereditary suicidal mania' (p. 36).

Bram Stoker drew heavily on le Fanu's malevolent animal motifs for his own 'The Judge's House', which appeared in the Christmas number of the *Illustrated Sporting and Dramatic Life* (1891). The story is about a young male student, cautioned by the locals about renting the creepy house of a notoriously harsh judge, who is ultimately forced to hang himself with the judge's rope after being haunted by an enormous rat. As in a number of le Fanu tales which are only able to end the haunting by the suicide of the haunted male protagonist,[35] this leaves unanswered the questions raised; as Harold Orel has argued in his discussion of the writer, 'it is curious...how often some form of suicide becomes the only possible solution to the problems created by abnormal tastes in living'.[36] The common motif of the anxious male professional forced to see suicide as the only way out again points towards feelings of impotence and desperation and the failure to 'discharge duties' as characteristic of a certain strain of middle-class Victorian masculinity.

In a Glass Darkly is also notable for its final, longer tale, 'Carmilla', about a lascivious female vampire, which anticipated many of the shocking scenes of violent undead women preying on innocent victims explored in Bram Stoker's *Dracula* (1897). Hesselius takes a back seat in this story; in the absence of a rational man, the narrator, Laura, is 'a rather spoiled girl' (p. 243), a lonely inhabitant of a Gothic Austrian castle 'studiously kept in ignorance of ghost stories' (p. 244), as both men and medical science fail to account for vampiric behaviour. The initial encounter with the vampire, when Laura is 'caressed' and 'soothed' to sleep by a young lady who appears as if in a vision at the side of her bed, a scene marred by the sensation of two needles being run deeply into her breast (p. 244), is repeated after that same young lady, Carmilla, comes to stay in the castle, claiming 'a right to [her] intimacy' (p. 257) because she too has experienced the vision. One striking scene, parading le Fanu's characteristic interest in the terrors produced by unearthly animals, depicts Laura's dream of a 'monstrous cat' about five feet long who springs onto her bed to suck her blood, exposing the malevolence of the vampire woman who has infiltrated the middle-class home. Although the more learned commentaries on vampirism come from the male characters, such as Laura's father and his friend General Spielsdorf, whose own daughter is one of Carmilla's victims, and although the final 'shocking scene' (p. 311) of the beheading and staking of Carmilla's body in its coffin can be described but not witnessed by a woman, what makes the narrative stand out is the viewpoint of a female narrator who is unable wholly to distance herself from her attraction to the supernatural figure.

It is almost impossible not to read Carmilla's 'passionate' gazes and the repetition of the idea that they will become 'very dear friends' (p. 258), coupled with the 'repulsion', 'the same faint antipathy...mingled with my admiration of her' (p. 259) experienced by the narrator, as indicators of a covert lesbian attraction between vampire and victim, despite the fact that same-sex desire, particularly between women, had not been openly acknowledged within the culture. le Fanu appears to have been ahead of his time in using the compressed scenes of the short-story form to hint at this taboo area of Victorian sexuality in representing the narrator's confused feelings, of 'excitement...mingled with a vague sense of fear and disgust' (p. 261), about another woman. While this does not present lesbianism as perversity, as it would later be categorised by medical 'experts', it does refuse to explain the feeling which the vampire inspires: even looking back with the knowledge of Carmilla's undead status, Laura does not apologise for her attraction. Glen Cavaliero, admiring the 'oddity' of the tale, has noted the ambiguity of the ending, 'for the narrator...is already dead, though whether to become a vampire in her turn is left unclear'.[37] Anticipating the focus in 1890s vampire fiction on the strange attractions of supernatural beings, the story can be used both to reveal and to conceal the taboo status of alternative sexualities embodied in figures defined by the culture as evil.

Witches, curses and female violence: Elizabeth Gaskell, George Eliot and Mary Elizabeth Braddon

The 1850s and 1860s witnessed a vogue for sensationalism in fiction, which prompted some realist writers to use the short-story form to step outside the safe parameters of social realism to probe deeper into controversial or shocking subjects in a more sensational mode. Elizabeth Gaskell, a regular contributor to *Household Words* throughout the 1850s, was known for her novels about the industrial poor, such as *Mary Barton*, published in 1848, and *North and South*, serialised in *Household Words* in 1855. She tended to work on her stories as a break from longer projects, ensuring that her shorter tales often reworked ideas she was exploring in her full-length fiction (for example, the plight of the fallen woman is treated extensively in her novel *Ruth* of 1853). Shirley Foster has noted that, in her innovative shorter works, Gaskell's representation of 'violence, both psychological and physical, within the content of dys-functional or fragmented familial relations' is used to explore 'poten-tially "unacceptable" topics such as child murder, sexual jealousy and revenge, and hatred of the Other'.[38] Gaskell's and Eliot's supernatural tales, like those of Thomas Hardy later in the century, are often struc-tured around Gothic paradigms, such as witchcraft, curses and demonic possession by a double, or doppelgänger, and examine such pseudo-sciences as clairvoyance and phrenology.

Gaskell's most anthologised piece, 'The Old Nurse's Story', published in the Christmas supplement to *Household Words* of 1852, is a haunted house narrative in which the sinister music from a broken organ and the appearances of a spectral child who leaves no footprints in the snow herald the return of half-buried but not forgotten family antagonisms. Narrated by the nurse, Hester, who has brought her newly orphaned young charge Rosamond to live in Furnivall Manor, the home of dis-tant relatives, the story chronicles the escalating fears of the servants about these ghostly happenings, with the no-nonsense tone of the nar-rator self-consciously echoing that of Nellie in Emily Brontë's *Wuthering Heights* (1847). One bitter-cold day Rosamond has to be rescued, half-frozen, after following the spectral child to be 'lull[ed] to sleep' (p. 28) by a weeping lady on the snowy Fells.[39] Old Miss Furnivall's 'wild warning' to Hester about the 'evil' nature of the 'wicked, naughty child' (p. 23) is followed by mutterings about forgiveness and mercy, which are later revealed to stem from her guilt about informing her father of her elder sister Maude's secret pregnancy, which prompted the death of the child in a snow-storm years earlier. The melodramatic scene describing the daughter's helplessness in the face of her father's anger, the 'great and violent noise' as he strikes the crying child and the disturbing image of 'Miss Maude sitting, all crazy and smiling, under the holly-trees, nurs-ing a dead child, with a terrible mark on its right shoulder' (p. 28), employs sensationalist tactics to expose family cruelty. Nevertheless, the anguish of the aging sister, Grace, is poignant. In this earlier scene she is standing by her father 'white and still as any stone', sighing with satisfaction at his actions (p. 28), but in its re-enactment later in the story she is forced to watch her proud younger self 'look on, stony and deadly serene', at the blow and the banishment, her 'wild entreaty' that her father spare the child unheard by the 'terrible phantoms' (p. 31). The repetition of this scene in more graphic detail at the climax of the tale adds to the horror of the conflict, forcing the reader to notice the way in which the mother's 'fierce and proud defiance' collapsed as 'she threw up her arms wildly and piteously to save her child' (p. 31) and dwelling on the violence of the blow. The final moral, repeated by the 'death-stricken' Grace in the last lines – 'Alas! Alas! What is done in youth can never be undone in age!' (p. 32) – reinforces the message about the sins of the father. Gaskell's unusual decision to make the phantoms in this final scene visible to all of the onlookers, subverting the convention of a single character seeing the ghost and having doubts raised about his or her sanity, was criticised by Dickens, who urged her to rewrite it before it appeared in *Household Words*, but she insisted that Grace must be '*visibly* confronted by her guilt'.[40] Perhaps this was a contrary impulse to accept the existence of the spiritual world in keeping with Hester's beliefs as a narrator, and also a conscious rejection and rewriting of the conventions of the mid-Victorian ghost story.

At a time when women's familial and domestic roles were being eagerly discussed in the press, the story can be seen as a commentary on their inferior positions within the Victorian household as daughters, sisters and mothers. Maude's helplessness, which is evocative of the unmarried mother stigmatised throughout the nineteenth century, is symptomatic of her era, and her desperate attempts to protect, and ultimately save, her child, whose death is prompted by her decision to bring her to live quietly in the family home, indicate the limited rights and powers of the mother in a patriarchal system. The cold-hearted spinster Grace, who does little more than sew and sleep, now wrinkled, deaf and treated 'as if she were a child' by her 'grey', 'stony' companion, Mrs Stark (p. 15), is hardly an appealing figure, and her constant association with stoniness serves to remind us of the dangers of rejecting a woman's natural roles as wife and mother. The feud with her sister, motivated by sexual jealousy, ultimately leaves her alone, and her punishment is to be imprisoned within the home. The story can be read as a plea for mercy towards illegitimate or unwanted children in the next generation, and as an acknowledgement of the powers of the nurturing woman: as an endorsement of this role, Hester becomes the 'old nurse' of the title, telling the story to Rosamond's children, the imagined readers significantly addressed in the first paragraph as 'my dears'.

Other of Gaskell's Gothic stories use the idea of the monstrous double or the figure of the witch to expose the stigmatisation that women are subject to, both those whose sexualities single them out for special attention and censure and those ostracised by the community for supposedly unnatural behaviour. In 'The Poor Clare', which appeared in three parts in *Household Words* in December 1856, Bridget's decision to live on the outskirts of her eighteenth-century community after the trauma of her beloved daughter's disappearance, coupled with recollection of 'her strong character and passionate anger', ensured that 'she was unconsciously earning for herself the dreadful reputation of a witch' (p. 57), which is later confirmed by her cursing of Squire Gisborne for shooting her daughter's dog. The loneliness of her existence in her 'desolate' home perhaps suggests the author's sympathy for the position of the 'helpless' widow, who, like the spinster, is an isolated and threatening figure for her rejection of social norms. Thus, the curse is seen as a bid for power in a society composed of the 'bad, cruel m[e]n' (p. 59) who condemn her in this way. Gaskell's ongoing interest in witchcraft set her apart from other writers because, according to Dickerson, in comparison to ghosts, 'the idea of witches was one that did not surface as often in the nineteenth century as one might suspect... perhaps because witches were so strikingly antithetical to the more current notion of the angel at the hearth'.[41] She is able to dissolve fears about the evil nature of Bridget, 'rather a wild and savage woman than a malignant witch' (p. 83), only by forcing her into the penitent position of a Poor Clare who willingly dies in her anguished attempts to undo the curse that tragically affects her own granddaughter, Lucy. The sympathetic treatment of the fearful witch figure is also evident in 'Lois the Witch' (also published in three parts in *All the Year Round*, in October 1859), which is set in 1692, the time of the Salem witch-hunts in New England, and focuses on the orphaned Lois, whose attractiveness and outspokenness result in her untimely death.

In both witch stories wildness and uncleanness haunt the borders of acceptable female behaviour, playing to fears about women outside the social norm. The use of the virtuous Lucy's monstrous double in 'The Poor Clare' anticipates techniques evident in vampire fiction by Sheridan le Fanu and Bram Stoker later in the century, where the sexuality of women, which has to be repressed in Victorian society, bursts out in the excessive lasciviousness and forward behaviour of the female vampire, an alarming alter ego for the angel in the house. Gaskell's Lucy struggles in the marriage market and is reproached by her father for her 'undue familiarity – all unbecoming a gentlewoman – with his grooms' (p. 77) because her mischievous double has no sense of social restraint. This existence of 'another wicked, fearful self' (p. 77) who has 'a loathsome demon soul looking out of the grey eyes, that were in turns mocking and voluptuous' (p. 78) draws on the kind of language used to describe prostitutes and signals male fears of the sexualised woman. Interestingly, as in 'The Old Nurse's Story', this apparition is visible to all, dissolving explanations based on insanity or hallucination. The rational narrator's initial disbelief in Lucy's story of her 'bewitchment' inclines him to the view that this is more likely 'the effect of a life of extreme seclusion telling on the nerves of a sensitive girl' (p. 78), though his scoffing at this 'belief in visions' is cut short by his own sighting of the ghastly figure behind her, which produces the expected reaction: 'my heart stood still within me; every hair rose up erect; my flesh crept with horror' (p. 78). A startling and uncharacteristic direct address to the reader of 1859 made in 'Lois the Witch' – 'you must remember, you who in the nineteenth century read this account, that witchcraft was a real terrible sin to her, Lois Barclay, two hundred years ago' (p. 211) – is perhaps revealing of Gaskell's fears of scepticism on the part of the reading public, a scepticism she attempts to challenge in her stories by appearing to demonstrate the working of curses or by showing her ghosts to more than one person.

George Eliot, the pseudonym of Mary Ann or Marian Evans, an intellectual writer and journalist with an interest in science and evolution, was more fascinated by the psychological effects of supernatural visions. She was a major Victorian author of realist novels such as *The Mill on the Floss* (1859) and *Middlemarch* (1871), which focus on education, marriage and gender inequalities. Her much anthologised 'The Lifted Veil' (1859), a disturbing exploration of the limits of scientific enquiry and the workings of psychology, is one of her rare forays into first-person narration. It is told from the perspective of 'a miserable ghost-seer' (p. 85), a clairvoyant second son 'cursed with an exceptional mental character' (p. 57) and able to read the minds of family and acquaintances and to foresee his own death after a marriage he predicts will be unhappy.[42] Oppressed by his vision of future events and the 'narrow thoughts' (p. 96) of his family circle, the sickly, feminised Latimer is used to question the benefits such 'double consciousness' (p. 95) could be imagined to offer – is it a 'strange new power' (p. 66) or a disease, a delirium? – again suggesting the unmanliness of supernatural experience. Eliot's publishers at *Blackwood's Magazine* found its subject matter 'strange' and were unwilling to publish it under her pseudonym of George Eliot lest it damage her growing reputation; Eliot herself initially dismissed the story as a *jeu de melancolie* (a melancholy game) which she herself thought nothing of.[43]

Yet this weird tale can also be seen as an intervention into the topical arena of medical science, posing questions about the visible world and our perceptions of the future. Eliot was intrigued by the new pseudo-sciences of clairvoyance, mesmerism and phrenology (the assessment of brain size in relation to moral character, which she drew on in her tale), and had been mesmerised herself in 1844, though she later rejected mesmerism as 'unscientific'.[44] Her exploration of clair-voyance cannot pretend to offer scientific evidence about such mental states, but Latimer's 'gift' does not appear to be open to alternative explanations, and his perceptions of the future – such as the photo-graphic image of Prague he 'sees' years before his actual visit – are more detailed and frequent than the dream-visions used by Dickens and Collins, suggesting that there is a scientific as well as a supernatural dimension to his unwanted powers, his 'super-added consciousness' (p. 71). His sense of the 'barrenness' of his existence and his future wife's 'bitter smile of contempt' for him, glimpsed in a 'moment of hell' in which he anticipates her desire that he kill himself, offer a sobering vision of marital despair (p. 74). He therefore enters the mar-riage with the knowledge of mutual contempt – 'she was my wife, and we hated each other' (p. 74) – destroying the possibility of future hap-piness. This 'hideous glimpse of the future' (p. 74) is even more hellish because his desire for Bertha has been sustained up to this point by the fact that her mind alone remained 'impenetrable' to him, leaving him helpless in the clutches of an evil, unnatural figure and therefore inviting his own death, again linking a troubled masculinity to the suicidal impulse.

This lurking evil of the Victorian wife also manifests itself in the spectacle, or threat, of female violence used by sensation novelists such as Braddon and Collins. The murderous intentions of the wife are revealed in a sensationalist final scene in 'The Lifted Veil' in which Latimer's medical friend, Charles Meunier, performs a blood transfu-sion, followed by artificial respiration, on the dead body of Bertha's servant, Mrs Archer, resulting in 'the wondrous slow return of life' (p. 94) and the animation of the body. Galvanism, temporarily restor-ing life to dead bodies through electro-magnetism, had been used to animate the creature in Mary Shelley's *Frankenstein* (1818), and such experiments, often performed on dead animals, were discussed in the medical press and intellectual journals of the day. But like the visions of the future seen as a curse rather than a gift, the reanimation of the body offers horror and the unwelcome revelation of secrets, as Archer points at Bertha and accuses her, 'You mean to poison your husband... you laughed at me, and told lies about me behind your back to make me disgusting... because you were jealous... are you sorry... now?' (p. 95). Rather than being a triumph for medical science, the experiment frightens the observers and unnerves the doctor. The lack of sympathy between Bertha and her servant is of a piece with the contempt which cements Latimer's marriage; the only brief comment he makes is that 'liv[ing] again' appears to be a form of waking up 'with our unuttered curses rising to our lips' (p. 95), another form of spiritual barrenness. Beryl Gray reads this scene as 'compounding the relationship between the power of evil and the story's realm of the Unknown', part of Eliot's 'serious attempt' to capture the horrors of visionary powers (and maybe of scientific progress), 'powers that a significant part of Victorian society believed in or was fascinated by, without, perhaps, fully considering the philosophical implications'.[45]

Female sensation novelists also exploited the conventions of the ghost story to comment more forcefully on sexual jealousy, betrayal and illicit desire by going beyond the limitations of what was acceptable in Victorian plots, in which feisty heroines had to be tamed or restrained. According to Jenny Uglow, their shorter fictions allowed them to avoid the conservative endings of popular novels demanded by publishers: 'in the novels the wayward heroines are cruelly punished and order is restored ... but in the stories the passionate women wreak vengeance on false, weak men, selfish betrayers of women's trust'.[46] Mary Elizabeth Braddon, a notorious former actress who set up home with a married man, John Maxwell, who was also her publisher, began her long writing career by producing detective stories and best-selling sensation novels, such as the much imitated *Lady Audley's Secret* (1862) and *Aurora Floyd* (1863), about women's willingness to commit bigamy or even murder to get what they wanted. Maxwell made Braddon editor of the magazine *Belgravia* (1866–76), and as the magazine's main attraction, Braddon used the space to serialise some of her own work. Her early sensationalist ghost stories, collected in *Ralph the Bailiff and Other Tales* (1867), sometimes featured erotic encounters with ghosts in order to explore revenge or women's inability to get what they wanted. In 'The Cold Embrace' a young student cannot escape from the 'cold and wet fingers' of his rejected lover, who has drowned herself and now takes sexual control only through death. Her revolting touch, a manifestation of the student's guilt, 'encapsulates Braddon's perception of the thin veneer of social life and sanity and of our vulnerability and isolation'.[47] 'Eveline's Visitant' tells the story of a new wife haunted by the phantom of a man her husband has killed in a duel, which makes her into 'the worst and vilest of women' as she is reduced against her will to 'one weird, unholy pleasure – the delight of his presence' (p. 123), though the narrator assures the reader that 'it was my wife's innocent heart which Andre made the instrument of his revenge' (p. 124).[48] Another level to both these stories is that the sexual frisson of the ghostly embrace overrides the tepid innocence of marriage. Eveline dies in the final sentence, 'sobbing and affrighted, that he was by her side' (p. 124), as the ghost is linked to guilt and unspoken pleasures.

Braddon's later stories employed sensationalist techniques more subtly to explore issues of class, money and work as they affected women's lives, in line with the fascination with the financial in women's supernatural tales of the 1870s and 1880s. In the thought-provoking story 'The Shadow in the Corner', published in *All the Year Round* in 1879, the haunted house is used to draw attention to the plight of those poorly paid and lonely women condemned to a life of domestic service. Servants featured prominently in supernatural tales, as they did in sensation fiction, sometimes as unreliable narrators whose testimonies should be treated with suspicion but also sometimes, as in this instance, to raise the public profile of a class of unacknowledged workers. 'The Shadow in the Corner', its title revealing the ways in which servants were effaced and depersonalised, describes the 'melancholy fate' of the 'pale and silent' Maria, who hangs herself after being forced to sleep in a 'big, lonely' attic room in which the master's brother hanged himself years before.[49] Eve M. Lynch has highlighted the correlations between the figures of the servant, reduced to a life of drudgery, and the phantom in Braddon's fiction: 'the working woman becomes a mere automaton, hollow and vague like the shadow in the corner'.[50] In a tale weighted towards his own viewpoint, the master's ridiculing of her bad dreams and the shadow of a dead body she sees as 'a silly fancy, bred of timidity and low spirits' (p. 61) attributable to the 'weak state' of her nerves (p. 57) functions to undermine her status within the household. Notwithstanding the master's 'compassionate' interest in the girl, he attempts to deny that he has had a similar experience in the room. This, combined with the other servants' insistence that she continue to sleep in the room, can be seen as contributing to the girl's own suicidal urges, though these are given the 'customary merciful verdict of "Temporary insanity"' (p. 68), a label often used to cover up the more class-based explanations for female suicides at the time. 'The Cold Embrace' also ends with the suicide of the male student, whose ghostly encounters coincide with his descent into starvation and feelings of guilt, suggesting Braddon's interest in the psychological elements of the suicidal impulse.

Another interesting story about class and economics is Braddon's excellent 'Good Lady Ducayne', published in the new magazine *The Strand* in 1896. The story uses the conventions of vampire fiction to address issues of women's work and the way in which the energy of the female labourer can be sucked out by over-demanding employers. The 'penniless' seamstress Bella Rolleston, first seen in one of the new employment agencies, takes a well-paid job as a lady's companion, only to discover that Lady Ducayne's previously healthy companions 'died in her service' under mysterious circumstances.[51] The girls have been bled during the night by the evil Dr Parravicini in order to keep their hundred-year-old employer alive, her vampiric status dependent on their labour. Bella's escape from 'cheap lodgings in a shabby street off the Walworth Road, scanty dinners, homely food, well-worn raiment' (p. 127) to the luxuries of an Italian hotel can be achieved only by sacrificing herself to the exacting conditions of her employer. The story protests against the growing numbers of young girls 'breaking down' under the strain of remaining financially self-sufficient at a time when women's wages and working conditions remained pitifully inadequate: despite her ailments, Bella will stay with the lady 'as long as she will go on paying me twenty-five pounds a quarter' (p. 144). The strange dreams she suffers from, the whirring of wheels and sinking into a 'gulf of unconsciousness' (p. 137), are explained as the result of the use of chloroform by 'that wretched Italian quack' (p. 143), as her class status means that she, too, operates as an object for medical experimentation. However, Bella is rescued into marriage by her doctor–suitor Herbert Stafford, whose commitment to her health might signify the triumph of modern medicine, but also perhaps underscores the recommendation that women withdraw from the dangers of the labour market.

Real *and* uncanny: Thomas Hardy

Thomas Hardy, a stonemason's son, was a realist novelist and poet whose narratives centred on the customs of rural Wessex, or Dorset, where he grew up. Late novels, such as *Tess of the d'Urbervilles* (1891) and *Jude the Obscure* (1895), are typical in their focus on working-class lives and traditions and their interest in education, marriage and female sexuality. Like Dickens and Gaskell, he published short stories throughout his career, the difference being in the range of British and American periodicals in which this work was first published in the 1880s and 1890s. His short fiction appeared in different forms in magazines and in the four collected editions of stories he later published, *Wessex Tales* (1888), *A Group of Noble Dames* (1891), *Life's Little Ironies* (1894) and *'A Changed Man' and Other Tales* (1913). Set in the 1820s, 'The Three Strangers', which first appeared in *Longman's Magazine* in 1884 before being serialised in the American magazine *Harper's Weekly*, tells a tale of three unknown men who each in turn take shelter from the rain at a christening party in a remote cottage. They are finally revealed to be a hangman, a condemned man who has escaped from prison, and the condemned man's brother, though the hangman remains unaware that he is drinking with the man whose life lies in his hands, whose brother suffers 'abject terror...his knees trembling' (p. 138) when he sees them together.[52] The impact of the story resides in the collective fear of the brothers and the villagers when they realise that 'an ominous public officer', 'the stranger of the deadly trade' (p. 137) and an embodiment of the threatening urban environment, is in their midst. One reviewer admired the story for 'the tension of its wild emotion'.[53] However, *Longman's* rejected what is now Hardy's most famous story, 'The Withered Arm' (also collected in *Wessex Tales*, after appearing in *Blackwood's Edinburgh Magazine* in 1888), for being too 'gloomy', suggesting a distaste for its focus on hanging and the supernatural. In his preface to *Wessex Tales*, Hardy defended himself against such charges by pointing out his commitment to realism, citing the importance of 'hanging matters' in the 'local tradition' and his knowledge of an old woman who had had her blood turned by the corpse of a hanged convict in the manner described in the story.[54] Like Dickens, Hardy was fascinated by public executions, which were banned only in 1868, and felt a keen sense of injustice about hanging for trifling crimes such as theft. His description of the eager spectators enjoying the event and of the 'line the colour of an unripe blackberry' (p. 264) surrounding the neck of the young male corpse adds to the shock factor of a tale that borrows from graphic criminal reports in the press, pushing at the boundaries of the genre by combining realism with horror.

In 'The Withered Arm', another powerful blend of folk tale and social realism, the jealousy of the milkmaid Rhoda Brooks, 'the supplanted woman' (p. 244), directed towards Gertrude, the new 'ladylike' wife of Farmer Lodge, the father of Rhoda's son, takes supernatural form in a vision in which 'the young wife, in the pale silk dress and white bonnet, but with features shockingly distorted, and wrinkled as by age, was sitting upon her chest as she lay' (p. 245). Struggling against this 'incubus', which mocked the half-suffocated supplanted woman with her wedding ring, Rhoda made physical contact, 'seized the confronting spectre by its obtrusive left arm, and whirled it backward to the floor' (p. 245). It is interesting that Hardy felt the need to tone down the ghostly nature of this incident by setting the encounter with the spectre within a dream; he admits in the preface that he had 'forgotten' that the real woman on whom he based the tale had been oppressed by the incubus 'while lying down on a hot day'.[55] However, this might say more about the climate of scepticism in which he was writing when he drew on these 'real' occurrences from earlier times. Kristin Brady has noted the minor changes Hardy made to the story after periodical publication. He added a 'few late-nineteenth-century scientific speculations' about the withering of the arm, keeping the superstition in line with his view that 'a story dealing with the supernatural should never be explained away in the unfortunate manner of [Gothic novelist] Mrs Radcliffe'.[56] The earlier setting of the story (in the 1820s or early 1830s) also means that Hardy can draw on the same association of witchcraft with uncontrolled female sexuality used by Gaskell, as Rhoda recoils from her actions:

> 'O, can it be,' she said to herself, when her visitor had departed, 'that I exercise a malignant power over people against my own will?' She knew that she had been slyly called a witch since her fall; but never having understood why that particular stigma had been attached to her, it had passed disregarded. Could this be the explanation, and had such things as this ever happened before? (p. 248)

In its exploration of the loss of physical beauty for women via Gertrude's desperate desire to cure her arm by having her blood turned by contact with a hanged corpse, the story attacks male expectations about marriage. As a sign of jealousy and female rivalry, rather than the domestic violence Gertrude imagines it to resemble, the arm remains uncured because at the scene of the hanging the 'delicate vitality' of the wife cannot withstand 'the double shock' (p. 265) of the closeness of Rhoda and her husband, who have come together to mourn the loss of their son, hanged for theft. The convention of withdrawing from the narrative in the final pages to question the veracity of supernatural events is abandoned, and the focus is instead on the gender divide between the husband's penitence after his wife's death and the aging of the bereaved, isolated milkmaid, whose 'impassive, wrinkled brow' (p. 266) reveals nothing of her secrets. The story therefore works as a variation on Hardy's recurring message in his longer fiction that 'the woman pays', as the suffering of the two women, brought on by sexual rivalry and the social stigmatising of the single mother, far outweighs that of the farmer, who abandoned his child until it was too late.

Sexual anxieties and the uncanny at the *fin de siècle*: Henry James and Vernon Lee

Reflecting the enduring interest in the paranormal, and a market more receptive to the short-story form, more collections of ghost stories appeared during the *fin de siècle*, the decadent period at the end of the nineteenth century. Many of these collections were by women writers, such as Margaret Oliphant's *Stories of the Seen and Unseen* (1889), Vernon Lee's *Hauntings* (1890), E. Nesbit's *Grim Tales* (1893) and Mary Molesworth's (1839–1921) *Uncanny Tales* (1896). The revival of Gothic at the *fin de siècle*, particularly among male writers, also produced a renewed interest in the figure of the monster, and a revisiting of the idea of 'the monstrous double signifying duplicity and evil nature', noted by Botting as a key nineteenth-century variant.[57] Henry James is an important figure in this period, primarily because of the publication of his well-known novella *The Turn of the Screw* (1898), a Gothic study of the nature of evil. Born in New York but resident in Britain for most of his adult life, James later became a British citizen, his reputation resting on his acclaimed, albeit complex, realist novels of the turn of the century, such as *The Portrait of a Lady* (1881) and *The Wings of the Dove* (1902). He published, and was well paid for, a number of ghost stories throughout his career (many in American periodicals), which, like his novels, showed a fascination with innocence and experience, with money and property, and with the figure of the young woman on the brink of marriage. In a preface to his stories, he identified the note he wished to emphasise in his supernatural fiction: 'that of the strange and the sinister embroidered on the very type of the normal and easy' (p. xlvi), which anticipates Freudian definitions of the uncanny, both familiar and unfamiliar.[58] 'Sir Edmund Orme', in the Christmas 1891 issue of the new London journal *Black and White*, appears to be a fairly normal courtship narrative, except that the narrator's pursuit of Charlotte Marden is punctuated by visions of the apparition of Sir Edmund Orme, a jilted lover of Charlotte's mother. What is more sinister is that the apparition appears in broad daylight, taking his silent place in the social scene, terrifying Mrs Marden and surprising the narrator, while Charlotte, the 'innocent child', remains oblivious. His appearances comment eerily on the artificiality and power dynamics of the courtship process, on both the mother's and the suitor's desire to hasten the suitable match. Being haunted by him is also the mother's punishment and her 'curse' for being a 'bad girl' (p. 6) in her past. The process of being haunted is closer to sexual excitement for the narrator, who describes Orme as a 'splendid presence' and 'exults' in being haunted 'as if it stood for all I had ever dreamt of' (p. 19). His final passionate embrace with Charlotte after she sees the presence, resulting in the mother's death and the sob of 'the exorcised and pacified spirit' (p. 35), underlines his acquisition of sexual power, which sits uneasily with the ghost's warnings about the dangers of female coquettishness.

In the more ambiguous novella *The Turn of the Screw*, serialised in twelve instalments in *Collier's Weekly* in 1898, James famously leaves it up to the reader to decide whether the ghosts are real. The unnamed governess, eager for romance and excited by her new role in the Gothic mansion of Bly, might or might not have seen the ghosts of former employees Peter Quint and Miss Jessel, whom she claims are trying to corrupt the innocence of her young charges, Flora and Miles. Although the story is framed by the authority of a male narrator, the narrative is primarily from the governess's slightly hysterical and obscure perspective, and it stops abruptly with no authorial comment, subverting the conventions of the supernatural tale and casting doubt on its authenticity. As a number of critics have discussed, the visions (or hallucinations) of the governess can be read in relation to contemporary theories about hysteria, frigidity and sexual repression. At a time when Sigmund Freud and other sexologists were beginning to examine and define sexual identity, and to normalise heterosexuality (preferably within marriage) at the expense of forms of 'perversion', writers took advantage of the avant-garde reputation of the short-story form to explore illicit desire and 'other' sexualities. The erotic encounters with the ghost of Quint, 'a living detestable dangerous presence', can be seen as showing the governess's desire to triumph over sexual repression without becoming a fallen woman; 'the wonder of wonders' is that 'there was nothing in me unable to meet and measure him' (p. 170). As in 'Sir Edmund Orme', the 'innocent' children, in danger of being 'lost', need to be protected from sexual knowledge, from what Quint and Jessel represent. The possible dangers of paedophilia, homosexuality, cross-class desire and unplanned pregnancy cluster around their ghostly figures; they have to be reconstructed from the fragments of conversation with the other servants, as nothing is directly specified. The ghost of Miss Jessel, the former governess, whom the narrator significantly sees sitting in her chair, can also operate as the new governess's 'monstrous double', her lascivious alter ego. In his preface, James distanced himself from contemporary research into the paranormal in the interests of keeping his story 'good', claiming, 'I had ... simply to renounce all attempt to keep the kind and degree of impression I wished to produce on terms with the today so copious psychical record of cases of apparitions' (p. lii). Obscurity was entirely necessary because 'it was clear that from the first my hovering prowling blighting presences, my pair of abnormal agents, would have to depart altogether from the rules' (p. liii). James desired the reader to '*think* the evil, make him think it for himself' (p. liv) rather than find it obviously within the story. The differences between the supernatural and the material worlds had to remain unclear: 'the importance of the supernatural was matched ... by the difficulty of speaking about it and by its resistance to definition'.[59] This shows how ghost stories were becoming more ambiguous, as authors had to break the rules to develop the genre, often in order to explore issues around sexuality, around ideas of the abnormal, which still remained taboo in late-Victorian culture.

Vernon Lee, the pseudonym of Violet Paget, an intellectual figure interested in art, travel and aestheticism who moved in the same circles as Oscar Wilde and Henry James, was probably influenced by James's work, and vice versa. Born in France, she spent much of her life in Italy, where many of her stories are set, reflecting her lifelong interest in Italian history: her first publication was a critical work, *Studies of the Eighteenth Century in Italy* (1880). The first of her three volumes, *Hauntings: Fantastic Stories* (1890), comprises four ghost stories, of which three are set in her beloved Italy. All narrated from a male perspective, stories such as 'Amour Dure' and 'Oke of Okehurst' record the male fascination with the *femme fatale* and the fatal consequences of erotic obsession with figures from the past; the protagonist of 'Amour Dure' becomes the last in a long line of dead lovers after a series of encounters with the ghost of the passionate sixteenth-century duchess Medea. Her later story 'The Image' (later reprinted as 'The Doll'), which appeared in the *Cornhill* in 1896 and is unusually narrated by a female collector of *bric-à-brac*, is also worth mentioning for the unnerving presence of the huge, lifelike doll dressed in the clothes of a beautiful countess who died in childbirth early in her marriage. The narrator's obsession and the revelation of the countess's story – kept 'secluded from the world' both as a shy, cosseted wife and as a dusty, blackening image confined to a closet – lead the narrator to purchase and ritually burn the doll, to 'put an end to her sorrows', a sharp comment on the sufferings of women buried alive in unfulfilling marriages.[60] In her preface to *Hauntings*, Lee explained:

> That is the thing – the Past ... that is the place to get our ghosts from ... my four little tales are of no genuine ghosts in the scientific sense; they tell of no hauntings such as could be contributed

by the [recently formed] Society for Psychical Research…My ghosts are what you call spurious ghosts (according to me the only genuine ones), of whom I can affirm only one thing, that they haunted certain brains, and have haunted, among others, my own and my friends. (pp. 39–40)[61]

One key difference between the uncanny tales of the 1880s and 1890s and those of the 1850s and 1860s is that the later ghosts take a less traditional form and are often used as a means to explore anxieties about gender and sexuality which troubled the *fin-de-siècle* mind. The existence of 'spurious ghosts', of what haunts the brain, also fits with the experiences of the unnamed narrator in *The Turn of the Screw*, in which the reader remains uncertain whether the governess's visions are indeed hallucinations or a sign of her hysteria, or some combination of the two. In his linking of supernatural fiction to psychical research, the journalist Andrew Lang concluded that 'even ghost stories, the delight of Christmas eve, have been ravaged and annexed by psychology'.[62]

The satisfyingly complex and unconventional story 'A Wicked Voice', from *Hauntings*, which is a rewriting of an earlier story, 'Winthrop's Adventure', first published in 1881, focuses on the experiences of a struggling composer of operas haunted by the 'ghost-voice' (p. 97) of a once-famous eighteenth-century singer, Zaffirino, who was allegedly able to kill women with the sweetness of his singing. Published in the same year as Oscar Wilde's decadent novel *The Picture of Dorian Gray* (1890), it also chronicles the male obsession with a beautiful image of another man in a portrait and explores the desires which lie beneath the surface of fashionable society. Obsessed by Zaffirino's portrait and 'sickened but intoxicated' by 'long-dead melodies' (p. 93), the narrator sees visions of the singer in the process of 'killing this woman, and killing me also, with his wicked voice' (p. 107). He is then thwarted in his feverish attempts to reproduce the unfinished cadence he has heard on the harpsichord, now broken and discordant, which the singer has been playing. 'A Wicked Voice' is also typical of the 1890s in daring to address alternative sexualities, albeit in a coded way. It has been read in relation to Lee's lesbianism at a time when same-sex desire was still a punishable offence. Rather than concluding with a commentary on his possibly delusional state of mind, the story ends with the distraught composer begging to be haunted again:

I am wasted by a strange and deadly disease. I can never lay hold of my own inspiration. My head is filled with music which is certainly by me, since I have never heard it before, but which still is not my own, which I despise and abhor: little, tripping flourishes and languishing phrases, and long-drawn, echoing cadences. O wicked, wicked voice, violin of flesh and blood made by the Evil One's hand, may I not even execrate thee in peace; but is it necessary that, at the moment when I curse, the longing to hear thee again should parch my soul like hell-thirst? And since I have satiated thy lust for revenge, since thou hast withered my life and withered my genius, is it not time for pity? May I not hear one note, only one note of thine, O singer, O wicked and contemptible wretch? (p. 108)

The process of haunting here is both deadly and invigorating, as the 'hell-thirst' to hear the despised music again mirrors the experience of unwanted sexual desire. The erotic nature of the music and the voice, 'languishing', 'exquisite', 'passionate' and 'voluptuous', which the composer tries to dismiss as 'wicked' and 'evil', recalls the language used to describe encounters with vampires, as does the idea that his life and genius are being 'wasted' and 'withered' by listening to the music. The idea of possession by the famous singer, then, functions to address unspoken anxieties about sexual desire. Throughout the tale Zaffirino is repeatedly described in feminine or in uncertainly gendered terms: people speculate 'whether the voice belonged to a man or to a woman' (p. 98), and he is seen as 'effeminate', 'decidedly a beautiful creature' (p. 92), with his 'wicked woman's face' (p. 93), and the narrator, 'overcome with shame' (p. 98), feels obliged to destroy his portrait. Carlo Caballero points out that Zaffirino is clearly a castrato, a castrated male singer, who, 'like other ghosts, ... erodes differences – those between the dead and the living, the past and the present, the male and the female'.[63] His own masculinity compromised by his fears, his lack of inspiration and the disease which renders him impotent, the composer's desire for the beautiful creature with the wicked voice borders on the homoerotic, though this is disguised by his disgust at his enjoyment of these ghostly encounters. More than the *femmes fatales* of the other stories in the collection, the castrato with his wicked voice allows Lee to explore and express the haunting experience of erotic obsession in a society unwilling to acknowledge her sexuality.

The Victorian ghost story can, then, be seen to range from the traditional haunted house tale narrated by a servant to the fragmented psychological case studies framed by doctors or other authoritative male figures. While the convention of the rational male narrator is used to raise concerns about gender roles within the household, both hysterical and more sober female narrators are also employed to comment on social relations. Fears around the exchange of reason for insanity in men, or the questioning of a man's ability to fulfil the demands of his occupation, often underpin ruminations on the type of person likely to see a ghost in these narratives, posing questions about contemporary definitions of Victorian masculinity and social progress. The influence of the Gothic on nineteenth-century authors is also clearly apparent in the fascination with strange animals, witches, monstrous doubles, vampires and eroticised violence, while the safe haven of the home can also harbour the uncanny.

4
New Woman Short Stories

The 1890s were the era of the New Woman, a type of modern femininity who began to appear regularly in the journals, magazines and literature of the *fin de siècle*. As Sally Ledger and Scott McCracken have argued in relation to the growth of imperialism, feminism and socialism, 'the process of cultural fragmentation that characterised the *fin de siècle* threw the norms of the Victorian age into crisis'.[1] The New Woman was a key element of the crisis in gender relations during this transitional period. Her potential feminism took the form of rebelling against the constraints of marriage and motherhood, rejecting domesticity and embracing the freedoms of new urban environments. Moreover, she challenged social norms by pursuing her own desires, acknowledging her own sexuality and agitating for better education and employment opportunities for women. In Sarah Grand's short story 'The Undefinable: A Fantasia', which appeared in the American magazine *Cosmopolitan* in 1894, the artist narrator rhapsodises about 'the glorious womanhood of this age of enlightenment, compared with the creature as she existed merely for man's use and pleasure of old; the toy-woman, drudge, degraded domestic animal, beast of intolerable burdens'.[2] However, the undefinable New Woman, who was everything that the stereotypical 'angel in the house' was not, was glorious only to those who embraced progress. Such a radical figure was held responsible for the breakdown of traditional gender roles; indeed, as Ann L. Ardis has argued, 'for her transgressions against the sex, gender and class distinctions of Victorian England, she was accused of instigating the second fall of man'.[3]

Numerous articles in the press condemned these developments in the character of woman. The prominent anti-feminist journalist Eliza Lynn Linton (1822–98) attacked her in a series of articles on 'The Wild

Women' which appeared in the mainstream journal *The Nineteenth Century* in 1891, arguing that modern woman's rejection of marriage and maternity threatened the social fabric. Echoing the pro-natalist views of her day, Linton claimed that 'the continuance of the race in healthy reproduction, together with the fit nourishment and care of the young after birth is the ultimate end of women as such; and whatever tells against these functions ... is an offence against nature and a wrong done to society'.[4] Despite her own independent lifestyle, Linton professed to find it inconceivable that women could choose to take up a career or study for a degree or live alone in rented accommodation – all options that were becoming available for young women at the turn of the century. However, such sentiments were balanced by the more forward-thinking views of journalists who welcomed women's new freedoms and helped to normalise these changes in gender identity. The novelist Mona Caird (1854–1932), whose New Woman heroines refused to settle for the traditional role of homemaker in novels such as *The Daughters of Danaus* (1894), defended the New Woman by questioning the current idealisation of maternity, arguing that 'we shall never have really good mothers until women cease to make their motherhood the central idea of their existence'.[5] Caird's discussions of the failure of marriage, which added fuel to a debate about the legitimacy of spinsterhood that had been simmering since mid-century, foregrounded the importance of economic independence for women and the need for a new kind of 'free marriage'. This ideal would help to provide a solution to 'the difficult problem of securing the real independence of women, and thence of the readjustment of their position in relation to men'.[6]

New Woman fiction became a popular genre in the decadent 1890s, following the decline of the mid-Victorian three-volume novel so beloved of circulating library users. This new type of fiction was most easily identifiable by the fresh kind of outspoken heroine who leapt from its pages, likely to demand education and employment as a woman's right, to seek to reform modern marriage or to reject dependency on men and follow her own desires, sexual and otherwise. In their discussion of possible commonality between the New Woman writers, Marion Shaw and Lyssa Randolph note their general 'insistence on the need to explore, redefine and celebrate women's sexuality' and their commitment to marital reform at a time when novelists were still battling the constraints of censorship.[7] Many of the new novels were closer to novellas in length or were more adventurous in form, anticipating the development of modernism in the early twentieth century. Nevertheless, Ann Heilmann has recently argued the importance of realism to the New Woman narrative: 'While moving into allegorical, utopian and non-realist, sensationalist, mythical, even dream-like and surrealist sequences of writing, New Woman fiction retained its links with realism in that it always located the conditions of women's oppression in contemporary social reality.'[8] This oppression included the brutality of husbands and women's confinement to the home at a time when the desire to break away from marriage altogether was still seen as radical, despite the growing number of single or 'superfluous' women in society. Moving beyond the constraints of the mid-Victorian marriage plot, which often used marriage and the birth of an heir as a reward in the closing chapters, New Woman narratives were less formulaic and more inconclusive; they were structured differently in order to focus on the experience of marital difficulties, messy divorces, working lives for women, the trials of motherhood or fluctuations in sexual desire.

Outlets

The vogue for short fiction at the *fin de siècle* was in part due to the desire for novelty: with its 'omissions, with the brevity of its allusiveness', Frederick Wedmore noted in 1898, 'the Short Story admits of greater variety of form than does the long novel'.[9] Picking up on the contemporary interest in psychology and sexology – the new science of sexuality – short stories often focused on isolated incidents, brief periods of time or a single conversation between two characters. This interest in the moment and fleeting emotion was reflected in the titles of stories and collections such as George Egerton's 'A Psychological Moment', Grand's collection *Emotional Moments*, and Ella D'Arcy's *Modern Instances* (1898).[10] One significant way of structuring the short story at this time was around a journey by train or omnibus or a short walk through the city. The use of a railway carriage as a setting for bringing together diverse characters in 'intervals of intensity, the beginnings of episodes – tragic, heroic, amorous, abject; or the conclusions, which make the turning point the crisis of a life' (p. 217),[11] as the first paragraph of Grand's story 'When the Door Opened...?' reveals, works particularly well in a narrative which mimics the experience of the short journeys more and more people were undertaking for work and leisure. Moreover, as Angelique Richardson suggests, 'inconclusive, openended, evasive short stories were a perfect fit for the modern woman, as she released herself from repressive social codes, and tried out new identities'.[12] As we noted in Chapter 1, the popularity of the short story increased to keep pace with the changing literary marketplace and what is now referred to as 'New Journalism', a newly commodified form of the periodical press that appealed to the masses with its illustrations, sensationalism and use of 'star' contributors.[13] New journals dedicated to short fiction, such as *The Strand*, *The Idler*, *Black and White* and *The Graphic*, all published their first editions in the early 1890s, at a time when, according to Clare Hanson, 'we can see the beginnings of the association between literary innovation and specialised coterie magazines'.[14] A proliferation of new magazines aimed at women readers, such as *Woman*, *Young Woman* and the American *Vogue*, which featured fiction predominantly by female authors as well as interviews and literary gossip, also began to appear. Like contemporary novelists such as Thomas Hardy and George Gissing, who opposed censorship and called for 'Candour in English Fiction',[15] short-story writers of this period also made use of what Elaine Showalter refers to as the 'flexibility and freedom' of the form to confront the complexities and inconsistencies of gender and sexual identities in a period of transition.[16] With the decline of the three-volume novel, fiction became more experimental. Around this time, changes in publishing also contributed to the development and greater popularity of short-story collections and anthologies, often with New Woman themes and titles.

However, the most significant new journal of this period in relation to the short story was the decadent and fashionable *The Yellow Book*, edited by Henry Harland and published in thirteen volumes between 1894 and 1897. With its first four covers designed by the art editor Aubrey Beardsley often featuring figures of indeterminate gender or sexuality, the journal embraced and inscribed the decadence and aestheticism of middle- and upper-class culture. As a new literary periodical aimed primarily at an elite of cultured intellectuals, it was prepared 'to take greater risks in terms of content'.[17] Harland set out to make himself 'the connoisseur of a true short story based on elusive impressions and suggestions whose difficulty bolstered the magazine's elitism'.[18] Although there were some topical articles, the magazine was devoted primarily to stories and poetry. Contributors included established authors such as Henry James, Arthur Symons (1865–1945) and George Gissing, but it soon became a showcase for the work of up-and-coming female writers such as Ella D'Arcy, Netta Syrett (1865–1943), Evelyn Sharp (1869–1965) and Ella Hepworth Dixon. As stories bordered on the controversial, examining issues such as female sexual desire, disillusionment within marriage and the chance encounters between men and women facilitated by the modern city, *The Yellow Book* quickly acquired a reputation for being risqué and shocking. It had a particularly urban slant; stories often opened with mysterious descriptions of London and went on to explore its freedoms and dangers. Like its offshoot, *The Savoy*, first published in 1896, the journal has also been seen as misogynist by modern critics, though, as Laurel Brake has argued, 'while...the subject of women in the *Yellow Book* is fraught with anxiety and misogyny, female readers seem to be among the audience addressed by its "get-up" and illustrated format'.[19] Although many of the stories certainly did seem to cater to and share the outlook of young men, with little respect for independent women, it evidently appealed to its intellectual female audience in its engagement with New Woman concerns (the American feminist writer Kate Chopin [1850–1904] had it specially delivered to St Louis).[20] The popularity of the journal helped to consolidate the generic features of the New Woman short story.

Motherhood and the failures of marriage: Sarah Grand, George Egerton and Netta Syrett

The desire to reform the institution of marriage or to reject it in favour of spinsterhood, lesbianism or a free union (the 1890s version of living in sin) was central to discourses about the New Woman. Sarah Grand, the pseudonym of Frances Elizabeth Bellenden (Clark) McFall, was a key contributor to debates about marriage at this time. Her best-selling New Woman novel *The Heavenly Twins* (1893) scandalously exposed the effects on women of marrying eligible but syphilitic husbands, and her journalism considered the possibility of married women's work and argued for marital reform. She proclaimed her belief in legal separation but not divorce, which she saw as having failed in both England and America, and she argued in *The Lady's Realm* for 1898 that the New Woman 'recognises [man's] infinite possibilities. She sees the God in him, and means to banish the brute'.[21] Discussions about the so-called woman of the future and the New Man developed in response to evolutionary thinking about gender, which is evident in Grand's views about the need for women to reform their partners: 'the man of the future will be better, while the woman will be stronger and wiser. To bring this about is the whole aim and object of the present struggle.'[22] Although she is known primarily for her long novels of the late Victorian period, her short-story collection *Emotional Moments* (1908), comprising stories previously published in a range of magazines, deserves attention for its daring discussion of marital problems, women's sexual desires and changes in women's roles. Its opening story, 'An Emotional Moment', is a candid confession by an actress of her passion for a man narrated to another man who finds her behaviour disgusting. 'The Man in the Scented Coat' is the adventure of a young woman taken to an illicit gambling den by some men she meets on the street. The more biting 'A New Sensation' pokes fun at a bored society hostess with 'a terrible dread of the future' (p. 231) who mistakenly believes she is sexually alluring to her young gardener.[23] Her failed attempt to make him into another of her 'conquests' makes her into a ridiculous older woman.

Grand's elliptical story 'When the Door Opened...?', which first appeared in the fashionable new magazine *The Idler* in 1897, before it was collected in *Emotional Moments*, explores the need for 'the right ordering of married lives' (p. 218), at the same time suggesting that men might find it hard to grant women their much-needed freedom. It opens with a disagreement between a husband and wife travelling by train, stemming from the out-of-date situation whereby he 'keeps her shut up, or only allows her out under escort, as if he thought that she would certainly misconduct herself if ever she had an opportunity' (p. 218). But the story we are told is not their story; it is the story of the marriage of an apparently enlightened male fellow-passenger who himself 'prefer[s] a free woman', believing a husband to be 'a companion, not a keeper' (p. 218), exactly the sort of partner to which a New Woman might aspire. His narrative, however, is about an occasion when he goes to check up on his wife at a fancy-dress ball at which he fears for her virtue: 'she might be dancing with some very undesirable partner' (p. 220). By wearing a mask himself, he is able to approach his wife as if he were himself such an undesirable figure, and he is horrified by her drinking, her dancing with him 'with the abandonment of a ballet girl' (p. 221) and her agreeing to come home with him. His fears about modern women's capacity to deceive their husbands while gaining their sexual satisfaction elsewhere – 'Was this the true woman, I wondered, and was that other to whom I was accustomed, only an actress earning her living?' (p. 221) – betray the would-be New Man's conventional nervousness about the new freedoms of the modern wife: 'O thrice accursed fool that I was to let her come alone!' (p. 222). Letting women out on their own in public at night lays them open to the 'fast' and 'vulgar' behaviour which tends to collapse the New Woman into the figure of the prostitute. The twist at the end of the tale is that the woman he brings home is not his wife but 'a creature with dyed hair, blackened eyelids and painted cheeks' (p. 224) who would damage his reputation, a presence he will have to explain to his wife, who is heard entering the house just after his discovery. This explanation is denied to the reader: Grand cleverly ends her narrative before the ensuing scene by having the husband stop mid-sentence to jump off the moving train at his station. The reader, like the narrator, is left 'tormented with conjectures as to what happened when that door opened' (p. 224), leaving the question of freedom within modern marriage unresolved.

The technique of leaving a story open-ended is employed elsewhere in Grand's *Emotional Moments*, as is perhaps suggested by the stories' titles. At the end of 'The Undefinable', the fast-talking artist's model, 'a free woman, a new creature' (p. 136), the subject of his brilliant but unfinished picture, vanishes, never to be seen again, though the artist searches in vain for her from his open carriage. He reads her 'coming and her going' throughout the story as 'a kind of allegory', to be interpreted as 'give me my due; and when you help me, I will help you!' (p. 136). This is a rather heavy-handed way of signalling the symbolic function of the central character here and the need for men to help the New Woman by recognising her as 'a creature of boundless possibilities' (p. 134), not just a beautiful muse. The unfinished thesis of 'When the Door Opened ... ?' is subtler and more complex. By leaving her narrator ungendered, merely informing us that it is someone who 'was coming home alone late one night by train from a distant suburb' (p. 217), she further complicates concerns about freedom of movement in public, as well as leaving her message ambiguous. Is Grand making the point that the husband's relish of his role makes it more likely that men will continue to endanger their wives by using prostitutes (one of the warnings of *The Heavenly Twins*), or is she suggesting that the modern husband shouldn't jump to conclusions about the potential 'wantonness' of their wives? Does the elided scene reinforce the view that men and women don't communicate or understand each other, hampering progress by restricting women's self-development?

Heilmann's argument about the 'experimentation' of New Woman writers and their explosion of narrative conventions[24] is particularly appropriate to the work of George Egerton, whose use of stream of consciousness anticipates the work of modernist writers such as Virginia Woolf. George Egerton was the pseudonym of the Australian-born writer Mary Chavelita Dunne, used to protect her reputation at a time when it was still commonplace for women writers to prefer to publish under male names or under initials. Although Egerton did initially contribute to *The Yellow Book*, it was her popular collections *Keynotes* (1893) and *Discords* (1894), featuring previously unpublished material, which sealed her notoriety. These launched the 'Keynotes' series of short works by new writers edited by John Lane, who also published *The Yellow Book*. Reviewers linked her writing to the current trend of 'erotomania' and complained about 'the hysterical frankness of its amatory abandonment'.[25] Now admired for their candour, Egerton's stories have been of particular interest to feminist critics because of their frank treatment of female erotic desire, but also for their readiness to confront contentious issues such as domestic violence, infanticide and marital rape. According to Sally Ledger, Egerton was unusual in providing 'a woman's-eye-view of womanhood',[26] part of her intention as a writer being to provide a more accurate version of femininity:

> I realised that in literature, everything had been better done by man than woman could have hoped to emulate. There was only one small plot to tell: the *terra incognita* of herself, as she knew herself to be, not as man liked to imagine her – in a word to give herself away, as man had given himself away in his writing.[27]

To map out the 'unknown' qualities of woman, many of her narratives, which are often entirely in the present tense, focus on 'psychological moments', thus linking her work to Freudian psychoanalysis and the development of the case history.[28] According to Laura Chrisman, Egerton used the short-story medium as 'a vehicle for dramatic epiphanies, life-changing sudden encounters, and melodrama'.[29] Her stories are often told from a female perspective, though she was just as adept at writing from the point of view of a man.

Egerton's most famous and frequently anthologised story 'A Cross Line', from *Keynotes*, is a strikingly candid and modern narrative of a woman's sexual fantasies and the decision she has to take about whether to leave her loving but dull husband for the attractive stranger she meets while fishing. To convey and explore sexual difference, Egerton's characters generally remain nameless, referred to in the text simply by pronouns or as the 'man', 'woman' or 'girl'. In 'A Cross Line' the woman is referred to as 'Gipsy' by her husband, but is more often simply 'she', an archetypal figure. The spirited and 'original' woman, showing her newness by her smoking and uninhibited conversation, is shown to be more at ease with the attractive stranger who appears to recognise her sexual nature than with her undemonstrative husband, who calls her 'poor little woman' and confides enthusiastically that 'being married to you is like chumming with a chap!' (p. 56).[30] Her need to express herself sexually makes her unfeminine, in keeping with contemporary fears that mannish New Women were unsexing themselves through their behaviour. The dialogue with her husband is punctuated with her caresses; she bites his ear and chin and kisses his eyes – 'fast' behaviour for a Victorian heroine.

The story is daring and original in both its subject matter and its style; the central section, one of the five psychological moments which make up its structure, is an extended fantasy sequence which takes the woman away from the endless routines of a wife, 'away from the daily need of dinner-getting and the recurring Monday with its washing; life with its tame duties and virtuous monotony' (p. 57). She imagines herself horseback riding in Arabia, then dancing in front of hundreds in an open-air theatre, scantily dressed with loose flowing hair:

> She can see herself with parted lips and panting, rounded breasts, and a dancing devil in each glowing eye, sway voluptuously to the wild music that rises, now slow, now fast, now deliriously wild, seductive, intoxicating, with a human note of passion in its strain. She can feel the answering shiver of feeling that quivers up to her from the dense audience, spellbound by the motion of her glancing feet, and she flies swifter and swifter, and lighter and lighter, till the very serpents seem alive with jewelled scintillations. One quivering, gleaming, daring bound, and she stands with outstretched arms, and passion-filled eyes, poised on one slender foot, asking a supreme note to finish her dream of motion. (pp. 57–58)

It is easy to appreciate how readers in the 1890s would have been shocked by the New Woman's 'amatory abandonment' here and the mention of her lips, breasts and voluptuous swaying. The language of quivering and shivering mimics the process of arousal – 'now slow, now fast', 'swifter and swifter, and lighter and lighter' – leading up to the female orgasm, 'a supreme note to finish her dream of motion'. The fantasy is also a celebration of the 'enigma' of woman, 'her complex nature' (p. 58), which is linked later in the sequence to 'the eternal wildness, the untamed primitive savage temperament that lurks in the mildest, best woman', 'the keynote of woman's witchcraft and woman's strength' (p. 59). The wildness and complexity of woman is posited as something man cannot comprehend, one of the sentiments for which Egerton has been accused of essentialism, of assuming that all men are the same and all women are the same. This story has also attracted attention for its handling of race; by casting her heroine as a Salome figure, admired by Eastern men, Egerton is seen to be demonstrating her 'instrumental and essentialist approach to cultural/racial otherness', colluding with an 'imperialistic orientalism' typical of her time.[31] Eroticising the Orient was a common feature of late-nineteenth-century fiction, used to reinforce European supremacy.

And yet the ending of the story sees the woman reconciled to her marriage as the growing realisation that she is pregnant persuades her to choose to remain with her husband rather than give the sign to the stranger that she will be his. This ending can be read in a number of ways. It could be a comment on women's choices at a time when they had little control over their marital partners or conception; other New Women heroines, like their counterparts in late-Victorian society, found their dreams of freedom curtailed with the coming of children, and feared the social ostracism associated with illegitimacy. Egerton was clearly interested in questions of maternity: Flo in 'Virgin Soil' (discussed below) complains about wives' lack of choices in their endless round of pregnancy and nursing, 'growing old, unlovely, with all joy of living swallowed in a senseless burden of reckless maternity' (p. 109). But maternity could also be seen as a genuine source of fulfilment for women.[32] The maternal instinct could be seen to override the sexual instinct. This can also be linked to 1890s imperialism and eugenics; as Ledger points out, 'the preoccupation with maternity in Egerton's, Schreiner's and Grand's feminist fiction strongly suggest[s] a complicity with the imperialist demand that women be responsible for the production of a pure strong British "race".'[33] One character in 'The Spell of the White Elf' even goes so far as to imagine conception without men: 'If one could only have a child...without a husband or the disgrace; ugh, the disgusting men!' (p. 80). Perhaps the story is commenting on the inability of men to satisfy women's needs, sexual and otherwise; neither the husband nor the stranger has everything the woman desires, so she has to compromise. The final conversation in 'A Cross Line' is between the heroine and her unmarried maid, Liz, who is able to pass on the baby clothes she saved after her own baby died. Their shared maternity forges a stronger link than that of sexual attraction, and the baby's white garment signals to the lover that his moment is ended. The woman remains 'impenetrable as a sphinx at the end of it' (p. 60) as her reasons for choosing her husband remain unarticulated, typically leaving the reader to decide how positive the outcome is for the New Woman.

'Virgin Soil', from the later and darker collection *Discords*, offers a more biting critique of Victorian marriage through a conversation between a mother and young daughter, Flo, who flees her husband's brutality and infidelity. The story composed almost entirely of a dialogue between two women was another of Egerton's innovations in the form. 'Virgin Soil' opens with the girl sobbing at her wedding ceremony and her mother's old-fashioned advice, 'marriage is a serious thing, a sacred thing...you must believe that what your husband tells you is right' (p. 103), before the drunken bridegroom makes her shiver with his 'curious amused proprietary air' (p. 105). In the dialogue, five years later, the girl, now a 'hollow-eyed sullen woman' (p. 107), is older and wiser, her face changed to 'a bitter disillusion' (p. 106) as she returns to blame her mother for keeping her ignorant of men. Her announcement that she is not going back to her husband, because of his infidelities, is likened to a bomb exploding in her mother's 'quiet, pretty room'. In this it is rather like Nora's notorious slamming of the door against the husband she despises in Henrik Ibsen's (1828–1906) shocking play *A Doll's House*, which premiered in London in the 1880s (possibly an intentional echo, given Egerton's admiration for Scandinavian writers). While her mother fears 'the disgrace, the scandal, what people will say' (p. 109), Flo's impassioned and radical speech about the inequalities of marriage and the potential for marital rape, reminiscent of Mona Caird, shocks in its candour: 'as long as man demands from a wife as a right, what he must sue from a mistress as a favour...marriage becomes for many women a legal prostitution, a nightly degradation, a hateful yoke under which they age, mere bearers of children conceived in a sense of duty, not love' (p. 109). The reader is left to wonder what has become of Flo's own children after five years of marriage and whether she is deserting them along with her husband. Egerton's attack on the enforced duties of marital sex and the 'degradation' experienced by wives (a word she uses again later in the story) is suggestive of the horrors of the bedroom for traumatised daughters, like Flo, left ignorant of the facts of life: 'Do you think that if I had realised how fearfully close the intimacy with him would have been that my whole soul would not have stood up in revolt, the whole woman in me cried out against such a degradation of myself?' (p. 111). But the ending of the story can be read more positively, as the wife is shown taking the train by herself in the opposite direction to both her marriage and her family home. As Sally Ledger has argued, 'What she is moving towards is unclear',[34] but the 'open-endedness' is more promising for the woman than for the unhappy wife Sue Bridehead in Thomas Hardy's *Jude the Obscure*, published a year later, in 1895, and for other women trapped in marriage at the time.

The horror of marital intimacy and the possibilities and difficulties of escape from unhappy marriages to an uncertain future recur in other New Woman stories of the time. Netta Syrett, a regular contributor to *The Yellow Book* and close friend of illustrator Aubrey Beardsley's sister

Mabel, published collections of stories with New Woman agendas and fairy tales. Her New Woman novels of the period, such as *Nobody's Fault* (1896) and *Three Women* (1910), examine the conflict between romantic desires and the need to achieve economic independence through work. As Ann Heilmann has noted, 'while few novelists came anywhere near to contesting the validity of heterosexuality as such, most [New Woman] texts were constructed around the collapse of heterosexual relationships', with the short-story format often allowing writers greater freedoms either to protest against marriage or to imagine a future without a husband.[35] 'Stifled' in her marriage to the slow, awkward and undemonstrative John Drayton, the nervous intellectual heroine, Kathleen, in Syrett's 'Thy Heart's Desire' (1894) is isolated in the Eastern camp where her husband works. Again the husband's presence leaves the New Woman 'torn by conflicting emotions', from 'pity and disgust' (p. 128) to horror: ' "No, don't touch me," she cried, shrinking back ... she had lost command of her voice, and the shrill note of horror in it was unmistakable' (p. 122).[36] News of his death arrives at the end of the fourth section of the story, leaving the reader to conjecture that her heart's desire might be found in Broomhurst, a more likely New Man figure who reads with her at the camp and appears to recognise her passion. The final section, set in England three months later, sees her turning him down, casting herself as a murderess. The 'loathing' she felt for her husband will not allow her to enjoy the release she had wished for: her first thought, that *'it was too good to be true'* (p. 138), gives way to the inevitability of being 'mad with self-reproach' (p. 139). Her nervousness ominously echoes that of the oppressed heroine of Charlotte Perkins Gilman's (1860–1935) well-known story 'The Yellow Wallpaper' (1893), which was based on the author's own experiences of an unhappy marriage and the rest-cure prescribed for hysteria. The ending of 'Thy Heart's Desire' also sees the woman accepting the blame for withdrawing her love from her husband, though Syrett leaves this ambiguous by describing Kathleen's final contemplation of the sea, after dismissing her lover, in terms of her regaining of self-respect. It is surely significant that both men refer to her as 'poor little girl' and want to take care of her by protecting her from the world; her rejection of men and marriage can, then, perhaps be seen as a prelude to acquiring the strength to live independently. In her later *Yellow Book* story 'A Correspondence' (1895), Syrett exposes the suitable match celebrated by society as a sham, as the beautiful Cecily, 'the orthodox engaged young lady', is neither clever nor accomplished enough to sustain the interest of her suitor once he learns that the cultured but less attractive governess Gretchen Verrol has been writing her love letters for her. The story ends on a note of sympathy for the 'patient' Cecily, who must endure her husband's desire for another woman, as their forced *ménage à trois* is a substitute for the happier life both women might have lived outside the rules of marriage.[37]

Also worth noting is 'A Story of a Wedding Tour' (1898) by the prolific Scottish writer Margaret Oliphant. Oliphant is generally viewed as a conservative figure. Reputedly Queen Victoria's favourite novelist, she often wrote about strong independent women but rarely proposed any solution other than marriage. 'A Story of a Wedding Tour' is an uncharacteristically progressive tale, in which the wedding tour ironically takes place without the husband. On a night journey through France, Mr Rosendale is left behind at a railway station, leaving his new young wife 'with a mingled sensation of excitement and terror and tremulous delight which words could not tell' (p. 428).[38] The 'private repugnances' (p. 430) of marriage for Janey are reinforced in the opening pages in the same language used by Egerton: her husband's proximity makes her 'frightened, horrified, and even revolted' (p. 427); 'she felt the horror of him, and his kind of loving' (p. 431). As a newly single woman she feels infused with 'energy and strength' and regains control over her own identity, becoming 'Janey herself, the real woman, whom nobody had ever seen before' (p. 431). Her decision to set up a home for herself without him conveys 'the blessed sensation of freedom – pleasure tinctured with the exhilaration of escape' (p. 433), and her subsequent life as a single mother is described more explicitly in terms of emancipation, though in the final pages she cannot forgive herself – an act of blaming perhaps added by Oliphant to tone down the subversive implications of the narrative. A variation on this plot is used by the American feminist writer Kate Chopin in the short but highly effective 'The Dream of an Hour' (sometimes called 'The Story of an Hour'), which was published in the daring new magazine *Vogue* in 1894. For a precious hour Mrs Mallard weeps and then allows herself to contemplate 'a long procession of years to come that would belong to her absolutely' after she is given the news that her husband has been killed in a railroad disaster. She feels herself to be 'free, free, free!', enjoying the 'feverish triumph' of her sudden release from a loveless marriage at a time when divorce remained a costly and unlikely option. The twist in the tale is the reappearance of the husband, who had not been involved in the accident after all, and the sudden death of the wife from the shock.[39] Although the conventional endings of some of these stories might have ostensibly set out to remind female readers that escape from unfulfilling marriages should remain a fantasy, the impact of their exposure of marital dissatisfaction could not be cancelled out.

Female independence and sexuality: Olive Schreiner and Ella D'Arcy

Independence was one of the key aims of the New Woman, to be achieved through paid work, the challenge to male authority, travel or escape from an enforced domesticity. As Mona Caird forcefully put it in her discussion of women's desire to earn their own money: 'if they desire the privilege of independence (a privilege denied them, work as they will, within the home), by what right does society refuse their demand?'[40] This demand for independence takes different forms in the short fiction of this period. Olive Schreiner (1855–1920) is sometimes credited with starting the trend for New Woman fiction with her startlingly modern novel *The Story of an African Farm* (1883) and its outspoken feminist heroine, Lyndall, who chafes against the restrictions of woman's sphere and hungers for the independence gained by education. A missionary's daughter from South Africa, Schreiner wrote about colonialism and imperialism but was also vocal in feminist and socialist debate. She lived in London from 1881 to 1887, where she was a prominent member of the radical discussion group the Men and Women's Club.[41]

Some of Schreiner's early short stories featured in the experimental collection *Dreams* (1890); others were published only after her death in 1920. Many of them stand out for their original use of form, their brevity and their marked departure from the confines of realist fiction. Some are utopian; others, allegorical, within the frame of a dream. In 'Life's Gifts', from *Dreams*, the shortest of the stories discussed in this chapter, only half a page of type, a woman dreams that Life offers her a choice between Love and Freedom. Her choice of Freedom is declared to be the right one, as Life explains: 'Now, the day will come when I shall return. In that day I shall bear both gifts in one hand' (p. 317).[42] This privileging of freedom over love recurs throughout Schreiner's writing, and the simple choice offered in this short allegory is an effective way of signalling the impossibility of the New Woman having it all: it is only in an unspecified future that love will not compromise a woman's freedom, and the final line of the story, 'I heard the woman laugh in her sleep' (p. 317), can be seen as derisive or affirmative, depending on how the allegory is interpreted. Comparing her stories to George Egerton's, Chrisman argues that Schreiner's more experimental, symbolic stories do not share Egerton's 'optimism about feminist self-realizability', as the idea of having it all has to be projected into an uncertain and distant future.[43]

'Three Dreams in a Desert', from the same collection, explores the reasons a woman struggles to shake off 'the burden of subjection' (p. 309) man has placed on her. The dreamer dreams of the Land of Freedom, where 'on the hills walked brave women and brave men hand in hand' (note the reversal of order here to privilege the importance of the female) and 'women also hold each other's hands' (p. 315), stressing the support of both female friendships and partnerships. The story sets out to counter the New Woman's isolation by likening women to locusts trying to cross a stream: the piled-up bodies of those who have tried and failed to cross enable others to pass over, and if women are able to build the bridge or are swept away in the process, this still will allow '*the entire human race*' (p. 315) to reach the other side, emphasising their reproductive contribution as mothers of the future race. This idea draws on evolutionary thinking about the ways in which women were being forced to adapt to survive. As mothers, women were training future citizens, a task it was becoming possible to achieve without men. In Egerton's final ambitious story from *Discords*, 'The Regeneration of Two', a bored society widow uses her money and resources to provide work for outcast women and single mothers, turning her home into a kind of commune. Promoting the vital importance of female self-reliance, she tells the disapproving pastor, 'the fathers were only an accident...man hasn't kept the race going, the burden of centuries has lain on the women...she has rocked the cradle and ruled the world, borne the sacred burden of her motherhood, carried in trust the future of the races' (pp. 206–7). These feminist visions of a more progressive society in which women support each other or, more radically, are able to live together without the need for men were later imagined more fully in Charlotte Perkins Gilman's radical utopia *Herland* (1915), where a community of brave women take sole control of reproduction, mothering, work and education.

One of Schreiner's most complex discussions of the choices available to independent women, and her own favourite story, is 'The Buddhist Priest's Wife', which dramatises gender divisions primarily through a dialogue between an unnamed New Woman and her male friend. Written in 1892, it remained unpublished, perhaps because of its radical content, until after her death, when it was collected in *Stories, Dreams and Allegories* (1923). In a single paragraph set apart from the main narrative, the story's startling opening is actually the ending, which seems to record the contemplation by an unknown speaker of an unburied female corpse: 'Cover her up! How still it lies!' (p. 84).[44] The speaker then asks a series of urgent questions about the life of a 'strong' but isolated woman who appears to have achieved a lot in the public world by sacrificing love and family:

She that had travelled so far, in so many lands, and done so much and seen so much, how she must like rest now!...did she ever need a love she could not have? Was she never obliged to unclasp her fingers from anything to which they clung? Was she really as strong as she looked? Did she never wake up in the night crying for that which she could not have? Were thought and travel enough for her? (p. 84)

Later in the story the New Woman figure imagines that dying might be a way to escape the restrictions of gender, 'to look round on the world and feel the bond of sex that has broken and crushed you all your life gone, nothing but the human left, no woman any more' (p. 93), though the opening perhaps refutes this, because in death she is still more woman than human. Set in the woman's lodgings, eight years earlier, in the 'London room' which Schreiner (anticipating Virginia Woolf) saw as crucial to the maintenance of female independence, the main narrative examines the choices New Women have to make about marriage, motherhood, work, travel and self-fulfilment. The heroine's newness is signalled by her uninhibited smoking, her receiving of a male visitor and her packing for a solitary one-way trip to India, where she will pursue her interest in the East and its 'complex, interesting life' (p. 88). Ann Ardis has suggested that the story is about the man's failure to recognise the woman's passion and his belittling of her ideals,[45] but it is also important to pay attention to questions about independence, about what constitutes a successful life for men and women and how they make their choices.

The discussion of marriage and parenting is intended to reinforce sexual difference, with the heroine functioning as a mouthpiece for feminist 'theories of the equality of men and women' (p. 93), a device which makes the conversation stirring but a little artificial. If the New Woman is to be shown aspiring to be the woman of the future, then it is fitting that she recognise both the limitations and the responsibilities of marriage. The man's view that, by his mid-thirties, 'it's not love, passion, he wants; it's a home; it's a wife and children' (p. 90) is in keeping with custom, but, in comparison, 'for a woman, marriage is much more serious than for a man' (p. 90), and the potential partner might appear at a point when it is not 'right or possible' (p. 90). The 'curious longing to have a child' (p. 90) as a woman gets older is then represented as 'a thing one has to get over' if she wishes to work, a rather chilling comment given indications in the story that the woman might be pregnant, as she is able to date her last meeting with the man precisely at seven months earlier. The man's dismissal of her 'idiotic' choice to live outside society, possibly in one of the new boarding houses for single women, 'burying yourself here with a lot of old frumps' (p. 88), is shown to be indicative of the patriarchal view that women should be wives and mothers rather than independent. Yet what the man sees as 'throw[ing] herself away' (p. 88) and wasting her time is in effect the woman's contribution to the world of work. Her 'squandering [her]self on every old beggar or forlorn female or escaped criminal' she meets (p. 89) implies that, like committed feminist figures such as Octavia Hill or Josephine Butler, she is involved with some form of social work, one of the new professions which women were entering in large numbers at this time. Some successful women, like Butler, were able to combine marriage and motherhood with paid work, but it was certainly difficult, and fictional heroines are often forced to choose between the roles of homemaker and professional woman, a choice foreshadowed in the opening paragraph's question about whether work was 'enough' for a woman.

The long speech the heroine makes at the centre of the story also shows the influence of evolutionary ideas about the laws of nature, which maintain 'the radical differences between men and women' (p. 91). In the comparison she sets up between friendship with men and sexual love, she argues that 'nature ordains that [a woman] should never show what she feels' because of the barriers this creates between men and women; therefore 'she must always go with her arms folded sexually' (pp. 92, 93). Friendship with men can be different because it can be on terms of 'perfect equality'. Such sentiments suggest the dangers of pursuing sexual desire. As opposed to Egerton's arguments against the social repression of women's sexuality, for Schreiner 'there is the possibility that sexual fulfilment is as much a threat to women's self-development as it is an expression of it'.[46] The possibility that the woman might suggest a free union with a man she is clearly attracted to disappears, perhaps because the reader is made increasingly aware of the man's failure to display the credentials for a New Man worthy of the name (the barbed comment late in the story that he looks down at her as one does 'at an interesting child or a big Newfoundland dog' [p. 95] clearly doesn't go in his favour). The title of the story is ironic; his joke that she will become a Buddhist priest's wife, when priests do

not marry, perhaps gestures to the New Woman as a similarly lone figure. The woman's departure after a surprising kiss and the man's wish
for future success – 'we'll see who succeeded best' (p. 96) – fades into
a reminder of her death. The man is left behind contemplating the
empty flat, asking the landlady when the woman will be back. Despite
applauding Schreiner's creation of a 'thoroughly grown-up' heroine 'in
control of her immediate, material life', Carolyn Burdett reads the story
as 'remorselessly bleak' in 'the gap it sees between what modernity can
open up for women, on the one hand, and, on the other, their prospects
for happiness in love'.[47]

The stories of Ella D'Arcy, though much less engaged with feminist
issues than Schreiner's, are notable for their examination of female
sexual independence and its relationship to urban culture. As assist-
ant editor for the majority of The Yellow Book's three-year run, whose
stories appeared in most of the volumes, D'Arcy was clearly abreast of
trends in the short-story form. However, though her stories touched
on daring topics and were candid about sexuality, as one might expect
in an avant-garde journal, they often remained ambivalent in their
treatment of the New Woman. Despite D'Arcy's reputation as a New
Woman writer, Anne M. Windholz suggests that 'her attitude toward
feminism was skeptical' and that she did not use her editorial position
to promote the publication of women writers.[48] D'Arcy's two collections
Monochromes (1895) and Modern Instances (1898) are 'honest, pessimistic stories' of difficult sexual relationships and unhappy marriages,[49]
often depicting the woman as a sexually confident figure who will
ultimately repel men. 'Irremediable', which appeared in the first issue
of The Yellow Book (1894), having been turned down by other editors
for its 'inappropriate' treatment of marriage, set the tone for the genre
in its frank portrayal of marital disillusionment and the 'sudden madness' (p. 81) of sexual desire.[50] With more than a nod to the work of
the naturalist writer George Gissing, whose story 'The Foolish Virgin'
(1896) also appeared in The Yellow Book, the terrifying consequences of
giving into the charms of the 'unrestrained' country girl Esther, with
her 'too friendly eyes' (p. 75), are that the hero, Willoughby, must suffer
the disgust and 'Hatred' he feels for his slatternly wife and his 'ago-
nising, unavailing regret' (p. 78) for his hasty marriage. Like most of
D'Arcy's stories, 'Irremediable' is told from a male perspective, which
allowed women writers to appeal to male readers while calling into
question the world-weary, pseudo-sophisticated stance of their narrators. Ada Leverson's (1862–1933) stories for subsequent issues, including
'Suggestion' (1895), a lively tale about an effeminate son's attempt to

prevent his father's second marriage, borrowed their witty and misogy-nist male characters from the work of her friend Oscar Wilde in order to parody and expose the limitations of upper-class masculinities.[51]

The perspective in D'Arcy's frequently anthologised 'The Pleasure-Pilgrim' (1895), which also appeared alongside 'Irremediable' in *Monochromes*, is that of the idle traveller Campbell, who is fascinated and repelled by the daring behaviour of American 'bad girl' Lulie Thayer on her European tour. It is a story which seems to borrow heav-ily for its plot and conception from Henry James's *Daisy Miller* (1879). As contemporary critics noted, D'Arcy, like James, raised questions about the sexual freedoms and independence of the new American girl, with her confidence in public and lack of reticence in conversa-tions with men. The 'magnificent apparel' (p. 141) and 'warm and friendly gaze' (p. 143) of this 'unique' creature increase Campbell's 'discomposure', and the story is interspersed with his conversations with his old friend Mayne, who tries to convince Campbell of her knowingness by claiming that he is only the latest in a long line. Lulie shares some of the attributes of the New Woman: according to Mayne, 'she's done everything', including cycling, nursing, studying art and dancing lessons, in order 'to extend her opportunities ... and acquire fresh sensations' (p. 147). But her challenge to social codes and the outdated system of chaperonage are linked to her uncontrolled sexual desires; she is 'an adventuress, but an end-of-the-century one', 'the most egregious little flirt', who 'makes love – desperate love, mind you, to every man she meets' (pp. 148, 149). The men's fluctuating desire for and fear of a woman who challenges social and sexual codes in this manner – Campbell feels himself 'so drawn towards her', despite his 'high ideal of Woman' (p. 147) – could be read as a pervasive nerv-ousness about the consequences of increased sexual independence for women as they pursue their pleasures in a masculine fashion. D'Arcy's decision about the girl's nationality would also have played on read-ers' awareness of the supposedly more advanced and outgoing types of femininity across the Atlantic, though this was not well received by American critics, who found Lulie to be 'an absurd caricature of the American girl as she exists in British fancy'.[52] The melodramatic ending of the story, in which the wide-eyed girl professes herself to be in love with Campbell and then shoots herself 'with her little tragic air' (p. 166) to prove this to him, suggests that D'Arcy might be playing with the caricature rather than accepting it, leaving her readers, like the bemused men in the story, unsure whether to take such exploits seri-ously. When it appeared in her first collection *Monochromes*, in Lane's

'Keynotes' series, it was generally felt to be inferior to 'Irremediable', though it is now her best-known story.[53] Its confusing criticisms of female sexual forwardness, showing the American girl as a potential 'wanton', are difficult to reconcile with the author's reputation as a New Woman writer.

The New Woman and urban culture: Charlotte Mew and Evelyn Sharp

We have already noted that *The Yellow Book* was central to shifts in how the short story was written, acquired and consumed during the early 1890s. *The Yellow Book* was also of its time in its fascination with urban culture, reflecting the rapid development of the modern city and exploring its impact on gender identity and sexual behaviours. Short stories of this period increasingly depicted the novelties and dangers of travelling by train or on the new omnibuses around London, or described purposeful walking across the city, all of which were relatively new experiences for women. As Deborah L. Parsons has argued in her fascinating study *Streetwalking the Metropolis*, 'Women's legitimate participation in city life was an extremely significant divergence from Victorian conventional belief.'[54] And the appearance of the New Woman in the urban space, whether for work or for leisure, was a significant sign of the times. Ella D'Arcy's *Yellow Book* story 'At Twickenham' (1897) satirises the stultifying 'somnolency' of suburban life for women through the viewpoint of Minnie's new husband, John Corbett, whose travels to do business in the city are mirrored in his wife and sister-in-law's shopping expeditions, their only valid reason for leaving the suburbs: 'the sisters suffered terribly from dullness, and one memorable Sunday evening, Corbett being away travelling, they took first-class tickets to Waterloo, returning by the next train, merely to pass the time'.[55]

The presence of middle-class women in the city, other than those engaged in satisfyingly feminine activities such as shopping, is shown to be unsettling and unstable, part of the process by which they were beginning to relieve the 'dullness' which had for too long been part of their lives. Grand's 'When the Door Opened...?' begins with a metafictional description of the 'curious glimpses of life...these intervals of intensity, the beginnings of episodes' (p. 217) visible to lookers-on in a great city, and it is these glimpses of life, these beginnings without endings, that allowed the writers of short stories to use the form to illuminate the unknowability of the urban or the chance encounters with strangers of different classes, races and sexualities which took place on the city streets.

The stories of Charlotte Mew (1869–1928), a *Yellow Book* author who went on to publish a collection of poetry, *The Farmer's Bride* (1916), illustrate this double-edged fascination with urban space. Her first published story, 'Passed' (1894), is a powerful narrative of a lone middle-class woman walking around the poorer districts of London and her struggle to overcome her antipathy to the ailing women she finds there. Although Mew has become better known for her poetry, her stories are notable for their dreamlike qualities and assault on the reader's complacency. 'Passed' is a striking first-person account which initially appears to be about the pleasures of walking, in which the unnamed narrator rejects domesticity by putting down her sewing and traversing the 'lonely squares' and thoroughfares of London. Notwithstanding the harrowing calls of children from a nearby prison and the 'sordid gloom' of the darkening city, her mood lightens once she leaves her home: 'the splendid cold of fierce frost set my spirit dancing' (p. 81); the stuffy church she visits leaves her 'longing for space again' (p. 84).[56] But the 'strange adventure' she will have on the streets does little to quench her appetite; in a nightmarish sequence she is dragged through the streets by a despairing woman from the church to see the dead body of another of the city's victims. In this strange company the 'hideous dark' (p. 85) and despair of the city intensify, as Mew cuts out all the dialogue to focus on the 'flaring booths', 'hoarse yells and haggling whines' (p. 87) and 'weirdly lighted faces' of her phantasmagorical vision.

In this vision, the streets, rather than serving as possible entertainment for the middle classes, are 'peopled with despair' (p. 85), and the narrator must confront her own 'apathy'. The beautiful body of a dead woman, reduced to destitution, 'extreme poverty' and a 'look of disillusion' (p. 87), might symbolise the failure of independence for lower-class women – she is clutching a torn letter in a man's hand, suggesting she has been abandoned – but the reader is left to piece her story together. Mew also limits the information we gain about the narrator and 'the eccentricity of her scheme' (p. 88) to do something for the women. Her situation evokes images of New Women socialists and philanthropists who worked tirelessly to ease the lives of the poor in urban areas,[57] but her struggle to escape from the 'alien presence' of the wraith who clings to her – 'the proximity was distasteful' (p. 87) – works against this. The ending of the story invites the reader to dwell on the distance the narrator is able to put between herself and the despairing women, a similar technique to that deployed in Mew's disturbing story for *Temple Bar*,

'A White Night' (1903), which taunts the reader with the 'temporary detachment' and voyeuristic 'inaction' of those who witness the burial alive of an unprotesting veiled woman in a Spanish church.[58] The final scene of 'Passed' sees the narrator caught up in a 'rapidly thickening throng' of prostitutes, 'decked out in frigid allurement', when she spots the woman from the church, now in the company of the man who had ruined the woman's dead friend, though the narrator does not recognise her. The question 'What place in the scene had I?' (p. 98) and the unspecified source of the terrible cry underline the uncertainty of the narrator's status in the city and the challenge to middle-class complacency mounted by the suffering women at the heart of the story. The narrator's ability to return home by taxi and dance the evening away cannot be separated from those female victims, desperate for money and security, for whom the city's freedoms are illusory.

Later examples of the New Woman's ambiguous position in the city as a worker and an activist appear in the work of the writer and journalist Evelyn Sharp, an active suffragette imprisoned in Holloway in 1911 and 1913 for breaking windows in protest at government refusals to grant women the vote. Originally a member of the *Yellow Book* circle, Sharp often explored ideas of freedom and constraint, of public transport and class divisions, for working women in her stories and in her New Woman novels of the late-Victorian period, such as *At the Relton Arms* (1896). Her *Yellow Book* story 'The Other Anna' (1897) is a clever variation on the narrative of an artist's model challenging the limited thinking of a male artist. In the story, the bored, respectable Anna poses as an unrestrained artist's model in order to talk freely to men. Finding her circle of friends on her 'At Home' day 'a very dull one' and the 'adventure', the 'new sensation', of modelling much more fun, Sharp's rebellious heroine ends the story engaged to the intrigued artist. Although she reaps the benefits of her 'absurd enterprise' by her union with a more interesting man, the story also raises awareness of the poorer women who depend on such compromising forms of work for survival.[59] Women struggling against the weariness induced by difficult working conditions for low pay are also analysed in Sharp's excellent *Yellow Book* story 'In Dull Brown' (1896), one of many short narratives of this period which describe the omnibus ride to comment on modernity and the figure of the woman worker.[60]

Sharp's later and powerful collection *Rebel Women* (1910) details the experiences of middle-class women rebellious enough to support the suffrage campaign by working in shops, collecting money or making speeches to the street crowds. The term 'suffragette' started to be

used in 1906 to describe militant pro-suffrage activists, and the importance of fiction to the campaign can be seen in the existence of the
Women Writers' Suffrage League, founded in 1908 by playwright
Cecily Hamilton. Hard-hitting short stories were seen to be an effective
mode for conveying suffrage themes to readers and fostering support
for the cause during the 1910s and 1920s, appearing in the new suffrage journals such as *Votes for Women*, which Sharp edited from 1912.
Like other suffrage writers, Sharp 'deliberately used her experiences in
print' to aid conversion to the cause.[61] *Rebel Women* was published by
the Women's Freedom League, which also published radical fiction by
fellow-suffragette Gertrude Colmore (1855–1926). One contemporary
review described the collection as 'a clever, brilliantly interesting and
amusing series of stories and sketches illustrative of the modern woman's movement ... putting the suffragette case in a fresh and convincing
manner'.[62] In *Rebel Women* the courageous female first-person narrators
voice the concerns of committed New Women and enlist the support of
readers through their observations of gender inequalities. The titles of
stories such as 'Patrolling the Gutter' and 'At a Street Corner' emphasise
women's new positions in urban culture, and their narratives explore
both the hesitancy and the determination of those new to the cause.
'Patrolling the Gutter' is unusually narrated in the first-person plural
from the perspective of a 'band of naturally timorous ladies' (p. 75) who
brave the Kensington rain and the insults and responses of passers-by in
their sandwich boards. By the end of the story they have gained courage
by their occupation of the city, becoming 'hardened to the perils and
vicissitudes of the road' (p. 81).

   One of the strongest stories from this collection, 'Filling the War
Chest', which is based on material that first appeared in the *Manchester
Guardian* newspaper in 1908, gives an account of the reactions of
passers-by to the figure of a lively 'militant suffragist of many and
strenuous experiences' (p. 342) seeking to fill her collection box for
the newly formed Women's Social and Political Union. Opening with
her self-conscious musing on the relative positions of the size of the
'gulf ... that separates the passer-by from those who are passed by' (p.
340), it goes on to contrast her chilly place outside a London Tube station with that of her 'boon companion[s]' such as the flower-girl, the
newsboy and the lady shoppers with their 'preposterous hats', all of
whom have an opinion to be recorded on women activists. The range of
short-sighted comments the narrator has to respond to – 'I quite believe
in your cause, but why do this sort of thing?' (p. 342) – are used to highlight the misunderstandings about women's fight for the vote, although

casting argumentative passers-by as 'the enemy' and 'the anti-suffragist' perhaps betrays the propagandist edge to the writing.

Sharp's dismissive descriptions of the idlers and loiterers who form part of the 'street crowd' and their ability to waste time and of the frivolous conversations of the lady shoppers are, however, nicely undercut by her recognition that surfaces can be deceptive, as the 'expensive dowager in sable and velvet' window-shopping beside the suffragette offers the most heartfelt support in her 'astonishing remark' 'If I were ten years younger I should be out in the street fighting with you' (p. 345). In jostling to maintain her position 'at the edge of the pavement' (p. 345), scrabbling on the floor to pick up stray coins thrown from the top of a passing omnibus, the suffragette figure, according to Maria DiCenzo, 'offers important insights into the challenges facing women activists in the public sphere', where their respectability might be compromised.[63] DiCenzo argues that whereas suffrage papers tended to glorify the act of street selling, a different story emerges in the fiction and autobiographies of the women involved. Certainly, 'Filling the War Chest' is typical of the suffrage short story in raising searching questions about acceptable forms of behaviour for women in public. The familiar taunt used in the story that suffragettes lack husbands also reminds the reader how threatening single women in this environment are still perceived to be. By the end of the narrative, when the narrator returns to the spot after her stint is over, she is met only with 'chilly civility' from her erstwhile companions and consequently feels that she has 'been put back in my place as a passer-by' (p. 345), reinforcing the temporary nature of her acceptance on the street. Buying flowers and papers from the sellers, she becomes just another lady shopper, surprised that class divisions are re-established. Shopping was clearly a more suitable occupation for a woman than activism or paid work, though not necessarily one that satisfied all women, as the story ends with a reinforcement of the different roles available for women in the new urban spaces of the *fin de siècle*. The activity of 'streetwalking the metropolis' threatened class divisions and allowed for 'an alternative perception of women's presence in the city'.[64]

As they appeared in the risqué *Yellow Book* and other new avant-garde journals of the 1890s, New Woman stories are noticeably more candid in their discussions of sexuality and their exposure of the trials of marriage than earlier nineteenth-century narratives. They also illustrate the new fascination with the urban and with the working woman: suffragettes, prostitutes, artists' models, shop-girls, journalists, and social workers become the new protagonists and narrators of the woman's short story. Some stories use realism to protest against women's oppression; others, such as Schreiner's short allegories and Sharp's politicised suffragette stories, adopt a more experimental form. Tending to mimic the brevity and intensity of a 'psychological moment', a dream, a journey on public transport or a key conversation between a modern couple, they also break the rules of Victorian fiction by including stream of consciousness, fragments and inconclusive resolutions, thus anticipating the development of the modernist short story.

5
Imperial Adventures and Colonial Tales

After the women-centred stories of Chapter 4, this chapter is concerned with a different dimension of the late-Victorian and Edwardian short story: versions of the male adventure romance, which, in its day, was an enormously popular (and potentially lucrative) sub-genre of fiction. In the 1880s, two bestselling novels – Robert Louis Stevenson's *Treasure Island* (1883) and H. Rider Haggard's (1856–1925) *King Solomon's Mines* (1886) – had helped set in motion a revival of this kind of writing. As Stevenson explained in 'A Gossip on Romance' (1882), the interest lay in 'clean, open-air adventure'.[1] Writers such as Rudyard Kipling, Joseph Conrad, Charles Hyne (1865–1944) and William H. Kingston (1814–80) were recognised, alongside Haggard and Stevenson, as the main romance writers, and in the 1890s and early 1900s they were joined from time to time by others such as William le Queux (1864–1927), Bram Stoker, Reginald Wray (W. B. Home-Gall, 1861–1936), W. J. Locke (1863–1930), P. C. Wren (1885–1941) and John Buchan (1875–1940).[2]

Summarising the characteristics of the adventure romance (or 'imperial romance', as it is sometimes termed), Deirdre David notes the form's emphasis on 'English national and masculine subjectivity', 'tropes of travel and hazardous adventure' and 'racism [which]...is unembarrassed and extreme', with race being a 'glamorous or demonic marker'.[3] Invariably the emphasis is on an exciting plot constructed around a virile (white) hero's adventures in far-flung exotic places: Africa, India or another outpost of empire. The plots tend to deal with adventurous men coping with violent situations: monsters or villainous 'savages', or 'non-white' masculinities more generally. And these events are invariably described in the same terms: 'them' and 'us'. Women, when they appear, tend to feature in one of two guises: innocent victim or *femme fatale*. The male-centred nature of these stories was later picked up on by Virginia Woolf in *A Room of One's Own* (1929), in which she claimed that as a woman reader she felt excluded from them and that reading Rudyard Kipling's stories was like 'eavesdropping at some purely masculine orgy'.[4]

Woolf's comment is significant because it flags up the extent to which the adventure romance – while exciting – also served an ideological function. Writers aimed to satisfy readers' desires for escapism, showing thrills and physical danger, but they also offered psychological reassurance and a familiar narrative coda as the hero and his solid English values emerged triumphant. As Rob Dixon points out in *Writing the Colonial Adventure*, supporters of these exciting romances also saw them 'as serving to deflect attention away from the dangerous unpleasantness of realism and decadence, which fostered introspection, unmanliness and morbidity'.[5] In an essay 'About Fiction' (1887), Rider Haggard condemned foreign 'Naturalistic' novelists such as Emile Zola and Guy de Maupassant for their interest in 'lewd', 'unmanly' subjects. In contrast, the supporters of 'King Romance' (as the contemporary critic Andrew Lang put it) aimed to write for men and to reclaim the territory of the English novel.[6] In 1891, the praise lavished on Rudyard Kipling's 'living, throbbing presentments of Indian life' by the *Aberdeen Weekly Journal* was presumably intended to imply that the search for realism *and* machismo had been successful – at least in this instance.[7]

The idea that the very act of writing about and representing distant lands could be part of the process of empire-building comes across in a good many commentaries. In 1893 Arthur Conan Doyle took a break from writing about Sherlock Holmes (another quasi-imperial hero) to deliver a lecture on 'modern fiction'. Of the Bristol leg of his tour, the local paper reported:

> Having characterised literature as a nation's most permanent glory, he [Conan Doyle] went on to point out a growth in English literature consequent upon the extension of the British Empire. Kipling in India, Olive Schreiner at the Cape, Stevenson in his self-imposed exile in the South Seas, Haggard in those frontier territories of South Africa where the pioneer and the savage were waging a constant struggle, Ralph Bolderwood in Australia, and Gilbert Parker and Robert Barr in Canada were enumerated as instances of the increasingly cosmopolitan character of our literature. There was something solemn, said Dr Doyle, and even touching, in that vast interchange of confidence, that calling of deep to deep all over our world-wide Empire.[8]

Doyle's comments suggest something of the idealism – and proprietorial attitudes – which often accompanied discussions of empire. The belief that the British had a civilising mission was regularly articulated in the press – and occasionally parodied, as in Conrad's 'An Outpost of Progress' (*Cosmopolis*, June–July 1897). In this story Conrad's would-be pioneers find an old newspaper 'which discussed what it was pleased to call "Our Colonial Expansion" in high-flown language. It spoke much of the rights and duties of civilisation, of the sacredness of the civilising work and extolled the merits of those who went about bringing light, and faith and commerce to the dark places of the earth' (p. 90).[9] Other story collections, such as Edgar Jepson (1863–1938) and Captain D. Beames's (nd) *On the Edge of Empire* (1899), Reginald Wray's (1861–1936) *Tales of Empire Told Round the Camp Fire* (1901), Mayne Lindsay's (nd) *Byways of Empire* (1904) and Charles Hyne's (1865–1944) *Atoms of Empire* (1904), are examples of the period's yarns of colonisation and consolidation played straight: muscular tales of jungle warfare, empire-building and the besting of both primitive peoples and European rivals. 'Don't abuse the English,' warns a character in Hyde's 'The Renegade', a story of slave-trading and mercenaries set in west Africa, 'they play fair.'[10] Writers of the period indulged their taste for landscapes full of exotic scenery and unfamiliar peoples, showing examples of ostentatiously heroic male behaviour while painting nightmarish scenarios in which the uncivilised (primal) self threatens to overwhelm the civilised if it is not held in check.[11]

Another relevant context is masculinity. As was noted in Chapter 4, what many *fin-de-siècle* stories have in common is their deep engagement with questions of how uncertainty and change in the modern world affect the roles of men and women. These questions were informed by political transformations and by what recent critics have recognised as a wider sense of a 'crisis' in masculinity that emerged during the *fin de siècle*, a widespread 'male malaise'.[12] The waning of Victorianism; the sudden 'plague' (as it seemed to many) of New Women, homosexuals and 'inverts' like Oscar Wilde; the continuing impact of urbanisation and the recruiting campaigns for the Boer War, which revealed that 60 per cent of men were physically unfit for military service – all meant that it was easy to regard hard-won standards of masculinity, like many other aspects of Victorian culture, as being in a state of transition and decay. One solution seemed to be to toughen up young men by sending them on colonial service. In the adventure romance of the 1890s and 1900s the codes and ideals that govern Anglo-Saxon gentlemanly behaviour invariably play a large part in the way in which characters are represented, helping bolster the consoling and extremely potent myth that the English deserved to be in charge and still were.

Many of these ideas are powerfully played out in the works of Rudyard Kipling, who, along with Joseph Conrad, is generally reckoned the most influential male exponent of the short story form in *fin-de-siècle* Britain. It is on these two writers that this chapter will focus primarily. Both writers were interested as much in the techniques of telling a story as in its content. In particular, both are notable for their experiments with the possibilities of frame narrative, or the use of a tale within a tale. Their stories often have an inner narrative, told in the first person, which is then enclosed in an outer frame narrative which is either told by or focalised through a Westerner who serves as a mediator between teller and audience. 'This is not a tale. It is a conversation which I had with a complete stranger' is how an 1890 parody of Kipling by Barry Pain begins.[13] The use of a narrator to frame the story allowed an unusual or impossible series of events to be told in a way which suggested some degree of actuality. Such events really had happened. The format could also serve another, more complex, purpose. In its subject matter, Conrad's 'Karain: A Memory' (1897) is – ostensibly at any rate – similar to other imperial romance stories: the clash of British trading interests and the Eastern 'other'. But, as David Adams has noted, the story also shows how it was possible to use 'one narrator (unnamed) to frame the story of another (Karain), framing that allows him [Conrad] to distance the cruder forms of imperial ideology while engaging the underlying psychological dynamic of imperial culture'.[14]

Bright oriental star: Rudyard Kipling

A writer who reserved special ire for the unmanly 'long-haired literati' seen to be cluttering up the drawing-rooms of London's literary scene, Kipling had established himself as a powerful exponent of the male-centred late-Victorian short story by the mid-1880s.[15] Born in 1865 in Bombay, where his father taught at the School of Art, Kipling was educated in England but returned to India in 1881 to take up work on a newspaper. Despite poor health, he published prodigiously, initially in local magazines intended for the Anglo-Indian community, notably the *Civil and Military Gazette* (1886–87) and *The Week's News* (1887–88), and subsequently in prestigious magazines based in Britain. These early tales were later collected and published in volume form as *Plain Tales from the Hills* (1888), *Soldiers Three* (1888), *Wee Willie Winkie* (1888) and *Life's Handicap* (1891). All were immediately popular, and Kipling was hailed as the next big thing. By the 1890s he was rumoured to command as much as £200 per story, not least because his appeal extended across social classes.

Kipling liked the money, but he was also driven by the desire to enlighten the British public ('savages living in black houses and ignorant of everything beyond the Channel'[16]) about the realities of British India. He saw himself – and came to be seen – as a voice of authority on imperial matters, particularly India, a country regarded as 'the linchpin' of Britain's world power, as Mrinalini Sinha puts it.[17] Devoid of many of the romantic illusions about colonial life which coloured numerous of the period's other colonial tales, Kipling nonetheless supported the imperial project (as, of course, did many of his readers) and had strong ideas about what he termed the 'White Man's [civilising] work' and about 'the business of introducing a sane and orderly administration into the dark places of the earth'.[18]

If we examine Kipling's early stories closely, it is easy to appreciate why contemporary reviewers saw him as doing something new with the short story form. Andrew Lang credited Kipling with the 'invention of the British soldier in India', and suggested that his snapshots served to 'reach more of India, of our task there, of the various peoples who we try to rule, than many Blue books [government reports]'.[19] Stylistically, Kipling is said to have modelled his early writing style on the official language used in civil service memos. 'He told his tale in few words, as it might have been an official report', notes the narrator in 'William the Conqueror'; 'Nothing sensational...but just plain facts about who is doing what.'[20] Moreover, the men of these stories, as Lang noted, are not necessarily chiselled public school heroes. Instead Kipling focused on what Raymond Williams called the 'functionaries' or servants of empire, not the British ruling class but those further down the social ladder who had to earn money to survive.[21] Often they are disreputable, as in the ironically titled 'The Three Musketeers',[22] one of the stories in *Soldiers Three*. Muvaney, Ortheris and Learoyd are 'the worst men in the regiment as far as genial blackguardism goes'; they are inarticulate, barely-literates whose hobbies are drinking and brawling. In 'The Madness of Private Otheris' the suggestion is made that such men are unable to function without the regimented discipline imposed by army life; as members of the working classes they need and want to be led. Uneducated and child-like, they carry out the useful function of killing in the service of empire, something Kipling demonstrates in 'On Greenhow Hill', in which the three wait in ambush for an Indian deserter who has been firing at them. Learoyd narrates. He recalls his youthful love for an English girl who died, and suggests that the deserter has run away because of love for a woman. The others scoff at his making excuses for the deserter, and the poignancy of Learoyd's love story is contrasted with the sensual excitement of killing, particularly as exhibited by Ortheris, a man who has encountered little in the way of female influence: ' "Ere's my chaplain," he said, and made the venomous black-headed bullet bow like a marionette. "E's going to teach a man all about which is which, an' wot's true, after all, before sundown".'[23] Killing, not caring, is shown as a way of making one's mark, of establishing a sense of self. The final words of the story describe Ortheris 'staring across the valley [at the dead soldier] with the smile of the artist who looks on completed work'. There is a sense that Kipling empathises with the underlying frustration and anger which lead to this attitude, and that he recognises that such characters are 'excluded from the larger possibility of life'.[24]

The actions of men like Otheris are a necessary part of policing the empire. This is significant because as readers of Kipling we do not have to travel very far to realise the extent to which he (like other writers of the time) was also preoccupied with the fragility of imperial rule. As Zohreh T. Sullivan notes: 'Kipling's work ... created alternative fictions of empire that demythologised while it venerated the work of the English in other lands.'[25] On the one hand, Kipling presents admiring pictures of British pluck and proper behaviour; 'The Man Who Was' (1891) and 'William the Conqueror' (1895–6) are just two notable examples. 'The Little House at Arrah' (1888) commemorates a famous moment of the 1857 Indian Mutiny when a small group of British civilians and their Indian servants, trapped in a house, defended themselves against 2,500 mutineers, barricading themselves into a billiard room – that symbol of British gamesmanship and fair play. On the other hand, and as the setting of 'The Little House at Arrah' reminds us, Kipling's India is a dominion permanently on the brink of chaos; there is always a fear that the country might be too much for the Englishman, that even if the indigenous population remains acquiescent about British rule ('good' Indians are those who respect the British), the Englishman himself might lose his grip, suffer a nervous or physical breakdown or, even worse, 'go native'. 'Without Benefit of Clergy' (1890) is an inter-racial love story remarkable for its lack of traditional moralising and racism, but the 'fallen' coloniser is treated much more conventionally in 'To Be Filed for Reference' (1888), in which an Oxford scholar, McIntosh Jellaludin, puts himself 'past redemption', and in 'Beyond the Pale' (1888), in which Trejago, an Englishman, has a love affair with Bisea, an Indian widow. He is punished by Bisea's uncle and is injured in the groin – it is implied that he is castrated – while Bisea's hands are cut off and the window to her cell is walled over. The titles of both stories have double-meanings, and the stories share the same moral. As the narrator of 'Beyond the Pale' explains: 'A Man should, whatever happens, keep to his own caste, race and breed ... This is the story of a man who willingly stepped beyond the safe limits of decent everyday society, and paid for it heavily' (p. 126).[26]

'On the City Wall' (1888) and 'Thrown Away' (1888) draw attention to the system's snobberies, the casual cruelty of many of those involved in it and the sense of alienation and disintegration experienced by sensitive male characters. At best, the colonial administrators are like those described in 'At the End of the Passage' (1890): 'lonely folk who understood the dread meaning of loneliness' (p. 139).[27] The result of such stories is, as Sullivan puts it, to 'transgress the official picture of India by centering on what Imperial society had marginalised – the dirt, the smells and the tastes of India, the British failure, the suicide, the syphilitic, the rebel'.[28] Thus there is invariably something double-edged in Kipling's treatment of the British in India. His characters are rarely the swashbuckling heroes of earlier imperial romances. Instead, they are often tormented individuals; their masculinities decaying or defeated, they are often tortured victims of forces they cannot control or of powers they have unwittingly offended. Sullivan suggests that it is useful to think in terms of a 'day-time' and a 'night-time' Kipling. The voice of the first, easily caricatured, defends imperial values and institutions; the voice of the second is 'dissonant and self-contradictory', at war with the other voice and ambivalent about the question of how to 'parent' India.[29]

This last point is significant because parenting and education pervade Kipling's stories. Famously, one way in which Kipling thought of Indians was as children in need of guidance, with Queen Victoria as a kind of benevolent imperial mother. Thinking in these terms was a way of legitimising imperialism and is put into use in works such as 'The Head of the District' (1888): '[T]hou art our father and our mother,' native soldiers tell a dying district officer (p. 95).[30] But Kipling also makes the point that, like any parent, Britain's representatives need to understand those they are seeking to govern. This is one of the messages of 'The Return of Imray' (1891; originally published as 'The Recrudescence of Imray'), in which a seemingly inoffensive official who spends all his time in his club is murdered by his servant after unintentionally cursing the servant's son. The murder is solved by one of Kipling's recurring characters, Strickland – a man whose familiarity with Indian life is frowned upon but whose knowledge of the country's customs and superstitions is what keeps him alive. Among the significant points made by Noel Annan in an important early essay was that Kipling's concern 'is society itself', that he 'sees human beings moving in a definable network of social relationships which impose upon them a code of behavior appropriate to their environment'.[31]

In Kipling's own day his version of India received surprisingly mixed responses. Some, like Edmund Gosse, admired Kipling's ability to capture – apparently accurately – 'the pathos, the splendor, the cruelty and the mystery'.[32] Robert Buchanan – not a particular fan of Kipling – praised his 'little Kodak-glimpses' which allowed readers to grasp something of 'the great and wonderful national life of India'.[33] Others were less fulsome, and more snobbish, in their praise. Oscar Wilde described Kipling as 'a genius who drops his aspirates', and he likened the experience of reading *Plain Tales from the Hills* to sitting 'under a palm tree reading life by superb flashes of vulgarity. The jaded, second-rate Anglo-Indians are in exquisite incongruity with their surroundings.'[34] Henry James came to despair over the '*violence* of it all, the almost exclusive preoccupation with fighting and killing'.[35] James also complained that in Kipling's work there was '[a]lmost nothing of the complicated soul or of the female form or of any question of *shades* – which latter constitute, to my sense, the real formative literary discipline'.[36] Yet the fact that Kipling's stories were not 'women-ridden' was, the novelist Gilbert Frankau (1884–1952) thought, a good thing, since such interest got in the way of the important work of empire-building.[37] This is a tad unfair. Women do play an important role in several of Kipling's works, notably his First World War stories (see Chapter 7). However, it is certainly true in the Indian stories that women tend to occupy either the nursery or the harem and rarely offer – or take – much comfort in either. Taken collectively these comments are important because they reveal Kipling as a writer who has always divided opinion, who provoked admiration, snobbery, anxiety and distaste in equal measure, but whose popularity with readers made him a literary force to be reckoned with.

In a book of this length it is obviously difficult to do justice to all Kipling's stories, so we will focus on two of the most striking, which were published in *The Phantom Rickshaw & Other Eerie Tales* (1888). These are the long story 'The Man Who Would Be King', adapted for cinema by John Huston in 1975, with Michael Caine and Sean Connery in the leading roles, and the supernatural title story, 'The Phantom Rickshaw' (1885).

'The Man Who Would Be King' is indicative of the sophistication inherent in Kipling's treatment of empire. The story opens with an unnamed narrator who works as a journalist for the *Backwoodsman*. He tells of meeting two adventurers, Peachey Taliaferro Carnehan and Daniel Dravot, who tell him that they plan to leave an India that 'isn't big enough for such as us' (p. 173).[38] They have entered into a contract to become kings of Kafiristan, a remote region in northeast Afghanistan. (Kafiristan means 'Land of the Infidel'.) Two years later Carnehan returns alone and updates the narrator. He relates how by exploiting different Masonic, religious and military rituals and superstitions, the men succeeded at first. In what is just one of a large number of biblical references Carnehan boasts: 'It's true ... True as gospel. Kings we were with crowns upon our heads', and they appeared god-like (p. 181). But when Dravot seeks to establish a dynasty via marriage to a girl from the local population, the god-like illusion collapses. In a striking example of the story's miscegenation, Dravot's flesh is ripped by the bite of the 'strapping wench' whom he plans to marry and his ordinariness is revealed: 'Neither God nor a Devil but a man!' (p. 198). Thus exposed, the men try to flee their furious 'shrieking' subjects, but are eventually ambushed by them in the hostile terrain. Dravot is marched to a ravine, where he is stabbed to death and pushed over; Carnehan is hoisted on a cross to be crucified, but he survives. He has now reappeared, marked by stigmata, 'a rag-wrapped whining cripple'; he produces his partner's 'dried withered head', together with a gold crown which he places 'tenderly on the battered temples', and speaks to it: ' "You be'old now," said Carnehan, "the Emperor in his 'abit as he lived – the King of Kafirstan with his crown upon his head. Poor old Daniel that was a monarch once!" ' (p. 203). Carnehan is now destitute and is last heard of dying from sunstroke as he staggers along the street. The final sentence of the story is typical of Kipling's narrative style: 'And there the matter rests,' announces the narrator, suggesting that a line has been drawn under these explosive events (p. 204).

How, then, does 'The Man Who Would be King' fit the pattern of Kipling's short stories? First, there is its frame narrative. The use of a narrator to frame the story allows an unusual or impossible series of events to be told. The slightly superior narrator seems to represent 'us'. He is of the 'real' world and holds values similar to those of his implied readers, and his job as a local reporter whose task it is to record what happened seems a further reason for trusting him. He gives us an exclusive into the underside of colonial life and also plays some small part in the action. The story told here is fairly fantastic, but Kipling's method is to give an ostentatiously bald account of some unlikely events; he adopts a very deliberate and 'spare' writing style, excising and blacking out all but the essential bits via a process he termed 'Higher Editing'. Kipling's economic prose – some called it journalistic – is one reason he has sometimes been seen as less of an artist than more verbose or more obviously self-conscious stylists such as Conrad, Joyce or Woolf. As a coda to this, one question which strikes the reader of 'The Man Who Would Be King' is whether the two men are making it all up; is theirs merely a tall tale? Is it possible that two Englishmen could really use Freemasonry to hold sway over the people of Kafiristan as kings? Thus, as Manfred Drandt has noted, the narrator has a dual function here, 'not only as a filter through which we view the two adventurers but also…as a mouthpiece for scepticism'.[39]

A second characteristic element of the story is the ordinariness of the characters themselves. Carnehan and Dravot are freer and quicker-witted than the heroes of *Soldiers Three*, but they are, nonetheless, unlikely king material; they are examples of Kipling's 'vulgar' characters (to use T. S. Eliot's phrase[40]). They are initially identified by the narrator as 'Loafers' or drifters, belonging to the 'Intermediate class' – a reference to railway travel but also social status, occupying a kind of mid-way between the rulers and the ruled (p. 172).

Like Nick Tarvin, the unscrupulous hero of another Kipling story from this period, 'The Naulahka' (1891–2), they are familiar Kipling characters: men on the make, chirpy and cynical about the British code of service, but with enough general knowledge to exploit others (and each other) for personal gain. Dravot – a kind of cut-price Cecil Rhodes – acts out a universal desire to dominate others. He is 'the man who would be king', and he achieves a kind of immortality via his resurrection in this story. Carnehan is more passive, and at the end is reminiscent of Samuel Coleridge's decrepit sailor who buttonholes the wedding guest in 'The Rime of the Ancient Mariner' (1798).[41] The men are arrogant and foolish and are severely punished for their actions – Carnehan is destroyed in both mind and body – but they also provoke admiration and pity in equal measure.

The third recognisable element of the story is its colonial dimension. Critics generally agree that the tale told by Carnehan to the narrator is a writing out of the 'myth of imperialism',[42] one which is both parable and parody of the British abroad. One influence for the story was the white rajahs of Sarawak, successive generations of the Brooke family who ruled part of north-west Borneo. At one point Dravot comments: 'Rajah Brooke will be a suckling to us', and he claims that Kafiristan is the 'only place now in the world that two strong men can Sar-*whack*...no-one has gone there' (p. 174). Kipling wrote the story at a key moment in the colonising process. Britain was competing with Russia for influence in Asia, particularly in Afghanistan, and skirmishes in Afghan territory were increasing. Dravot and Carnehan – soldiers of the Queen and agents of empire – use guns and a well-trained native army to end tribal warfare, bringing order to the weary local population and realising that 'a man who knows how to drill men can always be king'. Order out of chaos was the cornerstone of Kipling's moral support for the imperial project, and Dravot's declaration that having incorporated his empire he will need 'cleverer men than us' to administer things suggests good sense of the kind approved of by Kipling.

Nonetheless, Dravot's dream of being knighted by Queen Victoria for getting her this territory is also a reminder of how he is motivated as much by personal aggrandisement as by patriotic duty. Helen Bauer suggests that the two men 'lack commitment to the native population, to standards of justice, to honour. And the story reveals the fate of imperial designs without a moral centre.'[43] Yet the men are not condemned outright. There is an accompanying sense that the narrator approves of their scheme and is even a participant in their project, helping them with planning and giving his 'brother', Dravot, a compass. The reader becomes a witness to this fellowship at work and its possibilities. At its heart, however, the story is about what happens when rulers forget the responsibilities of their position, and it morphs into 'a parable of hubris, of empire over-reaching itself', as Jad Adams puts it.[44]

The difficulty in surviving hostile, unfamiliar territory also lies behind the impact of the 'The Phantom Rickshaw'. A supernatural *and* a psychological story (the two often coalesce in Kipling's work), 'The Phantom Rickshaw' is also a commentary on the British in India, in particular on the failure of the imperial project. The story's ironic opening ('One of the few advantages that India has over England is great knowability', p. 103) is followed by a description of India's excessive hospitality. The relationship is one of host and guest, but the English have abused it, travelling around without paying hotel bills, turning into '[g]lobe trotters who expect entertainment as a right', to the extent that they have 'blunted this openheartedness' (p. 103).

'The Phantom Rickshaw' is a ghost story – a popular nineteenth-century form, as we saw in Chapter 3. Kipling uses the form not simply to instil fear and wonder but, as Anjali Arondekar notes, to pass comment on how 'the incoherencies of colonial rule are secreted as haunting'.[45] In Kipling's story, a civil servant, Theobald Jack Pansay (the name suggests both a childlike and a feminine personality), is the only person who sees the ghost of Mrs Agnes Keith-Wessington. He does not understand why he is being haunted, even though everyone around him, including his fiancée, Kitty Mannering, and his doctor, Heatherlegh, regards him as a 'blackguard' (p. 119). Returning to India after vacationing in England, Jack has a casual shipboard fling with Agnes, but on reaching Bombay his 'fire of straw burned itself out to a pitiful end' (p. 106) and he breaks off the relationship: 'From my own lips, in August 1882, she learnt that I was sick of her presence, tired of her company, and weary of the sound of her voice' (p. 106). Agnes continues to try to see Jack, travelling in her yellow rickshaw drawn by servants in black-and-white livery. When he announces his engagement to Kitty, Agnes vows they will be reunited. Jack treats her sadistically: 'My answer might have made even a man wince. It cut through the dying woman before me like the blow of a whip' (p. 108). Jack is presented as a man completely lacking in empathy or compassion, and incapable of self-analysis. When Agnes dies, he announces himself 'the happiest man in India' (p. 109).

The apparitions that subsequently haunt Jack are of Agnes seated in her rickshaw. As they continue Jack demands an explanation for the haunting, and Agnes's ghost talks to him in death as she did in life: 'Jack! Jack darling! It's some hideous mistake...*Please* forgive me and let's be friends' (p. 111). No one else can see Agnes, and people begin to look at Jack strangely. When he tells them how he treated Agnes, they are repulsed; Kitty abruptly breaks off their engagement in a manner similar to Jack's break-up with Agnes. Abandoned and alone, Jack has only the vengeful Agnes for company, and he walks the streets alongside her rickshaw as if he is courting her all over again: 'a marvellously dear experience' (p. 126). Nothing else is real to him, and he accommodates himself to his double life with its 'persistent delusions' (p. 106). To others in Simla he is an object of ridicule – assumed to be an alcoholic or an epileptic – but when Jack eventually dies everyone is curious about the cause of death. The doctor, whose advice for everyone working in India is to 'lie low, go slow, and keep cool' (p. 104), thinks he merely 'went off the handle' (p. 104) through overwork. The narrator, on the other hand, more ominously suggests: 'There was a crack in Pansay's head and a little bit of the Dark World came through and pressed him to death' (p. 104).

Structurally, 'The Phantom Rickshaw' has two sections: the first part, narrated by Heatherlegh, sets up the willing suspense of disbelief necessary for ghost stories. Although Kipling thought this an unaccomplished and juvenile example of the genre, he admitted 'you can credit it from beginning to end'.[46] It is not clear whether the ghost exists or whether it is a product of Jack's guilt-ridden imagination. The second section is the ghost story, which is narrated as a kind of tortured confession by Jack on his deathbed for the benefit of the narrator, for Kitty and for us as readers. It is Heatherlegh who suggests Jack write down his fears, 'knowing that ink may assist him to ease his mind' (p. 105). Jack – feverish, 'half-crazed, devil-driven' and able to speak only in a kind of 'blood and thunder Magazine diction' (p. 105) – remains confused about what has happened to him, grasping only that he is being published as a 'condemned criminal' (p. 124) for having caused Agnes's death. He remains full of wonder 'that the seen and the unseen should mingle so strangely on this earth to hound one poor soul to its grave' (p. 127).

Kipling's stories are both about the problem of 'knowing' India and about what happens when Englishmen transgress boundaries or step over the mark. Thus 'The Phantom Rickshaw' has been read allegorically; that is, Jack's sexual exploitation of women brings punishment, madness and death in the same way that the ignorance, rapaciousness and lust for glory of the British Empire resulted in the death of British citizens. The fate of such men embodies the local (Indian) idea that people eventually pay for their misdeeds.

Experience pushed a little: Joseph Conrad

Joseph Conrad is often linked with Kipling as offering late-Victorian readers a sense of the issues at stake in Britain's imperial mission. Like Kipling, Conrad could boast first-hand experience of imperialism, and it is said that his stories frequently fictionalise some of his early experiences; 'Youth' (1898), with its naive young narrator, Marlow, is a notable example. Born Józef Teodor Konrad Korzeniowski, and orphaned at an early age, Conrad left Poland in 1874 to go to sea. This decision took him to Latin America (1875–76), the Far East (1883–88) and Africa (1890). By the 1880s, he had joined the British Merchant Service and become 'Joseph Conrad', taking British nationality in 1886. As a sailor Conrad travelled between great commercial centres and tiny 'outposts of progress'. Not surprisingly this gave him a distinctive perspective on the imperial project: he was an immigrant member of a colonising country.

According to McClure, the stories which followed engage with two major questions in the imperial debate: Were Europeans assuming the 'white man's burden' to save themselves and their savage kin? Or were they thronging to the darker continents on missions of economic or psychological exploitation?[47] Broadly speaking, Conrad is usually seen to be suggesting the latter. 'I think all ambitions are lawful except those which climb upwards on the miseries or credulities of mankind,' he wrote in his autobiography, *A Personal Record* (1912).[48] Like Kipling's, Conrad's stories seem designed to disabuse readers of their romantic ideas about life in the colonies, and also like Kipling's, his representations of colonial lives involve powerful images of helplessness and disturbance.[49] His novella *Heart of Darkness* (1902) is one of the most discussed of colonial texts largely for this very reason. At the same time, Conrad was also heavily influenced by some of the structural and ideological conventions of the popular imperial romance, including, or so it has been claimed, its racism. Certainly many of his stories trade off the popularity of this genre describing exciting happenings in foreign places. Conrad described his 'Amy Foster' (1901) as 'a story of adventure', albeit one 'written not exactly according to the usual formula for work of that kind'; it contains piracy, smuggling and shipwreck.[50] 'Youth', too, was created according to Conrad '[o]ut of the materials of a boy's story'.[51] 'Bangkok! I thrilled!', announces Marlow, the narrator of 'Youth', as he recalls his first overseas voyage (pp. 5–6).[52] Moreover, this was also how Conrad's work was seen by some contemporary critics. One reviewer of *Heart of Darkness* described its subject as 'life on the Congo and the Belgian ivory-hunt'.[53] In an 1896 article, 'Malayan Romance', the *Pall Mall Gazette* credited Conrad's 'impressionist pictures of a region previously unexplored by the novelist' with giving birth 'to what may be the new literature of the Indo-Malayan region'.[54] Conrad himself referred to his 'species of short story' as 'a sort of sea narrative without head or tail'.[55] Many of the stories – 'Youth', 'The Secret Sharer' (1910), 'Falk' (1903), 'An Outpost of Progress', 'Amy Foster' – involve sailing of some kind: ships, tugs, sailors, oceans and rivers loom large. His characters steer – or drift – unintentionally and symbolically into tragic or life-changing situations involving death, betrayal and confrontation. As in Kipling's work, his characters tend to be men who are thrust into circumstances which they are only half-capable of understanding, and the way characters meet these challenges is at least as important as the events themselves.

Something of this is apparent in 'Youth', one of the tales which introduced Conrad to the English reading public. Reputedly based on Conrad's 1881 voyage to the East on the ship *The Palestine* – here re-christened *The Judea* – this early story helped fashion an idea of Conrad as a writer of tales of adventure with a nautical flavour. Edward Garnett called

'Youth' 'a modern English epic of the Sea'.[56] Conrad himself, of course, wanted to be seen as someone rivalling the great modern masters of the short story – Gustave Flaubert (1821–80), Ivan Turgenev (1818–83) and Henry James – but this did not happen straightaway.[57]

'Youth' first appeared in *Blackwood's Edinburgh Magazine* in September 1898. *Blackwood's* was a conservative magazine with a well-established tradition of 'masculine' storytelling stretching back to James Hogg (1770–1835). Conrad, conscious of the cultural capital to be gained from appearing in such an august publication, recognised that he was in 'decent company', but, as we see in 'Youth', he was also keen to distance himself from the previous generation of writers. The most obvious way in which he did this was via his use of the frame narrative, in this case a situation in which a group of respectable men – a 'Director of companies, a Tory lawyer, a vicar' – sit round a table listening to Marlow, the 'narrator-participant' (as Norman Page terms him), tell his story.[58] We do not have to read many of Conrad's stories to realise how attracted he was by this narrative device – and by Marlow himself, a character who, it has been suggested, functions as Conrad's alter ego. As Norman Page notes, Conrad was

> attracted by the opportunity of being able to comment and ruminate on the action without resorting to the intrusive interpolations of an omniscient narrator beloved by Thackeray, Trollope, and other Victorian novelists but distinctly out of favour by the turn of the century. English, of course, was a foreign language to Conrad. The use of Marlow also enabled him to employ a more relaxed, informal semi-colloquial style that may have acted as a corrective to the tendency to over-writing that had inflicted the lush prose of his earliest work.[59]

In other ways, however, 'Youth' bears very definite traces of the adventure romance. Marlow seems modern, but the young Marlow as he presents himself in this story is a fairly recognisable type. His most obvious literary ancestor is David Balfour in R. L. Stevenson's *Kidnapped* (1886) and *Catriona* (1893), but he also carries traces of some of the more naive heroes of Walter Scott's fiction, for example Edward Waverley in *Waverley* (1814), and he wants to emulate the heroic deeds of these fictional heroes. His post as second mate on *The Judea* bound for Bangkok seems to offer an opportunity to do so, and even as the ship starts to sink and Marlow is frantically bailing water he recalls how 'there was somewhere in me the thought: By Jove! This is the deuce of an adventure – something you read about' (p. 12). Marlow copes with the situations he encounters – the cargo spontaneously combusting, the explosions, the gales, the steward's going mad – by imagining himself a hero in a story. As its title suggests, the story is a celebration of the 'strength ... romance ... glamour – of youth' (p. 42), but it is also a commentary on youth's naivety and ignorance. Marlow is undoubtedly brave, but his attempts at gloriously heroic deeds tend to fall rather flat, as, for example, when he tries to dig single-handed through the smoking coal to the fire. He arrives in the East in command not of *The Judea* but of a rowing boat. Here, his first impression is of a land 'impalpable and enslaving, like a charm, like a whispered promise of mysterious delight' (p. 37), but the first sound he registers is Captain Beard swearing at him because he thinks he is a local sailor – a comment perhaps on the way Europeans interact with the indigenous peoples of the territories they take over.

Before we look at other stories by Conrad, it is worth nothing some further important features of his writing. Conrad claimed not to distinguish between stories and novels, describing both genres as 'stories'.[60] His stories tend to be long: 'The Lagoon' (1897) is the shortest, coming in at 5,700 words; 'Karain: A Memory' (1902) is 14,500; 'Typhoon' (1902),28,000. Conrad uses highly poetic and very dense language. In the past he has been criticised for his 'adjectival insistence', a trait which has been labelled an 'un-English' quality.[61] There is considerable use of simile: 'The mysterious East faced me, perfumed like a flower, silent like death, dark like a grave,' says Marlow in 'Youth' (p. 38).

Somewhat awkwardly, given that he was a writer who resisted labels, the label 'impressionist' is also often bestowed on Conrad, encouraged by his own tendency to use this term. The term is most commonly used, of course, to describe a particular style of French painting of the 1880s and 1890s. One thinks of Claude Monet, Pierre-Auguste Renoir and Edouard Manet, whose paintings attempted to capture visual sensations and fleeting moments in life. Ford Madox Ford (1873–1939), Conrad's collaborator on the novel *The Nature of a Crime* (1909), claimed that he and Conrad developed the idea that the novel must be a rendering of impressions, not narration, because this gradual understanding of a character or event was more like life: 'life did not narrate, but made impressions on our brains. We in turn, if we wished to produce on you an effect of life, must not narrate but render impressions.'[62] When Conrad writes 'I am impressionist from instinct',[63] he is also referring 'to the use of episodic scenes, a strong reliance on sensory images – especially those of colour – and the shifts in narrative stance designed to emphasise the relativity of perspective and perceptual distortions brought about by alternating authorial or omniscient narrative with descriptive passages'.[64] Alongside this is a strong moral dimension: 'My task which I am trying to achieve is, by the power of the written word, to make you hear, to make you feel', Conrad explained, '– it is before all, to make you *see*.'[65] But here the term 'see' incorporates the act not just of visualising but also of understanding. His characters – who often, like Kipling, reappear in different stories (another innovation) – are frequently like blind men who 'see' imperfectly and then experience a sudden shock – what Conrad described as 'a flash of light into a dark cavern' – which brings with it 'such knowledge as comes of a short vision. The best kind of Knowledge because most akin to revelation.'[66]

'Youth', 'An Outpost of Progress' and *Heart of Darkness* all show characters reacting at some level to this kind of 'delayed decoding', as it is sometimes termed. In 'Youth', Marlow's description of the final explosion records his awareness of 'a queer sensation, of an absurd delusion, – I seemed somehow to be in the air'. He continues:

I heard all round me like a pent-up breath released – as if a thousand giants simultaneously had said Phoo! – and felt a dull concussion which made my ribs ache suddenly. No doubt about it – I was in the air, and my body was describing a short parabola. But short as it was I had the time to think several thoughts, in as far as I can remember, the following order: 'This can't be the carpenter – What is it? – Some accident – Submarine volcano? – Coals, gas – By Jove! we are being blown up – Everybody's dead – I am falling into the after-hatch – I see fire in it.' (p. 23)

As Ian Watt points out in his useful essay 'Conrad's Impressionism', the reader tends to be given details of sensations in the order in which they are experienced. Thus 'the reader finds it quite natural that there should be delay before Marlow's brain finally decodes his impressions into their cause: "We are being blown up." '[67] There is also comic contrast between what is actually happening and some of Marlow's expressions: the very British 'By Jove!' and the pompous 'my body was describing a short parabola'.

Conrad began writing in 1886 and entered (unsuccessfully) a short story, 'The Black Mate', into a competition run by *Tit-Bits*. He wrote intermittently through the 1880s and 1890s until the publication of the novel *Almayer's Folly* in 1895. This led to his being recognised as a new talent on the literary scene. *An Outcast of the Islands* followed in 1896, together with his first short story to be published, 'The Idiots', a lurid tale of murder heavily derivative in both its subject and way of telling of Guy de Maupassant. 'The Idiots' was published in *The Savoy* in October 1896, after rejections by at least two other magazines. Although Conrad had a tendency to dismiss popular magazine tales as 'silly', they were 'saleable' and paid well. Conrad was always short of money, and the successes of Conan Doyle, Kipling and Stevenson reminded him that '[s]hort stories – is the watchword now'.[68] He got £40 for 'Karain', £50 for 'An Outpost of Progress' and £75 for 'Typhoon'.[69] However, he was often undecided about where to submit his work. In 1897, he refused to send *Pearson's Magazine* 'The Return' on the grounds that it was 'much too good to be thrown away where the *right people* won't see it'.[70] By the 'right people' he meant those who would help make him part of the literary elite of late-Victorian Britain and who controlled the more prestigious literary journals, such as *Blackwood's*, *The Savoy* and *The New Review*. At other times, however, he was willing to set this ambition to be a highbrow/high-culture writer aside for the sake of ready cash. 'Do you think I am a lost soul', he asked Edward Garnett, after finishing 'The Lagoon' in 1897, before sending it off to the middle-brow *Cornhill*. 'I would bet a penny they will take it.'[71]

A good example of Conrad's take on the adventure romance is 'Typhoon', which was published in 1902 and characterised by the *Daily Mail* as a Robert Louis Stevenson-like 'sonata of ships and storms and breaking waves'.[72] In this story, a captain sails his ship, the *Nan-Shan*, into a hurricane. The foreign (Chinese) passengers panic and riot, the British crew restore order, the ship comes through the storm and the passengers' mixed-up belongings are shared out equally. Although some of Conrad's contemporaries thought his work too difficult and out of kilter with what 'the man in the street' could manage, 'Typhoon' is an example of how the same works can be seen to fit a long-established popular tradition of sea-faring stories. The British empire 'rests on trans-portation', wrote Conrad in 1919; 'the seamen hold up the edifice'.[73] 'Typhoon' itself can be read as a celebration of the strong sense of duty among Britain's sailors. (A similar call to patriotic feeling is made in 'Youth'.) The *Nan-Shan* is a microcosm of empire, and Captain McWhirr is the representative Merchant Navy captain whose very name seems to connote a smoothly working mechanism; his motto, 'Facing it – always facing it – that's the way to get through' (p. 89),[74] encapsulates his blind devotion to duty. To avoid the late arrival of the ship and the increased coal bill for taking a detour, McWhirr sails straight through the typhoon. 'A gale is a gale', he reasons, 'and a full-powered steam ship has got to face it' (p. 34). His 'frail and indomitable voice' heard above 'the shouting hurricane ... has an effect of quietness like the serene glow of a halo' (pp. 44–6). The ship is battered but arrives at Fu-chau as if she has sighted 'the coast of the Great Beyond whence no ship ever returns' (p. 91). British pluck saves the day. Of course, it might also be said that we are invited to be critical of the captain. One of the reasons that McWhirr shows no fear is that he is a fairly stupid man who has no imagination. The ship's first mate, Jukes, thinks that both captain and ship have 'the heavy obviousness of a lump of clay' (p. 16), and as the story progresses, the reader might start to question the usefulness of this tradition of stiff upper lips and doing the right thing. Was it necessary to sail into the typhoon in the first place? If these men are typical representatives of the British empire, isn't the empire ultimately doomed? This question proves difficult to answer, in part because Jukes is a xenophobic and unreliable witness.

In *Joseph Conrad and Popular Culture*, Stephen Donovan suggests that the central events of the *Nan-Shan*'s progress into the storm and the struggle to restore order below deck show Conrad doggedly following some of the rules for short-story composition set down in the writing manuals for would-be authors popular in his own day: 'a single predominating incident and a single chief character ... the whole treatment so organised as to produce a single impression'.[75] Conrad himself wrote of 'the single point of "suspended interest" ... One single episode out of a life, one single feeling combined with a certain form of action (you'll notice I say *action* not analysis) may give the quality of "suspended interest" to the tale of one single adventure in which the deepest sensations (and not only the bodies) of the actors are involved.'[76] Other stories also fit this pattern. 'Youth', for example, depicts one voyage being undertaken for a single purpose, and, with the exception of Marlow as narrator, there is one main character, Captain Beard. Within the stories, the 'single episode', then, takes on the status of metaphor, connected to the larger human experience.

Another feature of Conrad's writing which emerges strongly in these early stories is his use of setting. D. R. Schwartz makes the point that the physical conditions under which Conrad's people operate become a 'moral labyrinth which the characters are unable to negotiate and which not only shapes their destiny but also subsumes them'.[77] Conrad invariably chooses to set his fiction around a clash between one of his protagonists (usually a young man) and a remote, unfamiliar location, an encounter which is both physical and psychological. Thus what he offers his readers is not just the unknown but a new experience or new way of looking at something. Many Europeans, Conrad noted, had the idea that in 'distant lands all joy is a yell and a war dance, all pathos is a howl and a ghastly grin of filed teeth, and that the solution of all problems is found in the barrel of a revolver or on the point of an assegai'.[78] Conrad thought that the sense of difference or 'otherness' between East and West caused the Western writer's eye to be 'dazzled', with the result that it 'misses the delicate detail, sees only the strong outlines, while the colours in the steady light seem crude and without shadow'.[79] So his writerly style is also linked to ideas about how to *rep*-resent exotic lands as places which are more complex and elusive than readers are often led to believe. A story such as 'Youth' can be read as an ironic comment on Western ignorance of what the East is actually like. Re-visioning is also present in 'The Lagoon', one of Conrad's first stories, which was collected with 'Karain', 'The Idiots', 'The Return' and 'An Outpost of Progress' in *Tales of Unrest* (1898). The story is, as Conrad put it, 'very much Malay',[80] and he tended to be dismissive of its origi-nality, summing it up as follows: '[A] Malay tells a story to a white man who is spending the night at his hut. It's a tricky thing with the usual forests river – stars – wind sunrise, and so on – and lots of second hand Conradese.'[81] Nonetheless, the story was well received on its publication in the *Cornhill Magazine* ('not a bad mag. to appear in', Conrad noted[82]), where it earned its author £12. The *Spectator* saw it as a 'marvellous insight into certain types and phases of Oriental character...master-pieces of exotic portraiture'.[83] What the reviewer had in mind was this description of the jungle:

> The narrow creek was like a ditch: tortuous, fabulously deep; filled with gloom under the thin strip of pure and shining blue of the heaven...Here and there, near the glistening blackness of the water, a twisted root of some tall tree showed amongst the tracery of small ferns, black and dull, writhing and motionless like an arrested snake...Darkness oozed out from between the trees...mysterious and invincible; the darkness scented and poisonous. (p. 142)[84]

Although Conrad's use of this kind of description would later come in for parody, his contemporary readers expected a sense of menace in their exotic stories – a genre in which, as Rupert Ruppel has noted, 'the jungle is nearly always an antagonist'.[85] In this case, there is a liberal use of anthropomorphism – of water as well as land. Often in Conrad's work the exotic jungle stands for aspects of a country or continent which have been most resistant to the colonial project, or to humankind generally.

In this instance the landscape, which seems almost alive, might even be read as being akin to one of Sigmund Freud's hysterical subjects; the violence it embodies is a metaphor for a repressed (Eastern) psychic structure. This is why the country needs to be tamed. It represents a dangerous hiding place for the wild, uncivilised side of humankind.

In addition to its setting and the incorporation of what would become familiar Conradian themes – betrayal, remorse, moral blindness – 'The Lagoon' uses what would become a favourite structural device for Conrad: the tale within a tale. The story has an inner narrative, told in the first person. The frame narrative of 'The Lagoon' is the point of view of an anonymous white traveller, one of a number of masterful white men who populated adventure romances in the 1890s. He instructs his native crew – who are, in typical fashion, presented as childish and sulky – to tie the boat up for the night in a clearing near to where his old companion, Arsat, lives. Arsat is hated by the sailors not only 'as a stranger', but also because 'he is not afraid to live amongst the spirits that haunt the places abandoned by mankind' (p. 143). The crew refuses to leave the boat, so the white man goes alone. When he arrives at the hut, he finds Arsat's lover, Diamelen, ill with fever. Not having brought any medicine, he is unable to help her. As Rupert Ruppel notes, 'Arsat's reliance on, and admiration for, the white man at this point reflects another persistent imperialist idea that the whites know more about the colonial world than do the people who were born and raised there.'[86] Conrad represents Arsat as dog-like in his devotion, and as a brave fighter; he also gives him a form of speech which is elaborate, full of metaphors and flowery maxims (the sun is 'the eye of day'), which has the effect of making him – and by implication his culture – sound old-fashioned and thus in need of a guiding hand. Arsat and his visitor sit in silence until 'A plaintive murmur rose in the night; a murmur saddening and startling, as if the great solitudes of surrounding woods had tried to whisper into his ear the wisdom of their immense and lofty indifference' (p. 146). Although native peoples are generally not given much opportunity to tell their own stories in these tales, Conrad has Arsat recount how he fell in love with Diamelen, a serving-girl, and how he and his brother, sword-bearers to Inchi Midah, a chief, had planned to kidnap her from her mistress. When their attempt was discovered, Arsat abandoned his brother to certain death and ran away with Diamelen. Arsat is consumed by guilt and thinks Diamelen's death is payment for his behaviour. At first reading, Diamelen seems to be an exotic *femme fatale* who has come between two men and destroyed their relationship. However, the story also suggests a supernatural world: the cause of Diamelen's illness might be the vengeful spirit of Arsat's brother.

'The Lagoon' ends with Arsat talking of returning home to avenge his brother's killing, thus proving his bravery by dying honourably and achieving some kind of salvation – or so he thinks. The sun rises in the sky, the 'whisper of unconscious life' grows louder and a white eagle flies through the sky (p. 152). Arsat is seemingly paralysed, staring 'beyond the great light of a cloudless day into the darkness of a world of illusion' (p. 152). There have been many attempts to address the ambiguity of the ending; according to Laurence Graver, the light and dark motif 'suggests that though Arsat achieves a degree of relief by telling his story to the white man, he is merely substituting one illusion for another. Even if he goes back to avenge his brother... the return will be in no sense triumphant.'[87]

Written at the same time as 'The Lagoon', and with a similarly exotic jungle setting, 'An Outpost of Progress' is another story about human vulnerability and betrayal, but with 'a different moral attitude', as Conrad put it in his 'Author's Note' (p. 156).[88] With the publication of 'An Outpost of Progress' in *Tales of Unrest* Conrad was perceived to be breaking more 'fresh ground', although reviewers tended to be shocked by what they saw as the story's 'morbidity'.[89] 'To print all these miserable and tragic episodes on end in a single volume is artistically a mistake,' commented the *Westminster Gazette*.[90] Using a sardonic third-person narrator who offers external observation and social commentary, Conrad tells the story of two ineffectual Englishmen, Kayerts and his subordinate, Carlier, working for a 'Great Civilising Company'. Arriving in the company steamer ('an enormous sardine box with a flat-roofed shed erected on it', p. 68), they are dumped at a run-down trading post on the Kasai River (a tributary of the Congo) and left for six months to re-establish trade relations with the natives. They find an old newspaper article titled 'Our Colonial Expansion', a slogan which causes them to dream of a prosperous town on the site of their station replete with 'Quays, and warehouses, and barracks, and – and billiard rooms. Civilization' (p. 73). The company director predicts the two men will fail because they lack the intelligence, perception and drive necessary for such an undertaking. The narrator confirms this, explaining that the men are too small-minded and second-rate and therefore vulnerable; their 'every great and insignificant thought belongs' not to them 'but to the crowd' (p. 69). Thus isolated, the former administrator and former soldier both prove to be ignorant of the country; the narrator's labelling of them as 'the two pioneers of trade and progress' (p. 72) has a mocking tone. The men are scared to stray beyond the confines of their base; there is no communication with the outside world except via the river – and the steamer visits only twice a year. Gradually the hostile environment destroys the two British men: 'out of the great silence of the surrounding wilderness, its very hopelessness and savagery seemed to approach them nearer, to draw them gently, to look upon them, to envelop them with a solicitude irresistible, familiar, and disgusting' (p. 82). Makola is outwardly respectful ('a neat, civilised nigger' [p. 79]) but holds both men in contempt, and it is he rather than his slovenly 'superiors' who really controls the trading post. The men fail to apprehend the impending disaster. Conrad describes them as 'two blind men in a large room, aware only of what came into contact with them (and that only imperfectly) but unable to see the general aspect of things' (p. 71). When a group of armed traders arrive to sell a large stock of ivory, Makola negotiates a price: the compound's native labourers, who have ceased to flourish in the hostile climate but who have value as slaves. The labourers are drugged with alcohol and taken away in the night by the traders, who, it can be inferred, have acquired some of the white man's duplicity. The two white men themselves (typically) sleep through these events. When they discover what has happened, they are horrified, but their greed ensures that they accept the ivory even as they realise they are now participants in the slave trade. Eaten up by guilt, both men go mad. Their sense of isolation overwhelms them, food becomes short, and after a trivial quarrel over a piece of sugar Kayerts kills Carlier. He plans to bury him as a fever victim, but before he can do this he hears a ship's whistle ('the voice of progress and civilisation', as the narrator ironically puts it [p. 88]) signalling the return of the company director. When the director reaches the base he finds Kayerts hanging from the grave of the man who ran the station before them: 'his arms hung stiffly down; he seemed to be standing rigidly at attention, but with one purple cheek playfully posed on the shoulder. And irreverently he was putting out a swollen tongue at his Managing Director' (p. 89)

The story's final macabre gesture has been read as Conrad poking his tongue out at imperialism generally, at the greedy scramble for loot (disguised as 'civilising') and at 'the hubris of civilisation'.[91] 'In the post-Darwinian world... those who are "fittest to survive" prove to be not the Europeans but the family of Makola from Sierra Leone.'[92] Conrad himself told Edward Garnett that the story was written out of an incident he had heard about while in the Congo: 'All the bitterness of those days, all my puzzled wonder as to the meaning of all I saw – all my indignation at masquerading philanthropy – have been with me again, while I wrote.'[93]

Conrad's depiction of egotistical, ignorant men falling to pieces in an unforgiving environment has echoes of Kipling's 'The Man Who Would Be King', as well as anticipating *Heart of Darkness* (1899), although it lacks the technical sophistication of the more famous work. Lack of sophistication is not a charge which can be levelled against another early Malayan story, 'Karain: A Memory', the publication of which began Conrad's important five-year relationship with the prestigious *Blackwood's Magazine*. Conrad again dismissed the story as having 'something magazinish about it',[94] by which he meant that it once more contained many of the ingredients of popular romance: a Malay chief, a ghost, murder, betrayal against an exotic backdrop. Its subject matter is similar to that of the earlier stories: the clash of British trading interests and the Eastern 'other'. But its engagement with imperial attitudes is more complex. Skimming through the 'befogged respectability' (p. 5) of a newspaper, the narrator – a former imperial adventurer – notes an article on political unrest in the Malay Peninsula. This prompts him to recall his dealings with the Malay chief Karain, whom the *Daily Telegraph*'s reviewer described as 'a magnificent savage'.[95] Initially the narrator, faced with the grime of Victorian London, recalls the land of Mindanao romantically – even theatrically – in a series of flickering impressions which make the distant land seem more real than the present: 'Sunshine gleams between the lines of those short paragraphs – sunshine and the glitter of the sea. A strange name wakes up memories; the printed words scent the smoky atmosphere of today faintly... There are faces too... we seem to hear their soft voices' (p. 5). The narrator then tells how he and his crew went to Southeast Asia as arms dealers, illegally selling weapons to warring factions among the local population. The narrator does not seem to have any misgivings about this trade; it is a case of 'us' and 'them'. Karain, painted as a powerfully romantic exotic figure, was one of their clients: 'a petty chief of a conveniently isolated corner of Mindanao', where they 'could in comparative safety break the law against the traffic in firearms and ammunition with natives' (p. 7). Karain's kingdom appears magical, with sea on one side and a 'monumental amphitheatre of hills' (p. 10) on the other. Cut off from the outside world, it seems 'immense and vague' (p. 6).

Karain, who thinks the arms trade is sanctioned by the 'Great, Invincible, Pious and Fortunate' far-off Queen Victoria (p. 9), is an enigmatic, charismatic performer; the narrator describes 'the power he had to awaken an absurd expectation of something heroic going to take place... upon the vibrating tone of a wonderful sunshine' (p. 7). But it is also suggested that there is something not quite real about him: 'clothed

in the illusion of unavoidable success', in a setting of 'gorgeous spectacle' (p. 8), he is an 'actor ... treated with a solemn respect accorded in the
irreverent West only to the monarchs of the stage' (p. 7). The implication here seems to be that this respect need not be taken too seriously by
the Britisher; it is merely part of the excess surrounding the larger-than-
life non-European exotic. The narrator's claim of friendship carries with
it the assumptions of his class and nation. The narrator comments on
Karain's 'childish shrewdness'; sometimes the men catch sight of 'sombre glowing fury within him ... and a concentrated lust of violence which
is dangerous in a native' (p. 8).

One way in which 'Karain' fits the template of the adventure romance
is in its interest in the interplay between character and environment.
The men's early encounters with Karain are sensuous moments in a land
of golden beaches where 'green islets ... lie upon the level of a polished
sea, like a handful of emeralds on a buckler of steel' (p. 5). However,
during their final visit, the atmosphere changes: there is something sinister and unnamed lurking in the air, an uncanny stillness pervades the
place, and 'the trees far off stood in unstirring clumps, as if painted'
(p. 17). Storms are brewing, and Karain is nowhere to be seen. When
he does appear it is aboard the men's ship in the middle of the night.
He has swum from the shore, his face betraying 'the tormented weariness, the anger and the fear of a struggle against a thought ... a shadow, a
nothing, unconquerable and immortal, that preys upon life' (p. 20).

It is only at this point that Karain is given the opportunity to recount
his own story – 'the strange obsession that wound like a black thread
through the gorgeous pomp of his public life' (p. 11) and has more
hold on him than any human law. As with the portrayal of Arsat in
'The Lagoon', Conrad – or rather his narrator – has Karain speak in old-
fashioned English, in short sentences and faintly quaint metaphors (he
describes Dutch war ships as 'fire-ships' [p. 23]). He reveals that he is
haunted by the ghost of Pata Matara, a friend whom he killed during an
'obscure Odyssey of revenge' against Pata Matara's sister, who disgraced
her tribe by eloping with a Dutch trader (p. 32). Although the men track
down the sister, Karain has become so obsessed with the image of the
girl that he sacrifices Matara to save her life. Shortly afterwards he begins
to feel haunted by his murder victim's ghost. Only his devoted sword-
bearer can offer him protection, and with him he establishes his power as
ruler. However, the death of the sword-bearer exposes Karain again to the
'reproachful shade' (p. 34). Karain has come to consult the Western crew
because he has decided he needs a new form of protection, and these are
men from the 'land of unbelief, where the dead do not speak' (p. 35). He

hopes they will give him a 'Western' charm to see off the ghost. One of the crew members, Hollis, gives Karain a commemorative sixpence made out of gilt for Queen Victoria's Golden Jubilee celebrations in 1887. Karain is fascinated by the Queen, a woman who 'commands' a spirit, too – the spirit of her nation. The narrator recalls: 'The great thing was to impress him powerfully, to suggest absolute safety – the end of all trouble. We did our best' (p. 41). As Hollis places the counterfeit talisman round Karain's neck on a ribbon, Karain appears to have shaken off his ghosts; with the Queen as his guiding spirit he is restored to the 'illusion of unavoidable success', and his Malay subjects celebrate his recovery. The Englishmen meanwhile treat the idea of the sixpence as a magic charm ironically – as something with which to humour the primitive Malay ruler. The fact that he chooses to believe in its power is a sign to them of his stupidity.

The concluding scene of the story begins with the words 'But the memory remains' (p. 43). It has the narrator many years later back in London, where he meets his old crew mate Jackson in the Strand. The city is filthy: 'a broken confusion of roofs', streets 'deep as a well and narrow like a corridor full of a sombre and ceaseless stir'; '[i]nnumerable eyes stared straight in front, feet moved hurriedly, blank faces flowed, arms swung' (p. 43). The differences between London and Mindanao are obvious. The men stop outside a gun shop, and the sight of the fire-arms reminds Jackson of Karain: 'the sight of all this made me think of him' (p. 43). The narrator sees Jackson's reflection in the window, 'and I could see another man, powerful and bearded, peering at him intently from amongst the dark and polished tubes that can cure so many illusions' (p. 43). The story ends on a melancholy note, with Jackson asking whether Karain could truly have been haunted by a ghost. Jackson seems haunted by memories from the past. The memory of Karain is more real to him than the bustle of the great metropolis of London. As the narrator notes patronisingly: 'I think that, decidedly, he had been too long away from home' (p. 44).

Like all Conrad's stories, 'Karain' is rich in interpretive possibilities, and the final scene is complex and open-ended. Do we agree with the narrator's final comments or reject them as short-sighted? The fact that the events still loom large in the minds of the Englishmen, even when they stand in the busy streets of London, suggests a story about haunting. It has also been seen as a story about betrayal – a familiar Conradian theme. And it is a story about guilt – or gilt – and an exposé of an empire founded on violence and gun-running, and thus mor-ally and culturally bankrupt. Are the British about to have the guns they have sold turned back on them? Is the bearded man looking back out from behind the gun shop window really there? Is he the barbarian who lurks in the civilised English character? The narrator and his comrades believe in their own difference from Karain, but they are as violent and 'primitive' as he. None of this registers consciously with the narrator or Jackson, but the concluding descriptions of sunrise over Mindanao and sunset over London – creating the effect of an East–West 'split screen' – suggest the primitive and civilised societies overlapping. There are mysterious forces at work in London as well as in Mindanao.

Like many of the colonial stories discussed in this chapter, 'Karain' offers the reader a range of ideological positions, and as twenty-first-century readers we inevitably question some of them. However, part of the interest of this sub-genre of story – particularly as written by Conrad and Kipling – is its polyphony, its potential to avoid fixed readings. These stories carry many of the prejudices of their age, but they also expose some of the darker elements of the so-called New Imperialism of the late nineteenth and early twentieth centuries. We have also seen how the masculine situations or identities played out document some of the aspirations and anxieties of many late-Victorian and Edwardian men. Nonetheless, there is another side to both authors. As the discussion of 'The Phantom Rickshaw' suggests, in these same fictions Kipling at any rate is also concerned with the corresponding lives of women, and it is this concern which can give his works a very different feel from adventure romances by other male writers. In Chapter 7 we will focus on this dimension of Kipling's writing and explore some of the ways in which the texts engage with war-time ideas of 'Woman' and the feminine.

Part II

The Twentieth-Century Short Story

6
Introducing the Twentieth-Century Short Story

There is a particular way of describing the development of the short story in the early part of the twentieth century which has had enormous influence on studies of the form. Most surveys of the genre race towards the major figures of modernism in the period leading up to and immediately following the Great War – James Joyce, Katherine Mansfield and D. H. Lawrence, for instance – because, the argument goes, the short story is a modern form, and therefore it must be expected to operate within the experimental mode of modernism. The critical and aesthetic preferences in discussions of the form have been for what Clare Hanson has called the 'plotless fictions' of the early years of the twentieth century, where 'the primary distinction is between those works in which the major emphasis is on plot, and those in which plot is subordinate to psychology and mood'.[1] Although other commentators, notably Dominic Head in *The Modernist Short Story*, have sought to finesse this view, they have often done so in ways which focus strongly on the short story's formal features and on the technical innovations of the early part of the century.[2] There are a number of problems with this emphasis.

In the first place, there is a problem with the assumption that experiments only really began after 1900 – or, more likely, 1910, with the publication of Mansfield's first collection. As previous chapters of this book have suggested, the explosion of magazine publishing, the use of the short story for political ends by New Woman and suffrage writers in their periodical press, and a number of notable collections of short fictions (George Egerton's *Keynotes* and Joseph Conrad's *Tales of Unrest*, for instance) show the extent to which the end of the nineteenth century was also a fruitful period for the short story and for technical innovations in the form. The New Woman writers, for example, often eschewed novel publication because, as Jane Eldridge Miller has argued, the traditional realist plots of the nineteenth-century three-volume novel and a conservative publishing establishment did not suit their purposes at all. By way of contrast:

> the fragmentary and inconclusive nature of the short story made it the ideal vehicle for some of the most successful fictional explorations of modern women and feminism. It permitted writers to focus on individual episodes, or moments, instead of on causality and resolution, and thus it freed them from some of the narrative constraints of the novel.[3]

Among Eldridge Miller's examples of writers making use of the short form for political ends are George Egerton (pen name of Mary Chavelita Dunne), Victoria Cross (pen name of Anne Sophie Cory, 1868–1952), Ella D'Arcy, Ada Levenson, Evelyn Sharp and Edith Nesbit. Their experiments, although Mansfield and Woolf did not always acknowledge them as predecessors, were extremely significant for the next generation of women writers. As we have seen, in the 1890s a number of women published in experimental magazines such as *The Yellow Book* and also *The Savoy*, publications which favoured technical experiments with much more fragmented short stories than had been the fashion in the earlier part of the nineteenth century. That tradition of publication was picked up by the next generation in their work in organs such as *The Egoist*, which ran from 1914 to 1919 (renamed by Ezra Pound [1885–1972], having originally been a suffrage journal entitled *The New Freewoman*), and John Middleton Murry's (1889–1957) *Rhythm* (1911–13), which published a number of short stories by his wife, Katherine Mansfield. There were, in short, at least as many continuities as breaks with the Victorian past in the development of the twentieth-century short story. This is also true as it relates to figures such as Rudyard Kipling and H. G. Wells, who began writing as 'Victorians' but carried on writing well into the twentieth century: Kipling died in 1936; Wells a decade later, in 1946.

The critical consensus that modernism is what matters most risks falsifying literary history because it ignores those writers whose works are not deemed 'experimental'. In fact, as is also the case with the history of the novel, in the years immediately after the turn of the nineteenth century, the majority of short fiction published belonged to the popular genres that had been established in the Victorian periodical press – in particular, the detective story, the romance, the ghost story or weird tale, and the imperial adventure story, which developed into the war and spy stories of the inter-war period. In each of these genres, careful plotting is a driving force for the story, but that is not to say that such fictions do not also have an intense focus on psychological states (after all, a haunted character is in a state of psychological distress; a criminal pitted against a detective is an interesting psychological study; love and romance are periods of heightened psychological and emotional awareness). The distinction drawn by Clare Hanson, among others, between these traditional well-wrought (and sometimes highly wrought) tales and the works of modernism is the rejection of story in its shaped form. As Hanson puts it:

> Modernist short fiction writers distrusted the well-wrought tale for a variety of reasons... they argued that the pleasing shape and coherence of the traditional short story represented a falsification of the discrete and heterogeneous nature of experience... 'story'... seemed to convey the misleading notion of something finished, absolute and wholly understood.[4]

This account in part works to create an Aunt Sally: a simplified version of earlier forms of short fiction which enables the critic to dismiss them in favour of the innovative writing of the later period. As we saw in Chapter 2, H. G. Wells in 1905 managed to come up with a very long list of names of short-story writers he saw as important and readable but who have long since disappeared. If the critic ignores this range of popular short stories, published largely in magazines and periodicals, often aimed at women readers, the majority experience disappears from the literary record. Such an emphasis serves the interests of the academy, which likes its neat divisions and prefers the complex over the simple.

Finally, the distinction between a focus on technical experiments, psychological intensity and a fragmented narrative, on the one hand, and a neat tale with its twist and compressed sense of completion, on the other, is not actually that secure. There are very few modernist short stories which have no plot at all, and there are relatively few plotted or traditional short stories which are not also interested in point of view, psychological stresses and the necessary partiality of any narrative structure (as we saw in the previous chapter in the cases of Joseph Conrad and Rudyard Kipling). Experiment and tradition co-exist in the twentieth-century short story, as attested by the example of another pair of writers: George Moore (1852–1933) and Arnold Bennett (1867–1931).

Arnold Bennett and George Moore

It would be near-impossible to make any real claim for Arnold Bennett as a technical innovator in the short-story form, notwithstanding the fact that his first ever fiction publication was a short story for that most decadent and experimental of organs *The Yellow Book*. It was a sad little tale, called 'A Letter Home', published near the end of the magazine's life in 1897. In the story, a dying vagrant writes to his mother from his pauper's bed; his is a 'dead' letter in more sense than one, since it is never delivered, being used by the fellow-vagrant to whom it has been entrusted to light a pipe. It speaks of the futility of good intentions, and perhaps even of human life itself.

Despite his rather sombre beginnings as a short-story writer, the characteristic tone of Bennett's short stories is one of a gentle humour; this is in part a function of their origins as stories told to be sold to various periodicals and local newspapers for their original publication. Bennett joined the staff of *Woman* magazine in 1893, later becoming its editor, and he had a sure grasp of the market. His stories are light, popular reading rather than 'Art', although those terms and the judgements they imply are problematic. Bennett's key interest is in characters bounded by various forms of limitation – of opportunity, of horizon, of imagination, of empathy and, above all, of articulacy – themes that could well be at home in the modernist short story, too, as chapter 8 will suggest. The number of characters in Bennett's short fiction who do not speak (they choose not to because of a quarrel; they live lives of reticence because of their social milieu, which precludes speech; they do not have the words for the emotions they feel) is very striking. The difference between Bennett's tales and those of his modernist contemporaries, though, is that for the most part Bennett's narrators are articulate on behalf of the characters they describe, whereas the modernist narrator generally refuses the role of providing explanatory clarification. Bennett's narrators stand outside the frame of the story, poking gentle fun at the inhabitants of the Five Towns (his fictional name for the real-life conurbation of Stoke-on-Trent, where Bennett was born) and offering the insider's privileged but ironised view of the towns' denizens. Many of the stories are anecdotal or simply jokey, telling episodes in the lives of local 'characters' in the manner of gossip – a very nineteenth-century mode which owes much to the tradition inaugurated by Elizabeth Gaskell's *Cranford* stories, which began to be published as early as 1851. At the same time, there is an extended ambiguity and irony in Bennett's short fiction. They might not be experimental, but they are not simple or simplistic.

This is signalled from the very first line of his early collection *The Grim Smile of the Five Towns* (1907), in a story called 'The Lion's Share':

> In the Five Towns, the following history is related by those who know it as something side-splittingly funny – as one of the best jokes that ever occurred in a district devoted to jokes. And I, too, have hitherto regarded it as such. But upon my soul, now that I come to write it down, it strikes me as being, after all, a pretty grim tragedy. However, you shall judge, and laugh or cry as you please. (p. 7)[5]

The story is an anecdote, but when it enters the realm of literature (when it is written down as opposed to being disseminated orally), it gains not clarity but ambiguity, and possibly achieves the status of tragedy rather than simple humour. It tells of a young man who accidentally injures his younger stepbrother by falling down the stairs with the younger child in his arms. The older brother spends the rest of his life making amends for this unintentional act, giving up his own happiness, including the girl of his dreams, to his brother. The suspicion throughout the story is that the younger brother is faking the ongoing effects of his original injury for his own ends, and that the older brother is foolishly, blindly sacrificing his own life to the selfishness of the younger boy. The tone is light, but the subject matter is not. As we shall see in Chapter 8, in the hands of Katherine Mansfield or James Joyce, there would be no doubt of the tragedy, and comparing this story with the wasted lives of 'The Daughters of the Late Colonel' or 'Eveline' from *Dubliners* (1914) has a certain salutary force in defining the distinction between modernist and traditional short stories. But this is not to say that Bennett's stories lack artistry or effectiveness. What he provides is a sophisticated incongruity between tone and subject which is missing from the stories of the later writers, even if the signal of that incongruity is a little heavy-handed at the outset. 'The Lion's Share' ends traditionally, with a punch-line (or twist), as befits an anecdote: when the older brother returns from many years away, having lost his house, his business and the woman he loved in the service of his brother, the younger brother's little son asks: 'you carry me down-stairs, unky?' 'No,' says the older brother, 'I'm dashed if I do!' (p. 19). Is this the dawning consciousness of a wasted life or the simple learning of an uncomplicated lesson? The answer is not clear, and the ambiguity of the beginning is repeated in the story's end. It is an anecdote, but what exactly does it illustrate? The answer is in part the particular character of the Five Towns' inhabitants, whose inarticulacy is the symptom of an inability to live their lives fully.

One thing that all Bennett's Five Towns short fiction illustrates is the particular character of the district in which he sets his tales and its effects on the personalities of those who inhabit it. In this he is drawing on the nineteenth-century tradition of naturalism, a mode of representation aligned to realism, but which attempts to represent the real with a quasi-scientific attention to detail. We know that Bennett had read widely in the works of Émile Zola (1840–1902) (of whom he disapproved) and Maupassant (whom he greatly admired). He drew from them the view that the physical (geographical) environment and the moral environment of non-conformist Christianity *determined* the characters of the inhabitants of the Five Towns. The clay-pits, smoke, industry, pollution, crowds, transport, shopping, housing, drinking culture and temperance movements, the public amenities and the sanctioned and illicit amusements of the federation are the foundation of the characters' behaviour. 'We are a stolid and a taciturn race, we of the Five Towns,' Bennett writes:

> It may be because we are geographically so self-contained; or it may be because we work in clay and iron; or it may merely be because it is our nature to be stolid and taciturn. But stolid and taciturn we are. (p. 109)

This by way of introduction to a man who leaves his wife for more than twenty years, sends word that he is dead and then turns up, just to see how she is, for the entirely contingent reason that he has missed his train and happens to be in the locality. Her taciturnity and stolidity are indeed remarkable in these circumstances, particularly given that in the intervening twenty years she has bigamously remarried, had a daughter and been widowed:

> 'Well, well,' she murmured [when she sees him sitting in her parlour].
> But her capacity for wonder was almost exhausted.
> 'So ye've come back,' said Priscilla.
> 'Aye', concurred Toby.
> There was a pause.
> 'Cold weather we're having,' he muttered.
> 'It's seasonable,' Priscilla pointed out. (pp. 114–15)

The two did not communicate when they were first married. The story holds out no hope that they will do so if (and this is not certain) they come together again as husband and wife.

Much of the time, the communication failures in Bennett's stories are comic. We don't enter the minds of the protagonists, and the narrator keeps us and himself at a safe ironic distance. But in a couple of cases, irony shifts on its axis, particularly in the two extended stories 'The Death of Simon Fuge' (in *The Grim Smile of the Five Towns*) and the title story of *The Matador of the Five Towns* (1912). The narrator of both these tales is a named character, an outsider to the Five Towns from London, a man named Loring who works at the British Museum and is presented as an effete southerner. He is an acknowledged expert on pottery and china, but his knowledge is theoretical, in contrast to the much more practical knowledge of the Five Towns' citizens. (Stoke-on-Trent, of course, was the British centre for china and pottery production for around two hundred years.) In the former story, if there is a joke, it is at the expense of this outsider, who arrives in the Five Towns filled with prejudice and stereotyped notions of the place which are at first confirmed. The opening scene at the railway station is filled with working men and women rudely pushing their way backwards and forwards, and impatient with the southerner's indecision. It seems an uncivilised, barbaric place to Loring:

> My knowledge of industrial districts amounted to nothing. Born in Devonshire, educated at Cambridge, and fulfilling my destiny as curator of a certain department of antiquities at the British Museum, I had never been brought into contact with the vast constructive material activities of... Staffordshire. I had but passed through them occasionally... scorning their necessary grime with the perhaps too facile disdain of the clean-faced southerner, who is apt to forget that coal cannot walk up unaided out of the mine, and that the basin in which he washes... can only be manufactured amid conditions highly repellent... My impressions of the platform of Knype station were unfavourable. There was dirt in the air; I could feel it on my skin... the scene was shabby and rude... What I saw was a pushing, exclamatory, ill-dressed, determined crowd, each member of which was bent on the realization of his own desires by the least ceremonious means. (pp. 133–34)

This is the industrial version of what the *fin-de-siècle* critic Walter Pater had identified as the human condition: 'experience reduced to a swarm of impressions... through which no real voice has ever pierced on its way to us',[6] a statement which really does sum up many of the modernists' views of the limitations of personality and the impossibility of expressing it adequately. In Bennett's hands, this vision becomes an aestheticisation of naturalism, though there is also some gentle irony at the narrator's own expense, which is pursued in the rest of the story. On the train, Loring has heard of the death of the Staffordshire painter Simon Fuge, and this has set him off on a reverie about an anecdote he once heard the painter tell concerning a romantic boat trip on a lake by moonlight with two sisters. That evening the Londoner learns, first, that his initial impressions of the Five Towns are wrong – that this, in fact, is an intensely civilised and cultivated place where the middle classes at least can rival those of London for their knowledge and appreciation of culture and the arts. Second, he learns that the desire to impose his own romanticised meanings on the death of Simon Fuge cannot be sustained when confronted with other people's recollections of the man and the so-called romantic boat journey, for it was not romantic after all. The great painter was a fussy man, incompetent with oars, and he complained all night that his feet were cold. Loring must, from his confrontation with difference, learn to put aside his *indifference* to other people's emotions. He articulates this to his readers, but he cannot say anything about it, for reasons of propriety and reticence, to those most closely involved in the painter's story of the boat trip, the vulgar barmaid and her civilised sister whom he has made it is his mission to meet. Communication exists but is limited. This is a realist short story, but it makes use of the limitations imposed by the crisis of meaning that modernism operates within.

Bennett's Five Towns represent a landscape that is thoroughly exploited. Industry hums in all senses everywhere in Staffordshire. The people work hard, but they also play hard; some have rich cultural lives, all choose their religion, they rarely suffer from actual want, and they are proud of what they have made. The work of George Moore, an Irishman who lived in London for much of his life, tells very different kinds of stories. Take, for example, *The Untilled Field* (1903). This collection of stories has a much more clearly defined political purpose: this is not always gentle mockery; it is often a howl of pain against the conditions in rural Ireland in the latter years of the nineteenth century and early years of the twentieth century. The limitations in Moore's world are much more closely aligned to the context he writes about, a context of abject poverty, hopelessness and the suffocating embrace of religious belief which affects even those who are outside the realm of need. Thus the artists and middle-class politicians are just as stifled by the Church's strictures as are the inarticulate peasants. His picture of rural Ireland is of a land that is literally uncultivated and uncultured – hence 'untilled'. The collection opens famously with a broken statue, destroyed by the ignorance of two boys in thrall to the pronouncements of the priesthood. They have heard him adjudge the statue obscene, and they act unquestioningly upon his view, showing the extent to which even art is hemmed in by prejudice and narrow-mindedness. Beyond the relatively comfortable class of the bohemian artists (the artist Rodney is not actually hungry for food even if he does regard himself as poor), the effects of that belief system are even more strongly felt. The title of the collection is reflected in the story 'Julia Cahill's Curse', in which a middle-class observer, come to rural Ireland to encourage the development of industry, is shocked by the depopulated wreck of one of the villages he has to visit. The landscape is just as much a wasteland as T. S. Eliot's London would later be in his famous poem of 1922:

> They were scanty fields, drifting from thin grass into bog, and from bog into thin grass again, and in the distance there was a rim of melancholy mountains, and the peasants I saw along the road seemed a counterpart of the landscape. 'The land has made them,' I said, 'according to its own image and likeness,' and I tried to find the words to define the yearning that I read in their eyes. But I could find no words … Passing [on] I noticed that although the land was certainly better than the land around Culloch, there seemed to be very few people on it; and what was more significant than the untilled fields were the ruins, for they were not the cold ruins of twenty, or thirty, or forty years ago when the people were evicted and their tillage turned to pasture, but the ruins of cabins that had been lately abandoned. Some of the roof trees were still unbroken, and I said that the people must have left voluntarily.
> 'Sure they did. Arn't we all going to America?' (p. 121)[7]

The hand of history lies just as heavily on this land as it does on the smog-filled streets of Staffordshire, but this is a history of neglect, destruction, ignorance and superstition, which Moore identifies throughout the stories with unlettered oral peasant traditions, with the stranglehold of the Catholic Church and with the wilful neglect of the English, who nominally govern and often actually own the land as absentee landlords. In the words of Brendan Kennelly, 'behind Irish puritanism and repression stretches a long dark history of methodical English tyranny and futile

Irish protest that helps to account for the emotional and moral climate of *The Untilled Field*.[8] It is a landscape that permits no hope: the grass is thin, and where there is no grass, it is boggy and unproductive. It is bounded by mountains which narrow the horizon. There are 'no words' to describe its desolation. History, in the form of absentee landlords, has played some part in the scene, but so has the repressive religion which has led Julia Cahill to curse her native village, and so has the unquestioning belief of the people in that curse. The only hope of betterment is in America, the Promised Land – or, more negatively, a space of exile. (As the story 'Homesickness' suggests, America is not a land of milk and honey.) The labour of the peasants here produces nothing; pride, even in handiwork, is a sin; the body is denied its pleasures; and the result is emotional, geographical, spiritual emptiness.

To express this void, Moore experimented with the short-story form far more than Bennett did. His fictions are broadly realistic or even naturalistic in their depictions of the wasted land of Ireland. But they are also stories which eschew traditional plotting. Many have rambling structures; characters disappear and reappear in different tales. The conventional shape of a short story is one which implies progression: a lesson learned, for instance, or a problem solved, or a joke well told, or in genre fictions (detective stories, weird tales, ghost stories, romances) a particular elaboration of plot to a well-defined end (the criminal caught; the uncanny atmosphere evoked and explained; the lovers united – or sundered). Moore, however, sought to represent the stasis and stagnation of an environment where progress, both individual and social, was impossible. Nothing changes here, and therefore no hope is held out for a fictionalised resolution of the problems the collection charts. In several stories, resistance against those conditions is shown to be futile. When, in 'A Playhouse in the Waste', a local priest sets out to build a theatre to provide entertainment and employment for his parishioners, the building collapses following a storm and is never completed: the spirit goes out of the work because one of the girls who was to act in the miracle plays falls pregnant out of wedlock. Her child dies, and the village folk regard the collapse of the theatre as the work of the child's ghost. The narrator, the outsider of 'Julia Cahill's Curse', regards this as peasant superstition and identifies the car driver who tells him the tale as 'the legitimate descendant of the ancient bards' (p. 141). But the driver's anecdote does not bode well for the narrator's plans to bring modern work patterns to the people.

As for Bennett, despite the contrasts between the two writers, part of the problem for Moore and his characters is the problem of language – no words. This is not entirely the contempt for the English language to be found in Stephen Dedalus's statement that his 'soul frets' in the shadow of the English language in James Joyce's *Portrait of the Artist as a Young Man* (1916),[9] though Moore did work for Irish language education and did develop a version of English he called Anglo-Irish in these stories. The real point is that the conventional languages of polite society and of narrow Catholicism do not permit the expression of any but the narrowest of emotions. The people presented in *The Untilled Field* cannot communicate what they feel. Rodney, the sculptor, cannot express his artistic vision; Ned Carmady, the politician, cannot say what he wants to say about the future of Ireland without offending both his audiences and his wife, with whom silence on matters political and religious becomes the norm; beyond the comfortable middle classes, the priest, Father McTurnan, cannot use the Latin language to explain the necessity for repopulating the land – although the Latin is less the problem than the culture of utter conformity and obedience; Biddy M'Hale cannot communicate her vision of her stained-glass window, and the priest cannot even hear her talk of it without irritation; and even Kate Kavanagh, the wild Irish rose, 'had not strength to defy the priest' (p. 31), and although perhaps she finds strength in the end, it is only by leaving the land and choosing exile or freedom in America.

On the whole, this is not a seductive portrait by Moore of his native land. But it does make fascinating reading, in part because of the echoes it produces of later versions of narrowed-down lives which we will encounter in our examination of the modernists in Chapter 8: Joyce (who must surely have been thinking of Moore's story 'In the Clay' when he wrote 'Clay') and D. H. Lawrence (who similarly worked to express, often via symbolic means, the emotions that inarticulate characters could not speak for themselves). Both Bennett and Moore make use of the realist mode, but they do so with a modern sensibility. It would be a weakened history of the short story which did not include them, given that Moore influenced Joyce and that Bennett actually had a very wide readership for his stories.

* * *

In the early-twentieth-century part of this book the chapters focus on the short fictions of the First World War; modernist short fiction; and genre short fiction, taking Agatha Christie (1890–1976) and Daphne du Maurier (1907–89) as key figures. The argument we make is that although there were galvanising moments (the war being one particular example) which shifted the short story on it axis and meant it would never be 'quite the same again', there were also continuities. In juxtaposing the so-called high art short fiction of the modernist mode against some of the more traditional contemporary works, we suggest, first, that the modernist short story is best understood in its period and, second, that the distinction between high cultural and popular forms is not always as secure as it might initially appear. As we shall see in Chapter 9, the commercial fictions of writers such as Agatha Christie – works which get their effects from the repetition of plots and the familiarity they offer to the reader – might not make great claims for their status as 'Art', but they do offer more than a mere backdrop to the experiments of modernist writing.

7
The Short Story and the Great War

The First World War (1914–18) has held a prominent place in the British literary landscape for almost a century. It was, as Angela Smith notes, a 'cataclysmic conflict', very different from previous conflicts. On one day in July 1916, 60,000 British soldiers died, mowed down by the recently invented machine gun. It was also

> [a closer war than people were used to]: the guns of the Western front could be heard across the Channel; Zeppelins carried out bombing raids along the east coast of Britain. Men were conscripted into the combatant or non-combatant service. Women were encouraged to take the places of their men – in the workforce, in industry, on the land. Of the 5,215,162 men who served in the army, 44.4 percent were killed or wounded. Very few families escaped unscathed.[1]

In the war's aftermath, work began on building 'a land fit for heroes' (to quote Prime Minister David Lloyd George's 1919 electioneering slogan) and on commemorating the dead and trying to come to terms with the unprecedented slaughter that had taken place. The first national two-minute silence was held on 11 November 1919. War memorials were erected. The playwright and broadcaster J. B. Priestly (1894–1984) expressed the views of many when he wrote that 'nobody, nothing will shift me from the belief, which I shall take to the grave, that the generation to which I belong, destroyed between 1914 and 1918, was a great generation, marvellous in its promise'.[2] Autobiographies such as Siegfried Sassoon's (1886–1967) *Memoirs of a Fox-hunting Man* (1928), Robert Graves's (1895–1985) *Goodbye to All That* (1929) and Vera Brittain's (1893–1970) *A Testament of Youth* (1933) seemed to offer proof – if proof were needed – of the truth of Priestly's words, emerging alongside First

World War poetry as a means by which the conflict could be understood on an individual level but also mythologised and given a distinctive imagery. Fiction also played its part. By the end of the 1920s a tranche of best-selling novels – among them Ford Madox Ford's quartet *Parade's End* (1924–28), Richard Aldington's (1892–1962) *Death of a Hero* (1929) and Erich Remarque's (1898–1970) *Im Westen nichts Neues* (1929)– had prompted a good deal of discussion about how the war could, and should, be represented.

More than ninety years later, these few novels and autobiographies, plus of course, the period's poems, are still the best-known literary representations of the wartime experience. Yet British writers during and after the war also did powerful and immediate work in the short-story form. As will be seen, Rudyard Kipling's stories accommodate in complex ways his own rather tortured response to the conflict; Richard Aldington's story 'Deserter' (1930) might not rival the impact of his monumental series of novels comprising *Death of a Hero*, but it can be seen as equally thought-provoking, not least for its representation of the ordinary infantryman rather than the officer class. Marguerite Radclyffe-Hall's (Radclyffe Hall, 1880–1943) short stories ('Miss Ogilvy Finds Herself' [1926] and 'Fraulein Schwartz' [1934]) pack a far greater emotional punch than *The Well of Loneliness* (1928), the scandalous novel about lesbianism for which she is best known, and rank among her finest achievements. This chapter examines the kinds of war stories which found favour during the conflict and in the decade following – as well as some of those that did not. It also considers the themes which emerge and the different perspectives adopted.

A good place to start is with a discussion of what was perhaps the most popular First World War story – at least in the early stages of the conflict – 'The Bowmen', written by Arthur Machen (1863–1947), a journalist and writer of supernatural tales. His story, initially published in the *London Evening News* on 29 September 1914, was based on an apocryphal account of the ghosts of medieval soldiers coming to the aid of British troops on the verge of being overpowered by the Germans at the Battle of Mons at the end of August. In Machen's story, a young soldier remembers the motto on a plate in a vegetarian restaurant: *Adsit Anglis Sanctus Georgius* ('May St. George be a present help to the English' [p. 33]).[3] Uttering these words reveals 'a long line of shapes, with a shining about them. They were like men who drew the bows, and with another shout, their cloud of arrows flew singing and tingling through the air towards the German hosts' (p. 35). Machen seems to want to evoke another famous English victory – Henry V's victory at Agincourt, as told by William

Shakespeare – and the bowmen, with their seemingly musical arrows, carry a very definite chivalric appeal. With the help of these ghostly allies the British soldiers defeat an enemy army of 10,000. Afterwards, because the dead German soldiers have no visible wounds, the Germans decide that the British used poisonous gas.

In 1914 the story's journalistic style convinced many readers that Machen was relating real events. Moreover, there were plenty of people who claimed to be able to corroborate them. 'The Angels of Mons', the title under which the tale started to be known, was the talk of the day: vicars cited it in sermons, and when the story was issued in book form 3,000 copies were snapped up on the first day. Sales reached 100,000 within the year. The story's success surprised Machen, and his account of its composition downplays its artistry. Machen claimed that he had read an account of the battle in a newspaper and then had thought up the story while listening to a sermon during a church service, having also been reminded of Rudyard Kipling's 'The Lost Legion' (1893), in which a British unit in Afghanistan is helped by the ghosts of dead soldiers. As Machen saw it, his own story 'failed in the art of letters' but 'succeeded, unwittingly, in the art of deceit' (p. 297). The fact that the 'deceit' was so successful says a good deal about the reading public's need for solace and the ability of the written word to provide it. But as Adrian Eckersley notes, it also reveals 'the tensions under which the credulous and incredulous confronted one another in this era of materialism, when scientists were often appalled at the sheer inhuman mechanism of the cosmos they envisioned and religion became a counterweight and comfort against the inhumanity of their vision'.[4] Something of this is also apparent in another of Machen's stories, 'The Soldier's Rest' (1915), in which a soldier wakes up in a lavish hospital and is confused by the apparel of those who visit his bedside to praise him. Some talk to him in unfamiliar English; others, in foreign languages. The reader soon realises – as the soldier does not – that he is in the mythical Valhalla, resting place of the Norse warriors of old.

Both 'The Bowmen' and 'The Soldier's Rest' sound the theme of a whole raft of First World War stories, particularly those written in the first year of the conflict. The British government's War Propaganda Bureau (est. 1914) included J. M. Barrie, Rudyard Kipling, Arnold Bennett, John Buchan, H. G. Wells and Arthur Conan Doyle, all of whom were too old to fight but thought it their duty to write patriotically – whatever their private misgivings about the conflict or the way it was being run. One batch of war stories thus celebrated men participating in heroic activities: rescuing wounded comrades, catching spies, defending a stretch of no-man's land, sacrificing themselves for the national cause. Using the thrilling and reassuringly familiar conventions of imperial romances, it was easy for authors to fall back on old stereotypes about bullying foreigners versus upright, cricket-loving Englishmen, 'brothers in arms', God-chosen, fighting for democracy. In 'The Land of Topsy Turvey' (1916) by 'Sapper' (Herman Cyril McNeile, 1888–1937) a colonel addresses his regiment, telling his men: ' "Stick it, my lads ... Stick it, for the credit of the regiment, for the glory of our name ... Each one of us counts, men" – his voice sank a little – "each one of us has to play the game" ' (p. 264).[5] Despite the tremor in the colonel's voice – presumably he is overcome with emotion – there is no confusion about what is expected, and those who don't 'play the game' can look forward to being court-martialled and executed for desertion. The same kind of discourse ensured also that the Germans were invariably presented as 'swine' who didn't play the game or fight by the 'rules' of warfare. The propaganda was often crude and repetitive in its imagery, its purpose bloodthirsty. Only occasionally do cracks appear. In another story in this collection, 'The Motor-Gun', there is a graphic description of French infantrymen felled by a gas attack: 'a death of hideous torture, with the frothing bubbles gurgling in their throats and the foul liquid welling up in their lungs' (p. 38). The stories are given a powerful unifying tone by the recurrence of images of material and moral destruction and the sense that civilised values are on the verge of being lost altogether.

A sense that Britain's people need to be reminded what is at stake is also behind Arthur Conan Doyle's 'Danger!', which appeared in July 1914, at a moment when European diplomacy was in crisis. Published in *The Strand* magazine – the site of Sherlock Holmes's greatest detective triumphs – the story is intended to be disconcerting and unnerving, as it touches on a possibility too awful to contemplate: the invasion of Britain. The events leading to this too-awful-to-contemplate scenario are part of the log-book of a naval officer of an unnamed European foreign power who relates how he was tasked with 'bring[ing] proud England to her knees' (p. 4).[6] The story opens with his comment 'It is an amazing thing that the English, who have the reputation of being a practical nation, never saw the danger to which they were exposed' (p. 3). Britain finds herself under siege from new (unseen) weapons: submarines. The submarines attack merchant ships, food shortages follow, the population riots, the government is impotent, and England sues for peace, thankful that her opponent was not a bigger country. 'Of course,' writes the narrator, 'England will not be caught napping in such a fashion again! Her foolish blindness is partly explained by her delusion that her enemy would not torpedo merchant vessels. Common sense should have told her that her enemy will play the game that suits them best' (p. 19). The story finishes with what is supposedly a leading article from *The Times* lamenting 'this miserable business' and advocating the building of a railway line underneath the English Channel (p. 19). In the story's original publication format – that is to say, in the pages of *The Strand* – this blurring of discourses continued when the magazine drafted in a committee of 'experts', including naval commanders and engineers, to give their verdict on the plausibility of Conan Doyle's story. Could such events really happen? Much to Conan Doyle's annoyance, most of the admirals thought it 'fantastic', rather than 'realistic', 'more like one of Jules Verne's' stories'. They reassured readers that the likelihood of a 'civilised' nation behaving in such a sneaky, underhand way was slim, although they acknowledged that, yes, Britain was heavily dependent on the import of foodstuffs from her colonies.[7] Doyle thought he knew better; he later re-emphasised his point by remixing the familiar generic ingredients which had worked so well in the 1890s to bring Sherlock Holmes out of retirement for 'His Last Bow' (1917). Instead of Professor Moriarty, Conan Doyle pitted the seemingly ageless detective against the forces of German espionage and had him serve as a double agent. The opening imagery is striking: 'God's curse hung heavily over a degenerate world... The sun had long set, but one blood-red gash, like an open wound, lay low in the open west' (p. 155).[8] The Germans are confident of victory: 'They are not very hard to deceive, these Englanders,' laughs their chief spy, Von Bork (p. 156). Conan Doyle takes pains to present Britain as the underdog in every particular: Watson's 'little car' (an American Ford), for example, is up against a German Benz. However, at the end of the story, by which time the German spymaster has been foiled, Holmes does hint that England will pull through: 'You', he tells stolid Dr Watson, 'are the one fixed point in a changing age. There's an east wind coming all the same; some such wind as never blew in England yet. It will be cold and bitter, Watson, and a good many of us may wither before its blast. But it's God's own wind, nonetheless, and a cleaner, better, stronger land will lie in the sunshine when the storm has cleared. Start her up, Watson, for it's time we were on our way' (p. 172). Holmes's prediction of a redemptive re-establishment of English homes – the result of communal solidarity and the British capacity for bravery – naturally met with an appreciative audience.

Writing from the front line: Sapper and Richard Aldington

If one strain of the First World War short story has its roots in propaganda, adventure romance and, occasionally, fantasy, another accommodates the growing post-1915 need to talk about the conflict's darker effects. Not surprisingly, many of these stories tended to be written by men who had seen active service at the Front or as naval officers or airmen. The sex of these authors is significant here because it is a reflection of a powerful school of thought which held that only those who had experienced the horrors and mutilations of the trenches were qualified to write about them. Siegfried Sassoon's comment 'I had no tolerance for those who fought their country's battles from armchairs'[9] is generally seen as being directed against the infamous Jessie Pope, whose patriotic poems taunted young men with cowardice if they failed to enlist, but it also reflects a wider 'us versus them' mentality, with 'us' being those who had seen action – and thus knew what they were talking about – and 'them' being the ones who had stayed safely at home (women and conscientious objectors). Something of this mind-set is apparent in Sapper's 'Introduction' to his collection *Men, Women and Guns* (1916). Sapper (or rather his narrator), on leave from the front line, describes how he once attempted to put into words what it felt like to be shelled, only for his aunt to respond with a trite anecdote about a drunken deckchair attendant. Her inability to understand, together with her complete lack of imagination or even genuine interest, prompts the narrator to conclude that if women cannot understand the 'epitome' of the war, how can they begin to appreciate the horror of any of it (p. 15)?

Sapper is an interesting figure: widely read, with mass appeal, but largely forgotten today. After the war he was best known for his stories about the former army officer turned secret agent Bulldog Drummond. These stories were hugely popular during the 1920s and 1930s, in part because of the B-movie adaptations which were made of them. But, as we have seen, Sapper's work also included tales of the Western Front, notably about the stalemate which set in at the end of 1914, with the armies facing each other across 365 miles of trenches stretching from the Belgian coast to the French–Swiss border. He was astonishingly prolific: more than forty stories are collected in *The Lieutenant and Others* (1915), *Sergeant Michael Cassidy R.E.* (1915), *Men, Women and Guns* and *No Man's Land* (1917). The first two collections reached combined sales of 200,000 in their first twelve months of publication.[10]

It is not difficult to work out Sapper's appeal. His credentials for writing about life at the Front were hard to challenge, as he served with the

Royal Engineers. (A 'sapper' was a nickname for members of the engineering regiment, whose duties included tunnelling under enemy lines, and the pen name was given to McNeile by the newspaper magnate Lord Northcliffe when the stories began to appear in the *Daily Mail*.) The tone of his stories tends to be matter-of-fact, without much attempt to explore the feelings or moral dilemmas of his protagonists in any great psychological depth. Jack Adrian has written of their 'relentless facetiousness [which] makes the experiences he is describing less and less believable, at least to a modern reader'.[11] The stories – or episodes – are without much attempt to heighten their literary impact by subtle figurative or symbolic language, but many are notable for their sudden twist – or 'snap' – at the end. There is a strong sense of immediacy, and Sapper includes a good deal of army slang, as if he were trying to educate his audience in a new kind of literacy. Rather in the manner of 'boy's own' heroes, the characters do rather than think. The stories tend to be narrated in the first person by a series of identikit officer narrators, urbane and civilised men who carry a breezy sense that ingrained pluck will see the British forces victorious against a barbaric enemy 'whose standards are based on bombing or crucifying their prisoners and eating their own dead; on sinking unarmed liners and murdering an odd woman or two to fill in time... of crucifying an emaciated cat and stuffing a cigar in its mouth' (p. 1051).[12]

Sapper's *Men, Women and Guns* is a useful source for showing how some of the most resonant images of the conflict were created and perpetuated in fiction. The fiendishness of Germans is apparent in 'Retribution', in which the enemy sink *The Luciana*, a liner carrying women and children, and then shell the survivors in lifeboats before the tables are turned and they are shelled themselves:

> Like rats from a sinking ship the Germans were pouring up and diving into the water, and with snarling faces the Englishmen waited for them, waited for them with the dying proofs of their vileness still lying on the deck as one by one they came on board. Suddenly with a sucking noise the submarine foundered, and over the seething, troubled waters where she had been a sheet of blackish oil slowly spread.
>
> But Jerry spared no glance for the sinking boat – he did not so much look at the German sailors huddled fearfully together. (p. 182)

Sapper's representation of the Germans as 'gross and contemptible', full of swaggering bluster, made his stories popular, as, of course, did the affirmative and agreeable ways in which British soldiers are presented. In this sense his stories embody very neatly Paul Johnson's comments on the ways in which First World War propagandists 'were able to force-feed their ... audiences, nourishing their minds with politicised and militarised teachings that would help them grow into strong, loyal members of their respective states'.[13]

Similarly hostile is Sapper's representation of women, whose disloyalty is to the fore in stories such as 'The Motor-Gun', in which (in a moment of sheer coincidence) a soldier kills the German fiancé of the woman he himself wants to marry. In 'Henry James', a mother marries 'a sausage dog' (i.e. a German), her unpatriotic action capturing Sapper's sense of the war as an essentially male experience and as something with which women have only limited empathy. Elsewhere, there is the loving but naive wife in 'The Death Grip' who is nearly strangled by her sleepwalking husband, mirroring his killing of a Prussian officer in the trenches; in a more tragic vein, in 'The Fatal Second' Jerry Dixon, in a striking example of what he considers patriotic duty, shoots his fiancée's young brother 'through the heart from behind at point-blank range as I had trained myself to do' because the brother apparently showed glimpses that he might waver as his section launched their offensive. 'I knew fear had come,' he explains (p. 120). Jerry – whose very name creates a sense of ambiguity about whose side he is on – cannot bring himself to tell his fiancée any of this (the implication being that as a woman she is not strong enough to bear the details). Leaving the family to believe their son died a glorious death, he returns to the Front to be killed. This story, whose opening scene is set at Henley Regatta, is important social testimony; it is a celebration of upper-class English values and the institutions which support them told to us by a seemingly reliable narrator, who nonetheless provides an uncomfortable insight into the rigid codes of his class – which are assumed also to be those of upright Englishmen generally – and invites readers to question how war threatens the civilised behaviour it is pledged to defend.

More obviously, Sapper's stories contrive to tell – as Sapper himself put it – how 'self is sunk for the good of the cause – for the good of the community'. Sapper saw this as the basis of British militarism; King and empire and the status quo were unquestionably good things to be fighting for. Like Rudyard Kipling, Sapper viewed army training as a useful way of educating men to be men, teaching them lessons about 'playing for the side and unselfishness' and thus guiding them to maturity.[14] Yet embedded within the descriptions of army units and weaponry is an awareness of the pressures of the war on the individual and of the powerlessness of the combatants to control or protest. The focus is on survival and death, the relationships of men (and occasionally men and women) enacted in settings of ugliness and chaos, and 'the dirty details which go into winning or losing' (p. 1048).

These 'dirty details' are also much to the fore in the stories of Richard Aldington, whose work is part of a more sharply rebellious agenda. Nowadays, Aldington's literary reputation rests mainly on his novel *Death of a Hero*, but his ironically titled collection *Roads to Glory* (1930) also shocked some readers when it was first published. 'The roads of which his [Aldington's] title speaks are for the mind counterparts of the slimed and shell-holed plank roads nearing a battlefield,' announced *The Times*; 'the "glory" is an abomination of desolation in one form or another.' While the reviewer saw the stories as 'statements of the worst side' of the conflict, he admitted Aldington's strong sense of place, 'to which those who saw service will readily grant probability'. Moreover, some allowance might be made because the stories were, the reviewer believed, evidently the work of a damaged personality, 'a sympathetic spirit profoundly injured by events'. For those ignorant about the war, Aldington's 'hard, remorseless style and accumulation of sinister endings will arouse them'.[15]

Although there are some parallels with Sapper's stories – notably an appreciation of fallen comrades – Aldington's work is without the cultural certainties of the more mainstream writer, and his treatment of the conflict is more ambiguous. This shift is, of course, in part a matter of dates. The perception of the war changed, and the end of the 1920s saw a flood of books offering reflective, revisionist assessments. But as *The Times* noted (above), the highly wrought intensity of Aldington's stories was seen to be part and parcel of Aldington's own personality: passionate, quarrelsome and scornful of what he saw as British cant and hypocrisy. Moreover, by the time the Armistice was signed in November 1918, Aldington had been gassed and had also suffered from shell shock. He recorded that his 'nervous malady and insomnia increased rather than diminished' during the weeks which followed his return to civilian life. 'Every night as I read or lay sleepless I heard the raucous shouts and whoops of drunken revellers, a strange disorderliness in the decorous West End. I am not enemy to rejoicings, but this debauchery over two million graves seemed to me indecent. I saw nothing to rejoice about, having too many recollections of endless desolation.'[16] In *Roads to Glory* Aldington attempted to write out – albeit selectively – these horrors. Rather than comforting his readers, Aldington presented them with raw, nightmarish images in which men are robbed of human dignity: surrounded by rats and rotting cadavers they are left to die. Chaos reigns. Characters struggle to achieve any sense of order and become mere cogs in a vast inhuman system. Notable is the image of the unidentified soldier in 'Killed in Action', his nationality unclear, 'lying on his back with a bullet through his brain...feverishly and monotonously pawing with his right leg, and digging up the chalky soil' (p. 124).[17]

One way of understanding Aldington's stories is to consider how they map several of the concepts in another text of the period: Sigmund Freud's essay 'Mourning and Melancholia' (1917), which defines mourning as the painful but healthy process of severing the mourner from the deceased. As Freud sees it, effective mourning necessitates working through grief and thus freeing the ego so that it can attach itself to a new living person or ideal. When mourning is unsuccessful, a covert relationship to the deceased is retained; the mourner identifies with the lost object, with the result that 'object loss' is transformed into 'ego loss' and the mourner succumbs to melancholia, a state of grief, self-criticism and self-blame.[18] There is no evidence that Aldington studied Freud, but for many critics melancholia is one quality which defines writing about the First World War, and Aldington's writing in particular seems to embody this pattern. Writing was a form of exorcism, but Aldington also wanted to build what R. H. Mottram called a real cenotaph, a true war memorial – 'a record, at which gazing, our children may be able to imagine a way of settling disputes more intelligent'.[19]

This impetus to commemorate is apparent in the story 'Meditation on a German Grave'. Ronald Cumberland, a former army captain, becomes a successful publisher after the war but suffers a breakdown. He goes to a Mediterranean island to recover, but once there he starts remembering his visit to a German cemetery before the 1918 Armistice. He puts his arm around a German cross and speaks to the buried soldier about their mutual sacrifices: both have lost their lives – one physically, the other spiritually. What was it all for? Cumberland wishes he was lying beside his German 'brother', telling him:

> the years will pass...The young will not know; they'll be exploited by the selfish, rather stupid old men and greedy tradesmen and the venal journalists and the hysterical women. They'll be 'heroes' like you and me...they'll murder each other with yet more frightful weapons, for the honour of a country, the love of a whore motherland. They'll die all right. Sweet and decorous that they should die, a sacrifice to human stupidity and malevolence. (p. 32)

Aldington has his character exhibit a different kind of sensibility from that of Rupert Brooke (1887–1915), whose poem 'The Soldier' (1914) appears to be referenced here. Putting the word 'heroes' in inverted commas leaves the reader in no doubt of the irony of the term and questions its value as a title worth having in the modern world. At the same time, Aldington's scorn for the war's bogeymen – its profiteers, the elderly politicians and the women handing out white feathers – is made plain.

Other stories in *Roads to Glory* engage in what seems to be a process of defamiliarisation, their aim being to offer alternative representations of the war and to get the reader to discard naive notions of what winning the war involved. 'You ask about [the story] "Sacrifice Post",' Aldington wrote to a fan in 1958: 'Your Great War of 1941–45 was much more open than ours of 1914–18. It was siege warfare. In the spring of 1918, the British Army was carrying the burden of the western Front. The French had mutinied, and the Americans had (naturally) not arrived in any numbers...The British had to have outposts (nicknamed "sacrifice posts") to give warning of any surprise attack.'[20] The idea that the story is based on episodes from Aldington's own experience is strengthened by the similarities between the hero, Lieutenant Davidson, and Aldington himself. At the beginning of the story Davidson is sent to a school for training as a signal officer. Swept up in the beauty of the English countryside, he is overcome by a feeling of love for all humankind. This epiphany allows him to see through the propaganda spouted by his elders, but such is his education and upbringing that he finds it hard to articulate what he thinks: 'The trouble was that it was almost impossible for an ordinary educated Public School man to think coherently, let alone express his feelings...if only he could make others feel that vision, make them understand how they were duped into hatred under the guise of loyalty and duty' (p. 177). The word 'duty' is peppered throughout the stories, but whereas in Sapper's stories it carries all kinds of patriotic connotations, in those of Aldington it is an empty and sometimes sinister term. Typically, Davidson's moment of realisation fails to go anywhere. His private thoughts – which he has carelessly written down in a notebook – are discovered and he is sent back to the front line and (it is implied) eventual death.

Aldington's wish to reshape his readers' sense of the war is apparent, too, in 'Victory', which is set on the Mons road, where Aldington's division had halted on 11 November 1917. No glory was involved; rather, readers are told that the 'only victory that had resulted was in fact the victory of death over life, of stupidity over intelligence, of hatred over humanity' (p. 45), and Aldington provides some lacerating insights into military tactics. 'At All Costs' is similarly scathing; it details the dutiful acceptance of inevitable death by a group of officers who must hold their position 'at all costs' in the face of a German attack. The phrase and its implications reverberate in the mind of the central character, Captain Hanley: 'They were done for, napoo. No après la guerre for *them* – bon soir, toodle-oo, good-byeeee. The silly words repeated and repeated in his brain until he hated them' (p. 65). Ordered to do their duty, the members of the unit effectively receive a death sentence from their own side. They have to signal their artillery battalion to shorten its barrage as soon as the Germans enter their trench. Writing from Hanley's perspective, Aldington conveys the battle as a series of flickering cinematic images. Hanley's final felt emotion is loneliness as the unit is whittled down to just two men before they also are obliterated.

Both 'Victory' and 'At All Costs' encourage the idea that First World War military commanders were inept and out of touch. They also testify to the immense bitterness felt by Aldington at the treatment received by serving soldiers – 'integrity … perverted … comradeship betrayed', as Aldington had written in the preface to *Death of a Hero*. This sense of betrayal and abandonment is a common theme in the collection, as is the idea that the soldier's experience is one of fighting more than one enemy. 'Love for Love', 'Booby Trap' and 'The Lads of the Village' all feature sensitive characters destroyed not just by their experiences of war but by the indifference of civilians at home. In 'Deserter', Harry Werner, a friendless orphan, enlists in the army. During one period of leave he has an affair with a woman he picks up in a pub; she encourages him not to return to his unit but subsequently deserts him as soon as his money runs out. When Werner is handed over to the authorities, his fate is chillingly but succinctly revealed: shot in a field 'trembling and whimpering against the side of the barn', 'in the raw, drizzly dawn' (p. 88). The young officer in charge of organising the execution is almost sick. The story is told matter-of-factly, but the reader gets a feeling for Harry's confused sensations and slow thought processes. In some respects the story owes something to the pessimistic worldview of the naturalist writer George Gissing, whose characters struggle to survive in a brutal, uncaring environment. Aldington presents Harry as an innocent, destroyed by forces he cannot control. In refusing to go back to the Front, Harry seems to think he has found a kind of freedom, but of course he never has been free and has never had a choice. The convention of the patriotic young man off to help his country is overturned. Harry is technically guilty but never really grasps either what is happening to him or how he is being taken advantage of by all and sundry. Aldington does not offer a simplistic account of right versus wrong, and the 'Deserter' of the title can clearly refer to more than one person. Aldington's stories are not, like Sapper's, 'of the moment'; they are a response to something perceived to be overwhelming, the influence of which was felt long after it had finished.

War lover: Rudyard Kipling

Rudyard Kipling's letters testify to his virulent hatred of Germans, and indeed of anyone – conscientious objectors, pacifists, labour leaders – seen to be questioning the validity of the conflict. For Kipling the war was 'a matter which touches on the whole foundation and future of civilised life.'[21] His first war poem was a call to arms, 'For All We Have and Are', published in *The Times* and other newspapers on 1 September 1914: 'Stand up and take the war. | The Hun is at the gate,' Kipling wrote. Aged forty-nine, Kipling 'stood up'. Too old to enlist himself, he wangled his seventeen-year-old son, John, a commission in the Irish guards, cheering him off to France in August 1915. Denied active service, Kipling set off on a government recruiting drive, making speeches and advocating a 'brotherhood of service and sacrifice' by means of which victory would which be achieved.[22]

Almost everything Kipling wrote was connected with the war effort. 'I have given my son to the army: I am giving my time and substance to the work that lies before us,' he announced in the autumn of 1914.[23] Articles, government pamphlets and poems poured from his pen. Kipling visited the Front as correspondent for the *Daily Telegraph*, a trip which led to his book *France at War: On the Frontier of Civilisation* (1915). This was followed by *Sea Warfare* (1916), at the behest of the Ministry of Information. Kipling was thus seen by those in charge as a safe pair of hands into which to entrust the writing of the war for the home front. It seemed an added advantage that he believed wholeheartedly the reports of German brutalities in France and Belgium, including rumours that the advancing Germans had cut off the right hands of Belgian schoolboys to stop them joining the army. As Jad Adams notes, these 'atrocity stories were used to stimulate the British population into war fever'.[24] They also formed the inspiration for Kipling's first story of the war, 'Swept and Garnished', which was published in *Nash's Magazine* in January 1915. Frau Ebermann, a middle-aged German ill with a fever, is visited in her Berlin flat by the ghosts of five Belgian children killed in the invasion of their country. They tell her 'there isn't anything left' (p. 335) in their own county, which has been 'wiped out, stamped flat' (p. 336). There are thousands in their situation, and they have come to Berlin to wait for their parents to collect them. Her flat, along with the Kaiser's palace, has become a meeting point for dead children – presumably after the defeat of Germany – and so Berlin is occupied by allies. One of the girls pulls at the sleeve of one of the boys, at which point 'Frau Ebermann looked and saw' (p. 338).[25]

Most English readers would have known what she saw. The boy's severed hand reinforces the anti-German feeling stoked up by the press: 'There is no crime, no cruelty, no abomination that the mind of man can conceive which the German has not perpetrated, is not perpetrating, and will not perpetrate if he is allowed to go on,' announced the *Southport Guardian* in 1915.[26] Clearly the propagandist element of these stories was their immediate point, and Kipling later said of his wartime stories, 'I don't know what they are worth, I only know they ain't literature.'[27]

Two questions have tended to preoccupy critical accounts of a more complex story, 'Mary Postgate', first published in *Nash's Magazine* in 1915, soon after the start of German air-raids on English towns, and a month after John Kipling was posted to France. Both questions concern the events of the story. What has happened to Edna Gerritt, the injured young girl whom Mary and Nurse Eden find and watch die when the Royal Oak collapses? How do we explain, in a way that gives the story a coherent meaning, the presence of the 'German' airman at the end of the story and the central character's reaction to him? The plot is as follows. Miss Mary Postgate is a put-upon lady's companion, middle-aged and drab. She is devoted to her employer's nephew, Wynn, who joins the flying corps when war breaks out but is killed in a plane crash. Mary, who (misguidedly) views herself as Wynn's surrogate mother, is full of anger towards the German enemy. While buying paraffin to burn Wynn's clothes she witnesses the violent death of a child, Edna Gerritt, outside the Royal Oak pub. Back in the garden, with the fire ablaze, she comes across a German pilot seriously hurt by his fall through the trees. She tends the fire and studiously ignores his dying cries for help. Then, flushed and excited, she goes indoors to have tea.

Questions surround this story because, although it appears to be a recognisable piece of propaganda about Englishwomen doing 'their bit' in wartime, portions of it remain unclear. In part, this has to do with the death of the young girl Edna Gerritt (whose very name seems like a bad joke on Kipling's part). She is definitely dead – Nurse Eden's uniform is 'turned scarlet' by her blood – but exactly how she has died is not as clear as first appears. This is a point made by Norman Page in his article 'What

Happens in "Mary Postgate"?'[28] Page argues that Kipling deliberately raises doubts about Mary's reliability as a witness as she goes into the village ('it *seemed* to her that she could almost hear the beat of his propellers overhead but there was nothing to see' [p. 349, our italics]),[29] the idea being that Mary, in a state of (shell) shock following Wynn's death, is imagining scenarios which aren't true. This uncertainty is intensified in the conversation between Mary and the local medic, Dr Hennis, after Edna's death:

> Before she reached the house Dr. Hennis, who was also a special constable, overtook her in his car.
>
> 'Oh, Miss Postgate,' he said, 'I wanted to tell you that that accident at the "Royal Oak" was due to Gerritt's stable tumbling down. It's been dangerous for a long time. It ought to have been condemned.'
>
> 'I thought I heard an explosion too,' said Mary.
>
> 'You might have been misled by the beams snapping. I've been looking at 'em. They were dry-rotted through and through. Of course, as they broke, they would make a noise just like a gun.'
>
> 'Yes?' said Mary politely.
>
> 'Poor little Edna was playing underneath it,' he went on, still holding her with his eyes, 'and that and the tiles cut her to pieces, you see?'
>
> 'I saw it,' said Mary, shaking her head. 'I heard it too.'
>
> 'Well, we cannot be sure.' Dr. Hennis changed his tone completely. 'I know both you and Nurse Eden (I've been speaking to her) are perfectly trustworthy, and I can rely on you not to say anything – yet at least. It is no good to stir up people unless –' 'Oh, I never do – anyhow,' said Mary, and Dr. Hennis went on to the county town (p. 351).

According to the doctor there has been no air-raid, but Mary is convinced that there has. Who is correct? Is Mary being threatened into silence here? Is the doctor's tone menacing? Or does Dr Hennis recognise Mary as a mentally ill woman prone to fancies and in need of treatment?

Mary's encounter with the airman is also full of ambiguity. Mary behaves callously towards the airman, displaying an attitude which, it has been suggested, was Kipling's own; that is to say, it reflects his own fantasies about killing a German. The German airman falls into an Edenic garden where he pleads for mercy with an Englishwoman, but instead of giving way the virgin spinster gives him death. This Englishwoman is inspired by war and does her duty.

Other critics have suggested that it is rather more plausible to see the story as a psychological study of what the horrors of war do to seemingly civilised people. Mary's hatred and desire for revenge are governed by hatred of the havoc wrought by air-raids, though she overlooks the fact that Wynn died while in training to carry out similar raids. Again, the story contains various hints which invite the reader to question Mary's reliability. Mary mourns Wynn but forgets his cruel mockery of her. She is convinced that a bomb has fallen and killed the child, Edna, but no one else thinks this is the case. It is in part this belief that prompts her to let the young German pilot die, despite the fact that he speaks French and might not be German at all. It is also clear that having him at her mercy gives the resentful, frustrated spinster a sense of release after years of being patronised and put upon. The pleasure that Mary takes in a man's dying agony might even carry sadistic sexual overtones; there are hints that the act leaves Mary sexually excited, and it certainly gives her a new-found sense of power. According to this reading, Kipling does not support his protagonist's actions but merely records her response to the situation, leaving his readers to make up their own minds.

John Kipling was reported missing after the Battle of Loos (25–28 September 1915), which was one of a number of attempts to break the stalemate at the Front. His father's grief was acute. His hatred for the enemy intensified, and he threw himself into the war effort, reacting with satisfaction to the decision to intern British-based Germans. He described approvingly how 'a party of Huns – dog and three dry bitches [an old man and three elderly women]' had been hounded of out their coastal home because of a suspicion that they signalled to the enemy.[30] Meanwhile, those wanting to sue for peace Kipling regarded as 'dirt'.[31]

In 1917, Kipling became a member of the Imperial War Graves Commission, helping with the administration of the massive cemeteries required to hold the dead. This job clearly formed part of a need to remember his own son, whose body had proved difficult to trace, but it was also part of a growing interest in the causalities of war – those damaged physically but also mentally. This interest is apparent in *Debits and Credits* (1926), a collection which, as Donald Gray notes, focuses on 'the psychic damage of war and how friends or small communities protect or cure its victims'.[32] In 'The Janeites' (1924), the members of a Masonic lodge work together to help those who are unable to leave the war behind; the story records the sense of kinship created among men as a result of a shared passion for the works of Jane Austen, the embodiment of a particularly safe version of Englishness. 'A Madonna of the Trenches' (1924) focuses on the aftermath of the war, and in particular on a man whose mind has been shattered not only by what he has encountered but also by the experiences of his family life.

The most famous of these post-war stories is 'The Gardener', written after Kipling's trip to the war cemetery at Bois-Guillaume, near Rouen, in March 1925. Helen Turrell is a woman whom '[e]very one in the village knew', who 'did her duty by all her world', not least in the way she has given a home to her nephew, the son of her 'black sheep' brother (p. 277).[33] She raises Michael with great devotion and allows him to call her 'Mummy' at bedtime. In 1914, instead of going up to Oxford, Michael enlists in the army. He is soon listed as missing: 'a shell-splinter dropping out of a wet dawn killed him at once. The next shell uprooted and laid down over the body what had been the foundation of a barn wall, so neatly that none but an expert would have guessed that anything unpleasant had happened' (p. 281). This concept of covering things up is important in the story. Keeping a stiff upper lip, Helen adopts the role expected of her – 'manufactured into bereaved next of kin', like the shells she has seen made in a munitions factory (p. 282) – and she becomes accustomed to the routine of the mourner, recognising 'the ease with which she could slip Michael's name into talk and incline her head to the proper angle, at the proper murmur of sympathy' (p. 282). After the Armistice, the celebrations of which 'broke over her and pass unheeded' (p. 282), Michael's body is discovered and Helen decides to visit his grave in Belgium. On her journey Helen meets other bereaved women making similar pilgrimages, 'now strong in the certainty that there was an altar upon earth where they might lay their love' (p. 282). One woman from Lancashire is in search of her son, also illegitimate. She is distraught because she cannot locate his grave. The other woman, Mrs Scarsworth, claims to be visiting the cemetery to take photographs for those who cannot make the trip themselves. She appears to be something of a busybody and voyeur: 'when I've got enough commissions for one area to make it worthwhile, I pop over and execute them. It *does* comfort people' (p. 284). But she later confides that she has her own personal reasons for going: there is '*one*, d'you see, and – and he was more to me than anything else in the world'. Using her commissions as a smokescreen, Scarsworth visits her lover's grave: 'He was everything to me that he oughtn't to have been – the one real thing – the only thing that ever happened to me in all my life, and I've had to pretend he wasn't. I've had to watch every word I said, and think out what lie I'd tell next, for years and years!' Helen responds by reaching out to Mrs Scarsworth; the latter's reaction ('Is *that* how you take it?') suggests a bond between the two women (p. 286).

The following day Helen visits the cemetery, a 'merciless sea of black crosses'. She meets a man who 'look[s] at her with infinite compassion'. He asks her whom she is searching for. Helen tells him: 'Lieutenant Michael Turrell – my nephew.' The man answers by saying, 'I will show you where your son lies' (p. 287). Leaving the cemetery, she again sees the man. By this point most readers will have suspected from the clues given in the story that Michael is infact Helen's son. What remains unanswered is how the man knows Michael's identity. The story's final words are a biblical allusion to John 20:15, where Mary Magdalene, visiting the tomb of Jesus, turns to a man who asks her why she is weeping; she answers him 'supposing him to be the gardener' (p. 287). Kipling's use of the allusion has prompted considerable discussion. Does the oblique reference to Mary Magdalene point to Helen's own (illicit) past as a 'fallen' woman? Is Kipling condemning the lies and subterfuge that society uses to hide unpalatable truths? Is the man in the cemetery actually Jesus Christ? William Dillingham has argued that the story is 'a study of the excruciating and prolonged pain of bereavement'[34] in which religion provides no comfort. The idea that the Allies – and Britain's young men in particular – had offered themselves as a pointless sacrifice for the whole of humankind became an obsession for Kipling after his son's death, and he was increasingly prepared to highlight the personal costs involved. He wrote of the 'defrauded young', but by whom the young had been defrauded proved difficult to answer. The government? The generals? Imperialist poets? War-mongering short-story writers?[35]

Outsiders and misfits: Radclyffe Hall

If, as is often claimed, the short story deals with those on the margins, then Marguerite Radclyffe-Hall can claim to be the exemplary short-story writer. A lesbian who described herself as a 'congenital invert', who dressed in severe 'mannish' fashion and adopted the name John, Hall focused much of her writing on outsiders. In her own day she was most famous for her novel *The Well of Loneliness*, which became the centre of a highly publicised court case when it was banned on the grounds of indecency. The case did little to harm Hall's sales or fame. By 1928 she was reckoned 'the most easily recognised artistic celebrity in London' by one reporter.[36] Rebecca West described her as having 'a kind of austere, manly handsomeness which makes one think of a very beautifully made sporting rifle or golf club'.[37] Despite the comparison with weaponry, Hall's approach was rarely violent or polemical. She did not advocate feminism, as it is understood today; indeed, she thought that women's proper sphere was the home. Rather, as Claudia Stillman Franks has noted, her attention tends to be on 'the influence of irrational or insufficiently understood forces upon the individual, with obsessions and compulsions which preclude the characters' achieving ordinary forms of human fulfilment'.[38]

Hall's vision is also a religious one and, as Michael Baker notes, her stories 'demonstrate her preoccupation with a search for spiritual self-knowledge through suffering and denial' and deal with moments of crisis or turning points in this search.[39] Two statements Hall made help highlight other aspects her of writing. Fascinated by the 'new psychology', she wrote: 'My concern is always with the psychology of my characters as it would be affected by their circumstances and surroundings.'[40] And as someone who saw herself as a man trapped in a woman's body, she wrote: '[T]he loneliest place is the no-man's land of sex.'[41] Her mode is that of the realist, but she admired May Sinclair (1863–1946) and the stream of consciousness associated with Sinclair and other modernist writers such as Katherine Mansfield and Virginia Woolf.

Hall's reputation as a short-story writer rests on just one volume: *Miss Ogilvy Finds Herself* (1934). In the preface she wrote that the collection was in remembrance of 'the noble and selfless work done by hundreds of sexually inverted women during the Great War: 1914–1918' (p. 6).[42] This idea is exemplified in the much-admired title story, which describes the break-up of Miss Wilhelmina Ogilvy's ambulance unit at the end of the war. As she travels back to England, Miss Ogilvy remembers 'all that had gone to the marring of her from the days of her earliest childhood'. Gauche, lacking in confidence and shy, with a flat bosom and thick legs, Miss Ogilvy has been made painfully aware – as the young Radclyffe Hall also was – that she does not fit easily into the models of femininity expected of young women, and she views her psychological and biological make-up as 'the bad joke that Nature seemed to have played her' (p. 12). She prefers male sports to dancing. Her relationship to men is 'unusual', and she dislikes the thought of marriage. When her father dies, Miss Ogilvy unofficially assumes the role of head of the family, becoming – like many women in wartime – less subservient and more powerful. She finds a degree of contentment until the outbreak of the war. Her first reaction to news of war is ' "My God! If only I were a man!" ... Something in her was feeling deeply defrauded' (p. 10). Her sisters knit socks, but Miss Ogilvy wants to go to the front line and 'be actually under fire'. She achieves this by enlisting in a 'glorious' ambulance unit in France. These years working on the front line turn out to be happy ones, and Miss Ogilvy, who proves herself 'competent, fearless, devoted and untiring', experiences a sense of comradeship. The ambulance becomes 'the merciful emblem that had set [her] free' (p. 3). But the idea that people are fighting to change the world proves illusory when the war ends. Miss Ogilvy has to try to fit back into her former social and sexual straitjacket. In this sense Hall mirrors what many women of the time were said to have felt. David Mitchell notes: 'When the time came for demobilisation, many wept at the ending of what they now saw as the happiest and most purposeful days of their lives.'[43] Back in Britain, Miss Ogilvy is overwhelmed with a feeling of claustrophobia, even as she gazes out from her train window at the picturesque countryside fought for and won: 'The soft English landscape sped smoothly past: small homesteads, small churches, small pastures, small lanes with small hedges; all small like England itself, all small like Miss Ogilvy's future' (p. 6). Back home her unimaginative family crudely diagnose her as suffering from shell shock.

It is Miss Ogilvy's sense that she is lost in a kind of domestic no-man's land which prompts her to take a trip to a small island off the coast of Devon. She has never visited the island before but feels she knows it. The story now moves into the fantastical when, as she is shown some bones of a man shot in the Bronze Age, Miss Ogilvy dreams she is a young male warrior walking with a young woman. While unconscious, she finds herself for a second time. The narration focuses on the couple as they make their way to a cave to make love. The next morning, in a poignant image, Miss Ogilvy is found dead sitting at the mouth of the same cave. Hers is an abandoned and overlooked life, and the image is emblematic of the character's unhappiness with conventional lifestyles, as well as her inability to acknowledge her homosexuality and thus enter the cave herself.

The originality and importance of *Miss Ogilvy Finds Herself* lies in its subject matter and in the unusual form in which it is treated. As Hall noted, lesbians had begun to emerge from their 'holes' into the daylight during the war (p. 271). Hall supposedly based the story on a close friend, Barbara Lowther, the lesbian daughter of the Earl of Lonsdale, who ran an ambulance corps on the Western Front. The story's focus on awkward, unfulfilled female lives, on repressed (homo)sexuality, and its emphasis on a kind of 'herland' unsettled some contemporaries. One reviewer described the collection as unhealthy and depressing in its 'studies in frustration': 'lonely unappreciated, inarticulate individuals in conflict with a world too strong for them'.[44] However, the story is not simply about lesbianism. Indeed, as Heather Edwards has noted, 'what drives the story is not her [Miss Ogilvy's] sexual inversion but rather her outsider status and her frustrated attempts to feel at peace in a society that rejects those who do not conform to its expectations'.[45]

This is the unifying theme of the collection – although the characters illustrate it to different degrees. In 'The Rest Cure', Charles Duffell's financial troubles begin in the aftermath of the war, a time of 'black hating and blacker self-seeking'. In 'The Lover of Things', Harry Dobb is destroyed by his pursuit of beautiful objects which he compulsively acquires to relieve the monotony of his drab suburban life. The bleakest story in the book is 'Fraulein Schwartz', a powerful rendering of life in a shabby London boarding house in 1914. It tells of another unmarried, lonely woman and another character 'both limited and ennobled by her innocent nature', as Franks puts it.[46]

Fraulein Schwartz is a kind-hearted German teacher, a long-time resident in Mrs Raymond's 'Private Hotel', the sterility of which is encapsulated in a decaying rubber plant in the dining room – a reminder of the hotelier's earlier life as the wife of a colonial rubber merchant. As the story opens, we learn that until now Fraulein Schwartz has been sustained in her lonely life by her cat and by memories of her happy childhood in Germany. The outbreak of war changes everything. To the other residents she is suddenly a figure of some consequence – an enemy alien – and their incipient racism comes to the fore. Fraulein Schwartz discovers the world to be a harsher place. She is taunted by the other residents, and a speech in which she appeals to universal brotherhood is met with mockery. She remembers Germany from her childhood as 'a land of fairy tales, Christmas trees, and artless toys fashioned for little children' (pp. 154–55), but this is not how the English see it. For them Germany is the bully and the aggressor. The inhabitants of the boarding house hate all Germans with a savage passion that the Fraulein cannot comprehend. Hall seems to be making a comment on the powerful feelings generated by newspaper coverage of the war. The residents believe 'the real peril lay much less in men than in the vast, secret army of women; female spies masquerading as ladies' maids, private secretaries, and even as teachers' (p. 152).

Part of the pathos of Hall's story stems from the fact that the Fraulein is completely alone, adrift in an environment of hatred and cynicism which her experience has not equipped her to navigate. Her 'large overload of maternal affection' (p. 146) has no outlet, and she is unable to read with any degree of fluency the people she shares her lodgings with. She is 'innocent, blundering, bewildered and helpless', and, as Hall makes clear, disturbingly 'child-like' (p. 158). Unlike her fellow boarding-house residents who have quickly become hardened to the demands of war, Fraulein Schwartz underestimates the extent of anti-German feeling and tries to counter it by fussing around the other boarders, carrying out 'little acts of unwelcome kindness, and this at a time when war-wracked nerves would naturally lead to the worst interpretation' (p. 157). Her only allies are Alan Winter, a young man who has not enlisted (whether on the grounds of conscientious objections or cowardice is not made clear), and an Indian medical student who observes that the other inhabitants 'did not sound Christian' in their treatment of the German woman (p. 151).

Matters come to a head when the pregnant housemaid, mourning her fiancé, who has been killed in battle, poisons the Fraulein's cat. When she is faced with the intolerance of the boarding house – a kind of microcosm of British society – Fraulein Schwartz's own feelings change. She prays for a German victory and harbours feelings of revenge. Although this is not a story of self-discovery, Hall shows how the mind can become confused, principles can change and good intentions can vanish: 'from one of those dimly lit chasms of the mind there rushed up a mighty force fully armed, and it gripped Fraulein Schwartz and possessed her entirely, so that she who had been the friend of all the world was now shaken by gusts of primitive fury' (p. 139). The murder of her cat robs her of any purpose in her life. She carries it under her coat to the river, where she will also drown herself. The last description of the Fraulein conveys her sense of melancholy and defeat, and to onlookers she still cuts an absurd figure: 'even now she must walk lop-sided through the streets, looking as though some abominable growth had laid its distorting hand upon her' (p. 176). Hall does not romanticise her heroine; indeed, she seems to rob her of dignity. At the same time she conjures up links with those other female castaways, the suicidal 'fallen' women as mythologised in nineteenth-century poetry and painting. Fraulein Schwartz has not fallen in any sexual sense, but she represents innocence destroyed. Her brand of Christianity has no place in wartime, and her fate is shown to be 'the fate of all those who are too tender hearted' (p. 158). Death is the only liberation, and although Christian doctrine tells her she sins by committing suicide, she is confident that God will forgive her.

Hall did not, of course, know what it felt like to be a German woman in England during a time of war, but she knew what it felt like to be a lesbian and therefore an outsider to some degree. While it is generally agreed that *The Well of Loneliness* is her most significant achievement, the stories in *Miss Ogilvy Finds Herself* demonstrate the way in which the short-story form allowed a focus on individual moments of crisis which Hall (like other short-story writers before and since) felt unsustainable in a novel. These are portraits which are powerful in their sense of human suffering. As 'war writings' they give us portraits of another side of the conflict and open up a new tract of First World War literature for study. Later, it was just such a sense of the need for a fresh start which helped accelerate the new modernist generation's search for different ways of diagnosing and representing human experience.[47] The modernist sense of fragmentation, of fleeting glimpses, of loss, of exclusion and of estrangement, disintegration and instability is evident in the many of the stories written in response to the conflict.

8
Experiment and Continuity: The Modernist Short Story

What is modernism?

It is, of course, impossible to answer this question briefly, and it might be impossible to answer it at all. As with all the terms by which we identify movements in literature (Romanticism, the Gothic, realism, naturalism, postmodernism, for instance), it might be that modernist writings share little more than a certain amount of historical contiguity and a particular place in the mind of the literary critic. Like Romanticism, modernism is largely a retrospective term, applied by the academy after the event, and seldom used of themselves by those who appear under the label. It might even be that modernism is itself a 'short fiction', in the sense that it is a shorthand way of grouping writers and their works, taxonomising them for the purpose of imposing coherence on an otherwise messy literary history. That said, since the word is used by critics, some definition, however rudimentary and unsatisfactory, is probably necessary here, not least because the short-story form is often identified as a specifically modernist form.

The word 'modernism' has existed since at least the early eighteenth century.[1] In the sense in which we seek to use it here, however, as a description of the artistic innovations of the late nineteenth and early twentieth centuries, its first appearance is, according to the *Oxford English Dictionary*, in the work of Sidney Colvin, the art critic, in 1879. He used it disapprovingly – it is only 'fanatics' who are interested in 'realism and modernism' – but he did at least (conveniently for our purposes) also associate it with aesthetic 'experiments', which he cautiously welcomed. This is a useful hint. Modernism is almost always associated with artistic experiments, sometimes in the shape of new (and daring) subject matter, but much more often in terms of innovations in style and technique, in the visual arts and beyond. It might be an accident that Colvin was an art critic, but it also speaks an important truth. The first self-consciously modern movement in the arts was Impressionism, inaugurated by the scandal of Monet's *Impression: Sunrise*, which was refused official exhibition space when it was painted in 1873, but which was none the less widely seen that year in the *Salon des Refusés* (an exhibition of those excluded from the French Academy's exhibition). 'Impressionism' was adopted very early by writers to describe their comparable attempts to do in ink and with words what Claude Monet had done in painted images. (Joseph Conrad's efforts to do this are discussed in Chapter 5.) As Julia Van Gunsteren, writing about Katherine Mansfield, puts it:

> The aim [of literary impressionism] is to create an atmosphere, in subtle evocation, with discontinuous, retrospective or unfinished actions, in streams of consciousness, channelled by emotion, corresponding to the way in which we experience life. No analysis or inventory of set pictures or comments on the characters is given nor is there a chronological report with a definite beginning, middle and end. In its effect on the reader, it is highly suggestive...as early as 1894...H. Garland pointed out: 'It must never be forgotten, that they [the Impressionist painters] are not delineating a scene; they are painting a personal impression of a scene, which is vastly different.'[2]

This is not merely a description of a modernist technique in writing. It is also an extremely useful reference point for thinking specifically about how modernism inflected itself in the short-story form. Thus, one key element of modernism is technical experimentation with form, with genre and – though this is not always obvious to us, living in a much more 'free' age, at least with regard to sexual mores – with subject matter.

It is obvious that modernism is related to its root word, 'modern' (from the Latin *modo*, meaning 'just now; the present moment'). 'Now', however, is the ultimate moveable feast, always shifting, always becoming the past with immediate effect. None the less, the 'now-ness', and therefore newness, of the modern is an important way of thinking about its effects. Artists and writers of the early twentieth century often believed that they were living through a period of unprecedented change, and that artistic practices had to adapt to the new conditions: the watchword for modernism, in the words of the poet Ezra Pound, was 'make it new!' The moment of that change is variously dated. In a statement that is now so often quoted in introductions to modernism that it is almost a cliché of defining the literary field we now call modernism, Virginia Woolf wrote (in 1923):

> On or about December 1910, human character changed ... All human relations have shifted – those between masters and servants, husbands and wives, parents and children. And when human relations shift there is at the same time a change in religion, conduct, politics and literature.[3]

This is an absolute statement: there was a change, and we can date it pretty precisely. This is a feature often found in attempts to describe the origins of literary and cultural movements; a search for the precise moment at which something shifted makes explanation easier. The particular event in December 1910 to which Woolf refers was the first post-Impressionist exhibition, organised in London by Roger Fry – an exhibition, that is, that was self-consciously avant-garde, with modern art being displayed *as modern* for its audience. And that self-consciousness of deliberate newness is part of the modernist story. Other dates could do just as well as December 1910 to define the moment at which the world became 'modern' and art became modernist. There are equally sound reasons for dating a shift in human life to 1900 or to the aftermath of the first industrial-scale modern war, the Great War of 1914–18. As Frank Kermode argued in *The Sense of an Ending*, although 'this fuss about centuries can be seen to be based on the arbitrary calendar[,] it is known for a myth', 1900 certainly has several qualifications for being the date at which the world changed, at least intellectually:

> In 1900, Nietzsche died; Freud published *The Interpretation of Dreams*; 1900 was also the date of [Edmund] Husserl's *Logic*, and of [Bertrand] Russell's *Critical Exposition of the Philosophy of Leibniz*. With an exquisite sense of timing, [Max] Planck published his quantum hypothesis on the very last days of the century, December 1900. Thus, within a few months, were published works which transformed or transvalued spirituality, the relation of language to knowing, and the very locus of human uncertainty, henceforth to be thought of not as an imperfection of the human apparatus, but as part of the nature of things, a condition of what we may know.[4]

The significance of these writers is in terms of the thoughts they made it possible to think. Nietzsche had a major and often unacknowledged influence on the generation of writers who followed him; his philosophy is one which demands that the individual think for him- (or, possibly, her-) self rather than accept the conventional wisdoms handed down through the generations. Freud's significance is in part about his uncovering of the unconscious mechanisms by which individuals act: there are vast parts of the self that the individual does not know at all. But just as significant is his sense of the centrality of sexuality for an understanding of subjectivity – a topic that the apparently strait-laced Victorians did not discuss publicly. Husserl developed the philosophy of phenomenology – the concern with describing and accounting for personal experiences without recourse to metaphysical explanations (that is, to explanations beyond the observable world, such as God or Fate). Russell's explication of Leibniz's philosophy was similarly iconoclastic in that it, too, focused on the real, the observable and the scientific elements of philosophy as opposed to idealist or metaphysical ones. For all four of these writers, the key issues are the defiance of convention and the possibility for freedom (and for danger) that this opens up. Planck's quantum theory was galvanising in a slightly different way, for he set out to explain some of the areas of observable phenomena that could not be accounted for in the stable and knowable universe proposed by Isaac Newton. Not only did Planck lay the foundations for that most twentieth-century of theories Einstein's general theory of relativity, but he also demonstrated the extent to which Newton's view was limited or even mistaken.

For Kermode, then, the shift that the early twentieth century perceived in its own conditions of living is philosophical and scientific; for Virginia Woolf it is primarily aesthetic, but she suggests that the aesthetic shift also had material effects on the lives of those who lived through it (the relationships between masters and servants, husbands and wives, for instance). In both cases, the real point is that the conventions by which the past organised itself, its consciousness and its art forms are shown to be mistaken, or at least not immutable. Add to Freud, Nietzsche, Plank et al. the figure of Charles Darwin, who had as early as 1859 published his revolutionary theory of the *Origin of Species* (evolution), with the assault that this also implied on conventional religious belief – and one could also add the stirrings of revolutionary socialism and the increasingly significant campaigns for female suffrage across Europe on the political front into this mix – and it is relatively easy to see that the intellectual climate was one strangely willing to confront changes in artistic representation via experiment and innovation.

Change does not come from thinkers alone, however. One could equally easily make the case that technological innovation had major effects on the way that individuals saw and related to their world. The early twentieth century was 'modern' in the sense that a whole host of technical changes – from the availability of tinned food to the mechanisation of music (the gramophone) and of human communication (via the telephone, telegraph and typewriter); from improvements in domestic lighting (the electric light-bulb) to the invention of, and thence cheaper manufacture, of the motorcar; from the beginnings of tabloid journalism to the invention of a safe painkiller like aspirin – had revolutionised living conditions, at least for those with the material means to buy the new consumer goods.

These moves in the material and spiritual planes were marked by a profound ambivalence which is one of the hallmarks of modernism. Where the Victorians, in the words of Matthew Arnold, had sought to 'see things steadily and see them whole',[5] imposing perspective and coherence on their world through clear vision, the modernists often felt deprived of the stability of perspective, leading to a view of their world which was often incoherent and fragmented. This is a tendency that is also obvious in modern art, where perspective is often precisely what is missing from representational paintings by Pablo Picasso, Henri Matisse and Paul Gauguin. On the one hand, technologies that made life more comfortable were, of course, welcomed; on the other, one can certainly witness some profound anxieties about their effects on the human psyche: is swifter transportation (if it makes you dizzy and breathless) or tinned food (convenient but mass produced, tasteless and alien from the natural world which ought to have produced it) really an improvement? Does it do us good? As John Carey's *The Intellectuals and the Masses* suggests, part of what modernism articulates is pessimism about the direction of culture, a disapproval for the so-called new and improved versions of things.[6] Not all writers were pessimistic or even nihilistic, but many were, fearing that the mechanisation of the material sphere risked becoming a route to the mechanisation of human relations, and that it would lead to profound alienation from a world that the viewer could no longer see clearly and judge.

At its briefest, then, modernism is the cultural response to what were perceived as unprecedented changes in the *modus vivendi* of a majority of the populace; it is an aesthetic reaction to the condition of modernity as it was experienced by writers and artists in the early twentieth century. It represents an acceptance (though it is not always a cheerful acceptance) of the sense that the wholeness (and wholesomeness) and steadiness favoured by the Victorians were no longer obtainable. It speaks of the necessity for finding new conventions for representation.

If one could not see one's world according to the old conventions, which depended on the slower pace of life of an earlier period, then one could not represent one's world in the same way either. As Virginia Woolf put it in her essay 'Mr Bennett and Mrs Brown' (1923), 'The Edwardian tools [by which she means the tools of realism] are the wrong ones for us to use' because they lay too much stress on the 'fabric of things'; in other words, given the tenor of the rest of her essay, they are the wrong tools because the forms of realism produce the illusion of a stable and knowable world, an illusion that cannot be sustained in the face of so many forms of newness and mystery.[7] One of the places in which she locates that unknowability is the 'dark places of psychology'[8] – the unconscious – and thus another of the shifts one finds in prose fiction of the modernist mode is from external event to psychological evocation, from outside to inside. This means, too, that one often finds in modernist writing a preoccupation with the subjective nature of experience, with the effects that this has on the treatment of time and memory, as well as on the impressions that the individual inhabits.

In short, the shifts that modernism responds to are necessarily going to produce shifts in the conventions of representation. And another way of understanding the meaning of modernism is to see it as a reaction both to new conditions and against the conventions of the previous generation. Given that realism – the key conventional mode of representation for Victorians such as Anthony Trollope – is a totalising mode of representation (that is, it seeks to present a 'whole' world and its explanations), and given that totalisation often requires very great length for its elaboration (the Victorian three-volume novel is a notoriously lengthy production), it is perhaps no surprise that one of the key genres of a self-consciously innovative generation of writers should be the much more economical, shorter, more fragmentary and elliptical form the short story.

Symbols and stories: D. H. Lawrence

David Herbert Lawrence is far better known as a novelist than as a writer of short stories. Born in the Nottinghamshire village of Eastwood in 1885, one of the four children of a miner, he is unusual in the canon of English literature in that he came from a working-class background. Many of the details of his early life are recounted in his novel *Sons and Lovers* (1913). Lawrence is most famous as a writer on subjects connected with sex and sexuality, with novels such as *Lady Chatterley's Lover* (1928) provoking extreme reactions from contemporary audiences (this novel was prosecuted for obscenity and banned). His relationship with his German wife, Frieda, might in part have been responsible for his preference for this subject matter. She was not only a sexually liberated woman in her own right, but also a highly educated German speaker; well before Freud's ideas were popularised in the rest of Europe in translation, she knew about his work and discussed it with Lawrence. Many of Lawrence's writings, including his short stories, share themes with psychoanalytic discourse – especially questions of adolescent angst; the relationships between man and nature, man and man, man and woman; and the relationship between sex and power. Those themes are often also present in earlier short fictions of the kind we have been discussing so far, but they are repressed themes in those fictions – buried rather than explicitly described. Lawrence is, perhaps, best understood as a short-story writer who innovated in terms of technique. He was a poet as well as a novelist, and he used some of the techniques of poetry (image clusters, rhythm and symbols) in the making of his short stories. He can be described as a modernist writer, and the main thrust of his innovation is the technique of symbolism.

In literary terms symbol belongs to the realm of imagery and is related to other forms of imagistic writing, such as the simile or metaphor. Where a simile offers a comparison between two seemingly unconnected objects which is made grammatically explicit by the addition of 'like' or 'as' ('I wandered lonely *as* a cloud'; 'My love *is like* a red, red rose'), in a metaphor the equivalence between two things is implied rather than stated; the grammar does not alert the reader or listener to its existence. Metaphor pervades our language. In literary terms, symbols are closer to metaphors than to similes: the connection between the object that is named and the object that is alluded to is not made explicit. But more is going on with a symbol than the simple construction of equivalence whereby one object stands for another.

In its simplest sense, a symbol is anything which stands for, or represents, something beyond itself. Often a symbol works in a very conventional way; that is, a series of signs is recognised by the viewer in conventional (almost 'natural') terms. For instance, most British people will recognise the Union Flag as somehow representing the United Kingdom, although the meaning of the symbol depends, of course, on its context: the flag on top of Buckingham Palace means something different from the flag on a skinhead's T-shirt. When literary critics speak of symbols, however, they differentiate them from metaphors in terms of the type of relationship which is being implied between the signifier and the signified. A metaphor implies equivalence: one single thing (however indirectly) represents another single (one) thing. In symbol there is still a comparison between two unlike objects, but the range of connotations is wider: one thing represents a range of associations, not a single idea or image. Some symbols – for instance, the Cross – represent an entire religious and ethical framework. In literature, though, we use the words 'symbol' and 'symbolism' to focus on the ways in which an object can refer to a multiplicity of ideas beyond itself; where metaphor is about a one-to-one equivalence which is reasonably clear, a symbol's range of reference is much more indeterminate. Any writer who makes sustained use of symbols – through a whole narrative, for instance – can be said to be using a symbolist technique. This technique permits writers to create atmosphere in their writing, an atmosphere to which the reader responds emotionally rather than strictly logically. In his early novels and short stories, Lawrence made great use of symbol to discuss and evoke subject matter that could not be described in more explicit ways, particularly in relation to sexuality. In *Sons and Lovers*, for instance, Miriam's distaste for sexual relationships is consistently symbolised in her attitudes to flowers. She is at once fascinated by them and afraid of, even occasionally repelled by, them; through their symbolic associations are demonstrated her fears about a sexual relationship with Paul Morel.

This use of flowers as symbols is also found in the early, more or less realist short story 'Odour of Chrysanthemums' (1911). 'Odour of Chrysanthemums' is a transitional story, perhaps. It gets much of its effect from the careful enumeration of realist details about the house in which the Bates family – a miner and his wife and children – live in turn-of-the-century Nottinghamshire, as well as the houses of their neighbours. The 'detailism' is what is found in realist writing, and is typical of the style of realist writers such as Arnold Bennett. But the realism is overlaid with other forms of significance, among which the symbol of the flowers is key. The flowers, picked for pleasure by a small child, provoke an outburst of bitterness from his mother: 'Don't they smell beautiful?' the child asks, filled with innocent enthusiasm, only to receive the response 'No...not to me. It was chrysanthemums when I married him, chrysanthemums when you were born, and the first time they ever brought him home drunk, he'd got brown chrysanthemums in his button hole' (p. 93).[9] On this occasion, the chrysanthemums presage another momentous event. They have represented births and marriages; now they will represent death, for the father of the children and the husband of Elizabeth Bates has been killed in a mining accident. His dead body will later be brought back to a front parlour decorated by the child's chrysanthemums in vases, and one vase will be broken as fellow miners manoeuvre the body into the tiny room. The chrysanthemums are emblems of lost opportunity, lost love and death. Flowers are a conventional symbol for love. Lovers buy their girlfriends flowers as tokens of their affection, to stand in for, or to symbolise, their love, as Walter brings Elizabeth flowers for her wedding and her labours. But Elizabeth rejects them as symbols of love, and sees them as promises unfulfilled. Walter's death points to their emptiness and incapacity to articulate what they were meant to symbolise.

Lawrence himself described symbols thus:

> you can't give a great symbol a 'meaning' any more than you can give a cat a 'meaning'. Symbols are organic units of consciousness with a life of their own, and you can never explain them away, because their value is dynamic, emotional, belonging to the sense – consciousness of body and soul, and not simply mental.[10]

For him, the importance of the symbol is that its significance is evoked rather than stated. It gets its effects by illogical rather than logical means, which makes it particularly effective for providing atmosphere – an undefined feeling in the text. Lawrence's short fiction is modernist short fiction because it evokes rather than describes.

It is not all innovation in Lawrence's short fiction. He certainly made use of the traditions he had inherited from the Victorians, and thus represents continuity with the past as well as the innovations of the modernist present. In many ways, the relatively late story 'The Rocking-Horse Winner' (1926) is a traditional tale, structured in terms that Edgar Allan Poe would have recognised; it is focused on a single emotion, and has a powerful twist in the tail, when the child, Paul, is killed in his attempt to satisfy his mother's insatiable desire for money. Brian Finney has described this story as 'a neat parable of the acquisitive society's death wish', and he sees it as belonging to the Victorian tradition of short stories which, as we saw earlier, confuse the boundaries between the real world and the supernatural – as the ghost story also does:

> Lawrence seizes on the [short-story] genre as an excuse to upset normal expectations. He gives the contemporary obsession with material success a spectral insubstantiality that ultimately leads to the extinction of the innocent young recipient of these pernicious values...with James's *Turn of the Screw* in mind, Lawrence combines the genre of the supernatural with that of the fairy story. He internalises the supernatural and borrows from the fairy story its traditional simplification of life's complexities in order to draw attention to the moral of the story: 'lucky in money; unlucky in love.'[11]

In this story, the child is the victim of the inadequacies of his parents – the father whose prospects never materialise and the mother who has expensive tastes and who makes her disappointment felt by all around her. It is implied right from the start that this tragedy would not have occurred if the adults in the story had been either responsible or loving. The parents do not love each other, and they are incapable of loving their children. Uncle Oscar, who appears friendlier, is equally guilty since he exploits the boy's talent for his own gain, rather than seeking to understand and help him.

What this story articulates is the danger when emotional needs are displaced onto material objects, when money is mistaken for the route to satisfaction. Paul lives a life that is profoundly unsatisfactory in terms of his emotional needs. He learns from his mother that material things are the only real source of emotional satisfaction, and his attempts to satisfy his mother's emotional/material needs are clearly open to Freudian interpretation, in that he seeks to satisfy the yearnings that his father is manifestly incapable of meeting. In other words, the child takes on an adult responsibility which is simultaneously monetary and sexual, as the opening paragraph begins to make clear:

> There was a woman who was beautiful, who started with all the advantages, yet she had no luck. She married for love, and the love turned to *dust*. She had bonny children, yet she felt they had been *thrust* upon her, and she could not love them … And hurriedly, she felt that she must cover up some fault in herself. Yet what it was that she must cover up, she never knew. Nevertheless, when her children were present, she always felt the centre of her heart go hard. This troubled her, and her manner was all the more gentle and anxious for her children, as if she loved them very much. Only she herself knew that at the centre of her heart was a hard little place that could not feel love, no, not for anybody. Everybody said of her: 'She is such a good mother. She adores her children.' Only she herself, and the children themselves, knew it was not so. They read it in each other's eyes. (p. 444, our emphasis)

The emphases added to this passage suggest something of Lawrence the poet: the rhyming words link sex and death, which is in part the story's theme. As with the ghost story, and as with the Freudian explanation of child development, what is being evoked here is the trauma at the heart of the family. The narrative does not actually *explain* why the mother's marriage has been a failure, but it evokes a world in which emotional and sexual compatibility have broken down. The children, for example, have been 'thrust upon her', an action that has made her passive. They are the result of the marriage, but they are not the result of real love for her husband, which has 'turned to dust'. The father's sexual needs have rendered her impotent, and just as she has been powerless in the conception of her children, she becomes powerless to love them.

Because she is emotionally and sexually dissatisfied, the mother seeks satisfaction elsewhere by displacing her sexual needs onto material things. It is very telling that the father is basically absent from the events of the story, which provides the space for Paul to try to win his mother's love in an Oedipal game with deadly serious consequences. The competition between father and son is easier for the boy because the father is absent, but also more dangerous because it is unregulated by the norms of family life, whereby fathers would normally prevent such activity. The two things that the mother claims to want are the immaterial luck and the utterly material money: they are both the same thing in her mind, of course, and both replace what she really lacks, which is love.

Because money and luck are substitutes for affection and sex, it is beyond Paul's capacities to provide them for his mother. Paul discovers that he is able to predict the winners of horse races with preternatural accuracy by the frenzied riding of his rocking horse in his nursery. His Uncle Oscar takes full advantage of this ability. Paul's participation in gambling represents the taking on of adult responsibilities that are beyond him physically, emotionally and intellectually. His quest to uncover the names of winning horses places an intolerable strain on him both in mind and in body. The responsibility is too much for the child's mind: the rocking-horse journeys are too much for his body; he ends each 'race' worn out, we are told. And because the luck and the money are merely substitutes for what the mother lacks, they do not in fact resolve her cravings. What she needs is not more money, but to learn to feel, to replace 'the hard little place that could not feel love' in her heart (p. 444). When Paul takes his £5,000 to his mother as an anonymous gift, she remains unsatisfied; consequently, neither is the whispering house satisfied, and so, finally, neither is Paul:

> Paul's mother touched the whole five thousand. Then something very curious happened. The voices in the house suddenly went mad, like a chorus of frogs on a spring evening... the voices in the house, behind the sprays of mimosa and almond-blossom, and from under the piles of iridescent cushions, simply trilled and screamed in a sort of ecstasy: 'There *must* be more money! O-h-h! There *must* be more money! Oh, now, now-w! now-w-w! – there *must* be more money! – more than ever! More than ever!' (p. 453, emphasis in original)

The language here is intensely sexualised, which signals that money has become the substitute for love and affection, for sex itself, perhaps. Riding the horse, therefore, is a perverse form of sexual knowledge (horses and sex are often mixed up in literature), a knowledge the child should be protected from. Paul's riding is virtually masturbatory, which is why he worn out; he undertakes this activity in secret, and he is intensely protective of it. He is particularly clear that he doesn't want his mother to know – ostensibly about the gambling, but also about the means by which he gets his tips, implying a link between the horse-riding and other forms of illicit activity of which a small male child might be ashamed. Thus, although Paul begins his riding to help his mother, its result is that he turns further and further in on himself, and is eventually incapable of escaping from a vicious circle of obsession. The fact that the real problem is never tackled, but is displaced, causes the child's sickness. He eventually dies, we must suppose, effectively because of his parents' failure to love either each other or him adequately.

This symbolic and Freudian framework is located within yet another framework, that of the fairy tale. Much of the story is told in an impersonal way: the mother, the woman, the child, the sisters are archetypes rather than individuals. And in fairy-tale fashion, Paul appears to have bargained with evil powers to gain the knowledge that makes him 'lucky'. The difference between this story and the traditional formulation is that we never see Paul's bargain with the devil. That part of the story is effectively missing – the part that would have been climactic in other kinds of story. Instead, we get the following description:

> He went off by himself, vaguely, in a childish way, seeking for the clue to 'luck'. Absorbed, taking no heed of other people, he went about with a sort of stealth, seeking inwardly for luck. He wanted luck, he wanted it, he wanted it. When the two girls were playing dolls in the nursery, he would sit on his big rocking-horse, charging madly into space, with a frenzy that made the little girls peer at him uneasily. Wildly the horse careered, the waving dark hair of the boy tossed, his eyes had a strange glare in them. The little girls dared not speak to him. (p. 446)

Secretiveness, for Victorian and Edwardian families, is the hallmark of what they called secret vice: masturbation.

At the end, the question must be asked as to whether the child's death makes any difference to the living left behind. The answer is that it probably doesn't. As she watches her child die, after all, the mother still cannot feel: she suffers from 'tormented motherhood', but '[h]e talked and tossed, and his mother sat stonily by his side' (p. 456). And despite the crisis, both Bassett and Uncle Oscar still bet on the horse that Paul has named as the winner of the Grand National, making money more important to both of them than the child himself. Oscar's final remarks, which close the story, suggest that this is not a narrative from which any of the protagonists has taken any moral:

> And even as he lay dead, his mother heard her brother's voice saying to her: 'My God, Hester, you're eighty thousand to the good, and a poor devil of a son to the bad. But poor devil, poor devil, he's best gone out of a life where he rides his rocking-horse to find a winner.' (p. 457)

Oscar's syntactical priority (the money before the son in that first sentence) suggests where his moral priorities lie.

Stories as impressions: Katherine Mansfield

> It is simply the record of a young girl's thoughts and impressions, and consequently meant for publication. (Oscar Wilde, *The Importance of Being Earnest*)

reason is hateful ... Because it demonstrates ... that we, living, are out of life – utterly out of it. The mysteries of the universe made of drops of fire and clods of mud do not concern us in the least. The fate of a humanity condemned ultimately to perish from cold is not worth troubling about. If you take it to heart it becomes an unendurable tragedy. If you believe in improvement, you must weep, for the attained perfection must end in cold, darkness and silence. In a dispassionate view the ardour for reform, improvement, for virtue, for knowledge, and even for beauty is only a vain sticking up for appearances as though one were anxious about the cut of one's clothes in a community of blind men. Life knows us not and we do not know life – we don't even know our own thoughts. Half the words we use have no meaning whatever, and of the other half, each man understands each word after the fashion of his own folly and conceit. Faith is a myth and beliefs shift like mists on the shore; thoughts vanish; words, once pronounced, die; and the memory of yesterday is as shadowy as the hope of tomorrow – only the string of my platitudes seems to have no end. As our peasants say: 'Pray, brother, forgive me for the love of God.' And we don't know what forgiveness is, nor what is love, nor where God is.[12]

These two quotations are clearly different in their direction and tone. The first, from Oscar Wilde's *The Importance of Being Earnest* (1895), signals what several commentators have noticed about Katherine Mansfield: that she was profoundly influenced by the aesthetic movement of the late nineteenth century. Her early short stories are social satires in the manner of Wilde. As Clare Hanson notes, her 'early notebooks show that she developed a self-consciously symbolist aesthetic from her reading of Walter Pater, Wilde and in particular, Arthur Symons'.[13] Pater's *obiter dictum* that the purpose of life is to 'know one's impressions' thoroughly is key to Mansfield's themes and techniques, but in her choice of satire for most of her early collections, she shows an allegiance to the lighter touch that Wilde brought to the aesthetic table: the relativity of subjectivity can be – though it is not always – a source of humour. Conrad's vision, in contrast, is much darker. The letter quoted above is a response to his realisation of the implications of the second law of thermodynamics (the law of entropy, which asserts that there is a given amount of energy in the universe and that eventually that energy will dissipate itself, leading to the death of the universe through cold). For Conrad, as for others at the time, the possibility of the futility of human wishes in the face of an inexorable world and its inhuman physical laws represents the loss of all forms of order and all hopes for a better future. It is clothed in a language of despair which is also nostalgic for the old certainties, the old order.

Mansfield's writing inhabits both these worlds: the world of despair and loss, the sense that order has dissipated itself and disappeared coexists with an attitude which seems to state that if life is absurd and futile, let us celebrate its absurdity and futility. Thus, instead of voicing despair, Mansfield is often a comic writer, operating within a space of deliberate incongruity. As Mary Ann Gillies and Aurelea Mahood put it: 'The pivotal moment in a Mansfield story is the instant in which competing or contradictory impulses converge and conflict.'[14] It is the moment when 'order' is shown to be factitious. Sometimes this produces despair; sometimes it provokes a knowing laughter. There are very dark stories which border on the nihilistic (for example, 'The Woman at the Store' [1912] and 'Je Ne Parle Pas Français' [1920]), but there is also a will to bring humour out of pathos, waste, futility and the ridiculous. Her characters often desire the old order – the sense of things being in their place and the predictability of conventions. The sympathetic characters are, however, frequently those who are shown to be trapped by 'order' or who are in active revolt against it, as the stories discussed here suggest. We have chosen to explore Mansfield's later stories because it is here that her experiments are most clearly present in terms of form and style. The stories – 'The Garden Party' (1922) and 'Bliss' (1920) – also chart another of Mansfield's main themes, that of femininity and the specific limitations that society places on women. These tales cover the female lifecycle from puberty to maternity,[15] and show the different orders of sympathy and the different limitations demanded by and placed on these phases of a woman's life.

Katherine Mansfield was born in Wellington, New Zealand, in 1888. This fact is important: it renders her a writer of the British empire, and a kind of outsider to the mainstream of the British canon. (Lawrence and Joyce were similarly marginalised figures – Lawrence because of his working-class background and auto-didacticism, and Joyce because he, too, was a product of empire, having been born in Ireland at a time when Ireland was still ruled from London.) In Mansfield's case, her background matters both because it provides the backdrop for some of her most famous stories ('The Garden Party', for instance, is set in suburban Wellington) and because, as an outsider, her view of British life is interestingly eccentric. Unusually among writers, all Mansfield's fiction is in the short-story form. She never wrote a novel, preferring the shape of short fiction. In this she was probably influenced by Constance Garnett's translations of the short fictions of Anton Chekhov, which appeared in 1910[16] and which were widely admired and also treated with puzzlement when they were first published in England. As Charles E. May has suggested:

> Chekhov's short stories were first welcomed in England and America just after the turn of the twentieth century as examples of late-nine-teenth-century realism…they were termed 'realistic'…primarily because they seemed to focus on fragments of everyday reality – and so were characterized as 'sketches', 'cross sections' and 'slices of life'…they were widely noted as lacking the elements that constitute a really good short story, [but] critics saw that Chekhov's impressionism and freedom from the literary conventions of the highly plotted and formalized story marked the beginnings of a new or 'modern' kind of short fiction – one that combined the specific detail of realism with the poetic lyricism of romanticism.[17]

This quotation, describing Chekhov's work, contains much that could equally describe Mansfield's. The majority of her stories are fragments of everyday reality (sketches, cross-sections and slices of life) rather than fully plotted tales; they tend to be impressionistic rather than 'objective' – in part because they are often narrated not by a traditional first-person or third-person narrator, but by a narrator who passes in and out of the consciousnesses of the characters being described and evoked, in Mansfield's own version of free indirect style, a technique discussed below. The stories are also poetic and lyrical, requiring to be read as if they were lyric poems, with image clusters and rhythms that are at least as important as their plots. Thematically, there is a wide range of possibility. Some stories are focalised through children's eyes (for instance, 'Sun and Moon' [1920]); some through the eyes of problematic and often deeply unattractive narrators, such as Raoul Duquette in the previously mentioned 'Je Ne Parle Pas Français'. But her most intriguing works are the ones with more extensive plots in which the main protagonists are adult or adolescent females. These stories have much to say about how far the female protagonists have totally internalised the 'rules' of feminine propriety, to their own detriment (especially in the tragic and pathetic story of 'The Daughters of the Late Colonel' [1921]), or come into conflict with them (as with Bertha Young in 'Bliss' and Laura in 'The Garden Party').

A key question for anyone reading a story or a novel is always, Who is telling this story? It matters enormously how we answer that question because, depending on the nature of the narrated event (an event that is, say, fantastic or supernatural), who is telling the tale has an effect on the nature of the reader's response. When a story deals with fantasy, the cultural capital of the narrator is a major factor in the interpretation of the events that are narrated. There is, however, a problem with identifying the narrators of Mansfield's fiction as simply as one might identify those of an earlier kind of fiction. And this is the result of her innovative use of the technique known as free indirect style or discourse. Take the following example from the opening paragraph of 'The Garden Party':

> *And after all the weather was ideal. They could not have had a more perfect day for a garden party if they had **ordered** it.* Windless, warm, the sky without a cloud. Only the blue was veiled with a haze of light gold, as it sometimes is in early summer. The gardener had been up since dawn, mowing lawns and sweeping them, until the dark flat rosettes where the daisy plants had been seemed to shine. As for the roses, *you could not help feeling that they understood that roses are the*

only flowers to impress people at garden parties, the only flowers that everybody is certain of knowing. Hundreds, yes, literally hundreds, had come out in a single night; the green bushes bowed down as though they had been visited by the archangels. (p. 245, our emphasis)[18]

Some of the narrative is clearly written in the mode of a third-person narrator, observing the facts in a more or less dispassionate manner. But the italic passages are perhaps being spoken by someone else. We have the highly colloquial beginning – as if in the midst of things – with the word 'And'. There is a breathless enthusiasm to the first italic passage – the weather is ideal, it is perfect, it is as if they had ordered it. Then there is simple description – of the weather and of the activities of the gardener. Then we move back into another consciousness. One might suggest that the mind we move in and out of in this narrative is that of Laura, the main protagonist of the story. And the technique here insists on us recognising her voice and her views among those of the more objective omniscient third-person narrator. This has two important effects: it prevents the reader from settling on a given perspective and judging clearly, for we cannot immediately tell who is speaking; it also gives Laura's voice equal billing to that of the omniscient third-person narrator, meaning that her subjective impressions are valued the same as the impressions of the more dispassionate and objective voice that does the work of ordinary description. This is free indirect style. It is the technique of presenting as part of the main narrative the thoughts, impressions and emotions of a key character without explicitly signalling the change in focalisation (for instance, by inserting 'he said' or 'she thought' or by inserting the speech marks that tell us we are in another person's language).[19]

On our first reading of the opening paragraph of 'The Garden Party', we do not know that the consciousness we are entering is likely to be Laura Sheridan's, since we haven't met her yet. But as the story progresses, we discover that she is a young woman, filled with enthusiasm for life, from a particular social class (the New Zealand upper middle class – hence our double emphasis on the word 'ordered' in the quotation, because the word implies that the Sheridan family are used to ordering anything they want, and that they are people who live in a very ordered or regimented way), who is described by her mother as 'artistic'. Her focus on the natural world and the idiom in which that focus is described (slightly naive and faux poetic, perhaps) are both later identified strongly with Laura. Without any explicit marking of the narrative with phrases which identify who is speaking/feeling/describing,

Mansfield's technique is often directly associated with free indirect style where different voices compete. The stories are polyphonic (many-voiced) rather than mono-diegetic (a single voice orders its readers what to think).

In 'The Garden Party', although we are most concerned with Laura's consciousness, the shifts in focus of the narrative are significant, for they demonstrate the extent to which the heroine is being interpellated into a particular mode of being suitable to upper-middle-class femininity. Laura's is not the only voice we hear in the narrative passages: we also hear the tones and attitudes of Laura's mother, of the rest of her family and of her cultural milieu more generally – and Mansfield's point is presumably that the young woman feels herself free but is in fact hemmed in (ordered about, we might say) by the norms of her culture. In other words, the story uses a particular technique as a method of expressing something about gender. As Peter Childs has put it:

> Katherine Mansfield's stories frequently coalesce around the theme of the constraints on silenced or muted women within society and patriarchy. In terms of form, [her] work is characterised by obliquity and hiatus, such that what is not said in her stories is as important as what is. To create the effect of unspoken feeling, Mansfield uses symbolism, unfinished questions, indirect expression and partial revelation in a narrative filtered through the partial understanding of principal characters who are often marginalized figures: children, spinsters, women subservient to fathers, brothers and husbands.[20]

Although Laura is slightly different from her family – is in resistance against the norms they enforce on her – she is also made in their mould. At the end of the story it is not at all clear whether she will become like her mother or whether she will finally find a way to tread her own independent path. The ending, which is elliptical and inconclusive, does not give us a neat answer; the story breaks off, as it began, *in medias res*.

Laura Sheridan is presented as a character inhabiting a slight distance from her family, and especially from the rules of appropriate femininity that her mother represents. When she is sent to tell the workmen where to put the marquee, she copies her mother's voice: 'But that sounded so fearfully affected that she was ashamed' (p. 246) we are told. Her upbringing is training her in one way; her natural inclinations suggest other possibilities. But those possibilities are not quite realised, as the following passage suggests. Laura has just observed one of the workmen who is erecting the marquee picking a piece of lavender and smelling it:

> How many of the men that she knew would have done such a thing. Oh, how extraordinarily nice workmen were, she thought. Why couldn't she have workmen for friends instead of those silly boys she danced with and who came to Sunday night supper? She would get on much better with men like these.
>
> It's all the fault, she decided... of these absurd class distinctions. Well, for her part, she didn't feel them. Not a bit, not an atom... And now there came the chock-chock of the wooden hammers. Some one whistled, some one sang out, 'Are you right there, matey?' 'Matey!' The friendliness of it, the – the – Just to prove how happy she felt, and how she despised stupid conventions, Laura took a big bite of her bread-and-butter... She felt just like a work-girl. (pp. 247–48)

Although she might identify the class distinctions as absurd, she is trussed up by them. She romanticises the working men and the life of the working girl – and, in a typical moment, cannot express what she actually feels. Her training has given her no language to deal with the spontaneity of emotion, so her ideas trail off into ellipsis; the sentence is not completed. Her attitude patronises the working men, but Laura does not quite know this, and her attitude is certainly to be read as preferable to her mother's insistent distancing from working people generally (she sends Jose to deal with the cook, and Laura deals with both the marquee erecters and the family of the dead man at the end of the story, and Mrs Sheridan forbids her children to walk down the lane where the working families live). Laura, for all her attempts to refuse her training, is none the less part of the world her mother has made for her.

One of the ways in which Mansfield should, perhaps, be read is as a poet in prose. This story is carefully constructed around a series of symbolic images. The central subject of the story is the adolescent encounter with death. The death of the workman is a threat to the upper-class social world – or it would be if Laura's suggestion that the party should be cancelled were taken up. Her view of this death is that it should not occur in the same time and space as the celebration of a party. As Mansfield herself wrote of the story:

> [Laura] feels things ought to happen differently. First one and then another. But life isn't like that. We haven't the **ordering** of it. Laura says, 'But all these things must not happen at once.' And Life answers,

'Why not? How are they divided from each other?' and they *do* all happen, it is inevitable.[21]

The word 'ordering' is again emphasised here because it implies the extent to which Laura's privileged class position suggests to her that life is ordered and patterned rather than risky and contingent. It goes with giving orders and ordering goods, but it contrasts with the lives of the workers down the lane, where death might always be just around the corner. But, as Mansfield puts it, no one's life is completely ordered, even if material privilege sometimes gives that illusion. That is not, however, to say that the story itself is not ordered. And the way that images come together in the story is fundamentally poetic and symbolic. There are flowers: roses and lilies, associated respectively with love and death. There is also Laura's hat, which her mother uses as a distraction to get her daughter to forget her distress at the death of the workman. But it is a doubly symbolic hat, for all its practical effect in her mother's plot. It is part of Laura's training in femininity. When she accidentally sees herself in the mirror wearing it, she sees herself as someone different – as a proper young lady:

> [in her bedroom] quite by chance, the first thing she saw was this charming girl in the mirror in her black hat, trimmed with gold daisies and a long black velvet ribbon. Never had she imagined she could look like that. *Is mother right? she thought. Am I being extravagant?* Just for a moment she had another glimpse of that poor woman and those little children, and the body being carried into the house. But it all seemed blurred, unreal, like a picture in the newspaper. (p. 256, our emphasis)

The hat makes that other world of tragedy fade into the distance. This matters because when Laura later visits the family of the dead man, she is invited to view the body (something her mother has absolutely hoped she would not do, though she does not quite say so in case it puts ideas into her daughter's head). She feels the need to speak to the dead man's corpse. Her words are 'forgive my hat' – the hat which has made her forget the reality of his death and the tragedy he has left behind. Celebration and tragedy and comedy all come together. Similarly, when sister Jose is rehearsing a song for the party, the song focuses on death and dying:

> *Pom!* Ta-ta-ta!

> The piano burst out so passionately that Jose's face changed. She clasped her hands. She looked mournfully and enigmatically at her mother and Laura as they came in.

> This life is *wee-ary,*
> A Tear – a Sigh!
> A Love that *Chan*-ges
> This life is *wee-ary,*
>   A Tear – a Sigh! ...
>   A Love that *Chan*-ges
> And then ... Goodbye
> But at the word 'Goodbye' and although the piano sounded more
> desperate than ever, her face broke into a brilliant, dreadfully unsym-
> pathetic smile.
>   'Aren't I in good voice, mummy?' she beamed.
> This life is *wee-ary,*
>   Hope comes to Die. (pp. 250–51)

The language in which Laura views the dead body of the working man echoes this incongruous song. 'He was dreaming. Never wake him up again' (p.
261). Even her grief, which is heartfelt and real, is haunted by the limited
vocal models from Laura's home, and the limited thinking they imply.

Among the inheritances from the Victorian period is the presump-
tion of female sexual repression. Mansfield's 'Bliss' is about a woman,
Bertha Young, who has inherited that repression to a very great extent.
Bertha's name immediately alerts us to the possibility of a symbolic
reading of her story. She is a fashionable young woman of thirty, and
her name signals both her immaturity (Young) and the potential she
has for rebirth (*Birtha*). Although she is thirty, she sometimes has the
impulse to act like a child, as the story's opening reveals:

> Although Bertha Young was thirty she still had moments like this
> when she wanted to run instead of walk, to take dancing steps on
> and off the pavement, to bowl a hoop, to throw something up in the
> air and catch it again, or to stand still and laugh at – nothing – at
> nothing, simply.
>   What can you do if you are thirty and, turning the corner of your
> own street, you are overcome suddenly, by a feeling of bliss – absolute
> bliss! – as though you'd suddenly swallowed a bright piece of that late
> afternoon sun ...
>   Oh, is there no way you can express it without being 'drunk and
> disorderly'? How idiotic civilization is! Why be given a body if you
> have to keep it shut up in a case like a rare, rare fiddle? (pp. 91–92)

The story opens with the elliptical expression of a strong emotion which
is somehow outside the realms of Bertha's normal experiences. As the

story progresses, we discover that her apparently very happy life – her wealthy husband and lifestyle, her delightful baby, her comfortable surroundings and artistic friends – is not nearly so ideal as it at first seems. The way this is signalled in the text is by the number of places where ellipses and dashes interrupt the flow of thought. She is not nearly so happy as she would like to claim she is. Her comfortable lifestyle means that she is at the mercy of a dragon of a nanny who won't let her dandle her own child at will. And her husband appears to be a rather sensual but unloving man who has never awakened a reciprocal sexual desire in her. The night of the party is the first moment she has felt such desire spontaneously:

> For the first time in her life, Bertha Young desired her husband.
>
> Oh, she'd loved him – she'd been in love with him, of course, in every other way, but just not in that way... It had worried her dreadfully at first to find that she was so cold, but after a time it had not seemed to matter. They were so frank with each other – such good pals. That was the best of being modern.
>
> But now – ardently, ardently! The word ached in her ardent body. Was this what that feeling of bliss had been leading up to? (pp. 103–4)

Her desire, however, will be thwarted. On other occasions it has been dampened down by Harry's attitudes (his cynicism and sarcasm). On this occasion it will be destroyed by his betrayal of her with Pearl Fulton. But the whole story has set us up for this moment of betrayal. It was always going to happen. And the symbol of the pear tree makes this apparent:

> At the far end, against the wall, there was a tall, slender pear tree in fullest, richest bloom; it stood perfect, as though becalmed against the jade-green sky. Bertha couldn't help feeling... that it had not a single bud or faded petal... A grey cat, dragging its belly, crept across the lawn, and a black one, its shadow, trailed after. The sight of them, so intent and so quick, gave Bertha a curious shiver.
>
> 'What creepy things cats are!' she stammered, and she turned away from the window and began walking up and down. (p. 96)

A quasi-Edenic or pastoral image is coupled with a 'creepy' image. The perfection of the one is always already undermined and subverted by the haunting presence of the other. It might be a cat, not a serpent, it might be marital infidelity rather than the horrors unleashed by eating of the tree of knowledge, and it might be a pear tree not an apple tree, but the insistent focus on blossom and fruit in the story insists that we interpret the symbols in terms of the wider cultural references they connote. The story makes use of symbolism in much the same way as Lawrence's fictions do, but key differences exist in the technical method Mansfield uses and in the focus on femininity in her stories.

The partiality of revelation: James Joyce – epiphanies and symphonies in *Dubliners*

> All art constantly aspires to the condition of music. (Walter Pater, *Studies in the History of the Renaissance*)

Joyce's *Dubliners* had a very difficult birth and its painful parturition perhaps tells us most clearly that even those committed to the production of exquisite modernist aesthetic blooms could not escape the practical material considerations of fiction production. Joyce had completed his version of the narrative as early as 1904 and had a contract with the publisher Grant Richards for publication. However, as many others have shown,[22] Richards's printer objected to the content of the story 'Two Gallants' and refused to carry on setting type, fearing that he might well be prosecuted for obscenity. There followed a long (nearly ten-year) battle for Joyce to get his collection published, with a major too-ing and fro-ing of correspondence between Joyce and Richards about the aesthetic integrity of his stories versus the practical considerations of publication. Joyce did make alterations, though not always the kind that would reduce the risk of prosecution, and he violently defended his right to write as he pleased against the judgement of the printer, whom he identified as a mere tradesman. Only in 1914 was honour satisfied all round, and the collection finally saw the light of day.

Quite apart from those practical considerations, *Dubliners* offers a particular challenge to the conventions of the short story as a form. Although the individual stories can be read in isolation, the effect that Joyce was striving for was one in which the connections among the stories would be picked up by the reader, who has access to far more knowledge than any of the protagonists. The stories represent Joyce's diagnosis of his home city as a space of deathly paralysis. As in George Moore's *The Untilled Field*, the problems that hem his characters around are material (they are often materially very poor), emotional (they suffer emotional lack which comes out in the frustrations of violence and alcoholism), political (a number of stories focus on the fraught politics of a Dublin that was at that time seeking an outlet for its political ambition for Home Rule) and religious (Moore's countryside is priest-ridden, though some of his priests are well-meaning; Joyce's city is equally hidebound by the demands of Catholicism, and there are clear hints that the priests might not be quite so benign). And, like Moore, Joyce presents a number of stories which have very limited plots, producing an image of the city as fragmented, but also consistently bleak. The narratives are apparently episodic, but they operate as part of a larger structure. The limitations on personal freedoms that Joyce's characters experience are played out in different ways according to the age and social positioning, the temperament and the contexts of the characters, but they recur as a series of *leitmotifs* in the text. *Leitmotif* is a musical term referring to the repetitions (with differences and variations) of particular musical themes during the course of a symphony. At its simplest, in Joyce's work this device takes the form of repeated images which demonstrate the closed-in, limited lives that are being described. One example is in 'Eveline', where the phrase 'odour of dusty cretonne' is repeated. It describes the curtains in Eveline's home, curtains which close out the view and suffocate her ambition to escape to Buenos Aires and the arms of her romantic lover. The phrase represents, without explaining (it doesn't need to explain), her stasis and entrapment. But as a whole, the collection is also strongly focused on death – the end of life, but also lives wasted, in the Coleridgian phrase, in death in life.

In this section, then, we are suggesting that Joyce's collection overspills the limits of the short-story form. The one thing that all commentators are agreed on is that the short story must be *short*. For the early theorists of the mode, there were even attempts to state precisely how short it must be, as we have seen with Poe in particular. Joyce's individual stories obey Poe's rule about taking half an hour to two hours to read, but the collection as a whole tests the boundaries of that limitation and develops the genre in particular ways. The collection constructs a thematic coherence which is meant as a damning indictment of the narrowness of this paradoxically provincial capital city, a diagnosis of its many problems. As with Lawrence and Mansfield, and in common with many modernist writers, the diagnosis does not come with a cure. The collection is beautifully made, but it is also nihilistic. Compared with Mansfield's wit and occasionally joyous sense of the absurd, Joyce's is a much bleaker vision.

'The Sisters' is the first of the stories in Joyce's *Dubliners* collection. It opens, characteristically, with a death; it would appear that the modernists were much preoccupied with death, one way or another:

> There was no hope for him this time: it was the third stroke. Night after night I had passed the house (it was vacation time) and studied the lighted square window: and night after night I had found it lighted in the same way, faintly and evenly. If he was dead, I thought, I would see the reflection of candles on the darkened blind for I knew that two candles must be set at the head of a corpse. He had often said to me: *I am not long for this world*, and I had thought the words idle. Now I knew they were true. Every night as I gazed up at the window I said softly to myself the word *paralysis*. It had always sound strangely in my ears, like the word *gnomon* in the Euclid, and the word *simony* in the Catechism. But now it sounded to me like the name of some maleficent and sinful being. It filled me with fear and yet I longed to be nearer to it and to look upon its deadly work. (p. 1)[23]

The narrator is a man looking back on his younger self, describing that self from a perspective which is not precisely the same as the perspective he would have had at the time. He is remembering and recalling his feelings rather than reliving them. And there's much that we could make of the particular words that the narrating persona testifies fascinated his younger self: 'paralysis', 'gnomon' and 'simony'. Paralysis, as Joyce himself remarked in a letter to Constance P. Doran in 1904, was part of the schema of *Dubliners* – both its theme and its mode of writing: 'I am writing a series of epicleti – ten – for a paper ... I call the series *Dubliners* to betray the soul of that hemiplegia or paralysis which many consider a city.'[24] 'Epicleti' is a word from the Greek Orthodox Church; it refers to a moment during the service when the Holy Spirit is invoked. Joyce appears to be suggesting in *Dubliners* that there is no guarantee that the Holy Spirit will appear to order. Its sense also seems to be close to that of the word 'epiphany' as Joyce used it (see below), and the use of religious words does seem to speak to Joyce's sense of writing as a vocation. As he suggested in a letter to his brother:

> Don't you think ... there is a certain resemblance between the mystery of the Mass and what I am trying to do? I mean that I am trying ... to give some kind of intellectual pleasure or spiritual enjoyment by converting the bread of everyday life into something that has a permanent artistic life of its own ... for their mental, moral and spiritual uplift.[25]

On the one hand, then, the concern of the *Dubliners* collection is with paralysis – with stasis and immobility. Most of the characters we encounter are figured as trapped or stuck in a rut, often of their own making, though equally often the result of material circumstances beyond their control. Their individual failings make up the failings of the whole city, since a city, that most modern of spaces, must be the sum of its parts, and most of all the sum of its inhabitants and their failings. In addition, though, there is an attempt to see something spiritual in this world of squalor and despair (Joyce admitted that 'the odour of ashpits and old weeds and offal' hung around his stories[26]), though the epiphanies through which this spiritual dimension might be accessed are often vouchsafed not so much to the protagonists as to the reader. After all, many of the protagonists are inarticulate, able to feel their pains and pleasures but not to describe them.

But there are two other words which the narrator of 'The Sisters' focuses on with childlike wonder: 'gnomon' and 'simony'. A gnomon, according to the Concise Oxford dictionary, is a 'pillar, rod or pin, or plate of sundial, showing time by its shadow on marked surface; ... [or] part of a parallelogram left when similar one has been taken from its corner'. The focus here might be on a measure of time, or it might be on the 'something that is missing' from the shape, the point being that much of the *Dubliners* collection is about missing connections and missing links in the process of the narration – often figured by ellipsis (the typographical signal in three dots of something omitted, for instance from a quotation, or a convention for signalling hesitation in speech). For Dominic Head, the gnomon is certainly to be read as the geometric shape which is missing a section. This does not, however, provide the clue to the stories, as a missing jigsaw piece would complete the puzzle. The absence of the missing element is precisely the point of Joyce's 'gnomonic' principle, Head suggests, and speaks to 'an ambivalent narrative stance which precludes any simple interpretation because the ambivalence ... is usually an integral part of Joyce's purpose'.[27]

'Simony' is another religious term, this time referring to the sin of selling ecclesiastical preferment – jobs in the church or indulgences (attempts to circumvent periods in Purgatory after death). So paralysis is one of the things *Dubliners* is about, but so is ellipsis, and so is corruption, both religious and in other forms, the opening paragraph seems to imply. As we read on in 'The Sisters', this view of the story and the collection which it heads might well be cemented by the fact that it is certainly implied that the priest whose death is signalled by the third stroke is perhaps a corrupt and dangerous influence on the young boy who tells this story, as hinted at by the comments of Old Cotter, who regards Father Flynn as 'one of those ... peculiar cases ... but it's hard to say ...', and who comments but does not elaborate that 'I wouldn't like children of mine ... to have too much to say to a man like that' (p. 2, ellipses in original). The reasons for the distrust are not stated. The reader has to intuit or guess, as the reader has to intuit or guess with pretty much all the stories. There are explanations left out, and there are multiple instances of both corruption and paralysis in the fictions that *Dubliners* presents.

'The Sisters' also opens with a striking scene of haunting, a reference back to one of the traditional uses of the short-story form, the ghost story or weird tale, though it is extremely different from the hauntings to be found, say, in the Victorian short story. The young narrator suffers nightmare visions of the dead priest, Father Flynn:

> It was late when I fell asleep [...] I was angry with old Cotter for allud-ing to me as a child [and] I *puzzled my head to extract meaning from his unfinished sentences. In the dark of my room I imagined that I saw again the heavy grey face of the paralytic.* I drew the blankets over my head and tried to think of Christmas. But *the grey face still followed me. It murmured; and I understood that it desired to confess something.* I felt my soul receding into some pleasant and vicious region; and there again I found it waiting for me. It began to confess to me in a murmuring voice and I wondered why it smiled continually and why the lips were so moist with spittle. But then I remembered that *it had died of paralysis and I felt that I too was smiling feebly as if to absolve the simo-niac of his sin.* (p. 3, our emphasis)

The narrator is haunted both by the 'ghost' of the priest and by the uncanny feeling that there is something that he does not know – some-thing missing, as in the figure of the gnomon. He also notes both par-alysis and simony in his vision, returning to the theme that the story established in its first paragraph. 'The Sisters' is structured like a musical piece, repeating and returning to themes that at first seemed random. And the collection as a whole, and the last story in particular, operate in a similar way. Readers should note the number of characters haunted by dead people from their pasts – from Eveline, haunted by her mother's memory and paralysed because of it, to Mr Duffy in 'A Painful Case', who recollects the woman who might have been his mistress if only he had had the courage to pursue his desire, to Maria, the elderly spinster of 'Clay', who is unconsciously haunted and hemmed in by her own imminent mortality.

A collection that opens with an evocation of death and which contains the haunting of a young boy's dreams ends with a story explicitly entitled 'The Dead'. This story appears quite different from many of the others. Unlike much of the rest of the collection, which focuses on deprivation, material, moral, spiritual and emotional, and unlike most of the rest of the characters who appear in *Dubliners*, this story focuses on a protagonist whose material circumstances are more or less comfortable.Unlike in most of the other stories, the focus is not on the extremes that people go to when they are driven by circumstances to act (or not to act) in particular ways. This story is about a man who has choices, and the social setting of the story (a party) helps situate him as a middle-class man whose social and economic positions are secure – although he is not necessarily secure in other ways, as we shall discover.

The party and dance take place at the house of two ageing ladies, Gabriel Conroy's aunts, Julia and Kate Morkan, and their niece, Mary Jane, who is younger than they are, but who is none the less middle-aged (she has lived with her aunts for thirty years the narrative tells us); it is an annual event, a punctuation of the year – measuring time as the gnomon does in its primary meaning. This party is held in the days immediately after the Christmas festivities. Christmas, of course, celebrates a birth, but it is also a time for remembrance of things past, and for ghost stories (it is a typical setting and time of year for the telling of ghostly tales, as multiple examples from the Victorian period attest). Thus although the party is about pleasure, it looks both backwards and forwards – to the dead who have gone (Gabriel tells an anecdote about his dead grandfather) and to the new beginnings, which might also be endings, in the new year. Hints of mortality are everywhere in the very language that is used as part of the ordinary run of conversation (our emphasis):

– O Mr Conroy, said Lily... Miss Kate and Miss Julia thought you were never coming...
– I'll engage they did, said Gabriel, but they forget that my wife takes three *mortal* hours to dress herself. (p. 176)

Kate and Julia came toddling down the dark stairs at once. Both of them kissed Gabriel's wife, said she must be *perished* alive and asked was Gabriel with her. (p. 177)

He was their favourite nephew, *son of their dead elder sister*, Ellen, who had married T. J. Conroy of the Port and Docks. (p. 179)

– *The coffin*, said Mary Jane, *is to remind them of their last end.*
As the subject had grown lugubrious it was *buried* in a silence of the table ... (p. 202, a discussion over the dinner table of the habits of monks who sleep in coffins)

> – Close the door somebody. Mrs Malins will *get her death of cold*. (p. 207, at the end of the night)

These are small details, but they orchestrate the sense that death and dying are central themes, even in the midst of a party at which every year family friends and Mary Jane's musical pupils gather to enjoy the hospitality of the Morkan family. The key guest is the older ladies' nephew, Gabriel Conroy, who comes to the party as the oldest available male member of the family (and therefore as a kind of head of the family), to carve the goose, to ensure that none of the guests becomes troublesome through drink (another consistent theme of *Dubliners* is drunkenness) and to propose a vote of thanks to the hostesses.

The vote of thanks is about the past as well, in particular the Irish tradition of hospitality. But it is also about the loss of that tradition through death, figured via the imminent loss of those who represent the tradition. While Gabriel wants to celebrate the present in his praise of his aunts and cousin, he also – sentimentally and, it turns out, ironically – draws attention to the dead who are only present through memory:

> there are always in gatherings such as this sadder thoughts that will recur to our minds: thoughts of the past, of youth, of changes, of absent faces that we miss here tonight. Our path through life is strewn with many such sad memories: and were we to brood upon them always we could not find the heart to go on bravely with our work among the living ...
> – Therefore I will not linger on the past. I will not let any gloomy moralising intrude upon us here to-night. (p. 205)

Gabriel is, of course, wrong. He will brood on the past, because who he is is a function precisely of who he has been, and his own past and his wife's past intrude upon the present.

The party itself is evoked with careful attention to social detail that would grace any realist writer's need for detailism. The foibles and oddities of the various guests are dramatised. For instance, we see the anxieties of the older ladies about whether one of their guests, Freddy Malins,

is going to arrive inebriated (as indeed he does), and we see something of
the curious bad temper of the serving girl, who appears to be out of sorts
with men in general, though no reason is given for her display of irritation. There are multiple small details about embarrassment in social
situations and about anxieties provoked by them. The details all appear
to be random. Lily's bitterness about men – 'The men that is now is only
all palaver and what they can get out of you' (p. 178) – seems to come
out of nowhere. But as one reads through the whole story, it becomes
clear that this young woman's anger is a prolepsis (prediction or fore-
warning) of what Gabriel is about to discover about his own inadequacies in the present compared with his wife's first lover, Michael Furey,
who represents the virtues of the past. Thus, what seem to be random
details – even down to the fact that the two 'rivals' for Gretta's love
both have the names of archangels (Michael and Gabriel) – are actually
not random at all: this is a closely constructed story, and it completes a
closely constructed collection of stories in which themes and techniques
are repeated with differences throughout the set of tales. The party is a
great success, despite Freddy Malins's drunkenness, despite Lily's annoyance with men, despite the introduction of contentious political issues
into the party by Miss Ivors, and despite the refusal of the tenor Bartell
D'Arcy to sing for the company (he has a bad cold). But the real point of
the story is what happens after the ball is over. The party only appears
to be centrally important because it is the catalyst for other issues and
because it signals those issues, in part through the songs that are sung
and the music that is played – in other words, the message is produced
by allusion rather than by direct explanation. And this is a reversal
of the norms of narrative in the nineteenth century, in which large
social events are often central planks of plotting. Here, the real story is
slightly offstage; it is taking place elsewhere, in a manner which perhaps
Katherine Mansfield also picked up in her story 'The Garden Party'.

Because this is a party, music plays a central part – though it is also
slightly offstage in the narrative, since the protagonist on whom we
focus is not himself a musician. The purpose of the party, alongside the
general ideal of hospitality, is to provide a forum for Mary Jane's musical
pupils and for Mary Jane herself (she plays a virtuoso piece that Gabriel
doesn't listen to). But other music is also played, including the poignant
rendition by Julia Morkan of the opera song 'Arrayed for the Bridal' (by
Bellini). In this image of an elderly lady singing a song about waiting
for a marriage, there is, of course, an echo of the song sung by Maria in
'Clay': 'I Dreamt That I Dwelt in Marble Halls', which speaks of a desire
for material and emotional comforts of which Maria is so deprived that
she does not even recognise her own deprivation. In both cases, the

songs have ironic effects because they are evocations of the lives which both these women might have lived (if they had married) but did not live. Julia's song is about promise and hope, but this is elliptical because the song is evoked, not quoted:

Arrayed for the Bridal

Arrayed for the bridal, in beauty behold her
A white wreath entwineth a forehead more fair;
I envy the zephyrs that softly enfold her,
And play with the locks of her beautiful hair.
May life to her prove full of sunshine and love.
Who would not love her?
Sweet star of the morning, shining so bright
Earth's circle adorning, fair creature of light![28]

That hope has led nowhere for Aunt Julia. Her singing has been rejected by her church, and her own life has led to no wedding day. As Gabriel reviews the day's events at the end of the story, moreover, he predicts his aunt's death:

Poor Aunt Julia! She, too, would soon be a shade with the shade of Patrick Morkan and his horse. He had caught that haggard look upon her face for a moment when she was singing *Arrayed for the Bridal*. Soon, perhaps, he would be sitting in that same drawing-room, dressed in black, his silk hat on his knees. The blinds would be drawn down and Aunt Kate would be sitting beside him, crying and blowing her nose and telling him how Julia had died. *He would cast about in his mind for some words that might console her, and would find only lame and useless ones.* Yes, yes: that would happen very soon. (p. 224)

The words that are spoken are useless in situations such as this, but the words that are set to music evoke a whole different set of possibilities, memories and ideas. And this is the focus of one of the story's epiphanies. Aunt Julia is partially transformed by her song; she is an accomplished singer. But she is also a figure predicting her own death. This partial transformation of an older woman predicts the similar transformation of Gretta Conroy as she listens to the 'distant music' of Bartell D'Arcy's song. In both cases, the musical transformation is illusory and open to misinterpretation. The listener who hears Aunt Julia sing might believe her to be in her prime; the watcher who watches Gretta hear 'distant music' misinterprets that scene as well.

As the guests are leaving, then, one of the last to leave, Miss O'Callaghan, persuades Bartell D'Arcy to sing for her. He sings part of a song called 'The Lass of Aughrim' before his voice gives out because of his cold. While D'Arcy is singing, Gabriel, in the hallway downstairs, watches his wife, who is listening intently to the music, clearly moved by the song, and with tears in her eyes. His assumption is that it is the romantic sentiment of the song which has touched her, and he has great hopes that influence is going to mean the rekindling of the physical passion of their marriage. This image of the woman listening to music is what we might identify as a kind of epiphany in the story – though it is a misleading moment.

> He stood in the gloom of the hall, trying to catch the air that the voice was singing and gazing up at his wife. There was grace and mystery in her attitude *as if she were a symbol of something.* He asked himself, what is a woman standing on the stairs in the shadow, listening to distant music, a symbol of. If he were a painter, he would paint her in that attitude. Her blue felt hat would show off the bronze of her hair against the darkness and the dark panels of her skirt would show off the light ones. *Distant Music* he would call the picture, if he were a painter. (p. 211, our emphasis)

A quite mundane and ordinary scene – a familiar woman standing on the stairs listening to music – has become invested with significance and strangeness (and one could say that this is nearly uncanny). The significance of the woman, though, is obscure: Gabriel identifies her as a symbol, but he cannot say what she is a symbol of. He sees her as a painting, probably a Whistler,[29] a work of art, fixed in a single moment of perfection (wholeness, harmony and clarity). And he is roused (sexually, aesthetically and emotionally) by this image, though there is irony at work here, since his image of his wife is precisely that: *his* image. He has not understood the real meaning of her emotion at D'Arcy's song. In Joyce's aborted novel, *Stephen Hero*, we see a definition of the epiphany, and the scene at the party has all the elements that Joyce identified as significant in epiphanic moments:

> By an epiphany he meant a sudden spiritual manifestation, whether in the vulgarity of speech or of gesture or in a memorable phrase of the mind itself. He believed that it was for the man of letters to record these epiphanies with extreme care, seeing that they themselves are the most delicate and evanescent of moments.[30]

When they return to their hotel room that night, it becomes apparent that Gabriel has misinterpreted this apparently epiphanic moment. His interpretation (his wife is a symbol of, and therefore shares, his desire) has nothing to do with the emotions that are actually called into being by Bartell D'Arcy's song. The song, of which only snatches are quoted in the story, concerns an Irish woman betrayed by an English lord. She carries an illegitimate child back to her former lover, who refuses to acknowledge either woman or child. It is – one might say – a haunting melody. As in many Victorian short stories, the song's narrative of a romantic trauma could be the 'back story' for a haunting of a more literal kind. And so it turns out, though in this story the ghost is not realised as an actual figure. Michael Furey now exists only in Gretta's memory, and in the emotions which are recalled by the song and which are provoked by Gabriel's response to his wife's lost love. The song evokes the presence of the dead man both because he used to sing it and because the situation it describes is so similar to the last time that Gretta saw him. The scene on the stairs, then, far from rekindling the passion of the Conroys' marriage, points out its inadequacies. Gabriel is a fussy commonplace man, obsessed with health, comfort and 'taking care': he insists on his wife wearing galoshes, takes a room in a hotel rather than risk her catching cold in a taxi, and fusses over his children's health, making them take exercise and eat 'stirabout' porridge. His fear of mortality, signalled by these elaborate (and, of course, futile) gestures to stave off death, contrasts with the devil-may-care attitude of Michael Furey, who did not care about the minor issue of his own mortality, who got soaked to the skin and caught pneumonia in the service of a romantic gesture for the woman who has become Gabriel's wife. Michael Furey, then, appears – at least to Gretta – as heroic in his decision to court death for love. The story as a whole, though, perhaps reserves judgement. Since death is as general as the snow that cloaks the whole of Ireland at the end of the collection, perhaps the romantic gesture is as futile as the practical, pragmatic ones by which Gabriel lives his life.

Like a musical symphony, 'The Dead' operates by returning to what it has earlier described: words are used in part in the way a musical theme is used in classical music. The story also picks up *leitmotifs* from earlier parts of the collection. The dead in 'The Dead' are shown to be both others who have been significant in the past and have died and the living who are – it is the human condition – journeying towards death. As modernist short stories, the tales of *Dubliners* demonstrate the Janus-faced nature the modernist project: its explicit rejection of the conventions of the past alongside the fact that the past has a presence that cannot be wholly removed.

Are they short stories at all? Virginia Woolf

> it is impossible to say 'this is comic', or 'that is tragic', nor are we certain, since short stories, we have been taught, should be brief and conclusive, whether this, which is vague and inconclusive, should be called a short story at all.[31]

These are the words of Virginia Woolf, discussing and describing a story by Anton Chekhov. Her discussion is frankly approving, though this snippet perhaps does not make that clear. The story in question is called 'Gusev', and in Woolf's rendition of it, it tells of some Russian soldiers, ill onboard ship: 'we are given a few scraps of their talk and some of their thoughts; then one of them dies and is carried away' (p. 10).[32] There is more talk and another death, and the second dead soldier is thrown overboard. That is all. There is no message, and 'the emphasis is laid upon such unexpected places that at first it seems as if there were no emphasis at all' (p. 12). This is certainly an accurate description of Chekhov; there is also a sense in which it stands as a clear depiction of Woolf's own technique in the short story.

Virginia Woolf, a prominent member of the Bloomsbury set, is better known for her innovative and radical novels of the high modernist period, such as *Mrs Dalloway* (1925), *To the Lighthouse* (1927) and *The Waves* (1931), than for her short stories. However, as Laura Marcus and others have recently noted, her experimentation in the genre of short fiction not only enabled her to break from the conventions of the traditional novel but also contributed to the development of the modernist short story and her 'shaping of a modern aesthetic'.[33] With her ongoing emphasis on the experiences and rhythms of ordinary life, and her feminist commitment to mapping out women's territory in the modern world, she is a fit companion to Katherine Mansfield and shared the latter's admiration for Chekhov's technique: its refusal of 'emphasis' offered, she felt, a new way of writing fiction, in particular a form of fiction that was not to any significant degree in thrall to plot. Like Chekhov's, Woolf's short stories break new ground by refusing to dwell on the traditional grand narratives such as marriage, property or social progress. There is, however, a difference of tone between Woolf and the Russian writer. She described her writing of short stories as 'the treats I allowed myself when I had done my exercise in the conventional style'[34] at a time when she was struggling with writing one of her first novels, *Night and Day* (1919), and she frequently referred to the composition of short stories in terms of intoxicating freedom: Chekhov's works were never so light-hearted. Although she began writing stories in 1906, her most assured stories were produced between 1917 and 1920 and appeared in the only collection published in her lifetime, *Monday or Tuesday* (1921). She continued to earn good money from publication in American magazines such as *Harper's Bazaar* in the 1930s, which printed more satirical stories such as 'The Duchess and the Jeweller' (1938) and 'The Shooting Party' (1938). Unlike the stories of Chekhov and Mansfield, her narratives tend to fill only a few pages, with some distinctively pared down to only a few lines of print, notably the very unusual 'Blue and Green' (1921), which consists of two paragraphs of poetic descriptions of green and blue creatures, objects and moods.

As Tim Armstrong has argued, by the period of high modernism, around the late 1910s and early 1920s, 'the short story has become definitional to modernism: epiphanic, ambiguous, formally perfect – but still a basic unit of magazine publication', its quality unable to be dissociated 'from a consumer culture in which it identifies a particular audience'.[35] Since Woolf was also a publisher (she ran the Hogarth Press with her husband Leonard), she was more aware than most writers of this 'consumer culture', and deliberately tried to move away from the commercial considerations of printing presses in Hogarth's commitment to fine editions of her own and other writers' work. 'Kew Gardens', one of her best-known stories, was first published in 1919 as a Hogarth Press pamphlet with woodcuts by Vanessa Bell (Woolf's sister), before appearing in *Monday or Tuesday*. As the *Times Literary Supplement* reviewer noted of this original publication format, it was 'a work of art, made, "created" ... a thing of original and therefore strange beauty, with its own "atmosphere", its own vital force'.[36] The story consists of a series of fragments from the conversations of a disparate range of characters walking past an oval flowerbed in the Gardens one July day before the end of the war, and as such it predicts the interlocking dramatic monologues that make up T. S. Eliot's *über*-modernist poem *The Waste Land* (1922). It reveals isolated memories linked to the July day through the technique of stream of consciousness, such as the parallel lives which might have been for the married couple who remember earlier courtships and a first kiss. As the wife remarks, 'Doesn't one always think of the past, in a garden with men and women lying under the trees? Aren't they one's past, all that remains of it, those men and women, those ghosts lying under the trees ... one's happiness, one's reality?' (p. 12).

Woolf juxtaposes different kinds of conversation to evoke both social distinctions and the effects of war on society. The eccentric, possibly shell-shocked, older man 'murmuring about forests of Uruguay blanketed with the wax petals of tropical roses, nightingales, sea beaches, mermaids, and women drowned at sea' (p. 14) is moved on by his patient son, and is followed by two elderly women, pointedly bracketed as 'of the lower middle class', whose 'very complicated dialogue' is reduced to the names of family and friends and cheap food items such as kippers and sugar (p. 14). The framing of these conversations, which fade to the 'wordless voices' of the final paragraph, with the progress of a snail across the flowerbed and the careful patterning of colours and sounds conveys the impressionistic nature of the story and its proximity to the contemporary paintings of Matisse. As Adrian Hunter has argued, Woolf's open-ended narratives act as a 'deliberate provocation to the sort of unimaginative reader' who looks for clear signs of closure and resolution, so the short story becomes 'a form through which the practice of reading could be reformed', a reformation 'necessary to her own developing aesthetic project'.[37]

One such reader, perhaps, was novelist and occasional short-story writer E. M. Forster, who was particularly exercised by Woolf's story 'The Mark on the Wall' (1921). This story is another good example of the workings of stream of consciousness, the emphasis on the moment, on memory, on the rhythms of ordinary life, with the narrator's musings flowing from the nature of the mark in question (revealed in the final sentence to be a snail, though this revelation is, of course, far less important than the thoughts it throws up and inspires). Marcus characterises it as 'a highly self-conscious meditation on the ways in which narratives are constructed ... stand[ing] at the edge of the "stream of consciousness" so central to modernist narrative, so as to explore the extent to which identity and consciousness are separable'.[38] Woolf again signals that the story is about 'life', but here claims, in a suitably modernist analogy, that 'one must liken it to being blown through the Tube at fifty miles an hour – landing at the other end without a single hairpin in one's hair! ... Yes, that seems to express the rapidity of life, the perpetual waste and repair; all so casual, all so haphazard' (p. 4, ellipsis in original). The haphazard nature of experience, coupled with the rapidity resulting from huge advances in technology, signalled by the unprecedented speed of the new underground, produced the rather breathless, arbitrary collection of thoughts, from Shakespeare and the war to tablecloths, cows and water lilies we are presented with here. But characteristically the pleasant 'quiet, spacious world' (p. 8) that the narrator imagines cannot be sustained in the face of *Whitaker's Almanack*, 'an annually published book of factual information concerning the various ranks in public life', and marker of masculine materialism and conventionality,[39] which intrudes into the feminine sphere of Nature and the imagination.

Marcus's reading of this story accentuates its positive aesthetic effects. For Forster, on the other hand, it merely tells the reader that for Woolf, 'life is such a muddle, oh dear, the will is so weak, the sensations fidgety... philosophy... God... oh dear, look at the mark... listen to the door – existence... is really too... what were we saying?'[40] He does not damn her, but his mimicry of her style implies that he feels some limit has been reached. This is the same Forster who declared rather sadly that the novel had to tell a story; when the conventional story, in the sense of a narrative sequence of externally observable events, is missing, he finds himself perplexed and perhaps annoyed. Is something like 'The Mark on the Wall' actually a short story at all?

David Bradshaw asserts that in her stories Woolf 'focuses... on the disparity between an exterior, masculine world of action, fragmentation, and noise, and an interior feminine sphere of silence, contact, unity, and reflection', where the initial tranquillity of the narrative is often disrupted by loud reminders of 'the oppressive, ineluctable, mechanical grind of metropolitan experience'.[41] And that disparity between the masculine and the feminine is certainly part of what Woolf's stories emphasise. Sympathetic critics note her own view that 'the proper stuff of fiction is a little other than custom would have us believe it', and that she wished to escape the common constraints of fiction: 'to provide a plot, to provide comedy, tragedy, love interest, and an air of probability embalming the whole'.[42] Bradshaw's hint that she sought new material for fiction in the material conditions of modernity is a sensible one. Certainly, a number of her stories, such as 'Monday or Tuesday', 'Kew Gardens' and 'The Mark on the Wall', use the noise of public transport, the new omnibuses, trains, aeroplanes and underground, to signal mixed responses to the advances of recently urbanised culture. In 'An Unwritten Novel' (1920), the ungendered narrator speculates about the character of the woman sitting opposite on a train from London to the suburbs. Structuring a short story around a short train or omnibus journey was, as we have seen in previous chapters, an innovation of the 1890s which remained popular in the early twentieth century, allowing the reader the incomplete glimpses of other lives which travellers and commuters were rapidly becoming accustomed to. In this story the narrator cannot resist abandoning his or her reading of *The Times*, with its discussion of the end of the war, of railway accidents, murders and the cost of living, to imagine the details of the woman's life from their brief conversation: 'My eyes had once more crept over the paper's rim' (p. 18). The twist at the end of the tale is that the imagined identity of the woman traveller is far from the truth, prompting a reverie on the idea that such 'unknown figures' in any such urban encounter remain ineffable, unknowable:

> And yet the last look of them – he stepping from the kerb and she following him round the edge of the big building brims me with wonder – floods me anew. Mysterious figures! Mother and son. Who are you? Why do you walk down the street? Where tonight will you sleep, and then, tomorrow? Oh, how it whirls and surges – floats me afresh ... Wherever I go, mysterious figures, I see you, turning the corner, mothers and sons, you, you, you. (p. 28)

With a metafictional flourish, the story highlights the unknowability of others, while grounding this in the snap-shot nature of the short-story form, where what is omitted is essential to the meaning and depth of character can never be produced. Thus, it epitomises the modernist short story's compression of technique, which in turn implies a refusal to impose meaning.

As this chapter has suggested, the modernist short story is a very diverse cultural product and any attempt to define it in a few short sentences would belie that complexity. As the examples discussed here suggest, however, there are some common elements. The modernist form of short fiction emphasizes emotion and its evocation over event and its narration. It is more concerned with techniques of expression than its realist counterparts, making more explicit experimental use of the resources of language derived from poetry (image, symbol, rhythm and sound effects such as rhyme and assonance) for its emotional effects. It is not quite 'plotless' fiction but as the title question of the Woolf section implies, the modernist short story sometimes comes close to plot-lessness. At the same time, though, the modernist form is also indebted to its predecessors for both its topics and techniques. And as the next chapter shows, it had influences well beyond the cultural elites of the avant-garde, with its ghosts and echoes finding their way into even popular genre stories.

9
The Short Story and Genre Fiction: The Same Old Story?

> The magazine story is almost without exception a commercial article. Manufactured to a formula – those stories that show any art are seldom placed in magazines.[1]

> The two essentials for a story were a title and a plot – the rest was mere spade-work... The kind of story [the editor] wanted, and insisted on having (and incidentally paid handsomely for getting), was all about mysterious dark women, stabbed to the heart, a young hero unjustly suspected, and the sudden unravelling of the mystery and fixing of the guilt on the least likely person, by the means of wholly inadequate clues. (p. 224)[2]

The first of these two quotations is the answer of one of the respondents to a questionnaire sent out by Q. D. Leavis in the late 1920s when asked about the effect of magazine publication on short fiction. The respondents were all novelists, grouped by Leavis into a range from highbrow literary artists to those who were out-and-out commercial writers, avowing that they 'deliberately wrote fiction as a comfortable way of getting a good living, "with the minimum of exertion"'.[3] The second quotation is from one of Agatha Christie's non-detective short stories, 'Mr Eastwood's Adventure' (1932),[4] in which the eponymous hero is a writer working for the very magazines described in the first quotation. Mr Eastwood has writer's block, and is in search of a plot for his next commission; in the course of the story he embarks on a strange adventure which furnishes him with such a story, though he also ends up the victim of an audacious burglary, which is the result of precisely the kind of plot that his editor demands (a mysterious and beautiful woman in danger, himself as the hero apparently arrested for a crime, and so on). It shows the extent to which Christie, herself a very popular novelist and writer, was self-aware of the conventions of her chosen genres, to the extent even of making mockery of them in self-referential moments. In this chapter, then, we turn from the exquisite aestheticism and formal experimentation of the modernist short story to the popular forms of the short story in the twentieth century, though this contrast between what might be termed 'art' and 'craft' is not entirely secure, as the chapter will suggest.

The judgements made about popular genre fiction are often very harsh. Originality is highly prized both in the general culture and in the critical mind. If the writer is original, the critic has leeway to be original in his or her turn, noting the particular forms of newness which the writer has honed and crafted. But the short story's origins are in popular and profoundly unoriginal tales, beginning with oral story-telling traditions which, as Walter J. Ong suggests in *Orality and Literacy*, value tradition over innovation because the knowledge at the heart of the story is 'hard won' and meaningful in that it contains the lessons for survival in a dangerously contingent world.[5] As Jack Zipes has shown, those writers who made traditional folk tales into the far more 'literary' form of the fairy story from the seventeenth century onwards none the less maintained the formulae of the earlier oral form: the emphasis on patterning (three wishes, three little pigs, three tasks or trials), the location of the story in the 'long-ago and far-away' imaginary spaces of no place and no specific time, and characters who are stereotypical (handsome princes, beautiful princesses, wicked wolves, ghastly hags and witches) rather than the individualised and fully realised or rounded figures who are supposed to inhabit realist writing.[6]

The formulaic structure of a genre such as the fairy story has its virtues. Its usefulness for young readers, giving them a predictable structure for their first forays into reading, has even bred an entire critical tradition, of which Zipes is the leading figure. But there are disadvantages to it: it can be stale and moralistic, as the Saki short story discussed in Chapter 1 of this volume suggests. As readers become adults, they are increasingly expected to put away childish things, one of which is the predictable world of simple fictional forms. The critical weight in relation to fiction generally, and the short story in particular, is biased heavily towards writing which, in the terms of the Russian formalist critics, defamiliarises and destabilises the reader's expectations – for the formalists, indeed, this defamiliarised form of originality is the definition of literariness itself.[7]

Most readers, however, read for other reasons: for pleasure, for excitement and, paradoxically perhaps, for a certain kind of security. It is not accidental that in the early years of the twentieth century, despite the laments of the guardians of high culture (Q. D. Leavis's *Fiction and the Reading Public* of 1931 is a key text here), most readers turned to writing for entertainment. As Leavis notes, most people in the late 1920s and early 1930s read for the following reasons, and the ordering of her list is indicative of where the emphasis in their choices lay:

1. To pass time not unpleasantly.
2. To obtain vicarious satisfaction or compensation for life.
3. To obtain assistance in the business of living.
4. To enrich the quality of living by extending, deepening, refining, co-ordinating experience. (p. 48)

The primary choices of the general reading public in the 1920s and 1930s were the formulaic forms of genre fiction – in particular the detective story (which the twentieth century inherited and adapted from nineteenth-century precursors such as Edgar Allan Poe and Arthur Conan Doyle), adventure and spy stories (derived from nineteenth-century models in the magazines aimed specifically at gendered markets, such as the *Boys' Own* and *Girls' Own Paper* franchises, which saw a major resurgence in the wake of the First World War), the weird tale, which drew on the tradition of Victorian ghost stories, and the romance (the boy-meets-girl story which has been a staple of magazines aimed at women since the nineteenth-century). The detective story in particular had become a best-selling form, to the extent that its popular exponents in the inter-war period, Agatha Christie, Dorothy L. Sayers (1893–1957), Margery Allingham (1904–66) and the New Zealand writer Ngaio Marsh (1895–1982), combined popularity and huge sales with – in some cases – a measure of literary ambition, leading most critics of the genre to refer to the period as the 'Golden Age' of detective writing. And the detective form spawned its near-relative the thriller, in which the emphasis is on the excitement of the adventure rather than the quasi-intellectual enjoyment of solving the puzzle. The genres are very mixed up: detective fiction shades into thriller and spy story, for instance, and romance can be a backdrop to any of the other genres. But what they all share is being written so that readers can 'pass time not unpleasantly' and escape for a moment from the mundanity of diurnal existence.

For Leavis, this popularity of mass-produced genre fiction for a mass audience represents an expensive waste of time and a stilling of intellectual effort. She was, after all, the inheritor of a Victorian tradition which believed above all that the reading of fiction should be rationed and that when it was read, reading should be limited to the finest writing – the early-twentieth-century version of Matthew Arnold's phrase 'the best that has been thought and said', the discrimination of which he identified as the 'Function of Criticism' in an essay published as early as 1869. The detective story Leavis dismissed as the fictional equivalent of the cryptic crossword puzzle, which also became popular as a pastime in the newspapers of the 1920s. Her negative judgement on the value of pure entertainment is perhaps unwarranted, but Leavis was none the less an astute commentator on the reading habits of the general public. There is, for instance, certainly a link between crosswords and detection, as she suggests, which is clearly visible in some of the Agatha Christie 'Miss Marple' stories.[8] For example, in the story which first introduces this unlikely detective, an elderly spinster in a Home Counties village, 'The Tuesday Night Club', the clue that alerts Miss Marple to the identity of the murderer would not be out of place in a crossword. The murderer has been discovered, by means of blotting paper, to have written a letter containing the words *'Entirely dependent on my wife...she is dead I will...hundreds and thousands ...'.*[9] Most of the Tuesday night commentators regard this as a reference to the money the husband will inherit from the murder of his wife; only Miss Marple pays attention to the fact that the supper which poisoned the woman was rounded off with trifle. Her domesticated mind recalls what they have forgotten, that hundreds and thousands can also refer to the sugar strands which traditionally decorate this dessert. On this occasion, it is in these strands that the poison is placed on the trifle: for the others, it is indeed an unconsidered trifle, but for Miss Marple it is the telling detail. This is exactly how a crossword clue operates, misleading by contextual interpretation away from the real meaning. If the modernist story requires readers to interpret the tiny details of images and sound clusters poetically and thereby potentially uncover a version of life that is 'enriched, extended, deepened, refined', the reader of the detective short story reads the tiny details for the purpose of uncovering malefaction. Readers participate in the game for the intellectual satisfaction of uncovering the murderer and for the cosseting reassurance that murder and crime will always be detected, prosecuted and punished. The detective story in these terms is a conservative form, since it offers strong evidence for the ordering of the universe, in contrast with the absurdity and futility that modernist experimentation articulated.[10]

The reduction of violence to a puzzle, however, was also part of the objection to the detective form. As Stephen Knight puts it, violence is 'euphemized' out of existence by the puzzle struggle: 'The game-like features of the novel are forceful enough to dilute the real strength of the threats that are played with. Only the most technically and aesthetically strained processes can present so complete a puzzle.'[11] The force of Knight's remark is that the picture contained within the fiction falsifies the real, and that it does so by 'artificial' and 'strained' means; in other words, the detective genre is both aesthetically and technically weak.

This chapter focuses on two popular writers of the early twentieth century and beyond, Agatha Christie and Daphne du Maurier. Both women wrote a great deal of short fiction; du Maurier, indeed, began her career as a writer with short stories, believing that they would be easier to write than longer fiction, and she used them as a kind of apprenticeship.[12] Her early collections are not now much read, but, of course, du Maurier's short and long fiction – atmospheric, romantic and often weird or uncanny – has had an afterlife as the inspiration for film. In particular, 'The Birds' (1952) attracted the creepy black-and-white attention of Alfred Hitchcock, and 'Don't Look Now' (1970), a relatively late story, was filmed in equally creepy Technicolor by Nicholas Roeg in 1973 (the colour matters, since the red of a child's – or dwarf's – coat, glimpsed out of the corner of one's eye, is the symptom of what appears, at first glance, to be a haunting). Christie was the more popular and commercial writer, selling vast numbers of novels in large volumes and finding a ready market even for her short fictions, a form which is notoriously difficult to place in comparison to the novel.[13] What is significant in both cases here, though, is their relationship with popular genres: the detective story, of course, in the case of Agatha Christie; the romance and its offshoots in that of du Maurier.

Formulae and the power of fiction: Agatha Christie

Christie, in contrast to du Maurier, began with longer fiction, introducing her famous detective Hercule Poirot in his first case in a novel, *The Mysterious Affair at Styles*, in 1921. Miss Marple, on the other hand, makes her initial appearances in a number of short stories, originally commissioned for magazine publication in the mid- and late 1920s and later collected under the title *The Thirteen Problems* in 1932 (or *The Tuesday Night Club Murders* in America); only in 1930 does she become the heroine of the longer form. The structure of these stories is exactly what one would expect of genre fiction: they are formulaic and repetitive. For the point about genre is precisely that it is repetitive: only by repetition of structure and plot elements can genre itself be defined. And it is the repetition that readers enjoy while critics demur.

'Genre' is a word that is bandied about a lot in English studies. It comes from the French for 'type' or 'kind', and we use it in two distinct ways. First, it is used to define or describe the type or kind of form in which a given literary text is written. That is, the genre of a text is defined in terms of its form as poetry, drama or prose, novel, short story, sonnet, epic and so on. As this kind of designation is particularly obvious – we can usually tell straightaway what genre a text belongs to in terms of form – one might wonder why we bother. It does matter, though, even if it matters in somewhat instrumental ways. If, for instance, you happen to be the kind of reader for whom poetry has no attraction, a title such as *The Complete Poems of Sylvia Plath* is unlikely to fill you with excitement, and even more unlikely to make you part with your cash at the bookstore till. Within that basic formal division, however, there are always subdivisions. And it's the subdivisions that make the process of studying genre interesting.

Genre and its subdivisions matter for a number of reasons, some of which are purely practical. From a publisher's point of view, they matter because the genre of a novel, for example, determines how it is marketed – where on the shelves of the bookstore it is to be found. And they matter from a buyer's point of view because readers might not know much about literature, but they often know what they like. Most readers go back again and again to the types of fiction they know from experience that they like. What I'm buying when I buy a novel by, say, Agatha Christie, as opposed to one by Terry Pratchett, is the knowledge that I'm unlikely to be disappointed because I know what to expect: the very name of the author, as well as the book's cover (which is part of its marketing), provides what might be termed a 'horizon of expectation'. And if Agatha Christie had suddenly started to write bonk-busters, or sword-and-sorcery novels, or Mills & Boon books, her readership would have been very disappointed.

All of this sounds as though it might be trivial, but it isn't. These practical, economic considerations (the booking-buying market and its expectations) are (or should be) very important in literary studies. Because genre gives the reader a horizon of expectation, those expectations are extremely significant to how we read and judge. Any reasonably experienced reader would be able to identify the genre of a fiction from its cover, its author and its place on the shelves before the book is even opened. The introductory paragraphs will usually reassure us of the correctness of our identification. If we take the example of the detective story, we also know it belongs to that genre because we know other examples of that genre; we situate the novel or short story as a detective fiction because we know from other examples we have encountered that detective novels behave in particular ways. Genre thus teaches us how to read: what to look for, and what to think about what we find. The point is that form or genre can actually create meaning for the reader inasmuch as form or genre creates our perception of the text. Our expectations might be met or, in more interesting varieties, might be subverted. In either case the expectations have to exist.

For Christie, the short-story form was one on which she had interesting views. She felt that the form did not entirely suit the detective story, in addition to producing very practical problems in terms of finding a publisher, an audience and a commercially viable format. In her *Autobiography* (1977), she writes of the pragmatic as well as the aesthetic problems of the short form:

> Of course, there is a right length for everything. I think myself that the *right* length for a detective story [novel] is 50,000 words. I know this is considered by publishers as too short. Possibly readers feel themselves cheated if they pay their money and only get 50,000 words… 20,000 words for a long short story is an excellent length for a thriller. Unfortunately there is less and less market for stories of that size, and the authors tend not to be particularly well paid… The short story technique, I think, is not really suited to the detective story at all. A thriller, possibly – but a detective story no.[14]

This did not, of course, stop her from providing detective stories in the shorter form. Nor did it prevent her contemporary Dorothy L. Sayers writing short stories for her detective, Lord Peter Wimsey, and there must have been an audience for them because otherwise the publishers would not have played ball.[15] The majority of the Miss Marple stories come in at considerably fewer than the 20,000 words mentioned above (4,000–7,000 words is typical, and some are considerably shorter); like the quick crossword, they are coffee-break or bus-journey reading. This was almost certainly a response to the much more confined space permitted to short-fiction writers in magazines. But it was also a deliberate choice. The majority of the cases are relatively simple and do not require much elaboration.

In each of the early Miss Marple stories, one of six people, including Miss Marple, her nephew, his fiancé and a collection of local worthies (a doctor, solicitor and vicar), tells a story about a crime and requires his or her audience to solve it from the clues that are liberally scattered through the narrative. The nephew is an especially interesting minor character, since he is a novelist of the 'modern' tendency, with an interest in psychoanalysis and a strong assumption that all violent crime is basically motivated by sex. This, it would seem, is Christie's sly dig at the modernist avant-garde who sneered at her kind of fiction, for Miss Marple, of course, is much shrewder than her elderly persona and fussy demeanour would suggest and solves the crimes, whereas her nephew's more obviously intellectual approach does not. She has learned the fullness of human wickedness despite her closeted life in an English village – this is Raymond Williams's 'knowable community'[16] with a vengeance, and no one knows it better than Jane Marple – and she solves the problems offered on every occasion, much to the surprise of the audience of her supposed intellectual superiors.[17] Not only is the community knowable, but so too are the characters who compose it, characters who might have psychological complexity and secrets (why else would they commit crimes or unwittingly lay red herrings?) but who are still open to rational explanation. In the words of Marion Shaw and Sabine Vanacker:

> When everybody's identity has been established without a shadow of a doubt, it becomes easy to identify the motive for murder and hence the killer…a more secure world is created because the truth about everyone has been ascertained and any unease and doubt has been located and expelled in the figure of the murderer.[18]

With the first Miss Marple story, the pattern is *set* (that word is used advisedly). In later examples the Tuesday Night Club has been disbanded and Miss Marple works alone through problems brought to her door by a variety of troubled souls, but the basic situation remains the same: a story is told and interpreted by the arch-critic/detective Jane Marple, who knows her community and neighbours and by extension therefore also knows human nature and human society more generally. Both character and community are understood as stable and timeless (in fairly stark contrast to the versions of both elements in modernist writing). To some extent, the world Miss Marple lives in is a fairy-tale world of nostalgia for a past that never quite existed. Although Christie wrote in her autobiography that villages like St Mary Mead existed and continued (just) to exist, they also serve the function of 'long ago and [therefore] far away' which is signalled in the 'once-upon-a-time beginning'. Miss Marple herself is a fairy godmother (or a witch) – and what sharp eyes she has, and what a nose for scandal and what an ear for significant gossip. And one of the things her narratives embody for readers is, therefore, the nostalgia for a period of greater certainty than anything the modern or postmodern world can accommodate; this is the 'pleasant illusion that reality is intelligible and can therefore be controlled'.[19]

Miss Marple, and the narrator who describes her, regard her knowledge of human nature as incontestable, in stark contrast to the increasing sense among the modernists that human character is unknowable, unfathomable. She extrapolates, as realist writing tends also to do, from the particular case to the general, regarding individual behaviour as expressive of characterological types. Sometimes this has to do with class, sometimes with temperament. In her first outing as a detective, for instance, she spots the murderer early because '*A man of that Jones type – coarse and jovial*. As soon as I heard there was a pretty girl in the house I felt sure that he would not have left her alone. It is very distressing and not a very nice thing to talk about.'[20] Her experience – in the village, with other coarse and jovial men and with other equally identifiable types – is the key. Intellectually this view of character might be conservative,as Alison Light has observed,[21] but it is also quite impressively democratic in its refusal of some of the snobberies of the intensely realised English class system out of which Christie was writing. The perpetrator is almost always of the upper or upper middle classes, in a corrective to the view that it is the working classes who are most likely to be criminally inclined. Miss Marple is also astute in her recognition that when people are full of their own affairs, they do not notice middle-aged women of whatever class, and particularly they do not notice servants, who become, as it were, part of the furniture. This is not to say that the perfect criminal is in fact a middle-aged servant – but upper-class criminals who want to get away with something can do worse than to dress the part of the inconspicuous and unnoticed working-class figure, the servant, at the heart of the home or its equivalents (many stories take place in hotels).

There is a sense in which if you have read one of the Miss Marple stories, you have read them all. Christie did not, however, stick only to her tried-and-tested formula, though where she departs from her familiar and cosy village world into other stories of crime and weird phenomena, she none the less invokes the securities of genre even as she undermines them, and she is more self-conscious and knowing about genre than she is perhaps given credit for. In the stories that are not strictly detective stories, characters repeatedly refer to the detective genre, and to the power of stories more generally, to back up their suspicions and actions, and to provoke particular effects. In the title story of *The Listerdale*

Mystery (1934),[22] dismissing her brother's suspicions about the house her family has been able to rent at an absurdly cheap rent (incidentally one of the common tropes of the Victorian ghost story), the daughter of the house comments: 'That's just like you, Rupert, always making mysteries out of nothing. It's those dreadful detective stories you're always reading' (p. 17). The practical Barbara is equally dismissive of her fiancé's sense that there is something strange about the house:

> 'You know there's something queer about this house altogether, something uncanny and haunting.'
> 'Don't get like Rupert,' Barbara implored him. 'He is convinced that wicked Colonel Carfax murdered Lord Listerdale and hid his body under the floor.' ...
> 'I admire Rupert's detective zeal. No, I didn't mean anything of *that* kind. But there's something in the air, some atmosphere that one doesn't quite understand.' (pp. 23–24)[23]

In his sensitivity to the atmosphere, the boyfriend invokes the genre of the weird tale or ghost story, but it is invoked only to be dismissed, not only by Barbara's practical common sense but also by the denouement of the story. The strangeness is due neither to crime nor to ghostly activity; it is the result of a secret act of charity. The repetition of the tropes and traits of genre is a red herring for the interpretation of this particular tale.

In another story in the same collection, 'Philomel Cottage', other genres and intertexts are alluded to.[24] The newly married heroine, Alix, dreams of her husband's death and her former boyfriend standing over his dead body as Alix falls into his arms. The dreams suggest a portent of disaster. They are also perhaps bound up with a Freudian awareness of dreams as the site of both memory and desire: thus, although Alix identifies the dreams as horrible, she also recognises that even more horrible than her husband's imagined death is the fact that in the dream '*She, Alix Martin, was glad that her husband was dead*' (p. 38, original emphasis), and she is secretly more perturbed by its meaning 'than she liked to admit' (p. 39). The Freudian connection is not pursued, however, nor is that staple of stories of deceit: the diary happened upon by the eyes least appropriate to see it. Alix finds her husband's diary (it is, by the way, only a pocket diary, not the record of his innermost soul) in the garden and comments to herself: 'had this been a story, like those she had so often read, the diary would doubtless have furnished her with some sensational revelation. It would have had in it for certain the name of another woman' (p. 45). It does not contain any such incriminating evidence, and the only mysterious element is a date and time which Alix cannot explain. Yet she is unaccustomedly nervous in the wake of the dream and the discovery of the diary. That night, she asks her husband about his past; they have married very quickly, and she knows next to nothing about him. 'Do you think it wise, Alix,' he asks her, 'this Bluebeard's chamber business?' (p. 49). The reference to the fairy story in which a monstrous husband murders his many other wives, even as it sets out to dismiss her fears, does nothing to allay them.

Tortured by nameless suspicions, Alix goes in search of evidence about what kind of man her new husband is. There are moments of absurdity along the way: searching through one of his drawers she discovers a bundle of love letters from a woman, but in a moment that Catherine Morland, heroine of *Northanger Abbey* (1817), would recognise, they turn out to be her own letters to him, and so Christie's intertexts cover a wide range of possibility. Finally, she does find some more disturbing evidence of her husband's past. In another locked drawer she discovers a series of newspaper clippings about the notorious Charles Lemaitre, a serial bigamist suspected of murdering some of his many wives, who had escaped from an American prison at much the same moment Gerald Martin appeared to court her. The two pieces of clinching evidence are a vaguely familiar newspaper photograph and the newspaper's description of Lemaitre's distinguishing feature: a small scar on his wrist (Gerald has such a scar). Alix realises that she is about to become the latest in a series of victims and must *plot* (a story word) to save her own life.

She does so brilliantly by recourse to narrative: Bluebeard's wife becomes Scheherazade in yet another intertextual allusion. Knowing that her husband plans to murder her that night, she tells him the fabricated story of her own past – of a marriage with a much older man, whom she poisoned with hyoscine for the life assurance, and of a second marriage to a man her own age, similarly dispatched by means of their evening coffee. She keeps speaking in the hope that the clock will strike nine, for nine is the hour her rescuers will arrive. The unintended consequence of her story, however, is that her husband dies in the process of listening to it, killed by the power of suggestion which is the potency of narrative. (In another story already alluded to, Mr Eastwood is similarly beguiled by story-telling which distracts him sufficiently to enable a gang of thieves to make off with all his portable property.)

Genre, as we have seen, is repetitive as a structural formation. Repetition can be about the construction of security and comfort: we know what world we are in. But repetition can also be about terror – characters forced to repeat compulsive, destructive or violent behaviours. Gerald Martin – a serial murderer, it would seem – finds it only too easy to believe that he has become the victim of the self-same generic repetition which he had hoped to inflict on his wife.

Romance and atmosphere: Daphne du Maurier

'Genre' and 'gender' are related terms, both etymologically (they ultimately come from the same root, *genus*, Latin for 'type' or 'kind') and more practically. In the practical sense of the word 'genre', the version of it which relates most strongly to how the market functions, publishers know only too well that there are certain kinds of writing which appeal to men and certain kinds that appeal to women, and they market their books in that way. For a writer such as Daphne du Maurier, this was of practical benefit: she was a very high-earning novelist in part because of how she was positioned, as a woman's writer of romance, in the fiction market. But it was also an aesthetic and personal problem because the genre into which she was placed by her publishers and her public was that of romance. As Alison Light observes, quoting one of du Maurier's obituaries in April 1989:

> To be hailed nowadays as a popular romantic novelist or even 'the last of the great romantic writers' is an ambiguous tribute, especially for the woman writer, bringing with it the suggestion of a 'genre', the bestselling 'formula' fiction of the 'boy-meets-girl' variety, epitomised in Britain by the industrial output of Mills & Boon.[25]

Note again the slight distaste, even from a contemporary critic, for 'industrial' commercial fiction. But as Light also points out, if 'boy meets girl' is the definition of the romantic formula, then du Maurier is only very ambiguously connected with this most feminine of genres, since her best-known novels certainly resist the fairy-tale endings of the formulaic forms of such fiction. It could be that, if she were a romantic novelist at all, it is to an earlier meaning of 'romance' (one that Sir Walter Scott, say, might have recognised) that she returns – a version that combines the love story with wild adventure.

It is in her long fiction that du Maurier is most easily associated with the romance genre, but the designation affects how readers approach her shorter fiction, too, since there is an assumption (often quite wrong) that writers write always in a particular way. Du Maurier might best be understood as a writer who crosses genres and mixes them up, not quite in the arch and knowing way of Agatha Christie in 'Philomel Cottage' but more subtly. Her mixing of genres might also have something to do with her own troubled sense of gender identity. Margaret Forster[26] points out that du Maurier found adolescence particularly difficult because it put an end to her tomboyish ways; it forced – in du Maurier's own words – her 'inner boy' back into a box. And although she lived out the standard life for a woman of her class and time in that she married relatively young, gave birth to children and appeared to enjoy a stable and faithful relationship with her husband, in fact there was much more going on under the surface, including some very passionate affairs with women, one of whom was the actress Gertrude Lawrence, and also affairs with married men. Some would certainly have regarded those relationships as wild adventures, if not as romances. The short stories, however, show a fairly extensive range in du Maurier's fiction, and demonstrate, too, the extent to which the *cordon sanitaire* between high- and middle-brow forms is permeable.

Whatever else she was, Agatha Christie was not a stylist. Her effects come from ingenious, carefully constructed plots. Du Maurier, in partial contrast, certainly had ambitions to be thought of as an altogether classier kind of writer. She read the works of Katherine Mansfield, for example, with interest, and aspired to the high-cultural aesthetic of the modernist avant-garde. She wrote in a letter to her governess from her finishing school in France, as Margaret Forster notes, that 'she would probably not have thought about trying to write at all' if she had not read Mansfield's short stories.[27] The reader who comes to her short fiction expecting there to be an easily discernible connection between du Maurier and her modernist contemporaries, however, will not immediately find it, at least in terms of the style of her writings. But there are echoes none the less. In the story 'Panic', in which a sexual roué takes an inexperienced girl to a hotel in Paris for immoral purposes, one finds a different (and more sensational version) of Mansfield's story 'Je Ne Parle Pas Français', in which the obnoxious Raoul Duquette examines his responses to his observations of a friend's failed love affair and congratulates himself on his sensitivity to its tragedy, while providing multiple evidence that his sensitivity is entirely illusory. And in 'The Lover', a series of fragmented episodes from the life of another gigolo-type figure, something of Mansfield's elliptical technique is present as the narrative flits through a series of encounters between the titular lover and his multiple conquests.

As well as drawing on modernist technique, du Maurier was a fine writer of weird tales in which atmosphere was the key to the story's meaning, taking her cues from the popular short fictions of earlier periods. As Avril Horner and Sue Zlosnik have argued, she can perhaps most usefully be positioned as a writer in the Gothic mode.[28] There are wonderful ghost stories such as 'The Escort', in which a ship from Nelson's navy escorts to safety a ship menaced by U-Boats during the Second World War. 'The Fairy Tale' is actually a fairy tale, though one which refers closely to the material world and which conflates the roles of handsome prince and fairy godmother. And there are stories in the detective mode, too, of which 'No Motive' is the key example.[29]

If Mansfield is one influence whom she was proud to avow, then there is more than a hint that she was well-read in the works of the Edwardian ghost-story writer Algernon Blackwood (1869–1951). Blackwood wrote often about the uncanniness of nature (as in his famous story 'The Willows', 1907), and a repeated trope in his stories is that of the tree or trees that come to life. Du Maurier's story 'The Apple Tree' (1952) draws together the symbolic focus of Mansfield's 'Bliss', the pear tree with its 'perfect' blossom, and Blackwood's more self-evident horror. The story describes a widower who becomes haunted by the presence of his dead wife in the form of a misshapen apple tree in his garden:

> the likeness was unmistakable…The tree was scraggy and of a depressing thinness, possessing none of the gnarled solidity of its companions. Its few branches, growing high up on the trunk like narrow shoulders on a tall body, spread themselves in martyred resignation…How often had he seen Midge stand like this, dejected. (p. 114)[30]

The tree itself has been barren for years up to this point, but this particular spring and summer it is laden with blossom and then with fruit. Despite its resemblance to his hated dead wife, therefore, the widower is unable to cut it down (his gardener advises strongly against it, and the protagonist is a conventional man). It is partly hinted by the story that the widower is drawn into a loss of perspective by the resemblance of the tree to his wife; when it blossoms, he does not see it (as Bertha does in 'Bliss') as emblematic of beauty and hope; 'instead of blossoming to life, to beauty, it had somehow, deep in nature, gone awry and turned a freak' (p. 139). And he perceives the amazing harvest of apples through similarly jaundiced eyes:

> The tree was tortured by fruit, groaning under the weight of it, and the frightful part about it was that not one of the fruit was edible.

Every apple was rotten through and through. He trod them under-foot, the windfalls on the grass, there was no escaping them; and in a moment they were mush and slime, clinging about this heels – he had to clean the mess off with wisps of grass. (p. 144)

The story of the tree is fairly clearly an allegory for the story of the marriage. The dejected wife, whose every offering in terms of making a comfortable home for her husband (he designates her housework 'the dreary routine of unnecessary tasks she forced herself to do, day in, day out, through the interminable changeless years', p. 115) is rejected, has lived a blighted life. The blighted tree literalises that horticultural metaphor. As it makes one last effort to flower and fruit and please its owner, and that effort is also rejected when the widower refuses to eat the apples, has them stripped from the tree and simply gives them away, believing them to be inedible (they aren't – others eat and enjoy them), the tree resembles the drooping, dejected, rejected wife even more than before: 'The branches still sagged, and the leaves, withering now to the cold autumnal evening, folded upon themselves and shivered. "Is this my reward?" it seemed to say. "After all I've done for you?"' (p. 145). The widower finally cuts down the tree, and it takes its revenge by trapping him by the foot when he returns one night from the pub. He is left to die from hypothermia in its embrace, in a story that Nina Auerbach describes as 'the mutual murder that defines marriage in Daphne du Maurier's fiction'.[31]

The story is clearly more typical of the weird tales of the Victorian period than would be the case with Mansfield's fiction; although Bertha also takes the perfection of her tree as a symbol for the perfection of her marriage, she is clearly wrong. Sometimes, as Freud might have put it, a tree is just a tree. And though Bertha also has moments of Gothic shud-der (as the cat creeps through the garden, for instance), they are subject-ive not 'real' and cannot be mistaken for ghostly occurrences. The du Maurier story is much more ambivalent about the nature of what is hap-pening, in the manner of a Victorian ghost story, in which an internal psychological state is typically externalised onto an object or person who then becomes 'ghostly'. Comparatively, though, we can see the ways in which du Maurier had learned her technique from Mansfield. It is less thorough in its use of free indirect style than the New Zealand writer typically was, but in its use of focalisation (point of view) and its partial adoption of the free indirect mode, it shows the leakage between the aesthetic formalism of the modernists and the more straightforward narrative modes of popular writers.

'The Apple Tree' is a third-person narrative told almost entirely from the point of view of the widowed protagonist. Other voices intervene in direct speech, when he speaks to them and they reply, and readers can gauge something of the sense of his isolation from the widower's impression of their disapproval of him. But most of the narrative is carried through his consciousness, using his turns of phrase and judgements, just as we would find in the techniques of Mansfield:

> He went on staring at the apple tree. That *martyred bent* position, the *stooping* top, the *weary* branches, the few *withered* leaves that had not blown away with the wind and rain of the past winter and now *shivered* in the spring breeze like *wispy hair*; all of it protested soundlessly to the owner of the garden looking upon it, 'I am like this because of you, because of your neglect.' (p. 115, our emphasis)

The italic words in this passage are transferred epithets. They are the words the widower associates with his wife, whom he regards as sexually unattractive and paradoxically emotionally both cold and needy. They belong not to the tree – with the possible exception of 'withered' – but to a set of judgements that the widower has made about a woman: human emotions attached to an inanimate object. This tells us clearly that in some ways he always saw his wife as inanimate, so wrapped up was he in his own affairs and interests. At the end of the story, it is implied, she will wrap him up finally and fatally in her interests to avenge his earlier indifference. What the story never makes clear, which is the lesson that du Maurier learned from both the influences identified (modernism and the weird tale), is the extent to which he is deluded in his identification of the wife and the tree. Is this an illusion caused by psychological failings or an actual haunting with objective existence beyond his mind? The uncertainty is what the weird tale thrives on. It suggests the ways in which a genre, repetitive and formulaic as it might also be, can continue to unsettle the reader's horizons of expectation, can continue to mix its messages. Unlike Christie's knowable world, du Maurier's fiction presents us with a morally unstable universe via genres which emphasise their own instability, too.

Part III
The Post-War Short Story

10
Introducing the Post-War Short Story

It is often said that the short story declined during the second half of the twentieth century, following the end of the Second World War in 1945. A shrinking of the magazine market, coupled with the sense that the short story was 'for the most part middle-aged and graying around the temples', its main practitioners having been born before the First World War, led some observers to suggest that the short story's best days were over.[1] One such middle-aged and greying short-story writer was P. G. Wodehouse (1881–1975), who had been fabulously popular in the 1920s and 1930s on account of his comic stories of upper-class life featuring, among others, the (not so) bright young thing Bertie Wooster and his superior valet, Jeeves. In 1950, Wodehouse lamented the collapse of one of the mainstays of short fiction, *The Strand* magazine, asking, 'Where can [a writer] sell his stories?' He recalled seventeen magazines from his childhood, 'and probably a dozen more that I've forgotten'. Wodehouse's apparent inability to sell stories may well have had something to do with his dubious status in post-war Britain following his undistinguished war, in which he controversially made pro-German broadcasts before departing for the United States, but his own view was that magazines died of 'slanting' (the demand that all stories be written to a formula) and 'names' (printing anything by anyone famous even if it was substandard).[2]

The apparent decline in the popularity of the short story was one of the topics discussed in a special issue of the influential *London Magazine* in September 1966. Unlike Wodehouse, the short-story writer V. S. Pritchett (1900–97) was not unpopular. Indeed, he was much respected. He had had his first short story, 'Rain in the Sierra', published in the *New Statesman* in 1926 and was still going strong. But forty years later things had changed, and his faith in the short story as a form which 'concentrates an impulse that is essentially poetic' was being severely tested. In a long diatribe, Pritchett wrote that 'the periodicals on which the writer can rely have almost all vanished, driven out by expensive printing, by television and the hundred and one diversions of an extrovert and leisured society'.[3] In the same issue, Francis King (b.1923), author of *The Japanese Umbrella and Other Stories* (1964), noted how '[e] very apprentice writer has learned this dismal truth. *London Magazine, Encounter, The Cornhill,* two or three women's glossies, in which the author's name appears in smaller type than the most insignificant of photographers or nondescript of models – these are the only outlets for the short story writer in this country.'[4] Romantic fiction in magazines such as *Nomad, Woman's Journal, Secrets* and *She* was booming. Otherwise publishers and agents seemed to push their authors to move on from short stories towards the more profitable form of the novel.

The complaints made by Wodehouse, Pritchett and King are familiar ones, and for all their obvious one-sidedness they do accurately suggest something of the fluctuating fortunes of the British short story after 1945. This was all the more surprising given that during the war the form had seemed to gain a new lease of life. There was a marked increase in reading, with the result that 'literary magazines, such as *Penguin New Writing,* flourished when their mixture of short stories, articles and poetry was found to be particularly "war-friendly"'.[5] 'Short stories', as Anne Boston notes in the introduction to her anthology *Wave Me Goodbye* (1988), 'enjoyed an unexpected burst of popularity in wartime, when ordinary life was subject to constant interruption and time was at a premium.'[6] This was especially true in the early years of the war, when theatres and cinemas were closed and the blackout made it difficult to go out at night. The very shortness of the short story – the ability of realist fiction to capture a single brief incident or 'fragment' of life – was seen as one of its advantages. This in turn led to supporters of the genre having high hopes for its post-war existence. Writing about 'The Short Story in England' in *Britain To-Day* when the end of the war was in sight, Elizabeth Bowen predicted that the short story would emerge as 'the ideal prose medium for war-time creative writing', noting that 'war-time London, blitzed, cosmopolitan, electric with anticipation now teems, I feel, with untold but tellable stories, glitters with such scenes that cry aloud for the pen. So must our other cities, our ports and sea-coast, our factory settlements, our mobilized countryside.' 'I foresee', she added, 'a record crop of short stories immediately after the war.'[7] Yet these predictions failed to come true. After 1945, there was much less inclination on the part of writers to write the war than there had been to write the First World War, and there seemed to be much more resistance to retrospection generally.

Given all this, how do we describe the landscape of post-war short-story writing in a way that doesn't make it sound like a literary desert? One point to make is that although the market for short fiction was seen to dwindle during the 1950s and 1960s, it did not disappear altogether. The new publishers of paperback fiction Penguin, established in 1935 by Allan Lane, produced anthologies of both new and previously published stories which helped to establish the reputation of authors or to boost their careers. Nor did the short story itself disappear. After the Second World War there emerged a recognisably new kind of writing 'dominated by a mood of bitterness and defiance' and prompted by a sense of exclusion – often on the grounds of class or age.[8] In July 1957, the Conservative prime minister Harold Macmillan's famously complacent declaration 'Let's be frank about it: most of our people have never had it so good' struck a chord with some people pleased with their new car, television set and foreign holidays, but not with everyone.[9] Although Macmillan's line was that Britain had entered a new Elizabethan age of peace and prosperity and of reconciliation and rebuilding, the 1950s were also a decade of rebellion, frustration and resentment – particularly because the new dawn promised by the election of a Labour government in 1945 seemed to have disappeared.[10] Most disaffected was the younger generation who had not fought in the war and who, as Kenneth Allsop has written, 'suddenly made up its mind. Not so much to rebel against the old order of authority and standards [represented by that Edwardian gentleman of the old school, Harold Macmillan] but to refuse to vote for it.'[11] In literary terms one of the ways in which this refusal famously manifested itself was in the emergence of the group of writers labelled the 'Angry Young Men', who were seen to include John Braine (1922–86), Colin Wilson (b.1931), Kingsley Amis (1922–95), Alan Sillitoe (1928–2010), Stan Barstow (b.1928), David Storey (b.1933) and John Wain (1925–94). The most famous Angry Young Man was Jimmy Porter, (anti-)hero of John Osborne's (1929–94) lacerating play *Look Back in Anger*, which premiered in 1956. Porter is a character who rails loudly and self-importantly, but impotently, against middle-class pretension, at the same time revealing himself to be a misogynist and a bully. But a less self-indulgent, more authentically urgent (and longer-lasting) expression of this new mood came in the novella 'The Loneliness of the Long Distance Runner'.

'The Loneliness of the Long Distance Runner' is the bleak title story of a 1959 collection of stories by Alan Sillitoe, a writer whose working-class Nottingham background subsequently invited some inevitable – albeit rather lazy – comparisons with D. H. Lawrence. Like Sillitoe's most famous novel, *Saturday Night and Sunday Morning* (1958), 'The Loneliness of the Long Distance Runner' has its author adopting the persona, colloquialisms and imagined writing style of a young, badly educated working-class man, in this case Smith. (He is given no other name.) A seventeen-year-old from Nottingham, Smith sees the world as divided between Out-laws and In-laws ('them' and 'us') whose battles take place in institutions such as the borstal (reformatory) in the county of Essex to which he has been sent as punishment for robbery (p. 7).[12] Here power is represented by the borstal's governor, a patronising middle-class man who discovers that Smith has a talent for running ('I've always been a good runner') and has the idea of making him the winner of the national long-distance championship. Despite his contempt for the governor's plan Smith agrees to train for the race because running makes him feel mentally and physically free, as opposed to feeling like 'a cut-balled cockerel' (p. 19). However, he also decides to throw the race to hit back at the governor and publicly affirm his own independence. Organised sport, in this instance, seems to be associated with the establishment; talent is hijacked by those in charge for their own ends. As Smith explains: 'As soon as I got to Borstal they made me a long-distance cross-country runner' (p. 7). 'Our doddering bastard of a governor, our half-dead gangrened gaffer, is hollow like an empty petrol drum, and he wants me and my running life to give him glory, to put in him blood and throbbing veins he never had.' Smith does not see things quite the same way. He views himself as a human race-horse, running for 'a bit of blue ribbon and a cup for a prize' which will become the possessions of the institution, not himself (p. 8). Although 'The Loneliness of the Long Distance Runner' seems to be a story of defeat, it has also been read as a gesture of self-assertion and refusal on the part of a young (every)man to accept the smug, comfortable values of a decaying older generation – represented by the governor (a kind of surrogate father). 'I'm a human being and I've got thoughts and secrets and bloody life inside me that he doesn't know is there' (p. 13). One of the messages of the story is that the borstal system fails to work; men like the governor cannot hope to change Smith.

But Smith is not altogether a sympathetic figure. Sillitoe himself said that 'Smith is a...complex character. What his trouble is, we don't go into.'[13] Smith regards himself as outside the 'normal' boundaries of

society. He has no intention of making an honest living; he is motivated not by need but by pleasure and excitement. He is crude, callous
and self-centred ('They can drop all the atom bombs they like for all I
care ... You should think about nobody and go your own way'), and he
has a potential for violence – as we see when he imagines what he would
do with power: 'And if I had the whip-hand I wouldn't even bother to
build a place like this to put all the cops, governors, posh whores, pen-
pushers, army officers, Members of Parliament in; no, I'd stick them
up against a wall and let them have it' (p. 15). When he leaves borstal
he avoids national service because he has developed pleurisy, and he
is pleased by this; at time he is writing he has just stolen £628 and is
planning to steal again. Nevertheless, the story also invites us to register
sympathy for the young man. In part this has to do with the first-person
narrative: Smith confides in us, the readers, and encourages the feeling
that he is telling the truth (although we might wonder how truthful
or reliable a narrator he actually is). He is self-reliant and determined
but cannot imagine success because there will always be someone in
authority waiting to stop him. We learn something of his working-class
family: his father has died agonisingly from cancer of the throat; his
slatternly mother has a 'fancy man' and has squandered the insurance
money from her husband's death. Save for his friend Mike, Smith, we
are led to believe, has always been alone. As Smith recalls his father's
death during the last stage of the race he finds inspiration in his father
refusing medication and dying from choking on his own blood. 'If he
had guts for that then I've got guts for this' (p. 51). Clare Hanson reads
this moment of self-awareness as a form of rebirth. Smith 'comes alive
through the vision of his father's death, sight, sound, taste and smell,
as well as existential nausea come into play to emphasize his newfound
awareness'.[14] In this reading Smith achieves a status which is tragic and
almost heroic. As Bars argues: 'Running, the dominant, symbolic action
in the story, suggests three motifs: the experience of life, the endurance
test, and the lonely journey or pilgrimage.'[15] Penner has gone further
to suggest that rather than a sign of 'moral decay' Smith's rebellious
gesture is actually the demonstration of a 'Christ-like passion for a tragically deluded society suicidally hostile to life'.[16]

As well as being a powerful expression of working-class frustration,
'The Loneliness of the Long Distance Runner' is significant because it
embodies several key aspects of the short story as the form emerged and
developed after 1945 – particularly in the hands of male writers. It deals
with working-class, rather than upper- or middle-class, characters –
usually young men – who feel themselves to be on the margins of, or

estranged from, society and who are trying to come to terms with the pressures of family and environment. In this regard it fits Clare Hanson's explanation as to why the short story seems to appeal to sections of the writing population. According to Hanson: 'The formal properties of the short story – disjunction, inconclusiveness, and obliquity – connect with its ideological marginality, and with the fact that the form may be used to express something suppressed/repressed.'[17] In 1959 'The Loneliness of the Long Distance Runner' was a strong reminder that fiction could be written outside the narrow confines of literary London and that people north of Watford might have something to say about post-war Britain and how it operated. Stylistically, the story is also deliberately realist in its execution; that is to say, 'characters are lifelike, believably shaped by social and personal circumstances; the events of the narrative are similarly credible' and 'the language used and the syntax are unobtrusive, the self-effacing style preserving the illusion that what is offered is direct, unmediated access to real people and real lives'.[18] There is generally a refusal to romanticise male–female relationships, which are themselves described in explicit terms, and there is also an emphasis on how economics and class can often override the best of intentions. In terms of the history of the British short story such work might also be seen as a deliberate attempt to overturn – even stamp on – the modernist legacy established by Virginia Woolf *et al.* Part of the rebellion of the 1950s was literary – that is, against writing perceived as deliberately experimental, even pretentious, which seemed self-indulgent and elitist, written by people who had never done a day's work in their life and didn't have to.

This, then, was one of the paths taken by the post-war story. In 1958 Leslie Fielder, an American academic observing from across the Atlantic, wrote that this the new breed of writer represented predominantly 'a new class on its way into a controlling position in the culture of his country. He is able to define himself against the class he replaces: against a blend of homosexual sensibility, upper-class aloofness, liberal politics, and *avant garde* literary devices. When he is boorish rather than well-behaved...he can feel he is performing a service for literature liberating it from the tyranny of taste in a world of wealth and leisure which has become quite unreal.'[19] What is striking, of course, about Fielder's assessment is his use of the masculine pronoun 'he'. Fielder sums up quite nicely the tone of a good deal of post-Second World War writing by men (including the misogyny of some of its attitudes),[20] but implies that women had little to do with the changes taking place in Britain's literary landscape and had little opportunity to make their mark. This was far from being the case. In addition to the middle-brow, populist women's magazines mentioned rather sneeringly by Francis King (above), other outlets did remain, including more obviously 'literary' ones. One key editor of the mid-twentieth century, John Lehmann, set up the small-scale magazine anthology *New Writing* in 1936, which became *Penguin New Writing* in 1940, publishing forty paperback issues before the last edition in 1950. Other anthologies of modern stories, published by Penguin and the World's Classics series, took its place during the 1950s and 1960s, including 'classics' from earlier in the century and before, as well as stories by established writers such as V. S. Pritchett and H. E. Bates (1905–74). These anthologies also functioned to showcase the work of women writers, including Elizabeth Bowen, Elizabeth Taylor (1912–75), A. L. Barker (b.1918) and John Lehmann's sister, the popular novelist Rosamond Lehmann (1901–90). Mapping out the territory of middle-class family life that Taylor would explore at greater length, Barker and Rosamond Lehmann published their first collections in the 1940s; Lehmann's haunting volume *The Gipsy's Baby and Other Stories* (1946), with its disturbing images of illness, war-time privation and the trials of motherhood, included material previously published in *Penguin New Writing*. New periodicals which featured unpublished short fiction were also established during the war, including *English Story* (1941–50), *Horizon* (1940–50) and *Modern Reading* (1941–52). In 1951, Muriel Spark (1918–2006) entered and won the short-story competition organised by the *Observer* with her story 'The Seraph and the Zambesi'. The *Little Reviews Anthology*, edited by Denys Val Barker, which reprinted stories, as well as poems and essays, from a variety of these new periodicals, ran from 1943 to 1949.[21] John Lehmann was also responsible for founding the *London Magazine* in 1954, remaining editor until 1961. Despite Pritchett's complaints, this magazine published some key writing of the time, including work by Doris Lessing (b.1919) and some of the later, famous stories of Jean Rhys, such as 'Till September, Petronella' (1960), 'The Day They Burned the Books' (1960) and 'Let Them Call It Jazz' (1962).

The presence of Rhys, Bowen, Spark and Lessing in the post-war literary landscape is a reminder that the history of the British short story includes a tradition of women's short stories and the works of writers originating outside England in the old colonies (the West Indies, Ireland, South Africa) and also, it should be said, from the other countries making up the United Kingdom (Wales and Scotland). Moreover, the impact of this diversity gathered pace as the twentieth century progressed, particularly as the notion of a British empire governed from

London came to look increasingly untenable in the years after 1945. One sees the emergence of 'ex-centric' voices, cut off from the centre of power and influence (London). A notable example (though it falls outside the scope of the present volume) is the importance of the short story in Irish literary culture. C. L. Dallat, reviewing *The Faber Book of Best New Irish Short Stories 2004–5*, writes that the genre often becomes established out of 'the demands of societies in flux':

> where long-stable cultures in England and France led inexorably to the long-gestation novel, the new-founded 19th-century US, seismic 20th-century central Europe and post-independence Ireland all opted for brevity, the latter context producing a particular flourishing in the hands of O'Faolain, O'Flaherty and O'Connor, all more or less 'involved' in the early-20th-century struggle.[22]

In *The Lonely Voice: A Study of the Short Story*, the celebrated writer Frank O'Connor called the short story the genre of 'submerged population groups' who find themselves in 'frontier' or 'outsider' situations,[23] and perhaps making use of 'local colour' situations. O'Connor is talking about Ireland, but his comments are also applicable to the development of the short story in the United Kingdom in the post-war period, particularly during the past thirty years. In the late twentieth and early twenty-first centuries, short stories have tended to reflect radical changes in British society and in modern relationships, at a time when conventional ideas of the nuclear family, of what it means to be British, have seemed to be under threat. Many writers use their stories to dramatise the messy, traumatic aftermath of broken relationships – fathers struggling to come to terms with their roles as parents, for instance, or daughters gradually revealing the abuse they have suffered within the home. Urban living has become a key concern of short-fiction writers; many of the stories discussed in this section are set in London, Manchester or Glasgow, whether to explore the possibilities of mixed-race relationships or to revisit class and racial tensions which still underpin social divides. At the same time, reading the work of writers of mixed race or writers from Scotland or Wales who have been brought up in multicultural Britain has been seen as a means of re-examining the story's perennial ability to explore the role of the outsider and to reveal the lives of the ordinary, the dispossessed, the marginalised.

The stories discussed in this final section are also linked by their experimental nature and their stretching of the limits of the short-story form, in line with the changing directions of modern fiction in the twenty-first century. A number of factors have helped ensure the buoyancy of the form in recent years: the flourishing of small magazines devoted to stories and/or poetry, such as *Stand* and *Bête Noire*, often connected to the increasingly popular creative writing programmes at British universities; the continuation of mainstream newspapers such as the *Guardian* and the journal *Granta*, relaunched in 1979 with its lists of up-and-coming fiction writers to showcase new fiction; and the enduring popularity of Radio 4 and the increase in literary festivals and high-profile prizes for fiction (the BBC National Short Story Award, the Frank O'Connor International Short Story Award, the Bridport Prize), which are part of an increasing recognition that the short story deserves due critical (and financial) recognition and which broadcast and publicise the work of new and 'amateur', as well as established, writers. Recently started have been the Yorkshire and Humber Short Story Competition, the Bournemouth Short Story Competition and the competition launched at the National Eisteddfod in Bala in 2009. Elsewhere, there is the Hay Festival, in Hay-on-Wye, now sponsored by the *Guardian*, which features readings, screenings and events of a literary nature in a town dominated by bookshops; it first took place in 1988 and is now an important event in the fiction world. Anthologies linking authors to their home towns or countries, such as *The City Life Book of Manchester Short Stories, Children of Albion Rovers* (stories by Scottish writers), *Mama's Baby (Papa's Maybe)* (fifty-five stories by Welsh writers) and *Hard Shoulder* (1999), in which sixteen writers wrote stories about Birmingham, are now a much more regular fixture on the shelves of bookshops and libraries. At the same time, the emergence of the World Wide Web suggests that the short story need not be hidden away on a local bookshelf. To log onto that part of Web containing *Story* (theshortstory.org.uk), with its stock of new works by Ali Smith (b.1962), Will Self (b.1961), Nicola Barker (b.1966), William Boyd (b.1952) and Shena Mackay (b.1944), among others, together with invitations to enter the BBC National Short Story Award, is likewise to be reminded of the form's diversity and depth and to realise that it is not the exclusive property of the literati, that it takes in a variety of camps. The number of very different film adaptations of short stories is testament to this: Neil Jordan's *The Company of Wolves* (1984), sourced from Angela Carter's collection; Philip Haas's *Up at the Villa* (2000), from W. Somerset Maugham's novella; Patrice Chéreau's *Intimacy* (2001), based on a story by Hanif Kureishi; and Alvise Renzini's animated *Grande Anarca*, from J. G. Ballard's 'Answers to a Questionnaire' – currently viewable on YouTube. In the past ten years collections such as *All Hail the New Puritans* (2000) and *England Calling*

(2001) have helped re-enforce the possibilities of the genre, the latter, as its editors explain, not only offering twenty-four 'stories of the landscapes of England, but peeling back the layers of Englishness in the process – Englishness as it is now: multicultural, messy, survivalist'.[24] The former collection, whose contributors include Candida Clark (b.1970), Alex Garland (b.1970), Toby Litt (b.1968) and Scarlett Thomas (b.1972), carries a manifesto emphasising 'simplicity' and 'clarity' and promising 'to blow the dinosaurs out of the water' – a cheeky reference to an 'older' generation of British writers such as Martin Amis (b.1949) and Salman Rushdie (b.1947).[25] Taken collectively, such developments would seem to re-emphasise the short story's tendency to find a position 'in the vanguard of experimental writing'.[26]

11
Women's Stories, 1940s to the Present

One of the ways in which the period after the Second World War can be analysed is in terms of changes in women's material and psychic lives, registering the impact and repercussions of second-wave feminism. The 1950s housewife, presiding over 'homes fit for heroes', was a reference point for mid-century femininities, but women's association with the domestic space and their roles as wives, mothers and daughters are still important to late-twentieth-century and twenty-first-century gender formations. In an early feminist text, *The Second Sex* (1949), the French philosopher Simone de Beauvoir protested against the way in which woman was always defined in relation to man and therefore became his 'other'. Her famous line 'One is not born, but rather becomes a woman' also stressed the social, rather than the biological, process of acquiring femininity, throwing the emphasis onto social convention as a major factor in defining gender identity.[1]

The circulation of feminist concerns about inequality throws light on the development of post-war fiction. As Diana Wallace suggests, 'the resurgence of feminism in the late 1960s was a defining historical moment which changed and invigorated women's writing'. However, as she also makes clear, this does not mean that we should 'divide women's writing into "before feminism" and "after feminism" as this tends to obscure the fact that women writers of the 1940s, 1950s and early 1960s anticipate many of the political concerns of later authors'.[2] Some of the political changes which influenced discussions of family and sexuality in women's fiction were the Abortion Act of 1967, the greater availability of the Pill from the early 1960s and, by the 1980s, a wider social acceptance of lesbians and a recognition that traditional forms of heterosexuality need to be rethought and recast. Women also had greater access to higher education and the workplace, eased by the greater provision of crèches and nurseries, leading to discussions about the possibility of 'having it all', juggling a career with motherhood, becoming a 'super-woman'. In her discussion of women's new demands for 'agency, justice, equality, autonomy and freedom, in the workplace and at home', Mary Joannou notes the shift in realities and expectations of women's lives by the end of the 1970s, as many chose to 'cohabit... to have children outside marriage, to divorce, to live with same-sex partners, or to bring up children on their own'.[3]

New developments in anthology publishing, popular with modern readers, meant that with the revaluing and rediscovery of women's writing as a distinct category from the late 1970s onwards, more anthologies of women's short stories have appeared in the past twenty-five years, helping to create a new canon of female short-story writers. The establishment and growth of feminist publishing houses, including Virago and the Women's Press in Britain and the Feminist Press in the United States, contributed to this process.[4] Examples of these collections are *The Secret Self: A Century of Short Stories by Women* (1995) edited and chosen by Hermione Lee, *The Secret Woman: The Virago Book of Classic Short Stories* (1993) edited by Lynn Knight, and *The Mammoth Book of Lesbian Short Stories* (1999), edited by the Irish writer Emma Donoghue, all of which include writers from around the world. The important short-story writer Angela Carter, to be discussed below, also edited several collections of stories which celebrate female resourcefulness and transgression, as seen in the title *Wayward Girls and Wicked Women* (1986). These editors make some attempts to establish a tradition of women's short-story writing, though there is a tendency, as in other critical studies of the genre, to obscure potential differences between British and American writers, or among writers of different races, which might provide an alternative picture. Hermione Lee argues that twentieth-century women's stories 'come out of a double tradition': the oral tale, or handed-down fairy story, and the 'woman's story' entrenched in 'domestic realism, love interest, local colour' derived from nineteenth-century literary magazines. Although associations 'with a limited small-scale domestic range' can sometimes damage the reader's appreciations of women's stories, they retained the emphasis on liberation found in New Woman short stories of the 1880s and 1890s, recording 'revolutions, moments of change or possibility, openings-out'.[5] In her discussion of gender and genre in short fiction, Mary Eagleton has picked up on this 'double-bind which places women's writing in restricted categories', whereby women's adoption of the short-story form can be used to 'recognise women's social experience in our culture' but could also 'confine women once again in the personal', making the genre 'about all that women can manage'. She rightly highlights Lee's hesitancy about a female tradition of short-story writing, pointing out that 'the problem of finding a concept of gender that she [the woman writer] can relate to the short story proves intractable'.[6] The remainder of this chapter considers ways in which writers such as Elizabeth Taylor, Fay Weldon (b.1931), Doris Lessing, Angela Carter and A. S. Byatt approach these challenges.

Getting published

While many of the stories discussed in the following pages first appeared in journals and magazines, this is less commonly the case than in the nineteenth century. The sales and popularity of short-story collections, as well as anthologies, in the later twentieth century meant that readers were increasingly likely to read stories in volume form rather than in periodicals, or to access them via new technologies. As Dean Baldwin has noted, the gradual decline in periodical publishing of short fiction during the 1950s is synonymous with the rise of radio as 'an increasingly important outlet for writers wishing to reach a large audience', which also allowed writers to increase their 'exposure' by reading their own work.[7] Since the mid-1990s the Internet has made all forms of literature more widely available to readers, and author websites help to publicise new material. The uncertain British market fostered an increased tendency for British writers to publish their stories in American periodicals. *The New Yorker*, established in 1925, and still running, became one of the key spaces for showcasing new and often radical short fiction by British and American writers, including Ann Beattie, John Cheever, John Updike, Richard Yates, Elizabeth Taylor, Ian McEwan and Sylvia Townsend Warner. Edited by Harold Ross up to 1951, it was launched as a sophisticated humour magazine, offering a blend of serious journalism and fiction. It originally included two or three new stories per week, though this has now been reduced to one. Anthea Trodd points out that for women writers of mid-century fiction 'success in the American market was especially sought', with authors such as May Sinclair and Warner taking up the opportunities of lecture tours organised by their American publishers. Warner, who wrote stories throughout her long career, was able to support herself in her old age by regular short-story contributions to *The New Yorker*, on the basis of contacts made on a promotional tour of the States in the 1920s.[8] Women's fashion and lifestyle magazines, such as the long-running *Woman's Own, Company* and *Cosmopolitan*, the British version of which was relaunched in the early 1970s, continued to promote the work of women writers, providing an important space for up-and-coming feminist authors such as Fay Weldon and the Canadian writer Margaret Atwood in the 1970s and 1980s.

There is also a marked trend for major novelists to make their names by publishing collections, often experimental or provocative in nature, though other writers embrace, or revisit, this form later in their lives, or continue to write across a range of genres. Both Angela Carter and Ian McEwan began their prolific writing careers with radical and controversial collections which generated a mass of reviews and helped to reinvigorate the short-story form in the late 1970s and early 1980s. Carter's *Fireworks* (1974) and *The Bloody Chamber* (1979) and McEwan's *First Love, Last Rites* (1975) and *In Between the Sheets* (1978), all of which bordered on the pornographic in their frank representations of sexuality, also addressed taboo subjects such as incest, paedophilia, transvestism and sadomasochism.

Women and the city: Elizabeth Bowen and Jean Rhys

Woman's changing relationship with the city continued to be an important theme of mid-twentieth-century fiction. In her discussion of women writers, modernity and the city, Deborah Parsons has noted the 'backlash against female emancipation' in the inter-war period and the appearance of texts which present 'disorientating spatial movement ... the struggle of the woman as not so much to enter but to survive in the urban environment'.[9] London, as a site of devastation (caused by the wartime bombings) and as an arena for racial conflict and the commodification of lower-class women, offered a particularly interesting focus for women's explorations of their urban environment. Experiences of alienation and disorientation are common in the stories of women writing during and in the decades after the Second World War, a period of conservatism when the women's movement had gone underground. Emphasising its existence as 'a form of the margins', Clare Hanson has argued that 'the short story has offered itself to losers and loners, exiles, women, blacks – writers who for one reason or another have not been part of the ruling "narrative" or epistemological/experiential framework of their society'.[10] The alternative narratives provided by some of these marginalised figures write back to the official versions of Britishness and femininity produced during this period.

Elizabeth Bowen, a prolific Anglo-Irish novelist and short-story writer, began publishing fiction in the 1920s, with the short-story collections *Encounters* (1923) and *Ann Lee's* (1926) and her first novel, *The Hotel* (1927). Born in Dublin, but brought up in England, she later spent time in her ancestral home in County Cork; houses, furniture and domestic interiors are key features of her short fiction, in which place assumes a major importance. Her work of the 1940s, particularly the collection *The Demon Lover and Other Stories* (1945), engages with women's experiences of the Second World War and the attempts to convey the dislocation and fears of those living in London during the German bombings, known as the Blitz. Bowen remarked in the 1950 preface to the American edition of *The Demon Lover* that wartime experience produced not a solid, elaborately structured novel, but these 'flying particles of something enormous and inchoate that had been going on'.[11] Emphasising her commitment to the short story, Anthea Trodd likens Bowen to Katherine Mansfield (see Chapter 8), claiming that Bowen shared Mansfield's belief in the short story 'as the characteristic literary form of modernism, which permitted an escape from the novel's constricting structures and demand for coherent development of character, into other kinds of perception potentially truer to the fragmented experience of modern life'.[12]

The title story, 'The Demon Lover', which first appeared in 1941 in the magazine *The Listener*, a familiar outlet for Bowen's stories, is typical of the collection in its integration of uncanny elements into a realist mode. It describes the 'prosaic' Mrs Kathleen Drover's contemplation of her old London home, now boarded up, half empty and damaged by bombing, with her calm shattered by her discovery of a letter referring to an imminent meeting with the fiancé killed in the First World War. At the centre of the story is a flashback to an unnerving scene in 1916 between the young Kathleen and the brutal soldier she promises to wait for, in which she claims not to have 'ever completely seen his face' to the extent that she 'imagined spectral glitters in the place of his eyes' (p. 663).[13] The twist in the tale is that the taxi-driver who she imagines will convey her to safety in the final paragraph, it is implied, is the ghost of the dead fiancé, whose face she is forced to look at through the aperture. In the final sentence she 'continued to scream freely and to beat with her gloved hands on the glass all round as the taxi, accelerating without mercy, made off with her into the hinterland of deserted streets' (p. 666). This 'hinterland' evokes a sense of both a changed, deserted London and the 'complete dislocation from everything' (p. 664) brought on by her fiancé's presumed death; like the crumbling, half-empty structure of the house in which the story is set, from which her family had been 'driven out by the bombs of the next war', the character cannot cope with the instability. The bombing lays bare the fragility of her comfortable middle-class existence: 'The desuetude of her former bedroom, her married London home's whole air of being a cracked cup from which memory, with its reassuring power, had either evaporated or leaked away, made a crisis...the hollowness of the house this evening cancelled years on years of voices, habits and steps' (p. 664). As John Bayley has usefully argued in relation to Bowen's stories, she is less concerned with character than with 'a particular set of circumstances', and so effectively 'place comes before persons'.[14]

'The Happy Autumn Fields', first published in the long-established, middle-brow journal *The Cornhill* in 1944, is a more ambitious and satisfyingly complex war story, taking greater risks with the handling of time. Time and clocks are an important symbol in Bowen's war writing, as the awareness that men are constantly fighting and dying, or that the lives of civilians are constantly under threat from bombs, renders the future uncertain, which affects the experience of the present. The gaps in the narrative signal jumps in focus between a large Victorian family in their country house and a young woman sheltering from the bombs in a London terrace. What connect the two are the linked consciousnesses and perspectives of Sarah, one of the Victorian daughters, and Mary, the modern woman, who either imagines or dreams about the family through reading diaries she has found as an escape from the devastation of the 1940s. The ending of the story is the revelation by Mary's lover Travis that Eugene, to whom Sarah is attracted, had been inexplicably thrown from his horse and killed on his way home from the mansion, an event which suggests a possible link between the two eras, as wartime is more likely to deprive women of their future husbands. As if in sympathy or imaginative communication with the 1940s, it is Sarah who suffers from the dread that there will be no tomorrow, that this cannot be guaranteed, and a sense of doom haunts her narrative: 'how could she put into words her feeling of dislocation, the formless dread...How could she tell the others...she apprehended that the seconds were numbered?' (p. 681). As the bombs fall around Mary, 'the last soul left in the terrace' (p. 676), she also feels a sense of dislocation from her own body:

> Frantic at being delayed here, while the moment awaited her in the cornfield, she all but afforded a smile at the grotesquerie of being

saddled with Mary's body and lover. Rearing up her head from the bare pillow, she looked, as far as the crossed feet, along the form inside which she found herself trapped: the irrelevant body of Mary, weighted down to the bed, wore a short modern dress, flaked with plaster. The toes of the black suede shoes by their sickly whiteness showed Mary must have climbed over fallen ceilings; dirt engraved the fate-lines in Mary's palms. (p. 677)

As she blanks out the recognition that her home, with its 'fallen ceilings', is in fragments and returns to the past through her 'frantic' engagement with a moment of romance, war makes Mary experience herself as grotesque and irrelevant, 'saddled' with a lover who doesn't understand her. The happy autumn fields, according to Maud Ellmann, 'represent not only the historic past but the idealised world of childhood, unravaged by the blitz of sexuality', but overturned by the horse in the final paragraphs.[15] Like other Bowen heroines, both Mary and Sarah are shown to be confined and constrained within their societies, their perceptions of the future shadowed by a sense of doom. Gill Plain points out that this is typical of the pessimism of Bowen's writing about war: 'Mary's strategy [of freeing herself from the war by returning to the past] cannot ultimately empower her. Her vision concludes with a premonition of disaster.'[16]

'Mysterious Kôr', the final story in the *Demon Lover* collection and its keynote, opens with an arresting description of a moonlit deserted London, threatening and exposed, in which 'people stayed indoors with a fervour that could be felt' (p. 728). It first appeared in *Penguin New Writing*, 1944, a fitting space for its candid treatment of the effects of war on contemporary British society. Taking its title from the mythical city featured in H. Rider Haggard's late-Victorian adventure novel *She* (1887), which made a lasting impression on Bowen, the story uses a conversation between a soldier and his girlfriend, Pepita, to substitute this transformed and alienating London for the 'forsaken city': 'If you can blow whole places out of existence, you can blow whole places into it. I don't see why not. They say we can't say what's come out since the bombing started. By the time we've come to the end, Kôr may be the one city left: the abiding city' (p. 730). But these imaginings are exploded by the striking of midnight: 'Whereas in Kôr... In Kôr... Like glass, the illusion shattered' (p. 731, ellipses in original), the unfinished sentences revealing the author's (or maybe the character's) inability to sustain the vision. In an excellent reading of the story, Deborah Parsons emphasises the female view of 'a hallucinatory inner terrain that Bowen creates with her characteristic skill for evoking the psychological land-scape', contrasting with the male inability to imagine an 'unreal' city unmarked on a map.[17] The lovers' discussion of the need to populate Kôr thinly veils their frustration at being unable to find a private space away from Pepita's flatmate, Callie, to have sex on the man's first night of leave, finding themselves 'homeless...in London without any hope of any place of their own' (p. 731). In a surprising move the perspective then shifts to that of the waiting flatmate, whose conversation with the soldier while Pepita sleeps replaces the physical act. These two charac-ters are used to voice Bowen's pessimism about the war and its 'total of unlived lives' (p. 739), a state of affairs perceived by the man (Arthur) to be particularly hard on women. In Pepita's 'avid dream' (p. 739) of the final paragraph, Kôr, with its 'wide, void, pure streets' where the couple can find a place of their own, remains an illusion necessary to blot out the disruption of ordinary courting by war, when bars, streets, tubes and parks are packed and time is precious. As in her war novel *The Heat of the Day* (1948), 'these defences against the disruptions and chaos of war leave the characters emotionally isolated and distanced from their environment, but in Bowen's work alienation is frequently presented as an essential prerequisite of survival'.[18]

Feelings of isolation and alienation in the modern city also under-pin the writing of Dominican-born author Jean Rhys. Rhys's longevity makes her an interesting link between the modernists and the new, post-Second World War generation: she has a foot in both camps. Brought up in the West Indies but later educated in Britain before spending time in Paris and Vienna, Rhys inflects her stories with her experiences of Caribbean and European life and her sense of herself as an outsider, caught between cultures. Rhys is famous now for her last novel, *Wide Sargasso Sea* (1966), a rewriting of Charlotte Brontë's *Jane Eyre* (1847) partially from the perspective of the Creole Bertha Mason and set in the Caribbean. Yet, as we saw earlier, Rhys had actually been publishing fic-tion since the 1920s. As Helen Carr has argued, 'Rhys writes of an inbe-tween world, where identities are indecipherable, uncertain, confused. In her metropolitan fictions, her characters live in transitory, anony-mous boarding houses and hotels, surrounded by strangers, strangers to those who surround them.'[19]

Although Rhys's first story collection, *The Left Bank and Other Stories* (1927), with its fragmentary narratives and focus on the moment, illus-trates some of the techniques of modernism, the majority of her short stories were published late in her career in the collections *Tigers Are*

Better-Looking (1968) and *Sleep It Off Lady* (1976), both of which contained stories written much earlier; she also contributed to *Penguin Modern Stories* in 1969. Rhys's stories are particularly arresting for their assured use of first-person narrative, filtering events through the perspective of the alienated female outsider, who might be living under an assumed name, and often incorporating flashbacks and streams of consciousness. Some invoked her Caribbean childhood and were written from a child's limited point of view. 'The Day They Burned the Books', about a 'decent, respectable, nicely educated' coloured woman's burning of her white husband's books of English poetry, brought by Royal Mail steamer to the Caribbean, explored ideas of whiteness and racial identity.[20] The narrator's echo of her father's impatience with gradations of 'coloured blood' (p. 46) still does not wholly explain the significance of the burning. The story, according to Coral Ann Howells, 'poses the question, what is the white Creole child heir to in the Caribbean?'[21]

Most of the stories in *Tigers Are Better-Looking* originally appeared in the *London Magazine* in the early 1960s, helping to reignite Rhys's waning reputation and giving her a second lease of literary life long after her modernist contemporaries, Mansfield, Woolf, Joyce *et al.*, had died. In 'Till September, Petronella', the story's title refers to the empty promise made to the model Petronella that the man she picks up will return. The story centres on a typical Rhys heroine who relies on her sexuality to survive as she veers between drunken hysteria, blankness and depression. Reluctant city girl Petronella contemplates suicide as an escape from the 'grey nightmare' of the London streets and the old women in Camden Town market 'looking at you with hatred, or blankly, as though they had forgotten your language, and talked another one' (p. 12). As one of the more sympathetic men asks her, 'What's going to become of you, Miss Petronella Gray, living in a bed-sitting room in Torrington Square, with no money, no background and no nous?' (p. 17). His inadequate advice that she 'grow another skin or two and sharpen your claws before it's too late' (p. 17) underlines women's need for self-protection against the city and its unspecified dangers, and also links with the obsession with female appearance in Rhys's fiction. Parsons notes the disillusionment with the urban in women's fiction of this time, arguing that 'women's posture of urban knowledge and independence has become futile, sterile, and rather sordid', as their urban wanderings register 'confusion, bewilderment, and constant attempts at retreat'.[22] Distanced from her emotions and suffering from the 'dreadful blankness' of her mind, as in the terrifying moment of stage fright in the past when she failed to remember her only line, Petronella is positioned as out of control of her repetitive life, ever subject to the 'sneering expression' of the men she has to rely on.

In a similar way, the frequently anthologised 'Let Them Call It Jazz' includes a direct reference to the narrator's dislike for her London environment within the first few paragraphs: 'Don't talk to me about London. Plenty people there have heart like stone' (p. 47). It also announces itself as a tale of metropolitan discontent and disillusionment. However, the narrative voice, which Rhys referred to as 'stylized patois', is angrier, protesting about the alienation of the immigrant heroine, Selina, who is ostracised not only for her sexuality and her drunkenness, but for her race: 'At least the other tarts that crook installed here were *white* girls' (p. 57). This technique of 'writing back' through the voices of those of 'other' races, anticipating the narrative style of the best-selling *Wide Sargasso Sea* a few years later, was still fairly new in British fiction and particularly effective in the short-story format. In its exploration of the difficulties of racial integration, the story has similarities with the work of Flannery O'Connor (1925–64), who was born in Savannah, Georgia. The comparable title story of O'Connor's posthumous collection *Everything That Rises Must Converge* (1965) mocks the racist attitudes of the white travellers on a post-segregation bus journey through the less prejudiced perspective of a younger son, ending with the humiliation and distress of the racist white mother. Rhys's story achieves its attack on racism through the narrator's compelling articulation of her rights. Though the author feared such an episode might be unpublishable, Selina's time in Holloway Prison for being drunk and disorderly is based on Rhys's brief stay there in 1949, where she was haunted by the women's songs which feature so prominently in the story.[23] Selina's singing in her London home, seen by the neighbours as a 'disturbance', and the singing of the Holloway inmates register a refusal to bow to the forces of English authority. Although Selina is also the object of others' disapproving looks, this makes her angry. Rather than being cowed by her victimisation, her bawled response 'I have absolute and perfect right to be in the street same as anybody else' (p. 55) is a bold statement about the immigrant's desire to assert her claim to a new multicultural Britain. Even the appropriation of her Holloway song in the conclusion of the story, where it is jazzed up by a musician who sells it ('that song was all I had. I don't belong to nowhere really, and I haven't money to buy my way to belonging. I don't want to either', p. 67), is greeted with a shrug; the final clause offers an emphatic valuing of the position of the outsider, marginal to white middle-class culture. Howells is surely right to describe the story as 'a strong statement of female defiance against English racial prejudice and social exclusion'.[24]

Domesticity with a twist: Elizabeth Taylor, Doris Lessing and Fay Weldon

For women writers domesticity has often been a favourite theme, whether to record, to protest against or even to celebrate women's day-to-day experiences as wives, mothers and household managers. Like the 1890s stories by 'New Women' and suffragettes discussed earlier, domestic narratives from the 1960s onwards are particularly interesting in their reflections on the time when 'women ... began to look critically at their own lives and expectations and to recognise that their feelings of depression, entrapment and lack of fulfilment could, at least in part, be laid at the door of the society which did not recognise them as fully equal human beings'.[25] Elizabeth Taylor offers a realist examination of the domestic spaces inhabited by middle-class women and their roles within the family. Taylor began publishing novels in the 1940s, of which the best-known are *Palladian* (1946), a governess narrative which looks back to *Jane Eyre*, and *Angel* (1957). Wallace sees her as 'a writer in the quiet, domestic interior tradition which runs from Jane Austen to Barbara Pym and Anita Brookner',[26] and she has been coupled with Sylvia Townsend Warner as one of the *grandes dames* of the twentieth-century short story by Lynn Knight.[27] Her stories often first appeared in American magazines such as *The New Yorker* and those aimed at women, such as *Harper's Bazaar* and *Vogue*. The detailed concentration on motherhood, work, holidays and female friendship, on the trials and regrets of older, but not always wiser, women, in her four volumes of stories published between the 1950s and the early 1970s anticipates the debates about woman's position to be played out later in the century. The stories can be usefully read alongside the work of the American writer Betty Friedan (1921–2006), whose sociological study *The Feminine Mystique* (1963) is one of the first important polemical texts of second-wave feminism. Friedan's discussion of 'the problem with no name' of the typical middle-class housewife, 'a strange stirring, a sense of dissatisfaction, a yearning that women suffered', partially explains the hollowness and strain of domestic life as it is represented in some of Taylor's work.[28]

Taylor's first collection, *Hester Lilly* (1954), demonstrates a particular interest in the theme of motherhood, at a time when mothers were under pressure to look perfect and manage their perfect homes effortlessly. Although most of the stories are in the third person, they are often written from a female perspective, or they shift between the male and female points of view to register and explore the conflicts of interest and misunderstandings within a marriage or relationship. A. L. Barker refers to this technique as 'contrapuntal', 'revealing thoughts and emotions about the same situation or event – implacably, even comically opposed – to show how the value of experience fluctuates according to who has had it'.[29] One story typical of Taylor's interest in the older woman takes as its focus an eighty-year-old mother and her 'dejected, worn' son who 'might have been husband and wife' (p. 82). In ' "Taking Mother Out" ' the inverted commas around the phrase in the title signal that the balance of power in the relationship is not what it would seem. Although the mother 'displayed him, was indebted to him, gave credit to him, as she was doing now' (p. 79), the son's refusal to respond to her in the dialogue suggests his barely veiled irritation. In 'A Red-Letter Day', which focuses on a nervous divorced mother, Tory, taking her cringing son out for a day from school, the awkwardness of the mother–son relationship is evoked through stilted, artificial dialogue. The son's 'distant politeness' is matched by the 'fretful' mother's 'exasperation' as they struggle to communicate. Tory finds herself inadequate in comparison with the caricatured Mrs Hay-Hardy, with her 'teeming womb…like a woman in a pageant symbolising maternity' (p. 158), still carrying her mother's bag of sensible items. Outside the conventional pattern of the 1950s housewife, Tory's life with her husband has 'loosened and dissolved', leaving her love for her son 'painful, shadowed by guilt – the guilt of having nothing solid to offer' (p. 158). The conclusion of the story, with the son returning to the 'safety' of school, 'radiant with relief' (p. 166), is typical of the note of bitterness which creeps into Taylor's often-comic commentary on the strain and difficulties of family relationships. It also leaves the woman 'disappearing', and moves away from her perspective, which has dominated the story, as if to reinforce the male view. Other stories which sensitively address the feelings of older women are 'Mr Wharton', in *A Dedicated Man* (1965), about a nervous, over-excited mother helping to settle her duplicitous daughter into her new London flat, and the jubilant 'Flesh', from *The Devastating Boys* (1972), the comic holiday romance of 'massive' barmaid Phyl, unconsummated because of her sunburn and her lover's gout.

The final and more ambiguous story from Taylor's first collection, 'I Live in a World of Make-Believe', also ends with the husband's amused detachment from his wife's histrionics, characterising her despairing pose after her failure to impress her posh neighbours as 'Sarah

Bernhardt', a reference to the nineteenth-century tragic actress. The reader is uncertain whether to laugh at or sympathise with Mrs Miller, the fretful heroine of the story, whose frenzied attempts to prepare tea and cakes for Lady Luna are thwarted by her visitor's failure to appear after her daughter's sickness. Mother–son relations are again strained in the story, as Timmy seems to suffer from his mother's 'caprice and bitterness' (p. 207), while Mrs Miller, whose first name remains unknown, appears to find it an effort to behave 'like a good mother' (p. 207). Her martyrdom about her labour in the home and the stresses of visiting is at once comical and poignant, a fine balance achieved by Taylor's use of dialogue and interior monologue:

> 'Your mother' said Mrs Miller quietly, and as if she were not talking of herself, 'has no cook, nor house-parlour-maid, nor nanny ...'
>
> They waited still.
>
> 'She has only herself' she continued, 'to scrub the floors and bake ...'
>
> She produced a formidable vision of vast flagged floors and great bread ovens, her husband thought.
>
> 'And wash and mend,' she concluded. She drew her needle out to the length of the silk and, looking up at them, smiled bravely.
>
> 'But doesn't Mrs Wilson do the scrubbing?' Mr Miller asked, as if to erase this picture of intolerable human suffering.
>
> He could not understand the intricacies of housewifery, Mrs Miller implied by her brief look and her silence. (pp. 206–7)

The technique of presenting the husband's belittling comments and thoughts, and his perception of her anger as affected and misplaced, his need to 'erase' her suffering, might begin to prejudice the reader against him by the end of the story, but the darker moments, such as his imagining suicide, and his wish to protect his son, prevent a simplistic reading. Yet it is also possible to see Mrs Miller's bravery, her anxieties about status and appearance so typical of the 1950s wife, as masking the 'problem with no name' identified by Friedan as bound up with 'the intricacies of housewifery'.

The anxieties of the wife and mother about her family, her home and her sense of self were taken up with more polemical fervour by the feminist writers Doris Lessing and Fay Weldon later in the century. Lessing, an African-born novelist and campaigner, whose groundbreaking novels such as *The Golden Notebook* (1962) have become classic feminist texts, also published numerous collections of short stories, some dealing more obviously with gender roles and others focusing on her African heritage. Her enduring interest in the genre, despite her success as a novelist, has earned her the title of 'self-confessed short story junkie' from the critic Ellen Cronan Rose.[30] Early stories about men and women in conflict, struggling against sexual attraction, appear in her second collection, *A Man and Two Women* (1963), which questions monogamy, marriage and woman's fulfilment in the domestic sphere. This collection included material previously published in such avant-garde magazines as *The New Statesman, Partisan Review, Kenyon Review* and the *London Magazine*. The first story, 'One off the Short List', written from the unsympathetic perspective of a predatory married man enjoying his sexual conquests, is a radical attack on male sexual attitudes. When Graham's attempts to seduce a pretty actress are met with 'a smile of amusement' (p. 208), his seduction is transformed into attempted rape and the desire to master her.[31] However, the actress's passivity and boredom, and her refusal to be dominated, plus a determination '*to get it all over with*' (p. 214), instead make the scene 'the most embarrassing experience of his life' (p. 211). In 'A Man and Two Women', Lessing explores the difficulties of juggling motherhood and work through the situation of new mother Dorothy, who thinks that marriages are 'silly' (p. 253), though ultimately neither her husband nor her friend have the courage to attempt the liberated but dangerous *ménage a trois* she suggests. The sexual candour of Lessing's stories, their dramatisation of the battle of the sexes, reminiscent of the work of D. H. Lawrence, and their focus on ' "other woman" figures who feel the presence of "the shadow of the third", the wife'[32] indicate a development in the woman's short story, a more polemical impulse towards the debates which generated the rise of second-wave feminism.

One frequently anthologised story is 'To Room Nineteen', which is placed at the end of the collection *A Man and Two Women* (1963). This story addresses the stifling 'emptiness' of domesticity for a typical middle-class mother of four. Described in the first sentence as 'a story, I suppose, about a failure in intelligence' (p. 305), and chronicling the descent of the wife, Susan Rawlings, into madness, it is a painful cautionary tale of a couple who 'had everything they had wanted and had planned for' (p. 306) yet still felt unfulfilled. In the midst of marriages breaking up around them, a sign of the times when the divorce rate was growing, the couple looked 'in secret disbelief at this thing they had created – marriage, four children, big house, garden, charwomen, friends, cars' (p. 307) – and the anxieties of keeping it all going. By punctuating their story with the modern tenets by which they lived their lives ('Children needed their mother to a certain age, that both parents knew and agreed on', p. 308), Lessing's analysis of Susan's growing sense of panic at the 'flatness' of their existence is all the more poignant. Once the children all reach school age and are 'off her hands', this panic becomes more acute, as she feels both unable to escape her domestic responsibilities and then deprived of a sense of purpose by her charwoman and the new home help. Room 19 is the room of her own (to pick up on Virginia Woolf's well-known demand), 'more her own than the house she lived in' (p. 327). The room, in a sordid hotel, is where Susan goes to sit alone and do nothing, rather than indulging in the adulterous sex for which the room is usually used. Significantly, Susan is obliged to ask her husband to pay for the privilege of renting the room.

One way of approaching this story is to draw on Simone de Beauvoir's arguments about the need for women to pursue their own liberty. Susan Watkins, in a detailed reading of this 'angry text', notes the difficulties readers might have in responding to Susan's inability to act: 'the extent of her power to act suggests a crucial problem about agency which is also present in *The Second Sex*... Exactly how free does de Beauvoir believe women are to change their situation?'[33] Lessing encourages the reader to question the extent to which her heroine is in control of her life. By the end of the story, after fabricating an affair to match her husband's infidelity, because the real explanation would be 'too terrifying' (p. 329) for both of them, Susan commits suicide in the room, which could be variously interpreted as a means of escape, a bid for liberty or control or a recognition of her own victimisation. Drawing the obvious parallel with Sylvia Plath's writing, Mary Joannou notes 'the metonymic links between mental illness and the post-war feminine mystique'[34] in women's fiction of the 1960s, which reflected the 'quiet dissatisfaction' with the role of 'happy housewife' identified by Friedan.[35]

Primarily known as a novelist whose early work includes *Female Friends* (1975), *Praxis* (1978) and the best-selling *Life and Loves of a She-Devil* (1983), Fay Weldon has also published four collections of short stories, including *Polaris and Other Stories* (1985) and *Watching Me, Watching You* (1981). A former advertising copywriter, Weldon is distinctive as a writer for her short paragraphs and sentences, use of the present tense and repetition of slogan-style phrases to draw out the irony, a device which is particularly effective for the short-story form. Her work, like that of Marilyn French, has been seen as 'consciousness-raising', making women aware of their oppression, in its deployment of 'black humour to articulate energizing anger'.[36] Labelled as controversial in their blatant attacks on men, her stories can also be seen as typical of the particular feminist moment of the late 1970s and early 1980s when sexual explicitness in fiction was both shocking and making a particular feminist point. Many of her stories first appeared in women's magazines such as *Woman's Own, Company* and *Cosmopolitan*, all of which were ideal spaces for interrogating female attitudes to the domestic. The newly launched British version of *Cosmopolitan* was also shocking readers at this time with articles about the female orgasm, the single woman and male centrefolds, and the stories it published were selected to be in dialogue with its feminist and provocative agenda. Weldon's short stories often dealt with adultery, from the point of view of both the mistress and the wife, and the pressures on busy wives to be 'superwomen', a word coined in the 1980s. References to the women's movement and the 'assertive women' who have emerged underpin the stories, though the reader sometimes remains unsure about the attitude she is being invited to adopt towards the 'traditional woman'. In 'In the Great War', a tale of female rivalry set in the 1950s, before women became 'allies', the mistress-turned-wife Enid sets out 'with perfection in mind':

> Doing better! Oh, how neat the corners of the beds she tucked, how fresh the butter, how crisp the tablecloth! Her curtains were always fully lined, her armpits smooth and washed, never merely sprayed. Enid never let her weapons get rusty. She would do better, thank you, than Patty, or Helene, or Rosanne. (p. 137)[37]

Yet by the end of the story the husband returns to his first wife, and Enid brings up her daughter alone, going back to college in order to 'earn a good living' (p. 143). Even those who excel in the bedroom and the kitchen are not guaranteed to keep their men.

'Weekend', a frequently anthologised story, first published in *Cosmopolitan* in 1978, before appearing in *Watching Me, Watching You*, is a darkly comic account of the exhausting domestic work undertaken by the wife and mother figure to achieve a relaxing weekend away for the family. Rather like Elizabeth Taylor's 'I Live in a World of Make-Believe', it deploys the hard-hitting device of including the husband's criticisms in brackets after the wife's endless tasks as part of its attack on the inadequacies of the modern husband: 'Then supper – pork chops in sweet and sour sauce ("Pork is such a *dull* meat if you don't cook it properly": Martin), green salad from the garden, or such green salad as the rabbits had left ("Martha, did you really net them properly? Be honest, now!": Martin)' (pp. 372–3).[38] Its use of lists reinforces the anxieties experienced by women

about their responsibilities for keeping everyone happy and the une-
qual division of labour within the typical home: 'smile, Martha, smile.
Domestic happiness depends on you' (p. 379). These lists are similar to
those featured in 'Christmas Lists – A Seasonal Story' in *Polaris and Other
Stories*, in which the husband ridicules the wife for her 'Christmas file'
begun in September and the lists of chores, presents and family members
to be supported which punctuate their lives. As in other Weldon narratives, the unhappy wife compares herself unfavourably with younger,
thinner female rivals. In 'Weekend', Martin admires Katie, for whom his
friend has left his wife, with her 'lean, childless body', a type of working woman stereotypically oblivious to the messy world of motherhood,
which is driven by 'organising, planning, thinking ahead, side-stepping
disaster, making preparations, like a mother hen, fussing and irritating'
(p. 379). Katie's attempt to help out and prepare lunch by pulling out of
the fridge 'all the things Martha had put away for the next day's picnic
lunch party' (p. 378) means that the careful organisation and preparations are thwarted, leaving the wife more open to the husband's criticisms. Underpinning these criticisms are little comments about Katie's
place in the workplace, her love of work, 'a piece of cake' in comparison,
and her rising wages, reflecting changing social trends. The story ends
with Katie imploring Martha not to clear the coffee cups after Martin
has reproached her for the 'unforgivable offence' of 'the appearance of
martyrdom in the face of guests' (p. 381) before Martha finally cries
uncontrollably at her daughter's first period. These tears are for the next
generation, who will grow up to struggle to maintain what pundits now
call the work–life balance, for the roles women have to fulfil. '[H]er daughter, Jenny: wife, mother, friend' (p. 383) is the final, cryptic one-sentence
paragraph, and it strikes a more sombre note than Taylor achieved. As
one *Guardian* reviewer noted of Weldon's short fiction, 'the sheer sparki-
ness and vitality of the narration hide the depth and pessimism of the
analysis'.[39]

Feminist fairy tales: Angela Carter and A. S. Byatt

A particularly important influence on the development of short stories
has been the fairy tale, with its gender conventions of male power and
female passivity. In the late twentieth century, women writers subverted
such conventions to produce alternative versions of the fairy tale, many
of which can be interpreted as feminist in their revaluing of female
experience. As Hermione Lee has noted, this tradition 'breaks rules,
adapts to circumstances, advises, warns and frightens, gives power to

its stoic and crafty heroines, mixes lies, fantasy and realism'.[40] Female writers who have published stories and/or collections in this subgenre include Angela Carter, A. S. Byatt, Marina Warner, the American novelist Joyce Carol Oates (b.1938) and Margaret Atwood. Irish writer Emma Donoghue's (b.1969) sparkling collection *Kissing the Witch* (1997) rewrites the fairy tale from a lesbian perspective, downplaying the roles of princes and kings and privileging the perspectives of witches, stepmothers and female Rumpelstiltskins. In the opening story, 'The Tale of the Shoe', 'all very fairy-tale', the Cinderella figure chooses the fairy godmother over the prince, throwing the glass slipper into the brambles because it was 'digging into my heel'; in the final tale the lonely witch demands a kiss from the red-haired girl even though 'kissing a witch is a perilous business'.[41]

The most important single collection of fairy tales in this vein has been Carter's *The Bloody Chamber* (1979), seen by some as a landmark in the short-story form, 'as shocking today as when the collection first appeared', according to Helen Simpson, writing in the *Guardian* in 2006.[42] Feminist critics have been divided over whether Carter's rewritings of fairy tales, with their far from passively subordinate heroines, can be seen as an effective challenge to patriarchal values or whether, as Patricia Duncker famously argued in 1984, gender roles and female sexuality ultimately remain static, as 'Carter is rewriting the tales within the strait-jacket of their original structures'. Duncker takes issue with their representation of female sexuality and Carter's notion of the erotic, arguing that 'Carter's tales are, supposedly, celebrations of erotic desire. But...Heterosexual feminists have not yet invented an alternative, anti-sexist language of the erotic.'[43] Or, to put it another way, as Susan Sellers asks in her study of fairy tale and myth in contemporary women's fiction, 'Is feminist rewriting possible?'[44]

Angela Carter has been described as one of the most original writers of her generation; her candid explorations of female sexuality, from sado-masochism to transsexuality, earned her a reputation as an avant-garde author. The same year that *The Bloody Chamber* was published, Carter also published *The Sadeian Woman: An Exercise in Cultural History* (1979), about the types of femininity used in the pornographic novels of the Marquis de Sade, which 'helped set the agenda for the anti-censorship wing of the "sex wars" that divided much feminist campaigning around pornography in the 1980s'.[45] Novels such as *The Magic Toyshop* (1967), *Nights at the Circus* (1985) and *Wise Children* (1992) borrowed from magic realism and irreverently mixed fantasy, myth and the Gothic. Her enduring interest in the fairy tale is evident in her translating of the

works of Charles Perrault, one of the early transcribers of these traditionally oral narratives, and her editing of three collections of fairy tales for
Virago, the newly formed feminist press, later in her career, including
the celebratory *Wayward Girls and Wicked Women*. In the introduction
to *The Virago Book of Fairy Tales* (1990), Carter remarked on the potential
for female resourcefulness: 'The qualities they recommend for the survival and prosperity of women are never those of passive subordination,
[for example] women are required to do the thinking in a family and to
undertake epic journeys'.[46] Her selection serves to back up this thesis.
The selected tales demonstrate, in her words, 'the richness and diversity with which femininity, in practice, is represented in "unofficial"
culture: its strategies, its plots, its hard work'; it is surely significant that
tales about 'Clever Women, Resourceful Girls and Desperate Stratagems'
vastly outnumber tales about 'Good Girls and where it gets them'.[47] For
Carter, good girls are the least interesting characters in this form, so her
own collections examine female vampires, girls transformed into beasts
and women unafraid of violence, demonstrating the strategies women
need to adopt to free themselves from passivity and a heterosexuality
which is always on male terms. She denied that her stories were 'versions' of the fairy tale or, as they are sometimes described, 'adult fairy
tales', claiming that her intention was rather 'to extract the latent content from the traditional stories and to use it as the beginnings of new
stories ... and the latent content is violently sexual'.[48]

The title story, 'The Bloody Chamber', an alternative version of
Perrault's tale of Bluebeard, who keeps his murdered wives locked away
in his castle, is the longest and one of the best, its startling first-person
narrative an obvious means of turning the traditional fairy tale on its
head. The voice of Bluebeard's newest wife, opening the story 'in a tender, delicious ecstasy of excitement' on the train which takes her 'away
from girlhood, away from the white, enclosed quietude of my mother's
apartment, into the unguessable country of marriage' (p. 7), is immediately engaging.[49] The transition from girlhood to womanhood, the
separation from the mother and sexual desire as the unknown are all
traditional Carter territory, as are the luxurious descriptions of clothing
and the modern references to phones, New York agents and gold taps in
what the reader knows is supposed to be a nineteenth-century castle. The
Bluebeard figure here is a marquis, a clear-cross reference to the Marquis
de Sade and his sadomasochistic tendencies. Shocking in its explicitness about the sexual violence of the wedding night, which follows on
directly from the heroine's bewilderment at the pornographic pictures
in her husband's library, the story describes the sexual objectification

of the innocent bride, who is made to wear a ruby choker symbolis-ing the guillotine before she is kissed and reflected in the mirror: 'A dozen husbands impaled a dozen brides' (p. 17). Images of penetration and impaling link sex to the murdered wives in the bloody chamber, 'a little museum of his perversity', 'a room designed for desecration and some dark night of unimaginable lovers whose embraces were anni-hilation' (p. 28), where the Romanian countess is 'pierced, not by one but by a hundred spikes' (p. 29) inside the Iron Maiden, an instrument of torture. As an *Observer* reviewer noted, the collection 'shows Angela Carter taking the opportunity to give her own particular twist of sexual unease to the vivid, cruel world of the fairy story... as surprising and disconcerting as the original unbowdlerized Grimm'.[50]

And yet the tale also chronicles the heroine's loss of innocence and the strategies she uses to outwit the marquis. Determined not to be the next victim, she 'retained sufficient presence of mind' (p. 29) to cover her traces in the chamber, and she feels herself animated by the spirit of her tiger-defying mother as she finds out the worst. As a way out of remaining a sexual object, she learns to acknowledge and wel-come her own desires for her monstrous husband, but she is also able to dupe him by performing her own sexuality: 'I forced myself to be seductive. I saw myself, pale, pliant as a plant that begs to be trampled underfoot, a dozen appealing girls reflected in as many mirrors, and I saw how he almost failed to resist me' (p. 35). This perhaps goes some way towards the creation of a new language of the erotic which Patricia Duncker hoped for. Queer theorist Judith Butler's arguments about gen-der as a performance, '*a stylized repetition of acts*', are also relevant here,[51] as it is the heroine's performance of a pliant heterosexual femininity which allows her to alter her fate. (Sex, mirrors and gender performance are also key elements of an earlier story, 'Flesh and the Mirror', which appeared in Carter's first collection, *Fireworks*). The heroine of 'The Bloody Chamber' is nurtured and helped by a blind piano tuner, who will love her without fetishising her beauty. Carter replaces the broth-ers who rescue the bride in the original Perrault tale with the return of the mother, likened to Medusa, who turned men to stone. As a woman rescues a woman, gender categories are overturned and male power is deflated: 'The puppet master, open-mouthed, wide-eyed, impotent at the last, saw his dolls break free of their strings, abandon the rituals he had ordained for them since time began and start to live for themselves; the king, aghast, witnesses the revolt of his pawns' (p. 39). The ending is not as black and white, however; the mother has had to use the father's gun, a man's weapon, to kill the marquis, and the daughter retains a mark of her shame at the end, which could be interpreted to mean that sexual knowledge is shaming, rather than liberatory, for women.

Other stories in *The Bloody Chamber* work in groups or pairs: there are two versions of 'Beauty and the Beast', and three wolf stories loosely related to 'Little Red Riding Hood'. These stories focus on transformations, looking at the boundaries between beast and beauty, and the moments of empathy with what, in 'The Bloody Chamber', Carter refers to as 'the atrocious loneliness of the monster'. In 'The Tiger's Bride', the second, more subversive rewriting of 'Beauty and the Beast', readers are told how '[t]he tiger will never lie down with the lamb; he acknowledges no pact that is not reciprocal. The lamb must learn to run with the tigers' (p. 64). In the ending, rather than continuing 'to perform the part of my father's daughter', where she is bartered in the marriage market, the heroine is transformed into a beast, who 'shrugged the drops off my beautiful fur' (p. 67).

Critics have also been particularly interested in the story 'The Company of Wolves', not least because it was made into a successful film directed by Neil Jordan in 1984. Opening with a series of mini-narratives about werewolves before offering a version of the familiar tale of 'Little Red Riding Hood', this is one of the most complex stories in the collection, as the narratives work against each other in their characterisation of the wolf. 'Fear and flee the wolf; for, worst of all, the wolf may be more than he seems' (p. 111), the reader is cautioned, yet the ending of the story sees the heroine sleeping soundly in her grandmother's bed, 'between the paws of the tender wolf' (p. 118), naked and animal-like. Not heeding the danger, the 'wise child' delivers her lines, 'What big eyes you have', but learns to embrace her fate, 'since her fear did her no good, she ceased to be afraid' (p. 117). The wolf here is represented in terms of an aggressive heterosexuality, stripping off before the grandmother ('His genitals, huge. Ah! Huge') and showing 'a remarkable object in his pocket', but he is also the object of the girl's curiosity, once she learns not to take his aggression seriously and to burst out laughing at his desire to eat her up: 'she knew she was nobody's meat' (p. 118). She then helps to undress him and 'freely gave the kiss she owed him' (p. 118), acknowledging her desires rather than always taking the cue from him. Shedding her clothes as an act of liberation also recalls 'The Tiger's Bride' and the later story 'Wolf-Alice.' These echoes serve to link the stories together. As Helen Simpson notes, 'Images of meat, naked flesh, fur, snow, blood unite, giv[e] these stories an unmistakable family resemblance.'[52] While some critics labelled the explicitness of the stories pornographic, others admired their daring and liberating representations of female sexual identities: 'Until we can take on board the disturbing and even violent elements of female sexuality, we will not be able to decode the full feminist agenda of these fairy tales.'[53]

One writer strongly influenced by Carter and sharing her interest in fairy-tale traditions from around the world is her contemporary A. S. Byatt (b.1936), who, like Carter, first began publishing fiction in the 1960s. Byatt's high-brow novels, often partly set in the nineteenth century, include *The Virgin in the Garden* (1978), *Angels and Insects* (1992), which is about Darwinism, and the Booker Prize-winning *Possession: A Romance* (1990), about academics researching the lives of Victorian poets. She has also published five collections of short stories, *Sugar and Other Stories* (1987), *The Matisse Stories* (1993), *The Djinn in the Nightingale's Eye* (1994), *Elementals: Stories of Fire and Ice* (1999) and *Little Black Book of Stories* (2003), and has edited editions of *New Writing* and *The Oxford Book of Short Stories* (1998). All her collections are beautifully illustrated with vibrantly coloured covers featuring related paintings, reflecting Byatt's fascination with visual art. Borrowing from postmodern techniques, her typical meta-fictional tale plays with convention and 'attempts... to unsettle its readers by thwarting expectations both as to the twists and turns generic fairy tales are supposed to take as well as to any presuppositions such readers may have entertained about the teller'.[54] Less concerned with female sexuality than Carter's stories, and usually adopting the familiar 'Once upon a time' format, Byatt's stories nevertheless draw the reader into an entirely fabulous world. This world sometimes features fairy-tale characters in modern settings, as in the long title story from *The Djinn in the Nightingale's Eye*, where the djinn, or genie, appears in the Turkish hotel room of the narratologist Dr Gillian Perholt, whose 'business was storytelling' and who is attending a conference on 'Stories of Women's Lives'. With tongue firmly in cheek, Byatt begins this long tale with the sentence 'Once upon a time, when men and women hurtled through the air on metal wings, when they wore webbed feet and walked on the bottom of the sea...' (p. 95), establishing her modern setting within the fairy-tale framework.[55] Meta-fictional jokes about how the heroine responds to and learns from the djinn are linked to the series of stories about male power told at the conference (Gillian significantly tells that of Chaucer's long-suffering Patient Griselda) and the more revisionary stories exchanged between Gillian and the djinn. It is interesting that despite her initial panic that she has 'no story' and is therefore irrelevant, Gillian goes on to narrate a tale about her perception of her body as a younger woman, in which the first of the three wishes granted by the djinn is to have her body return to the state when she last liked it, underlining one of the answers to what women desire and the narratives about female beauty dominant in her culture.

In one of the best-known stories from the same collection, 'The Story of the Eldest Princess', Byatt uses a quest narrative to examine the choices available to young women and the ways in which they can seek to alter their destiny. She was commissioned to write the story for a collection of contemporary fairy tales and fables published by Vintage, *Caught in a Story* (1992), and chose this theme as she had 'always been worried about being the eldest of three sisters' (p. 280). To restore the blue colour of the sky, the eldest princess is sent off through the forest to find a single silver bird with an inexhaustible water bottle and a sword, though the quest is never fulfilled and she never returns. What makes the narrative postmodern is the princess's awareness of quest narratives: 'she had read a great many stories in her spare time, including several stories about princes and princesses who set out on Quests' (p. 47). A common pattern is that the older sisters, or brothers, are doomed to failure and can only be rescued by the third royal person. 'She thought, I am in a pattern I know, and I suspect I have no power to break it, and I am going to meet a test and fail it, and spend seven years as a stone' (p. 48). Persuaded to leave the path by a series of increasingly horrible creatures, including a scorpion, a cockroach and a toad who promises not to turn into a prince, she ultimately arrives at the house of an old woman, having rejected a handsome woodcutter with a taste for domestic violence en route. The old woman congratulates her with having 'the sense to see that you were caught in a story, and the sense to see that you could change to another one' (p. 66). Older women, who are free because they 'have no story of [their] own', have escaped narratives of princes and kings, marriages and succession. The old woman also offers her the brief stories of the younger princesses, though the second princess's completion of the quest and succession to queen is dull in comparison to the third princess's unfinished story, which, like Scheherazade's tales, holds the reader's interest by its withholding of the ending. Sellers has drawn attention to the unsatisfactory position of women 'not having or being outside the story' in Byatt's tales, something which she sees as being as problematic as those 'trapped within narratives that hinder them'.[56] The moral of Byatt's tale might be that trying to change your own story, as well as rejecting narrative patterns seen as restricting, is a means of emancipation. As the character Gillian Perholt remarks in 'The Djinn in the Nightingale's Eye', 'consider this…in almost all stories of promises and prohibitions, the promises and prohibitions carry with them the inevitability of failure, of their own breaking' (p. 111). Failure, to live up to expectations about femininity, to observe rules, becomes important and necessary.

In her later collection *Elementals*, Byatt uses opposing images of fire and ice to comment on women's perceptions of their lives, again mixing modern settings with fairy-tale themes and including tales within tales. Reviewing the collection in the *Independent on Sunday*, Michele Roberts admired the 'rich physical details, lush sensual descriptions of people and places...Byatt's engaging message is that art, curiosity and stories save us'.[57] In 'Cold', the princess Fiammarosa, who grows thinner and whiter as she grows up, presents 'a picture of lassitude and boredom, or, just possibly, of despair' (pp. 120–21), only coming to life when the temperature cools. In an erotically charged passage she creeps out in the night into the snow, 'her body...full of an electric charge, a thrill, from an intense cold' (p. 125), takes off her clothes, lies in the ice and then dances a strange leaping dance. She is then slowly transformed into a frozen icewoman, like Fror, who is imprisoned for witchcraft and has to give up her son, the subject of the embedded story told to her by her tutor, Hugh. Although her coldness is equated with her inability to love, 'there was more life in coldness. In solitude. Inside a crackling skin of protective ice that was also a sensuous delight' (p. 133). In a fascinating passage about princesses at the centre of the story, Byatt debunks myths and appears to grant her heroine a freedom from commodification before bowing to patriarchal requests:

> Princesses, also, are expected to marry. They are expected to marry for dynastic reasons, to cement an alliance, to placate a powerful rival, to bear royal heirs. They are, in the old stories, gifts and rewards, handed over by their loving fathers to heroes and adventurers...It would appear, Fiammarosa had thought as a young girl, reading both histories and wonder tales, that princesses are commodities. But also, in the same histories and tales, it can be seen that this is not so. Princesses are captious and clever choosers...They do have, in real life, the power to reject and some power to choose. They are wooed. She had considered her own cold heart in this context and had thought that she would do better, ideally, to remain unmarried. She was too happy alone to make a good bride. She could not think out a course of action entirely but had vaguely decided upon a course of prevarication and intimidation, if suitors presented themselves (pp. 135–36)

Uncertain whether they are reading an old story or a slice of real life, readers now expect the princess to have some power to reject or choose, but not, it seems, to remain unmarried, as in the next paragraph we are told that the king's own idea was that 'his daughter needed to marry more than most women' (p. 137). The cold list of reasons why princesses have to marry and become commodities, taken for granted in the fairy tale, cannot be escaped, as the princess has to fulfil the role of 'good bride'. The glass gifts from Prince Sasan which help to win her heart are the prelude to a difficult marriage in which sex brings her out in red marks and she loses her unborn child after being exposed to the heat of the glass-blowing furnace. But in an unexpected happily ever after ending their marriage is saved by her husband's building of a glass palace for them to live in and the birth of twins, rewriting the Fror narrative in more enabling terms, though still tinged with loneliness and compromise: 'And if Fiammarosa was sometimes lonely in her glass palace, and sometimes wished that Sasan would come more often, and that she could roam amongst fjords and ice-fells, this was not unusual, for no one has everything they can desire' (pp. 181–82). As Sellers concludes, 'feminist rewriting can thus be thought of in two categories: as an act of demolition, exposing and detonating the stories that have hampered women, and as a task of construction – of bringing into being enabling alternatives.'[58]

Women's stories after the Second World War can, then, be seen to respond to the concerns of feminism, to debates about work and domestic space, often through their focus on the alienated perspective of the frustrated housewife and mother. The renewed interest in the fairy-tale form from the 1970s onwards has allowed female authors to embrace an enabling process of feminist rewriting by revisiting the gender stereotypes of the originals and finding an alternative narrative voice. While some stories, particularly those of Bowen and Rhys, look back to modernist writers such as Mansfield in their use of fragmentation and stream of consciousness, others adopt more postmodern techniques of meta-fictionality, drawing the reader's attention to the short-story form and its limits, a technique used by other twenty-first-century writers such as A. L. Kennedy (b.1965) and Ali Smith, to be further discussed in the next chapter.

12
The British Short Story Today

Changes in British society, including mass immigration, the recruitment of new workers from the West Indies and a rise in mixed-race relationships, contributed to the growth of multiculturalism after the Second World War, ensuring that post-war fiction came increasingly to address issues of race, ethnicity and mixed-race relationships. In his discussion of the development of the British novel between 1950 and 2000, Dominic Head has commented on the complex questions of identity and national affiliation at the end of empire, in which fiction 'has proved to be a fruitful site for investigating the hybridised cultural forms that might be produced in an evolving, and so *genuinely*, multicultural Britain'.[1] Hybridity, referring to the process of the mixing of races theorised by Homi Bhabha, becomes a key concern, but though it can sometimes be celebratory, 'the migrant identities that are fictionalised in post-war writing are often embattled and vulnerable'.[2] Large-scale post-war migration and xenophobia influenced notions of national identity; as Mark Stein has written, 'black British authors record both a confrontation between their protagonists and Britain, its institutions, its people, and some of the strategies that were employed in this situation'.[3] In his discussion of the politics of recognition, Charles Taylor[4] contends that racial identity needs to be recognised, acknowledged in its diversity and difference, to combat the process of 'othering', which marginalises those who do not fit easily into conceptions of whiteness. Postcolonial critics such as Stuart Hall have argued for a new understanding of 'the margin as a space of productive negotiation', so that we can celebrate rather than attack difference.[5] This chapter will focus specifically on narratives of multicultural life, of racial conflict or new ethnic identities, often centred on a moment of crisis that acts as a revelation of the complexities of integration into the community. It also addresses the ways in which the short-story form has been used to reflect on national identities. To narrow down a potentially very broad discussion of the multiple strands and concerns of the contemporary short story, we have decided to focus on Scottishness, as the genre has proved particularly malleable in the hands of a new generation of Scottish writers who have been prepared to take risks with the parameters and conventions of the form.

The experience of the immigrant, often represented as an alienated outsider, has been a common theme of the British short story, allowing writers to explore and protest against this process of othering. Although it has been argued that the race question has been a more important focus for Irish and American short-story writers,[6] it is still a vital concern in Britain, and is particularly appropriate to the contemporary short story. Women writers discussed in the previous chapter such as Jean Rhys, who moved from the Caribbean to Europe in the 1920s, and the South African-born Doris Lessing, who arrived in London in 1949, as well as first-generation children of immigrants growing up in a predominantly white environment, have 'a curiously mixed perspective on English culture ... simultaneously that of outsider and insider'.[7] Stories about race and multiculturalism are often written in the first person in order to rewrite events from the oblique point of view of the insider/outsider figure. The postmodern techniques of contemporary short-story writers, including a conscious questioning of the expectations readers have of stories, suggest a return to the experimental, with authors such as Jackie Kay and Ali Smith withholding information about their unnamed and sometimes ungendered narrators, leaving the sexual orientation of characters purposefully unspecified or obscure until the end of the story. While place is necessarily a key component of stories interested in ideas of nation and community, this, too, is sometimes significantly unspecified to throw readers off balance and make them question their assumptions about racial identity and what constitutes 'home'.

Black British writers and multiculturalism: Jackie Kay and Hanif Kureishi

The collections of black Scottish writer Jackie Kay, *Why Don't You Stop Talking?* (2002) and *Wish I Was Here* (2006), offer a range of monologues, mostly from the female perspective, on motherhood, breastfeeding, adoption, rejection, jealousy and 'day-to-day paranoias and prevarications ... affording glimpses into frail private worlds which are both familiar and strange'.[8] Born in Edinburgh, adopted by a white Scottish family and growing up in Glasgow before moving to the more multicultural Manchester, where she now lives and works, Kay negotiates the role of outsider as well as setting out to normalise mixed-race and/or lesbian relationships between women. Alex Clark has noted the author's 'remarkable... ability to write about lesbian relationships and racial identity without ever seeming to be pushing an issue on us'. Clark argues that the dissection of 'human ordinariness' overrides this, as 'Kay's characters challenge themselves and us to make sense of their oddball lives, to find a meaning in all the comic (and cosmic) chaos and fertile chatter'.[9] Kay's experimentation with narrative perspective had already been demonstrated in her poetry collection *The Adoption Papers* (1991) and her acclaimed only novel *Trumpet* (1998), both of which shift among narrators of different races. In *Why Don't You Stop Talking?* some of the narrators are black, such as Rose McGuire Roberts in 'Out of Hand', who looks back on her life in England as a nurse, having stepped off 'that huge fiction of a ship' (p. 169)[10], the *Windrush*, in 1948. Like many other immigrants who came to 'the mother country' on this vessel, her dreams of 'England, England, England!' (p. 160) fail to match up with the reality of racism and marginalisation and the shouts of 'Go back to your own country!', leaving us with the question, 'How come she thought England was her country? How did that happen?' (p. 168). Kay's use of Scottish dialect and idioms for some of these narrator figures gives authenticity and works in tandem with the focus on black identity to interrogate standard notions of Britishness, as in the compelling two-part story 'Wha's Like Us', half a third-person description of 'The oldest woman in Scotland' and her great-grandchildren, half a monologue in dialect examining 'A guid Scots death'. In the first part, the fleeting reference to the 'brave' act of white parents adopting a black child, mirroring Kay's own upbringing, steers the story away from a standard version of Scottish identity. Stories such as 'Big Milk' in her first collection, named after the larger of the lover's breasts, in which the black female narrator struggles with her rejection by her white mother and her jealousy of the breast-feeding baby of her female partner, address the experiences of parenting from a lesbian perspective: 'At night I lie in bed next to the pair of them sleeping like family. The mother's arms flung out like a drowned bird. The baby suckling like a tiny pig... I lie next to the sleeping mother and baby and feel totally irreligious. They are a painting. I could rip the canvas' (p. 24). Milk is used to symbolise both the comfort and complications of maternity: the final image of the narrator drinking sour milk on her own estranged mother's doorstep in Scotland encapsulates the (often frustrated) need to be nurtured and part of the family which many of her characters express. This ending also, as Joanne Winning notes, brings together the anxious positions of non-biological lesbian parent and displaced Scot, questioning how 'one might be able to fulfil one's longing for an authentic "home" identity'.[11]

Kay's second collection, *Wish I Was Here*, dissects the experience of jealousy and the breakdown of relationships from the perspectives of both lesbian and heterosexual characters, using race as a complicating factor in some of the stories. Focusing primarily on women's experiences of fulfilment, frustration or isolation within the domestic space, on the strains and stresses of maintaining relationships or surviving their breakdown, Kay's subtle humour and inventiveness nevertheless tend to rescue the stories from the bleakness and despair they sometimes approach: the woman who repeatedly and gleefully uses quotes from Martin Amis novels as a form of abuse against her affronted lover in the opening story, significantly titled 'You Go When You Can No Longer Stay', will no doubt make the literary reader smile. The lesbian narrator finds it odd that 'Martin Amis should be coming into our lives in this way' (p. 3), as if Kay is self-consciously distancing herself from the fiction of her contemporary Amis, whose frank depictions of aggressive heterosexuality are a million miles away from the kinds of relationship she herself wishes to depict. Aimed at exactly this kind of knowing middle-class audience, many of these stories first appeared in newspapers and magazines such as *Granta* and the *Guardian*, and on Radio 3 and Radio 4, as well as in anthologies of Scottish writing. With a nod to Angela Carter, the mother in 'My Daughter the Fox' gives birth to and breastfeeds a fox, struggling to ignore the screams and horror of family, friends and midwife, focusing instead on the nurturing process. This could, perhaps, be read in terms of the community's reactions to white parenting of black children ('They were all shaking and quaking like it was the most disgusting thing they had ever seen', p. 87), but it is also one of a number of stories in which a transformation into some kind of animal (like the depressed mother slowly transforming into a tortoise in 'Shell' in the first collection) shatters the illusion of cosy domesticity in order to symbolise the strains and challenges of motherhood. Like many of the narrators of other stories, the fox's mother is on her own, with an absent partner, and her bitterness drives the tale. The deluded and rejected lover of 'Wish I Was Here', awaiting the arrival in a foreign resort of her ex with her new lover, tells us in the first paragraph of her increasingly excruciating narrative that 'I'll be a nice surprise for them'

(p. 27), as she is unable to stop herself describing the togetherness she and her ex have shared, though this is, of course, now locked within the past she cannot reclaim. These abandoned and unloved narrators look back to their past relationships with poignancy in these sad but sometimes also darkly comic tales of the effects of desire that has been outgrown.

Hanif Kureishi, born and brought up in Kent by a white English mother and a Pakistani father, has published a number of short-story collections addressing the state of multicultural Britain, focusing on mixed-race relationships and intergenerational conflict between traditional parents who moved to Britain from Asia and more liberated British-born children. Dominic Head has discussed Kureishi's fiction in relation to metropolitan experiences and the flight from suburbia, admiring the ways in which his work engages with 'issues of ethnicity and opportunity'.[12] Kureishi uses his opinionated, sympathetic male narrators to epitomise and confront the challenges of hybridity in contemporary London, the problems and opportunities generated by being 'black British' or half-Asian, half-English. The problems of definition or split allegiances to two different cultures which figure in these narratives also apply to the author; as Stein has asked, 'Is Hanif Kureishi...a "black" writer, and if so, what does this mean?'[13] In discussing the shift to a multicultural society around the 1980s, Kureishi amends this to 'black or Asian':

> This wasn't merely a confrontation with simple racism, the kind of thing I'd grown up with, which was usually referred to as 'the colour problem'. When I was young, it was taken for granted that to be black or Asian was to be inferior to the white man. And not for any particular reason. It was just a fact. This was much more than that. Almost blindly, a revolutionary, unprecedented social experiment had been taking place. The project was to turn – out of the end of Empire, and on the basis of mass immigration – a predominantly white society into a racially mixed one, thus forming a new notion of what Britain was and would become.[14]

The author has always had a fairly prominent media presence, winning awards for early screenplays such as *My Beautiful Launderette* (1985), a controversial film about the secret homosexual relationship between a white working-class teenager and his educated Asian friend in Thatcherite London. His narratives not only 'altered the popular perception of Asians in mainstream culture' but also inspired other writers:[15] the popular British film *East Is East* (1997), about a mixed-race family in 1970s Salford, was based on a play by the Asian writer Ayub Khan Din (b.1961), who appeared in one of Kureishi's earlier films and was evidently inspired by his work.

Kureishi's confrontation of the difficulties of a racially mixed society forms the basis of a significant number of his short stories. One of the most hard-hitting stories from his first collection, *Love in a Blue Time* (1997), is 'My Son the Fanatic', which first appeared in *The New Yorker* in 1994 and was adapted into a BBC film, released in 1998 – one example of the increasing adaptability of short stories to screen in the late twentieth and twenty-first centuries. Focusing on the troubled relationship between the Pakistani Parvez and his increasingly sharp-tongued teenage son, the narrative perspective is that of the father, bewildered by the eccentric behaviour of his son, Ali, who throws out his material possessions, the electrical equipment usually beloved of teenagers, and finishes with his English girlfriend. The twist in the tale is that, rather than earning his father's anger by readily embracing Western ideals and habits, becoming a drug addict as his father suspects, the son is fervently following the rules of the Koran, praying regularly and later denouncing his father for drinking and eating pork. 'Yet Parvez felt his son's eccentricity as an injustice. He had always been aware of the pitfalls which other men's sons had fallen into in England. And so, for Ali, he had worked long hours and spent a lot of money paying for this education as an accountant' (p. 119).[16] Had his son gained a good job and married 'the right girl', 'his dreams of doing well in England would have come true' (p. 120), with the suggestion that it is the father who would prefer a mixed-race marriage, not necessarily the son. The situation alienates him from his Punjabi friends, who become 'oddly silent. They could hardly condemn the boy for his devotions' (p. 123). The father's desire to 'fit in' (p. 125) and his allegiances to England distance him from the son (as the title of the story suggests), leading to his violent drunken attack on the unresisting boy in the final paragraph, with the boy's retort, 'So who's the fanatic now?' (p. 131), thrown out of the story to the reader. Demonstrating the difficulties of 'fitting in' in England, and the violence within the family born out of frustration, this powerful and very contemporary tale subverts some of the stereotypes about black British identity. Other stories in the collection address these stereotypes in both comic and serious terms, protesting against the reluctance of the white British to accept immigrant families. In 'We're Not Jews' (1997), which first appeared in the *London Review of Books*, Azhar and his white mother, Yvonne, are bullied on a bus

252 The Post-War Short Story

by the racist Billy family, whose verbal abuse, the 'renewed might of names new to Azhar: sambo, wog, little coon' (p. 43), repeats that used at school. He struggles with his mother's explanations of the inferiority of 'black and brown people' across the world, 'vertiginously irrational and not taught in his school' (p. 45), which echo through his dreams. And yet the story goes on to show the inadequacies of available hybrid identities: Yvonne refuses to use the word 'immigrant' about her husband, because 'in her eyes it applied only to illiterate tiny men with downcast eyes and mismatched clothes' (p. 45), and both parents lack a stable sense of 'home', as neither Pakistan nor England, 'the new country' (p. 46), offers them security and acceptance. In interview Kureishi refers to the contemporary nature of his work, which he labels 'state of Britain' narratives, reflecting the time in which they were written. However, he also brackets them as pre-7/7 texts (referring to the bombing of London by terrorists in July 2005), and fears that they might be seen as 'frivolous' in light of negative perceptions of Muslims in Britain hardened in the wake of the feared terrorist threat.[17]

Stories foregrounding the concerns of mixed-race families in Britain before 7/7 are interspersed with narratives which capture the strains and petty bickering of married life and the heady, life-affirming qualities of secret, sordid affairs, with a particular focus on the perspective of the anxious or estranged father. In the short, rather melancholic 'Nightlight', in *Love in a Blue Time*, the unnamed male narrator reflects on his own 'random desolation' in an existence organised around picking up his kids three times a week before returning them to a house his wife now 'forbids him to enter' and his Wednesday night 'inexplicable liaison[s]' (p. 140) with a passionate woman of unknown address who keeps her cab waiting outside. With the dialogue reduced to a brief exchange of abuse as he leaves his wife's house in the middle of the night, tripping over the TV as he goes, and the questions he formulates but never asks of his lover, the story, punctuated by his unanswered questions about life and 'Success', describes his thwarted desires and shabby sense of hopelessness with a touching honesty: 'The shame of loneliness, a dingy affliction! There are few creatures more despised than middle-aged men with strong desires, and desire renews itself each day, returning like a recurring illness, crying out, more life, more!' (pp. 143–4). Ending with the characteristic impasse that even though sex is all you want it is never sufficient, the narrative is typical of Kureishi's portraits of the desires of middle-aged men, tired of their families but dissatisfied by what else remains. Critics have read his work in the context of the 'male testimonial', with Bradley Buchanan arguing that his 'heroes' rejection of the shackles [of marriage and shared responsibility] is never more than a partial escape from the torments of adulthood', with the collections serving as 'sad, angry, despairing testaments to the difficulties that attend one's adult obligations, whether one accepts them fully or not'.[18]

His second collection, *Midnight All Day* (1999), 'not a book you would read in bed to cheer yourself up', according to Susie Thomas,[19] resounds with the laments and dissatisfactions of absent or reluctant father figures, recording their ambivalent feelings about their families. The strangely titled 'Morning in the Bowl of Night' describes the peculiarity of an absent father's attendance at his son's nativity play and his strained exchanges 'for the public show' (p. 197) with his estranged wife. In the poignant tale 'The Umbrella', the inappropriately dressed father waits in the dripping porch of his former home with his two small sons, shut out by changed locks, until his sneering wife returns and refuses to lend him one of his own umbrellas, punches him and pushes him out into the driving rain. This frustrated violence, a recurring marker of the desolation of broken marriages, is only partially offset by Roger's final walk to a party in the soaking rain in his dishevelled suit: 'It would not stop raining for a long time. He could not just stand in the same place for hours. The thing to do was not to mind. He started out then, across the Green, in the dark, wet through, but moving forward' (p. 192). In 'That Was Then', about the passionate reunion of former lovers Nick and Natasha, their past 'exotic interests' and the 'new fears and transgressions' of the AIDS period (p. 80) are set against Nick's new role of father and the memoir he has written about his own father and 'what men, and fathers, could become, having been released, as women were two decades earlier, from some of their unconventional expectations' (p. 68). In flashbacks to their heady days as sexual outlaws, he remembers the artificiality of the moment: 'Like actors unable to stop playing a part, as though they could be on stage for ever, he and Natasha wanted to remain at a dramatic pitch where there was no disappointment, no self-knowledge or development, only a state of constant, narcissistic emergency and a clear white light in the head' (p. 81). But the end of the story sees the return to the security of his wife, son and excessively large freezer, after an afternoon drugged and tied to his ex-lover's bed, with the familiar reference to unprotected sex and the ambivalence towards pregnancy leaving the reader uncertain of Kureishi's message. Stein argues that some of his later stories can be seen as 'postethnic', in that they self-consciously sidestep concerns about migration, race and ethnicity, in order to tease the reader, 'provoking questions such as: "Why does the ethnicity of the character matter? Or, why does it not matter?"[20] While these metropolitan narratives, with their evocation of both the liberation and sordid underside of millennium London, could be read as 'speculative, incomplete attempts to make some sense of unpromising relationships',[21] they also offer a dark vision of mid-life crisis, of the stifling nature of domesticity and the failure to return to the lost, careless hedonism and numbing drug culture of the consumerist 1980s. The undisclosed Britishness, 'black' or otherwise, of Kureishi's anxious fathers works in tandem with the foregrounding of ethnic markers in other stories in the collections to question the links between ethnicity, family and masculinity.

Scottish short stories: James Kelman, A. L. Kennedy and Ali Smith

One of the things that becomes evident in looking at the landscape of the contemporary short story is that old-fashioned and stereotyped ideas about 'merrie England', with the short story 'marooned amongst buffers and buffoons, bucolics, butties and Blimps', as A. S. Byatt has put it in her introduction to the most recent edition of *The Oxford Book of English Short Stories* (1998), are no longer tenable.[22] The contemporary short story carries with it deeper political and cultural dimensions, particularly as these relate to ideas about what it means to be English, but also Scottish, Welsh or Irish. There is a long tradition of short-story writing in Wales in both Welsh and English, and also in Ireland.[23] William Trevor, born in Mitchelstown, County Cork, remains one of the pre-eminent Irish practitioners of the genre, alongside such writers as Colm Tóibín (b.1955) and Bernard MacLaverty. Born in Belfast, MacLaverty has published five collections, including *Walking the Dog* (1994) and *Matters of Life and Death: And Other Stories* (2006), as well as a number of novels, though his move to Scotland in 1975 has served to complicate any easy assessment based on meanings of Irishness in his work. Trevor, who has published an impressive twelve collections of short stories, from early works such as *The Ballroom of Romance and Other Stories*(1972) to the more recent *Hill Bachelors* (2000) and *Cheating at Canasta* (2007), also moved away from Ireland, emigrating to England in 1954, but, as Joyce famously proved, being exiled from one's country, perhaps particularly in the case of Ireland with its troubled history of religious and political conflict, does not necessarily restrict its influence on an author's writing. Many of Trevor's and MacLaverty's stories are set in Ireland or focus on journeys to or from Ireland. They rely on a strong sense of place to evoke its enduring traditions, its sense of family and community, and are often narrated by or interested in those who do not fit neatly into the identities associated with these structures. Neil Corcoran has admired the melancholy of Trevor's stories, effective in such early stories as 'The Ballroom of Romance', set in the 1940s and 1950s, when the lower-middle-class Protestant Irish provincial class was in the process of disintegration, as well as in those which engage more directly with Irish political history, such as 'The Distant Past' and 'The News from Ireland'.[24] Concerns about Irishness, and the vexed relationship with England, are filtered through outsider figures – the forgotten spinsters, the hill bachelors – and those trapped within cultural and religious conventions, such as disillusioned brides and soldiers.

The focus of this section, however, is Scotland. The vibrancy and diversity of the contemporary Scottish short story can in part be attributed to the renaissance in Scottish literature since the 1980s, with a crossover into popular films such as *Trainspotting* (1996), based on Irvine Welsh's internationally successful 1993 novel. Other influential writers, such as Alasdair Gray and James Kelman, with their proud use of local dialect and swear-words associated with a particular kind of Scots idiom, have helped to shape perceptions of Scottish identity and given direction to fictional forms and styles. Welsh, Kelman and Duncan MacLean (b.1964), author of the prize-winning collection *Bucket of Tongues* (1992), toured the United States and Australia in the mid-1990s, boosting the profile of Scottish fiction. A popular – if simplistic – way of reading Scottish fiction since the 1980s is to connect recent success with political developments, in particular the campaign for independence from England. In 1979, there was a good deal of disappointment and anger when the Devolution Bill, which was intended to give Scotland its own parliament, was defeated, but in the following decades fiction began to thrive, even before Scotland's achievement of a devolved parliament in May 1999.[25] As with discussions of the Irish and Welsh short story, it has become commonplace to argue that when a country struggles politically to establish its sovereignty, it is literature that works to safeguard national identity. Ian Bell sees in Scottish writing of the past twenty years 'a radical literature of [political] resistance and reclamation'.[26] And yet, as Berthold Schoene has asked in his discussion of post-devolution 'Scottishness', 'Ought Scottish literature to continue to be burdened with an alleged national specificity, or should it be allowed to go cosmopolitan rather than native?' How helpful is the label of Scottishness at a time when 'Scotland evidently holds postethnic potential?'[27] What it means to be Scottish, like what it means to be

British, Welsh or Irish, might need to be reconstituted in a multicultural postethnic world, where writers resident, but not born and raised, in a country necessarily adopt new personas which might or might not be influenced by the fiction of their new homeland. MacLaverty, Irish but resident in Scotland for the past thirty-five years, is eligible to win Scottish literary prizes. Kay's sense of her own Scottishness is shot through with her status as outsider: 'That sense of being outside with being inside Scotland – with being very proud of the country and very proud of being Scottish, and also being outside in terms of receiving a lot of racism from other Scottish people – is what fuels my sense of how and what I write.'[28]

Scottish short-story specialists have been particularly interested in reclaiming the marginal, telling the forgotten stories of ordinary people. As Douglas Dunn has argued in his introduction to an anthology of Scottish short fiction, despite the perennial focus on middle-class existence, '[o]n the evidence of the Scottish short story there is a marked pull towards under-expressed, under-described lives; but this is also a commonplace of the form as practised almost everywhere, though rarer in English than in American stories'.[29] Since the 1930s Scottish writers have set out to write realistically about the privations of working-class people and the cultural antagonisms between those from different areas. Unlike famous Scottish writers of previous generations – Margaret Oliphant, Arthur Conan Doyle, Muriel Spark – who tended to make only intermittent and sometimes indirect use of their Scottish backgrounds, Kelman, Welsh and others describe the Scottish cities they know well in their work. Glasgow-born James Kelman tends to set his stories in urban spaces and to force the reader to confront contemporary youth culture as it is, plagued by violence, unemployment, crime and AIDS. In an essay on 'The Importance of Glasgow in My Work', he has claimed: 'I wanted to write as one of my own people, I wanted to write and remain a member of my own community... Whenever I did find somebody from my sort of background in English literature there they were confined to the margins, kept in their place, stuck in the dialogue. You only ever saw or heard them. You never got into their mind.'[30] He rejects the idea of 'some "mystical" national culture', preferring to focus on the local Glaswegian context rather than the national one.[31] Duncan Petrie has read his work in terms of disaffection and despair, seeing the author as 'relentlessly focussed on the specific details of life on the margins in contemporary Glasgow, rendered in a language that explicitly challenges metropolitan cultural hegemony'.[32]

Kelman has published seven collections to date, from *An Old Pub Near the Angel* (1973) to *Not, Not While the Giro* (1983) and *The Good Times* (1998), which won the 1999 Stakis Prize for Scottish Writer of the Year, and several novels, including the controversial *How Late It Was, How Late* (1994), with its innovative and acclaimed use of working-class voices. A fairly early story, 'Home for a Couple of Days', from *Greyhound for Breakfast* (1987), about a Glaswegian returning to his earlier drinking haunts, included alongside Dilys Rose's (b.1954) 'Street of the Three Terraces', from *Red Tides* (1993), about a young homosexual boy beaten to death by teenagers from the 'grimy tenements', in Dunn's anthology contrasts the under-described lives of those from different parts of the community, and those who have moved away from Scotland with those who stayed behind. 'Home for a Couple of Days' focuses on Eddie Brown's return to Glasgow, fondly describing his reading of Scottish newspapers, reminiscing about Scottish football and visiting local pubs, the main thrust of the story consisting of dialogue in the pub and in his hotel. Now living in London, Eddie regards his home town from the viewpoint of an outsider, though, as the title suggests, it is still 'home'. Although his old 'skint' friends perceive that he is better off and better dressed than they are, he still fits into the local scene because, in a passage which underlines his outsider status in England, his voice betrays his origins:

> Although it was busy at the bar he was served quite quickly. It was good seeing as many working behind the counter as this. One of the things he didn't like about England was the way sometimes you could wait ages to get served in their pubs – especially if they heard your accent. (p. 397)

Like many other contemporary Scottish narratives, the story is punctuated by street names and locations – Chancellor Street, Sauchiehall Street, the Springwell Tavern, the Green Park hotel – which might be familiar to readers, producing a topography of the city. The ending, which sees Eddie asleep in his hotel uncertain what to do – 'maybe we would just leave tomorrow. He would if he felt like it' (p. 402) – does not give us information about the purpose of his visit or his future intentions, which are left purposefully hazy. The importance of place, of rural versus urban, and 'such strong local identities' for the Scottish writer[33] helps to shape their narratives and the contrasting perspectives of their characters and voices; Petrie talks about Kelman and others as involved in the crucial process of 'reimagining Glasgow', opening up 'a range of fresh approaches and aesthetic strategies for the representation of Scotland'.[34] In her discussion of the evolving tradition of Scottish women writers of short fiction, Alison Lumsden has noted that 'Kelman's work has given a new-found credibility to the short story in Scotland, and suggested ways in which it may be developed', not least in terms of its function as a vehicle for analysing national identity, the power of language and the politics of space.[35]

Renowned for her ability to mould language into new forms, A. L. Kennedy, born in Dundee and now based in Glasgow, has won numerous awards for her fiction and is seen as one of the most important Scottish writers of her generation. She has now published five short-story collections, the first of which, *Night Geometry and the Garscadden Trains* (1990), won the John Llewellyn Rhys Prize, the Scotsman Saltire Award and the Scottish Arts Council Book Award, and she appeared on the Granta lists for Best Writer of Fiction in both 1993 and 2003. Duncan Petrie couples her with Janice Galloway as an uncompromising writer addressing the concerns of women 'from a perspective that was unequivocally contemporary and urban', mobilising 'a vibrant new female presence in Scottish writing'.[36] Her later collections, *Now That You're Back* (1994), *Original Bliss* (1997), *Indelible Acts* (2002) and *What Becomes* (2009), have been interspersed with five novels, including *Paradise* (2004), a first-person narrative of a young female alcoholic, tackling a subject associated with Scottish identity in order to break down some of the stereotypes about drinking. She has also been active in journalism, publishing in the *Scotsman* and the *Glasgow Herald*, as well as writing a column for the *Guardian*, and some of her stories have appeared in anthologies of *New Writing* and been broadcast on Radio 4. Although she prefers not to be pigeonholed as a Scottish writer, she does admit the influence on her work: 'My nationality is beaten together from a mongrel mix of Scots, Welsh, Scots-Irish and Midlands English. Because I love Scotland I will always seek to write about it as enough of an outsider to see it clearly.'[37] As Kaye Mitchell concludes: 'Whilst rejecting the tag of "Scottish writer", stressing its vapid and tautological nature, she nevertheless constructs an "outsider" identity for herself (as one not from London, not from the literary scene) which is necessarily reliant on her "Scottishness," at least in the way that this is construed by others.'[38] In the title story of her first collection, set in her native Glasgow, the female narrator muses, 'Why do so many trains terminate at Garscadden?'(p. 24), before the unfolding of a story of marital infidelity which is organised around her standing at her station every morning for years, as if to mark the stages of a relationship also considered to be 'unrepeatable, remarkable and entirely unique. So I thought' (p. 30).[39] And yet her union with her husband has the inevitability of waiting for a train – 'Before I met him, I was waiting to love him' (p. 27) – and the sexual act, their 'night geometry', is described in a similar way: 'But when we slowed to a stop, when we terminated, the geometry had changed ... the following morning, I waited on the westbound platform and the smell of him was still on me, even having washed' (p. 28). She discovers her husband's infidelity, a process which has been 'repeating itself for years', only because her train is unusually 'Not in Service'. In her excellent reading of the 'banality' of intimacy in this story, Mitchell has emphasised 'the focus, in much of Kennedy's work ... on the minor, everyday tragedies which blight individual lives but never make the headlines'; this is a story of 'what nearly happened ... but in fact she doesn't kill her husband, instead merely injures herself on the knife while handling it'.[40] The final paragraphs, as the narrator compares her insignificance and the demise of her relationship to the predictability of public transport, reinforce the Scottish setting:

> But the silent majority and I do have one memorial, at least. The Disaster. We have small lives, easily lost in foreign droughts, or famines; the occasional incendiary incident, or a wall of pale faces, crushed against grillwork, one Saturday afternoon in Spring. This is not enough. (p. 34)

The reference to the Hillsborough stadium disaster, in which ninety-six football fans were crushed to death in 1989, and the emphasis on the 'small lives' of those in local communities, coupled with the fierce declaration 'This is not enough', act as a kind of manifesto for the direction of the Scottish short story, which will go on to record and chronicle the small lives to which Kennedy draws our attention. Questioned about this phrase in interview, she countered: 'I've never met anyone with a small life. It pains me that lives would be perceived as small. I don't think I write to remedy a lack of perspective in other places, but I certainly write about the people who interest me in a way that would show the largeness of the interior we never really see.'[41] Her isolated, unemotional narrators ponder the meaning of their far-from-small lives in libraries, on buses, or in bed as their partners sleep, interweaving the present with their strongest memories, offering snapshots of past lives which the reader has to work hard to interpret (it is surely significant that photographs and photographers, potentially misleading images of family life, recur in many of the narratives). In 'Star Dust', narrated by an old woman who loves cinema, the narrator imagines the films she might make of 'ordinary' people, 'because they have good stories too. Some one should remember them' (p. 88). Other stories in the collection circle around lost or abandoned children, or controversial issues of sexual abuse and domestic violence, such as the chilling 'The Moving House', which allows the reader to understand the reality which lies behind Gracie's sickness and the lines 'a door, opened smoothly on a room with the curtains drawn. The familiar dream' (p. 35) from the opening paragraphs only after the aggressive threats and humiliation of the final dialogue with her mother's boyfriend: 'Nobody's gonny believe you. Who are you? You're fuckun nothun' (p. 41).

This interest in 'the interior we never really see' runs throughout her disturbing narratives, which often make innovative use of stream of consciousness, in the form of italics, bold or capitals standing out from the main text, to comment on the fragility and fragmentation of modern identity. Perhaps her darkest collection, *Indelible Acts* describes awkward or painful moments in the complicated lives of ordinary narrators struggling with their identities in various ways, or unable to communicate with their families and partners. In 'An Immaculate Man', Howie the solicitor is unable to interpret the physical connections made by his married male colleague Salter or to reconcile himself to his homosexuality: '*I don't hate the idea, the actions, the thought. Being gay as a concept, that's probably something I love. I do, very probably, love that I am gay. I only hate me*' (p. 40). Italics and capitalisation are used to follow the thought processes of the central character, here interspersing intentionally banal descriptions of the office with explicit descriptions of repressed sexual desire and unanswered questions: 'I HAVE AN ERECTION I DIDN'T MAKE. *I am not responsible*' (p. 43). In the moving and rather frightening 'A Bad Son', which examines the tortured inner world of shy schoolboy Ronald as he plays in the snow with a friend, the italics are used only towards the end of the story, as he worries about staying away overnight, leaving his mother to the mercy of his violent father. Repeated phrases such as '*It wasn't my fault*', '*Please make her safe*' and the single word '**Fuck**' (sometimes in bold) punctuate the increasingly nervous narrative, at one point running into a single desperate mantra in his mind: '*Please make her fucking safe please make her safe pleasemakeherfuckingsafepleasemake hersafe please*' (p. 84), an effective means of signalling his inner turmoil. Ronald's attempt to embrace his Scottishness by adopting the persona created by his friend, who admiringly refers to him as 'Ronnie, mad as fuck' after an unintentionally fast and dangerous sledge ride signals his bravado, and his increased use of language such as 'aye' can also be seen as a desire to both counter and copy the stereotype of the alcoholic violent Scottish man represented by his father. By becoming 'a bad son', he could conquer his own fear and helplessness: 'It wasn't about wishing, or pretending, and there were no miracles. It was about concentrating until you can turn into somebody new, somebody your father wouldn't expect' (p. 87). His desire to become someone new, to '*not feel a thing*', repeated in the closing pages as his taciturn father drives him home, is symptomatic of the Kennedy narrator's need to close himself or herself off from emotional intimacy, from the fear of identity, like the female narrator of 'Elsewhere', who periodically sets fire to her possessions to 'burn her sadnesses away' before moving on to a new life with no memories and no regrets: 'It saved having to pack' (p. 129).

Admired by Jeanette Winterson and other writers for her originality, Ali Smith, born in Inverness but now living in England, has published four short-story collections, *Free Love and Other Stories* (1995), *Other Stories and Other Stories* (1999), *The Whole Story and Other Stories* (2003) and *The First Person and Other Stories* (2008), plus four novels, including *Hotel World* (2001). While some of the stories are set in Scotland, others describe Scottish characters travelling through England, or significantly contain minimal references to place and location. Lumsden suggests that though Ali Smith is less interested in national identity than other Scottish writers, she shares an interest with Kennedy 'in the nature of fiction itself',[42] and one reviewer has admired her 'bittersweet' writing, 'twisting her tales in unexpected directions, pushing the possibilities of the short story and delighting us'.[43] Her work has appeared in the *Times Literary Supplement*, the *Scotsman*, *Scottish Book Collector* and other magazines, and has been frequently anthologised. Her quirky, experimental and rather surreal stories are often told from two or more perspectives, like 'Being Quick' and 'May', both of which juxtapose first-person accounts of everyday life by female lovers in a style reminiscent of Jackie Kay. 'Paradise', opening with a poetic vision of Loch Ness and its monster, gives the viewpoints of the three McKinlay sisters – two of them realist descriptions of mundane working lives, the final one an alcoholic reverie. Several of the stories in her recent collection *The Whole Story and Other Stories* (whose very title characteristically plays on the conventions for naming short-story collections while giving nothing away about its subject matter) announce their own fictional status. The opening tale, called 'The Universal Story' (the collection doesn't actually include one called 'The Whole Story' as the reader expects), makes several false starts, trying out a number of different characters and settings:

> There was a man dwelt by a churchyard.
> Well, no, okay, it wasn't always a man; in this particular case it was a woman. There was a woman dwelt by a churchyard.
> Though, to be honest, nobody really uses that word nowadays. Everybody says cemetery. And nobody says dwelt any more. In other words:
> There was once a woman who lived by a cemetery. Every morning when she woke up she looked out of her back window and saw –
> Actually, no. There was once a woman who lived by – no, in – a second-hand bookshop. She lived in the flat on the first floor and ran the shop which took up the whole of downstairs. (p. 1)

Such an opening to a collection indicates the creative process at work, the decisions writers might make about their characters, as well as subtly suggesting the shift towards the female perspective in the stories: 'it wasn't always a man'. The lives which are rejected in favour of the tale of the bookshop owner, selling all her copies of *The Great Gatsby* to a smiling young man who makes ill-fated boats out of them, are briefly referred to in the closing lines, though Smith teasingly tells us that what the woman who lived by a cemetery saw out of her window is 'another story' (p. 13) which cannot be revealed. 'Erosive' plays on the expected structure of a narrative by using the scrambled subtitles 'middle', 'end' and 'beginning' in that order, after an opening section which demands of the reader what information he or she needs to know about a character in a short story: 'What do you need to know about me for this story? How old I am? How much I earn a year? What kind of car I drive? Look at me now, here I am at the beginning, the middle and the end all at once, in love with someone I can't have' (p. 115), though all of these identifying factors are ultimately withheld. The woman's need to get rid of the ants on her apple tree ends not with her pulling up the tree in frustration, but with the description of her, 'dazed and glowing', falling in love, so that the final moment (from the beginning) is when she lies on the floor, staring at the ceiling and its 'flystuck old electric fitting and at this point in the story even the ceiling is glorious' (p. 122). Similarly, 'The Book Club', about a woman's taxi ride home shot through with memories of the books she borrowed as a child, a gruesome murder and her last conversation with her aging father, invites us to form our own ideas about her character from the clues scattered through the conversation about the benefits of satellite navigation. In the final sentence we are denied access to the home she enters in an unnamed small town as she closes the front door behind her. These meta-fictional narratives, playing with time and memory and breaking down simple notions of identity, show the short story at its more experimental and postmodern.

Smith's most ambitious work to date, *The First Person and Other Stories*, is further evidence of her stretching of the form of the short story, as the fragmented, playful stories, which resist linearity and realism, remind us of both the freedoms and the boundaries of the form. In 'The Child', a surreal commentary on the ticking of the biological clock, a childless woman finds a baby in her supermarket trolley which then miraculously begins to ask questions, swear and tell sexist jokes as she drives him home, before she feels compelled to return him. In another story a woman has a conversation with her fourteen-year-old self, as Smith reflects on the complex processes and fears which make up female identity and memory. The opening piece, 'True Short Story', which according to the acknowledgements was 'written in 2005 in playful response to a speech given by *Prospect*'s deputy editor Alex Linklater on the inauguration of the National Short Story Prize' and appeared in *Prospect* in the same year, makes a series of jokes about the short-story form – 'Why is the short story like a nymph?' (p. 11) – following a discussion overheard between two men in a cafe comparing it with the novel.[44] It ends with two pages of definitions of the short story by leading practitioners and critics of the form from Kafka to Alice Munro, as if to parade the genre's malleability, before a few lines return us to the two men in the cafe and to the terminally ill friend who features in the tale. Announcing its own fictionality while acting in many ways as a manifesto for the short story (with a nod to the new literary prize recognising the merits of this undervalued fictional genre), the list of definitions serves to offer the reader a way to interpret the tales which follow. Grace Paley's comment, for example, that short stories are more appropriate to life because 'short stories are, by nature, about life, and...life itself is always found in dialogue and argument' (p. 17) is surely relevant to the strange dialogues and arguments between unnamed lovers in several of the stories in this collection which open out their relationship in revealing but elliptical ways. One character in a story talks significantly of 'all the years of dialogue between us' (p. 123). The clues which reveal that the lovers are both female are often withheld until near the end of the story, and the names are kept out of the story, leaving the characters as 'I' and 'you', a

particularly effective way to both complicate and universalise the relationships. As Katy Guest notes in her *Independent* review of the collection, short stories, like love affairs, have beginnings, middles and ends,
but 'both contain multitudes of fictions', as Smith's work reinforces
the importance and necessity of story-telling, of surviving by fictions
or creating new ones, for both the relationships she describes and her
own task as a writer.[45] 'The Second Person' constitutes an elaborate dialogue between lovers in which both try to capture their lover's identity
by telling a story about how the other would behave in a music shop,
a contest which is hilarious and poignant, as both women are hurt,
surprised and elated by the shifting directions of the stories: 'You suggested I'm wasteful and whimsical. You suggested, in your story of me
buying musical instruments I can't play, that I'm completely ridiculous
and laughable' (p. 125). The links between identity and the stories we
tell ourselves and others are pursued further in the final story, 'The
First Person', which centres around the fabrication of stories a new couple will choose to tell their friends and family about how they met,
which then both reveals and conceals the kind of relationship they
(think they) have. The impossibility of becoming 'story-free' (p. 202),
where 'there is no story', is proved when the narrative itself takes a
characteristic leap to an earlier point in the narrator's life, describing
a clichéd episode of the 1970s series *Tales of the Unexpected* which she
has recently watched again, a leap which allows the reader to continue
to form a view of her character, though as the form dictates, this will
only ever remain partial (as it will for her lover). Commenting both
profoundly and playfully on the complexities of living in (and leaving)
Scotland, the joys and difficulties of lesbian relationships and the ways
in which stories both sustain and fail us, Smith's work is a useful place
to end our narrative of the evolution of short fiction and its exploration of national, sexual and racial identities.

The contemporary British short story can, then, be seen to be characterised by a renewed interest in the perspective of the outsider, who
might be an anxious lesbian lover, a mixed-race character adjusting to
a new multicultural community or a disillusioned single or separated
parent. Black British, Scottish and Irish authors have been particularly attentive to the vagaries of national identity, the politics of space
and 'home', as their stories urge us to reconsider standard notions of
Scottishness or Irishness and to problematise our assumptions about
what it means to be British in a new, potentially postethnic world.
Contemporary stories also exhibit a postmodern playfulness in their

withholding of information about the identity of their narrators, their fragmented time sequences and their self-conscious references to the form in which they are written, demonstrating the possibilities and vitality of the genre in the early twenty-first century.

Notes

1 Introduction: What Is a Short Story?

1. Ian Reid, *The Short Story* (London: Methuen, 1977), pp. 9, 1.
2. Dominic Head, *The Modernist Short Story: A Study in Theory and Practice* (Cambridge: Cambridge University Press, 1989), pp. 13–15.
3. Valerie Shaw, *The Short Story: A Critical Introduction* (London: Longman, 1983), p. 16.
4. William Boyd, 'Brief Encounters', *Guardian* (2 October 2004), http://www.guardian.co.uk/books/2004/oct/02/featuresreviews.guardianreview38.
5. Harold Orel, *The Victorian Short Story: Development and Triumph of a Literary Genre* (Cambridge: Cambridge University Press, 1986), p. ix.
6. Letter to Charles Anthon, October 1844, in *The Letters of Edgar Allan Poe*, ed. John Ward Ostrom, 2 Vols. (New York: Gordian Press, 1966), Vol. 1, p. 268.
7. Edgar Allan Poe, review of *Twice-Told Tales*, rpt. in *The New Short Story Theories*, ed. Charles E. May (Athens: Ohio University Press, 1994), p. 61.
8. Edgar Allan Poe, review of Edward Bulwer Lytton's *Night and Morning*, 1841, rpt. in May, p. 65 (emphasis in original).
9. Edgar Allan Poe, 'How to Write a *Blackwood's* Article', in *The Collected Works of Edgar Allan Poe*, ed. Thomas Ollive Mabbott, 3 Vols. (Cambridge: Harvard University Press, 1978), Vol. 1, 336–57, p. 340.
10. Orel suggests that the baseline length of the Victorian British short story was around 12,000 words; Poe's stories tend to come in at considerably fewer than 3,000 words.
11. Dean Baldwin, ed., *The Riverside Anthology of Short Fiction: Convention and Innovation* (Boston and New York: Houghton Mifflin, 1998).
12. Henry James, 'Preface', in *The Reverberator; Madame de Mauves; A Passionate Pilgrim; etc.* (New York: Library of America, 1989).
13. Roger Luckhurst, *Science Fiction* (Cambridge: Polity, 2005), p. 17.
14. Tim Killick, *British Short Fiction in the Early Nineteenth Century* (Aldershot: Ashgate, 2008).
15. Wendell Harris, *British Short Fiction of the Nineteenth Century: A Literary and Bibliographic Guide* (Detroit: Wayne State University Press, 1979), p. 108.
16. Brander Matthews, 'Short Stories', *Saturday Review* (8 July 1884), 33–34, p. 33.
17. Orel, p. 2.
18. Clare Hanson, *Short Stories and Short Fictions, 1880–1980* (London: Macmillan, 1985), p. 6.
19. Frederick Wedmore, 'The Short Story', *Nineteenth Century* 43 (1898), 406–16, pp. 407, 411, 409.
20. Quoted in Shaw, p. 23.
21. Jane Eldridge Miller, *Rebel Women: Feminism, Modernism and the Edwardian Novel* (London: Virago, 1994), pp. 24–25.
22. Angelique Richardson, 'Introduction', in *Women Who Did: Stories by Men and Women, 1890–1914* (Harmondsworth: Penguin), p. xlv.

23. Dennis Vannatta, ed., *The English Short Story, 1880–1945* (Boston: Twayne, 1985), p. 35.
24. Woodrow Wyatt, *English Story*, 4th series (London: Collins, 1943), pp. 5–6.
25. Dennis Vannatta, 'Introduction', in *The English Short Story, 1945–1980* (Boston: Twayne, 1985), pp. xvii, xviii. Vannatta notes that three of the four contributors to this volume 'express serious reservations about the state of the contemporary short story', though this appears to be changing with a new generation of writers who began to publish in the 1970s.
26. Hanson, *Short Stories and Short Fictions, 1880–1980*, p. 172.
27. All quotations are taken from Saki [Hector Hugh Munro], 'The Story-Teller', in *The Penguin Complete Saki*, intro. Noël Coward (Harmondsworth: Penguin, 1976).
28. John Bayley, *The Short Story: Henry James to Elizabeth Bowen* (Brighton: Harvester Press, 1988), p. viii.
29. Cited in Harriet Lane, 'Just Stick to the Brief', *Observer* (5 September 2004), http://www.guardian.co.uk/books/2004/sep/05/fiction.features.
30. Andrew Levy, *The Culture and Commerce of the American Short Story* (Cambridge: Cambridge University Press, 1993), p. 27.
31. Clare Hanson, ed., *Re-Reading the Short Story* (London: Macmillan, 1989), p. 6.
32. Shaw, p. 2.
33. Letter, 26 July 1917, quoted in David Bradshaw, 'Introduction' to Virginia Woolf, *The Mark on the Wall and Other Short Fiction* (Oxford: Oxford University Press, 2001), p. xii.
34. Bradshaw, pp. xii–xiii. Woolf's now well-known ideas about 'the task of the novelist' and the need to focus on 'the ordinary course of life' to which the mind is exposed are taken from an essay originally published in the *Times Literary Supplement* as 'Modern Novels' on 10 April 1919, which was revised to become 'Modern Fiction' in 1925.
35. Elizabeth Bowen, 'Introduction', in *The Faber Book of Modern Stories* (London: Faber & Faber, 1937), pp. 7, 6, qtd. in Hanson, *Re-Reading the Short Story*, p. 5. Hanson goes on to link this to the unconscious: 'Both short story and film reject or deny certain levels of narrative, a certain kind of discursive "explanation", preferring instead to work on a level on which unconscious desires and motives may be explored via "associations not examined by reason".'
36. Qtd. in Helen Simpson, 'Femme Fatale', *Guardian* (24 June 2006), http://www.guardian.co.uk/books/2006/jun/24/classics.angelacarter (accessed 4 July 2010).
37. Bayley, p. viii.
38. Shaw, p. 2.
39. Lynda Prescott, 'Preface', in *A World of Difference: An Anthology of Short Stories from Five Continents* (Basingstoke: Palgrave Macmillan, 2008), p. xv.
40. Derek Hudson, 'Introduction', in *Modern English Short Stories, 1930–1955* (World's Classics, 1956; Oxford: Oxford University Press, 1985), p. xii.
41. See, for example, Emma Donaghue, ed., *The Mammoth Book of Lesbian Short Stories* (London: Robinson, 1999); David Leavitt and Mark Mitchell, eds., *The Penguin Book of Gay Short Stories* (London: Penguin, 1991); Ra Page, ed., *The City Life Book of Manchester Short Stories* (Harmondsworth: Penguin, 1999).
42. Prescott, p. xvi.

43. Mary Eagleton, 'Gender and Genre', in Hanson, *Re-Reading the Short Story*, 55–68, p. 66.
44. Margaret Beetham, *A Magazine of Her Own? Domesticity and Desire in the Woman's Magazine, 1800–1914* (London and New York: Routledge, 1996), pp. 1, 2. Beetham argues that 'readers may be relatively less powerful than writers but they can still accept or resist the meanings the writer produces. Writers are powerful in relation to language and the reader but less so in relation to the editor, the publisher or the advertiser. Editorial power is itself limited, discursively and economically, by pressure from advertisers and from readers' (p. 2).

2   Introducing the Victorian and Edwardian Short Story

1. Deborah Thomas, *Dickens and the Short Story* (Philadelphia: University of Pennsylvania Press, 1982), p. 3.
2. Linda Hughes and Michael Lund, *Victorian Publishing and Mrs Gaskell's Work* (London: University Press of Virginia, 1999), p. 118.
3. Anthony Trollope, *An Autobiography*, ed. David Skilton (London: Penguin, 1996), p. 230.
4. Harold Orel, *The Victorian Short Story: Development and Triumph of a Literary Genre* (Cambridge: Cambridge University Press, 1986), p. 101.
5. In 1901, Brander Matthews, one of the first critics to analyse the genre in any depth, suggested: 'It is the three-volume Novel which has killed the Short story in England.' See Brander Matthews, *The Philosophy of the Short Story* (New York: Longmans, Green, 1901), p. 60.
6. W. M. Thackeray to Anthony Trollope, 28 October 1859, qtd. in Trollope, p. 91.
7. Winnie Chan, *The Economy of the Short Story in British Periodicals of the 1890s* (London: Routledge, 2007), p. 5.
8. Cited in Orel, p. 79.
9. Unsigned review, 'New Novels', *The Times* (13 August 1857), p. 13.
10. Unsigned review, *Saturday Review* 30 (13 August 1870), pp. 211–12, in David Skilton, *Anthony Trollope and His Contemporaries* (London: Longman, 1972), pp. 59–60.
11. James Kincaid, *The Novels of Anthony Trollope* (Oxford: Clarendon Press, 1977), p. 43.
12. Anthony Trollope, 'The Spotted Dog', in *Anthony Trollope: The Complete Short Stories*, ed. Betty Brewer 5 Vols. (Fort Worth: Texas Christian University Press), Vol. 1.
13. Richard Holt Hutton, 'The Golden Lion of Grandpere', *Spectator* 59 (18 May 1872), p. 631.
14. Letter to W. M. Thackeray, 15 November 1860, in *The Letters of Anthony Trollope*, ed. Bradford A. Booth (Oxford: Oxford University Press, 1951), p. 78.
15. Cited in Julia Briggs, *Night Visitors: The Rise and Fall of the English Ghost Story* (London: Faber & Faber, 1977), p. 15.
16. Fred Warner, 'Stevenson's First Scottish Story', *Nineteenth Century Fiction* 24.3 (1969), 334–44, p. 337.
17. See Penny Fielding, *Writing and Orality: Nationality, Culture and Nineteenth-Century Scottish Fiction* (Oxford: Clarendon Press, 1996).

18. See Paul March Russell, *The Short Story: An Introduction* (Edinburgh: Edinburgh University Press, 2009), p. 47.
19. Reginald Pound, *Mirror of the Century: The Strand Magazine, 1891–1950* (New York: A.S. Barnes, 1966), p. 30.
20. See Chan, p. 5.
21. All quotations are taken from Edwin Pugh, 'The Decay of the Short Story', *Fortnightly Review* 84 (October 1908), 631–42.
22. Entry for 8 May 1892, in *The Notebooks of Henry James*, ed. F. O. Matthiessen and Kenneth Murdock (New York: Oxford University Press, 1947), p. 120.
23. H. G. Wells, 'Three Yellow-Book Storytellers', Pall Mall Gazette (1 June 1895), p. 730, rpt. in Patrick Parrinder and Robert M. Philmus (eds.), *H. G. Well's Literary Criticism* (Hassocks: Harvester Press 1980), p. 189.
24. H. G. Wells, 'Preface', in *The Country of the Blind and Other Stories* (London: Nelson, 1911), p. v.
25. Wells, p. v.
26. Cited in Chan, p. 62.
27. Orel, p. 101.
28. Bliss Perry, 'The Short Story', *Atlantic Monthly* 90 (1902), 245–52, p. 250.
29. Kristin Brady, *The Short Stories of Thomas Hardy: Tales of Past and Present* (London: Macmillan, 1982), p. 35.
30. Edmund Gosse, 'The Speaker's Gallery', *The Speaker* 2.295 (13 September 1890), in *Thomas Hardy: The Critical Heritage*, ed. R. Cox (London: Routledge & Kegan Paul, 1979), p. 177.
31. William Minto, 'Thomas Hardy', *The Bookman* 1.99 (December 1891), in Cox, p. 175.
32. Henry James, 'Greville Fane', in *The Real Thing* (London: Macmillan, 1893), pp. 258, 252, 251, 254.
33. Vernon Lee, 'Lady Tal', in *Daughters of Decadence: Women Writers of the Fin de Siècle*, ed. Elaine Showalter (London: Virago, 1993), pp. 213, 259.
34. Elaine Showalter, 'Smoking Room', *Times Literary Supplement* (16 June 1995), p. 12.
35. Nicole Fluhr, 'Empathy and Identity in Vernon Lee's *Hauntings*', *Victorian Studies* 48 (2006), 287–94.
36. Cited in Mary Buran, 'The Feminine Short Story in America', in *American Women Short Story Writers*, ed. Julie Brown (New York: Garland, 1995), 269–80.
37. Elaine Showalter, *Sexual Anarchy* (London: Virago, 1992), p. 142.
38. Perry, p. 251.

3 Victorian Sensations: Supernatural and Weird Tales

1. Nicola Bown, Carolyn Burdett and Pamela Thurschwell, eds., *The Victorian Supernatural* (Cambridge: Cambridge University Press, 2004), pp. 1–2.
2. Fred Botting, *Gothic* (London: Routledge, 1996), p. 5.
3. Lyn Pykett, *The Sensation Novel* (Plymouth: Northcote House, 1994), p. 196.
4. Botting, p. 2.
5. Julia Briggs, *Night Visitors: The Rise and Fall of the English Ghost Story* (London: Faber & Faber, 1977), p. 19.
6. Elaine Ostry, ' "Social Wonders": Fancy, Science and Technology in Dickens's Periodicals', *Victorian Periodicals Review* 34.1 (2001), 54–78, p. 56.

7. Alex Owen, *The Darkened Room: Women, Power and Spiritualism in Late Victorian England* (Philadelphia: University of Pennsylvania Press, 1990), p. 1.
8. Mary Walker, 'Between Fiction and Madness: The Relationship of Women to the Supernatural in Late Victorian Britain', in *That Gentle Strength: Historical Perspectives on Women in Christianity*, ed. Lynda L. Coon, Katherine J. Haldane and Elisabeth W. Sommer (Charlottesville and London: University Press of Virginia, 1990), pp. 231–32.
9. Vanessa Dickerson, *Victorian Ghosts in the Noontide: Women Writers and the Supernatural* (Columbia: University of Missouri Press, 1996), p. 5.
10. Owen, p. 8.
11. Diana Basham, *The Trial of Woman: Feminism and the Occult Sciences in Victorian Literature and Society* (Basingstoke: Macmillan, 1998), p. 158.
12. Briggs, p. 14.
13. Qtd. in *Nineteenth-Century Short Stories by Women: A Routledge Anthology*, ed. Harriet Devine Jump (London and New York: Routledge, 1998), pp. 76–77
14. Lyn Pykett, *Charles Dickens* (Basingstoke: Palgrave, 2002), pp. 126, 156.
15. Louise Henson, 'Investigations and Fictions: Charles Dickens and Ghosts', in Bown *et al.*, p. 59.
16. Ostry, p. 57.
17. John M. L. Drew, *Dickens the Journalist* (Basingstoke: Palgrave, 2003), p. 147.
18. For a full list of the stories and contributors to the Christmas supplements, which ran from 1850 to 1867, see Deborah Thomas, *Dickens and the Short Story* (Philadelphia: University of Pennsylvania Press, 1980), Appendix A, pp. 140–45.
19. Henson, p. 56.
20. Briggs, p. 42.
21. All quotations are taken from Michael Hayes, ed., *The Supernatural Short Stories of Charles Dickens* (London: John Calder, 1978).
22. Drew, pp. 118, 151.
23. All quotations are taken from Charles Dickens, *Mugby Junction*, ed. Robert Macfarlane (1866; London: Hesperus Press, 2005).
24. The story appears in *The Penguin Book of Classic Fantasy by Women*, ed. A. Susan Williams (Harmondsworth: Penguin, 1992).
25. Bown *et al.*, p. 13.
26. Henson, p. 58.
27. Macfarlane, p. vii.
28. Macfarlane, p. x.
29. Alison Milbank, *Daughters of the House: Modes of the Gothic in Victorian Fiction* (Basingstoke: Macmillan, 1992), p. 25.
30. All quotations are taken from Wilkie Collins, *The Dream-Woman and Other Stories*, ed. Peter Miles (London: Orion, 1998).
31. All quotations are taken from Wilkie Collins, *Miss or Mrs? The Haunted Hotel and the Guilty River*, ed. Norman Page and Toru Sasaki (Oxford: Oxford University Press, 1999).
32. Harold Orel, *The Victorian Short Story: Development and Triumph of a Literary Genre* (Cambridge: Cambridge University Press, 1986), p. 91.
33. Milbank, p. 160.
34. All quotations are taken from Sheridan le Fanu, *In a Glass Darkly*, ed. W. J. McCormack (1872; Gloucester: Alan Sutton, 1990).

35. See, for example, 'Squire Toby's Will' from *Temple Bar* 22 (January 1868), pp. 212–36 and 'Mr Justice Harbottle' from *In a Glass Darkly*. Both follow the pattern of a professional man haunted by an animal which goads and frightens him into self-destruction. The latter appeared in *Belgravia*, edited by Mary Braddon, in January 1872; it was based on an earlier version called 'An Account of Some Strange Disturbances in Aungier Street' which was printed in the *Dublin University Magazine* in 1853

36. Orel, p. 42.

37. Glen Cavaliero, *The Supernatural and English Fiction: From the Castle of Otranto to Hawksmoor* (Oxford: Oxford University Press, 1995), p. 43.

38. Shirley Foster, 'Violence and Disorder in Elizabeth Gaskell's Short Stories', *Gaskell Society Journal* 19 (2005), 14–24, pp. 14–15.

39. All quotations are taken from Elizabeth Gaskell, *Gothic Tales*, ed. Laura Kranzler (Harmondsworth: Penguin, 2000).

40. Quoted in Kranzler, p. 344.

41. Dickerson, p. 119. She also argues that 'the curse in supernatural stories appears to be a distinctly feminine phenomenon': Lois's trial, in Gaskell's 'Lois the Witch', is in part 'explained' by the fact that as the parson's daughter, she has been singled out of the crowd and cursed by another woman being half-drowned (see p. 131).

42. All quotations are taken from George Eliot, 'The Lifted Veil' (1859), in Williams, pp. 57–96.

43. Beryl Gray, 'Pseudoscience and George Eliot's "The Lifted Veil"', *Nineteenth-Century Fiction* 36 (1982), 407–23, pp. 407, 408.

44. Dickerson, p. 89.

45. Gray, p. 420.

46. Jenny Uglow, 'Introduction', in *The Virago Book of Victorian Ghost Stories*, ed. Richard Dalby (London: Virago, 1988), p. xiv.

47. Uglow, p. xiv.

48. All quotations are taken from Jump.

49. All quotations are taken from Michael Cox and R. A. Gilbert, eds., *The Oxford Book of English Ghost Stories* (Oxford: Oxford University Press, 1986).

50. Eve M. Lynch, 'Spectral Politics: The Victorian Ghost Story and the Domestic Servant', in Bown *et al.*, p. 82.

51. All quotations are taken from Leslie Shepherd, ed., *The Book of Dracula* (New York: Wings Books, 1991).

52. All quotations are taken from Thomas Hardy, *Outside the Gates of the World: Selected Short Stories*, ed. Jan Jedrzejewski, with an introduction by John Bayley (London: J.M. Dent, 1996).

53. See 'Books: Mr Hardy's Wessex Stories', *Spectator* (28 July 1888), 1037–38.

54. See Jedrzejewski, pp. 398, 381.

55. Jedrzejewski, p. 398.

56. Kristin Brady, *The Short Stories of Thomas Hardy: Tales of Past and Present* (London: Macmillan, 1982), p. 22. These changes may have been in response to criticism by Leslie Stephen, who argued that 'the tale was weakened by the lack of a material explanation for its less believable aspects'. Brady suggests that Hardy's refusal to take Stephen's suggestions on board 'reveals his own artistic purpose in presenting the story as a believed folk tale'.

57. Botting, p. 2.

58. All quotations are taken from Henry James, *The Turn of the Screw and Other Stories*, ed. T. J. Lustig (Oxford: Oxford University Press, 1992). This edition includes the Prefaces to the Collected Stories.
59. Bown *et al.*, p. 3.
60. Vernon Lee, 'The Image', *Cornhill Magazine* 26 (1896), 516–23, pp. 520, 523.
61. All quotations are taken from Vernon Lee, *Hauntings and Other Fantastic Tales*, ed. Catherine Maxwell and Patricia Pulham (Peterborough: Broadview Press, 2006).
62. Andrew Lang, 'Ghosts up to Date', *Blackwood's Magazine* 155 (1894), 47–58, p. 47.
63. Carlo Caballero, ' "A Wicked Voice": On Vernon Lee, Wagner, and the Effects of Music', *Victorian Studies* 35.4 (Summer 1992), 385–406, p. 389.

4   New Woman Short Stories

1. Sally Ledger and Scott McCracken, eds., *Cultural Politics at the Fin de Siècle* (Cambridge: Cambridge University Press, 1995), p. 1.
2. All quotations are taken from Elaine Showalter, ed., *Daughters of Decadence: Women Writers of the Fin de Siècle* (London: Virago, 1993).
3. Ann L. Ardis, *New Women, New Novels: Feminism and Early Modernism* (New Brunswick and London: Rutgers University Press, 1990), p. 31.
4. Eliza Lynn Linton, 'The Wild Women: As Politicians', *Nineteenth Century* (July 1891), rpt. in *Criminals, Idiots, Women and Minors: Nineteenth-Century Writing by Women on Women*, ed. Susan Hamilton (Ontario: Broadview Press, 1995), p. 188.
5. Mona Caird, 'A Defence of the So-Called "Wild Women" ', *Nineteenth Century* (May 1892), rpt. in Hamilton, p. 296.
6. Mona Caird, 'Marriage', *Westminster Review* 130.2 (1888), rpt. in *The Fin de Siècle: A Reader in Cultural History, c.1880–1900*, ed. Sally Ledger and Roger Luckhurst (Oxford: Oxford University Press, 2000), p. 79.
7. Marion Shaw and Lyssa Randolph, *New Woman Writers of the Late Nineteenth Century* (Plymouth: Northcote House, 2007), pp. 9, 12.
8. Ann Heilmann, *New Woman Fiction: Women Writing First-Wave Feminism* (Basingstoke: Macmillan, 2000), p. 9.
9. Frederick Wedmore, 'The Short Story', *Nineteenth Century* 43 (1898), 406–16, p. 409.
10. Angelique Richardson, 'Introduction', in *Women Who Did: Stories by Men and Women, 1890–1914* (Harmondsworth: Penguin, 2002), p. lxviii.
11. Richardson, p. 217.
12. Richardson, p. lxvi.
13. Laurel Brake, *Print in Transition, 1850–1910: Studies in Media and Book History* (Basingstoke: Palgrave, 2001), pp. 154, 160.
14. Clare Hanson, *Short Stories and Short Fictions, 1880–1980* (London: Macmillan, 1985), p. 11.
15. This was the title of an article by Walter Besant, Eliza Lynn Linton and Thomas Hardy in *New Review* (1890), rpt. in Ledger and Luckhurst, pp. 111–20.
16. Showalter, p. viii.
17. Hanson, p. 11.

18. Winnie Chan, *The Economy of the Short Story in British Periodicals of the 1890s* (London: Routledge, 2007), pp. 54, 62. See also Henry Harland, 'Concerning the Short Story', *Academy* (5 June 1897), p. 6.
19. Brake, p. 165.
20. Showalter, p. xi.
21. Gillian Kersley, *Darling Madame: Sarah Grand & Devoted Friend* (London: Virago, 1983), p. 101.
22. Sarah Grand, 'The New Aspect of the Woman Question', *North American Review* 158 (1894), rpt. in Ledger and Luckhurst, p. 90.
23. All quotations are taken from Richardson.
24. Heilmann, p. 67.
25. Qtd. in Showalter, p. xii.
26. Sally Ledger, *The New woman: Fiction and Feminism at the Fin de Siècle* (Manchester: Manchester University Press, 1997), p. 187.
27. George Egerton, 'A Keynote to *Keynotes*', in *Ten Contemporaries: Notes towards Their Definitive Bibliography*, ed. John Gawsworth [Terence Armstrong] (London: E. Benn, 1932), 58–60, p. 59.
28. See Richardson, pp. lxviii–lxxi.
29. Laura Chrisman, 'Empire, "Race" and Feminism at the *Fin de Siècle*: The Work of George Egerton and Olive Schreiner', in Ledger and McCracken, p. 46.
30. Quotations from 'A Cross Line' are taken from Richardson; quotations from all other stories are from George Egerton, *Keynotes & Discords*, ed. Martha Vicinus (1893/4; London: Virago, 1983).
31. Chrisman, p. 55.
32. See Emma Liggins, '"With a Dead Child in Her Lap": Bad Mothers and Infant Mortality in George Egerton's *Discords*', *Literature & History* 9.2 (2000), 17–36, pp. 32–35.
33. Ledger, pp. 69, 82.
34. Ledger, p. 192.
35. Heilmann, p. 67.
36. All quotations are taken from Joan Smith (ed.), *Femmes de Siècle: Stories from the 90s: Women Writing at the End of Two Centuries* (London: Chatto & Windus, 1992).
37. Rpt. in *Nineteenth-Century Short Stories by Women: A Routledge Anthology*, ed. Harriet Devine Jump (London and New York: Routledge, 1998), pp. 325, 328.
38. This first appeared in the collection *A Widow's Tale and Other Stories* (1898). All quotations are taken from Jump's anthology.
39. Rpt. in Richardson, p. 138.
40. Caird, 'A Defence of the So-Called "Wild Women"', qtd. in Hamilton, p. 291.
41. Ledger, pp. 73–74.
42. All quotations are taken from Showalter.
43. Chrisman, p. 46.
44. All quotes are taken from Showalter.
45. Ann Ardis, 'New Women and the New Hellenism', in *The New Woman in Fiction and in Fact: Fin-de-Siècle Feminisms*, ed. Angelique Richardson and Chris Willis (Basingstoke: Palgrave, 2001), p. 108.
46. Chrisman, p. 57.
47. Carolyn Burdett, *Olive Schreiner and the Progress of Feminism* (Basingstoke: Palgrave, 2001), p. 110.

48. Anne M. Windholz, 'The Woman Who Would Be Editor: Ella D'Arcy and the *Yellow Book*', *Victorian Periodicals Review* 29.2 (1996), 116–30, p. 121.
49. Jump, p. 282.
50. All quotations are taken from Ella D'Arcy, *Monochromes* (London: John Lane, 1895), except for those from 'The Pleasure Pilgrim', which are taken from Richardson.
51. See Jump, p. 306.
52. Qtd. in Benjamin Fisher, 'The American Reception of Ella D'Arcy', *Victorian Periodicals Review* 28.3 (1995), 232–48, p. 236.
53. Fisher, pp. 239–41.
54. Deborah L. Parsons, *Streetwalking the Metropolis: Women, the City and Modernity* (Oxford: Oxford University Press, 2000), p. 43.
55. Rpt. in Smith, p. 8.
56. All quotations are taken from Charlotte Mew, 'Passed', in Smith.
57. See Ledger, pp. 36–37, 44–45.
58. See Showalter, pp. 134, 135.
59. Evelyn Sharp, 'The Other Anna', in Jump, p. 387.
60. Other contemporary examples of this are Netta Syrett's later story 'The Last Journey', from *The Venture* (1905), and Katherine Mansfield's early story 'The Tiredness of Rosabel' (1908), which is reprinted in Richardson.
61. Angela V. John, ' "Behind the Locked Door": Evelyn Sharp, Suffragette and Rebel Journalist', *Women's History Review* 12.1 (2003), 5–13, p. 8.
62. This quotation appears in the Spring List at the back of the 1910 edition. Quotations from the stories are also taken from Evelyn Sharp, *Rebel Women* (London: A.C. Fyfield, 1910), except for 'Filling the War Chest', which is reprinted in Richardson.
63. Maria DiCenzo, 'Gutter Politics: Women Newsies and the Suffrage Press', *Women's History Review* 12.1 (2003), 15–33, p. 16.
64. Parsons, p. 43. See also Ledger, pp. 150–57.

5   Imperial Adventures and Colonial Tales

1. Robert Louis Stevenson, 'A Gossip on Romance', from *Memories and Portraits*, in *The Works of Robert Louis Stevenson* (New York: Charles Scribner's Sons, 1922), Vol. 12, pp. 188–89.
2. Lynda Dryden, *Joseph Conrad and the Imperial Romance* (London: Palgrave, 2000). See also Patrick Brantlinger, *Rule of Darkness: British Literature and Imperialism, 1830–1914* (New York: Cornell University Press, 1993).
3. Deirdre David, 'Empire, Race and the Victorian Novel', in *A Companion to the Victorian Novel*, ed. Patrick Brantlinger and William Thesing (Oxford: Blackwell, 2002), p. 96.
4. Virginia Woolf, *A Room of One's Own* (London: Panther, 1984), p. 97.
5. Rob Dixon, *Writing the Colonial Adventure* (Cambridge: Cambridge University Press, 1995), p. 4.
6. Dixon, p. 4.
7. Unsigned article, 'Toujours Perfide', *Aberdeen Weekly Journal* (2 September 1891), p. 5.
8. Unsigned article, 'Dr Conan Doyle in Bristol', *Bristol Mercury and Daily Post* (7 December 1893), p. 8.

9. All quotations are taken from Joseph Conrad, *Tales of Unrest*, ed. Antony Fothergill (London: Everyman, 2000).
10. Charles Hyne, *Atoms of Empire* (London: Macmillan, 1904), p. 288.
11. On boys' adventure fiction, see Kelly Boyd, *Manliness and the Boys' Story Paper in Britain: A Cultural History, 1855–1940* (New York: Palgrave Macmillan, 2003); Joseph Bristow, *Empire Boys: Adventures in a Man's World* (London: HarperCollins, 1991); and Jeffrey Richards, ed., *Imperialism and Juvenile Literature* (Manchester: Manchester University Press, 1989).
12. See Elaine Showalter, *Sexual Anarchy* (London: Virago, 1992); Harry Brod, 'The New Men's Studies: From Feminist Theory to Gender Scholarship', *Hypatia* 2 (1987), 179–96, cited in J. Kestner, *Masculinities in Victorian Painting* (Aldershot: Ashgate, 1995), p. 8.
13. Cited in Jad Adams, *Rudyard Kipling* (London: Haus, 2005), p. 64.
14. David Adams, 'Remorse and Power: Conrad's "Karain", and the Queen', *Modern Fiction Studies* 47.4 (2001), 723–52, p. 724.
15. Harry Ricketts, *The Unforgiving Minute: A Life of Rudyard Kipling* (London: Chatto & Windus, 1999), p. 154.
16. Qtd. in Ricketts, p. 152.
17. M. Sinha, *Colonial Masculinity: The Manly Englishman and the Effeminate Bengali in the Late Nineteenth Century* (Manchester: Manchester University Press, 1995), p. 24.
18. Ricketts, p. 231.
19. Andrew Lang, 'Plain Tales from the Hills', *Daily News* (1889), rpt. in *Kipling: The Critical Heritage*, ed. R. L. Green (London: Routledge, 1971), p. 48.
20. Rudyard Kipling, *The Day's Work* (Leipzig: Tauchnitz, 1898), pp. 250, 230.
21. Raymond Williams, *George Orwell* (New York: Viking, 1971), cited in John McClure, *Kipling and Conrad: The Colonial Fiction* (London: Harvard University Press, 1981), p. 9.
22. The collection from which the story is taken is Plain Tales from the Hills (1888). Rudyard Kipling, *Plain Tales from the Hills*, ed. Andrew Rutherford (Oxford University Press, 1987), p. 53.
23. Rudyard Kipling, 'On Greenbow Hill', in *Life's Handicap*, ed. A. O. J. Cockshutt (Oxford: Oxford University Press, 1987), p. 69.
24. McClure, p. 21.
25. Zohreh T. Sullivan, *Narratives of Empire: The Fictions of Rudyard Kipling* (Cambridge: Cambridge University Press, 1993), p. 10.
26. All quotations are taken from Rudyard Kipling, *Plain Tales from the Hills*, ed. Andrew Rutherford (Oxford: Oxford University Press, 1987). Other cautionary stories feature opium dens ('The Gate of the Hundred Sorrows'), brothels ('The City of Dreadful Night'), suicides ('At the End of the Passage'), madness ('The Mark of the Beast'), syphilis ('Love-o'-Women') and death from overwork ('In the Pride of His Youth').
27. Kipling, 'At the End of the Passage', in *Life's Handicap*.
28. Sullivan, p. 17.
29. Sullivan, p. 15.
30. Kipling, 'The Head of the District', in *Life's Handicap*.
31. Noel Annan, 'Kipling's Place in the History of Ideas', *Victorian Studies* 3 (1959–60), 322–48, rpt. in *Kipling's Mind and Art*, ed. Andrew Rutherford (Stanford: Stanford University Press, 1964), 97–125, p. 102.

32. Edmund Gosse, 'Rudyard Kipling', *Century Magazine* (1891), rpt. in Green, p. 117.
33. Robert Buchanan, 'The Voice of the Hooligan', *Contemporary Review* 86 (December 1899), rpt. in Green, p. 236.
34. Oscar Wilde, 'Plain Tales from the Hills', *Nineteenth Century* (1890), rpt. in Adams, *Kipling*, p. 42.
35. Ricketts, p. 205.
36. Ricketts, p. 253.
37. Gilbert Frankau, 'Rudyard Kipling', *London Magazine* 61 (August 1928), 130–34, rpt. in Green, p. 365.
38. Quoatations in this discussion are taken from Rudyard Kipling, 'The Man Who Would Be King', in *Wee Willie Winkie, The Phantom Rickshaw and Other Stories* (London: Macmillan, 1913), Vol. 3 of the Bombay Edition of *The Works of Rudyard Kipling*.
39. Manfred Drandt, 'Reality or Delusion? Narrative Technique and Meaning in Kipling's "The Man Who Would Be King"', *English Studies* 65.4 (1984), 316–26, p. 316.
40. T. S. Eliot, 'The Years Between', *Athenaeum* (9 May 1919), 297–98, rpt. in Green, p. 322.
41. See Tim Bascom, 'Secret Imperialism: The Reader's Response to the Narrator in "The Man Who Would Be King"', *ELT* 131.2 (1988), 162–73, p. 167.
42. Louis Cornell, *Kipling in India* (New York: St. Martin's, 1966), p. 163.
43. Helen Bauer, *Rudyard Kipling: A Study of the Short Fiction* (New York: Twayne, 1994), p. 40.
44. Adams, *Kipling*, p. 54.
45. Anjali Arondekar, 'Lingering Pleasures, Perverted Texts', in *Imperial Desire: Dissident Sexualities and Colonial Literature*, ed. Philip Holden and Richard J. Ruppel (London: University of Minnesota Press, 2003), p. 67.
46. Rudyard Kipling, *Something of Myself: For Friends Known and Unknown* (London: Macmillan, 1981), p. 45.
47. McClure, p. 99.
48. Joseph Conrad, *A Personal Record* (1912; London: Dent, 1919), p. 20.
49. However, Kipling once wrote critically of Conrad that 'the intensity of fear and terror' among his characters is 'above the English norm'. Cited in Jan Perowski, 'On Conrad and Kipling', in *Conrad under Familial Eyes*, ed. Zdzisaw Najder, trans. Halina Carroll Najder (Cambridge: Cambridge University Press, 1983), pp. 162–63.
50. Letter to J. Pinker, 7 November 1901, in *The Collected Letters of Joseph Conrad*, Vol. 2, ed. Frederick Karl and Laurence Davies (Cambridge: Cambridge University Press, 1986), p. 357.
51. Letter to William Blackwood, 31 May 1902, in Karl and Davies, Vol. 2, p. 417.
52. All quotations are taken from Joseph Conrad, *Youth, Heart of Darkness, The End of the Tether*, ed. Robert Kimbrough (Oxford: Oxford World's Classics, 1984).
53. Unsigned review, *Athenaeum* (20 December 1902), p. 824, in *Joseph Conrad, The Critical Heritage*, ed. Norman Sherry (London: Routledge, 1973), p. 139.
54. Unsigned review, 'Malayan Romance', *Pall Mall Gazette* (1896), p. 165.
55. Letter to E. L. Sanderson, 15 June 1898, in Karl and Davies, Vol. 2, p. 71.
56. Edward Garnett, 'youth', 'Heart of Darkness', 'The End of the Tether', *Academy* (6 December 1902), p. 606, qtd. in Norman Sherry (ed.), *Joseph Conrad: The Critical Heritage* (London: Routledge and Kegan Paul, 1973), p. 98.

57. Samuel Hynes, 'Introduction', in Joseph Conrad, *The Complete Short Fiction* (London: Pickering & Chatto, 1992), p. xv.
58. Norman Page, *A Conrad Companion* (London: Macmillan, 1986), p. 141.
59. Page, p. 141.
60. See Gail Fraser, 'The Short Fiction', in *The Cambridge Companion to Joseph Conrad*, ed. J. Stape (Cambridge: Cambridge University Press, 1996), 25–44, p. 25.
61. F. R. Leavis, *The Great Tradition: George Eliot, Henry James, Joseph Conrad* (Harmondsworth: Penguin, 1962), pp. 204–77.
62. Ford Madox Ford, 'Literary Impressionism', in *A Personal Remembrance* (London: Duckworth, 1924), p. 194.
63. Letter to E. L. Sanderson, 17 October 1897, in *The Collected Letters of Joseph Conrad*, Vol. 1, ed. Frederick R. Karl and Laurence Davies (Cambridge University Press, 1983), p. 398.
64. Adrian M. De Lange, 'Conrad and Impressionism: Problems and (Possible) Solutions', in *Conrad's Literary Career*, ed. Keith Carabine, Owen Knowles and Wieslaw Krajia, 2 Vols. (New York: Columbia University Press, 1992), Vol. 1, p. 28.
65. Joseph Conrad, 'Preface', in *The Nigger of Narcissus*, ed. Jacques Berthoud (Oxford: Oxford University Press, 1984), p. xlii.
66. Letter to Edward Garnett, 10 March 1897, in Karl and Davies, Vol. 1, p. 343.
67. Ian Watt, 'Conrad's Impressionism', in *Joseph Conrad's Heart of Darkness: A Casebook*, ed. Gene M. Moore (Oxford: Oxford University Press, 2004), p. 177.
68. Letter to J. B. Pinker, 12 May 1905, in *The Collected Letters of Joseph Conrad*, Vol. 3, ed. Frederick R. Karl and Laurence Davies (Cambridge University Press, 1988), p. 243.
69. Cedric Watts, *Joseph Conrad: A Literary Life* (London: Macmillan, 1989), p. 65.
70. Letter to T. Fisher Unwin, 5 November 1897, in Karl and Davies, Vol. 1, p. 405.
71. Letter to Edward Garnett, 14 August 1896, in Karl and Davies, Vol. 1, p. 301.
72. Unsigned review, ' "The Sea between Covers": Mr Joseph Conrad's New Book', *Daily Mail* (22 April 1903), p. 4, rpt. in Sherry, p. 146.
73. Joseph Conrad, 'Notes on Life and Letters', in *Complete Works of Joseph Conrad* (London: Heron Books, 1969), Vol. 9, p. 202.
74. Joseph Conrad, *Typhoon and other Tales*, ed. Cedric Watts (Oxford: Oxford University Press, 2002).
75. J. Berg Esenswein, *Writing the Short Story: A Practical Handbook on the Rise, Structure, and Sale of the Modern Short-Story* (London: Melrose, 1912), p. 40, cited in Stephen Donovan, *Joseph Conrad and Popular Culture* (Basingstoke: Palgrave, 2005), p. 182.
76. Letter to E. N. Doubleday, 21 December 1918, in *The Collected Letters of Joseph Conrad*, Vol. 6, ed. Laurence Davies, Frederick R. Karl and Owen Knowles (Cambridge: Cambridge University Press, 2003), p. 333.
77. D. R. Schwartz, *The Transformation of the English Novel, 1890–1930* (New York: St. Martin's, 1989), p. 22.
78. McClure, p. 99.
79. McClure, p. 100.
80. Letter to Edward Garnett, 4 August 1896, in Karl and Davies, Vol. 1, p. 296.

81. Letter to Edward Garnett, 14 August 1896, in Karl and Davies, Vol. 1, p. 301.
82. Letter to T. Fisher Unwin, 7 June 1896, in Karl and Davies, Vol. 1, p. 286.
83. Unsigned review, 'Recent Short Stories', *The Spectator* (13 August 1898), 218–19.
84. From Conrad, *Tales of Unrest*.
85. Rupert Ruppel, ' "The Lagoon" and the Popular Exotic Tradition', in *Contexts for Conrad*, ed. Keith Carabine, Owen Knowles and Wieslaw Krajia (New York: Columbia University Press, 1993), p. 180.
86. Ruppel, p. 18.
87. Laurence Graver, *Conrad's Short Fiction* (Berkeley: University of California Press, 1969), p. 28.
88. Taken from Conrad, *Tales of Unrest*.
89. Unsigned review, 'Impressions from East and West', *Pall Mall Gazette* (27 May 1898), p. 7.
90. Unsigned review, 'An Outpost of Progress', *Westminster Gazette* (4 May 1898), in Sherry, p. 14.
91. Cedric Watts, *Joseph Conrad* (Plymouth: Northcote House, 1994), p. 15.
92. Watts, p. 15.
93. Letter to T. Fisher Unwin, 22 July 1896, in Karl and Davies, Vol. 1, p. 294.
94. Letter to R. B. Cunninghame-Graham, 14 April 1898, in Karl and Davies, Vol. 2, p. 57.
95. Unsigned review, 'Tales of Unrest', *Daily Telegraph* (9 April 1898), p. 8, rpt. in Sherry, p. 101.

6 Introducing the Twentieth-Century Short Story

1. Clare Hanson, *Short Stories and Short Fictions, 1880–1980* (London: Macmillan, 1985), pp. 5, 6.
2. Dominic Head, *The Modernist Short Story* (Cambridge: Cambridge University Press, 1992), 'Introduction' and *passim*.
3. Jane Eldridge Miller, *Rebel Women: Feminism, Modernism and the Edwardian Novel* (London: Virago, 1994), pp. 24–25.
4. Hanson, p. 55.
5. All quotations are taken from Arnold Bennett, *The Grim Smile of the Five Towns* (1907; Harmondsworth: Penguin, 1946).
6. Walter Pater, *The Renaissance: The 1893 Text*, ed. Donald L. Hill (Berkley and London: University of California Press, 1980), pp. 187–88.
7. George Moore, *The Untilled Field* (1903; no place: Biblio bazaar, 2006).
8. Brendan Kennelly, 'George Moore's Lonely Voices: A Study of His Short Stories', in *George Moore's Mind and Art*, ed. Graham Owens (Edinburgh: Oliver and Boyd, 1968), 144–65, p. 153.
9. James Joyce, *A Portrait of the Artist as a Young Man* (Harmonsdworth: Penguin, 1996), p. 205.

7 The Short Story and the Great War

1. Angela Smith, *The Second Battlefield: Women, Modernism and the First World War* (Manchester: Manchester University Press, 2000), p. 2.

2. J. B. Priestly, *Margin Released* (London: Methuen, 1962), p. 231.
3. All quotations are taken from Arthur Machen, *The Bowmen and Other Legends of the War* (London: Simpkin Marshal, 1915).
4. Adrian Eckersley, 'Arthur Machen', in *British Short-Fiction Writers, 1880–1914: The Romantic Tradition,* ed. William F. Naufftus (Dictionary of Literary Biography, Vol. 156; New York: Gale, 1996), p. 222.
5. All quotations are taken from Sapper, *Men, Women and Guns* (London: Hodder, 1916).
6. All quotations are taken from Arthur Conan Doyle, 'Danger! Being the Log of Captain John Sirius', *Strand* 48 (July 1914), 3–19.
7. Unsigned article, 'What Naval Experts Think', *Strand* 48 (July 1914), p. 20.
8. All quotations are taken from Arthur Conan Doyle, *His Last Bow,* ed. Owen Dudley Edwards (Oxford: Oxford University Press, 1993).
9. Siegfried Sassoon, *Siegfried's Journeys: 1916–1920* (London: Faber & Faber, 1945), p. 53.
10. Jack Adrian, 'Introduction', in Sapper, *The Best Short Stories* (London: Dent, 1984), p. x.
11. Adrian, p. xi.
12. Sapper, *Sapper's War Stories* (London: Hodder, 1930).
13. Paul Johnson, *Land Fit for Heroes: The Planning of British Reconstruction, 1916–1919* (Chicago: Chicago University Press, 1968), p. 61.
14. *Sapper's War Stories,* p. 1050.
15. Unsigned review, 'New Novels: The War and After', *The Times* (12 September 1930), p. 7.
16. Richard Aldington, *Life for Life's Sake* (London: Viking, 1941), pp. 207, 215.
17. Richard Aldington, *Roads to Glory* (London: Chatto and Windus, 1930).
18. See Patricia Rae, *Modernism and Mourning* (Lewisburg: Bucknell University Press, 2007), pp. 13–14.
19. Christopher Ridgeway, 'Introduction', in Richard Aldington, *Death of a Hero* (London: Hogarth Press, 2004). p. v.
20. Mikhail Urnov, 'Aldington in Russia', in *Richard Aldington,* ed. Lionel Kelly (Reading: University of Reading, 1987), p. 46.
21. Thomas Pinney, ed., *The Letters of Rudyard Kipling,* 6 Vols. (London: Macmillan, 1990–2004), Vol. 4, p. 254.
22. *Brighton Observer* (11 September 1914), cited in Harry Ricketts, *The Unforgiving Minute: A Life of Rudyard Kipling* (London: Chatto & Windus, 1995), p. 315.
23. Cited in Ricketts, p. 317.
24. Jad Adams, *Rudyard Kipling* (London: Haus, 2005), p. 169.
25. All quotations are taken from Rudyard Kipling, *A Diversity of Creatures,* ed. Paul Driver (London: Penguin, 1987).
26. *Southport Guardian* (25 June 1915), cited in Ricketts, p. 321.
27. H. Rider Haggard, *Record of a Friendship,* p. 84, cited in Morton Cohen (ed.), *Rudyard Kipling to Rider Haggard: The Record of a Friendship* (London: Hutchinson, 1965).
28. Norman Page, 'What Happens in "Mary Postgate"?', *English Literature in Transition 1880–1920,* 29.1 (1986), 41–47, p. 42.
29. Taken from Kipling, *A Diversity of Creatures.*
30. Letter to Stanley Baldwin, 21 September 1918, in Pinney, Vol. 4, p. 511.
31. Letter to Sir Almoroth Wright, 1916?, in Pinney, Vol. 4, pp. 421.

32. Donald Gray, 'Rudyard Kipling', in Naufftus, p. 194.
33. All quotations are taken from Rudyard Kipling, *Debits and Credits*, ed. Sandra Kemp (London: Penguin, 1987).
34. William Dillingham, *Rudyard Kipling: Hell and Heroism* (London: Palgrave, 2005), p. 68.
35. See Adams, pp. 176–77.
36. Cited in Terry Castle, *Noel Coward and Radclyffe Hall* (New York: Columbia University Press, 1996), p. 19.
37. Rebecca West, *Ending in Earnest* (New York: Doubleday, 1971), p. 6.
38. Claudia Stillman Franks, *Beyond The Well of Loneliness: The Fiction of Radclyffe Hall* (Aldershot: Ashgate, 1982), p. 123.
39. Michael Baker, 'Marguerite Radclyffe Hall', *New Dictionary of National Biography* (Oxford: Oxford University Press, 2005), Vol. 24, p. 638.
40. Qtd. in Sally Cline, *Radclyffe Hall: The Woman Who Was John* (London: John Murray, 1997), p. 100.
41. Qtd. in Cline, p. 226.
42. All quotations are taken from Radclyffe Hall, *Miss Ogilvy Finds Herself* (London: William Heinemann, 1934).
43. David Mitchell, *Women on the Warpath* (London: Jonathan Cape, 1966), p. 380.
44. Unsigned review, 'Miss Ogilvy Finds Herself', *Times Literary Supplement* (8 March 1934), p. 160.
45. Heather Edwards, 'Miss Ogilvy Finds Herself', in *A Companion to the British Short Story*, ed. Andrew Maunder (New York: Facts on File, 2007), 287–88.
46. Franks, p. 137.
47. David Goldie, *A Critical Difference: T.S. Eliot and John Middleton Murray in English Literary Criticism 1919–28* (Oxford: Clarendon Press, 1998), pp. 29–30.

8   Experiment and Continuity: The Modernist Short Story

1. The *Oxford English Dictionary* cites its first use in print as dating from 1737, in the writings of Jonathan Swift, though he was not using the word in quite the way that contemporary critical thought does. For Swift it meant roughly 'neologism' – the coining of new or slang terms, which he disapproved of as the 'corruption of English ... abominable'.
2. Julia Van Gunsteren, *Katherine Mansfield and Literary Impressionism* (Amsterdam: Rodopi, 1990), pp. 51–52.
3. Virginia Woolf, 'Mr Bennett and Mrs Brown', *Nation and Athenaeum* (1 December 1923), rpt. in Virginia Woolf, *A Woman's Essays*, ed. Rachel Bowlby (Harmondsworth: Penguin, 1992), Vol. 1, 69–87, pp. 70–71.
4. Frank Kermode, *The Sense of an Ending: Studies in the Theory of Fiction* (Oxford: Oxford University Press, 1968), p. 97.
5. Matthew Arnold, 'The Modern Element in Literature', rpt. in *Selected Poems and Prose*, ed. Miriam Allott (London: Dent, 1993), p. 136.
6. John Carey, *The Intellectuals and the Masses* (London: Faber & Faber, 1992).
7. Woolf, 'Mr Bennett and Mrs Brown', p. 82.
8. Virginia Woolf, 'Modern Fiction', in *The Crowded Dance of Modern Life, Selected Essays*, Vol. 2, ed. Rachel Bowlby (Harmondsworth: Penguin, 1992), p. 10.
9. All quotations are taken from D. H. Lawrence, *Selected Short Stories*, ed. Brian Finney (Harmondsworth: Penguin, 1982).

10. D. H. Lawrence, 'Introduction to The Dragon of the Apocalypse', in *A Selection from Phoenix*, ed. A. A. H. Inglis (Harmondsworth: Penguin, 1979), p. 543.
11. Brian Finney, 'Introduction', in D. H. Lawrence, *Selected Short Stories* (Harmondsworth: Penguin, 1982), p. 26.
12. Joseph Conrad, letter to Cunninghame Graham, 1898, in *Joseph Conrad's Letters to Cunninghame Graham*, ed. C. T. Wells (Cambridge: Cambridge University Press, 1969), p. 65.
13. Both Clare Hanson and Saralyn Daly make this point. See Clare Hanson, *Short Stories and Short Fiction, 1880–1980* (London: Macmillan, 1985), p. 78; Saralyn Daly, *Katherine Mansfield* (New York: Twayne, 1994), p. 3.
14. Mary Ann Gillies and Aurelea Mahood, *Modernist Literature: An Introduction* (Edinburgh: Edinburgh University Press, 2007), p. 50.
15. Mansfield also has a number of virtuoso short stories on menopausal women: 'Miss Brill', for instance, and the stunning 'Daughters of the Late Colonel', both of which are strongly recommended.
16. Both German and French translations of Chekhov appeared earlier, and it is highly likely that Mansfield had read a German translation in the early part of the century.
17. Charles E. May, *The Short Story: The Reality of Artifice* (New York and London: Routledge, 2002), pp. 15–16.
18. All quotations are taken from Katherine Mansfield, *The Collected Stories*, ed. and intro. Ali Smith (Harmondsworth: Penguin, 2007).
19. For a useful description and analysis of the workings of free indirect style, see H. Porter Abbott, *The Cambridge Introduction to Narrative* (Cambridge: Cambridge University Press, 2002).
20. Peter Childs, *Modernism* (London: Routledge, 2000), p. 136.
21. *Letters of Katherine Mansfield*, qtd. in 'Introduction', in Katherine Mansfield, *Selected Stories*, ed. Angela Smith (Oxford: Oxford World's Classics, 1999), p. xxix (our bold).
22. The reader who wants more information should consult the Norton Critical Edition of *Dubliners*, ed. Margot Norris (New York: W.W. Norton, 2006).
23. All quotations are taken from James Joyce, *Dubliners*, ed. Terence Brown (Harmondsworth: Penguin, 1992).
24. Joyce, letter to Constance Doran, 1904, in *Letters of James Joyce*, Vol. 1, ed. Stuart Gilvert (New York: Viking, 1957), p. 55.
25. Stanilaus Joyce, *My Brother's Keeper*, ed. Richard Ellmann (London: Faber and Faber, 1958), p. 116.
26. Joyce, letter to Stanislaus Joyce, 1906, in Gilvert, Vol. 1, p. 63.
27. See Dominic Head, *The Modernist Short Story* (Basingstoke: Macmillan, 1992), p. 44.
28. Quoted by Lindsay Warren, 'An analysis of the Use of Musical Allusions in James Joyce's *Dubliners*', internet, The Modern World, www.themodern-world.com/joyce/joycepaper/warren.html (accessed August 2009)
29. James Abbott McNeill Whistler (1834–1903) was a major figure at the end of the nineteenth century. His figurative paintings are impressionistic portraits of young (and beautiful) women, and the titles of his works often allude to music, for he too was influenced by Walter Pater. Thus one can find 'Symphony in White' and a whole series of 'Nocturnes' among his oeuvre.
30. James Joyce, *Stephen Hero* (London: Jonathan Cape, 1969), p. 218.
31. Woolf, 'Modern Fiction', p. 11.

32. All quotations are taken from Virginia Woolf, *The Mark on the Wall and Other Short Fiction*, ed. David Bradshaw (Oxford: Oxford University Press, 2001).
33. Laura Marcus, *Virginia Woolf* (Plymouth: Northcote House, 1997), p. 21.
34. Letter to Ethel Smyth, 16 October 1930, in *The Letters of Virginia Woolf*, Vol. 4, ed. Nigel Nicolson and Joanne Trautman (London: Harcourt, 1981), p. 231.
35. Tim Armstrong, *Modernism: A Cultural History* (Cambridge: Polity, 2005), pp. 52–53.
36. [Harold Childs], *Times Literary Supplement* (29 May 1919), p. 293, qtd. in *Virginia Woolf: The Critical Heritage*, ed. Robin Majumdar and Allen McLaurin (London and Boston: Routledge & Kegan Paul, 1975), p. 66.
37. Adrian Hunter, *The Cambridge Introduction to the Short Story in English* (Cambridge: Cambridge University Press, 2007), p. 71.
38. Marcus, p. 18.
39. Hunter, p. 66. Hunter's incisive analysis of this story is particularly illuminating in terms of its focus on opposing kinds of knowledge: 'By contrast with Whitaker's four-square certainties stand the narrator's hesitant, sensitive enquiries into her environment, her puzzling over minutiae, the quality of air in the room, and the size of thoughts' (p. 67).
40. E. M. Forster, *Aspects of the Novel* (Harmondsworth: Penguin, 1927), pp. 35–36.
41. Bradshaw, 'Introduction', in *The Mark on the Wall*, p. xxiii.
42. Woolf, 'Modern Fiction', p. 8

9   The Short Story and Genre Fiction: The Same Old Story?

1. Qtd. in Q. D. Leavis, *Fiction and the Reading Public* (1932; London: Bellow Publishing, 1978), p. 47.
2. All quotations are taken from Agatha Christie, 'Mr Eastwood's Adventure', in *The Listerdale Mystery* (1934; London: HarperCollins, 1997).
3. Leavis, p. 45.
4. This story was first published as 'The Mystery of the Second Cucumber' in *The Novel* magazine in August 1924.
5. See Walter J. Ong, *Orality and Literacy: The Technologizing of the Word* (London: Routledge, 1981) for an outline of this argument.
6. Jack Zipes, *Fairy Tales and the Art of Subversion: The Classical Genre for Children and the Process of Civilisation* (New York: Routledge, 1985).
7. See Lee T. Lemon and M. J. Reis, eds., *Russian Formalist Criticism: Four Essays* (Lincoln: University of Nebraska Press, 1965) for more information about the Russian Formalist tradition.
8. This link between puzzles and detection is picked up by the contemporary detective novelist Colin Dexter, whose Inspector Morse prides himself on the speed with which he can complete the *Times* crossword each day.
9. Agatha Christie, 'The Tuesday Night Club' (1932), in *Miss Marple: Complete Short Stories* (London: HarperCollins, 1997), p. 8. This story was first published in December 1927 in *The Royal Magazine*.
10. See Chapter 8 for comments on Katherine Mansfield's use of the word and concept of 'order' in 'The Garden Party', and the section on James Joyce in that chapter for comments on how 'puzzles' are not solved in modernist writing.
11. Stephen Knight, *Form and Ideology in Crime Fiction* (London: Macmillan, 1980), p. 127.

12. Margaret Forster, *Daphne du Maurier* (London: Arrow, 2007), pp. 42–43.
13. Christie's works too have been multiply filmed, though not for quite the same reason as du Maurier's fictions. Du Maurier attracted film makers who were interested in the evocation of atmosphere. Christie's stories, in contrast, are attractive as much more straightforward adaptations: it is their relatively simple narrative form and concentration on plot which make them suitable for film treatment.
14. Agatha Christie, *Autobiography* (London: HarperCollins, 1993), p. 352.
15. Sayers's short-story collections include *Lord Peter Views the Body* (1928), *Hangman's Holiday* (1933) and *In the Teeth of the Evidence* (1939). They are largely detective stories, but there are also some notable examples of the weird tale in the last of these collections, for those who want to follow up the connection between these genres.
16. Raymond Williams, *The English Novel from Dickens to Lawrence* (London: Hogarth Press, 1985), p. 141. Williams uses the phrase to describe the ship in the fiction of Joseph Conrad, but he extends from this to argue that the village (or small community) is the archetype of the knowable community in the traditional English novel.
17. Poirot too gets several excursions in the shorter-form detective story, and his little grey cells are just as effective there as they are in the more extended narratives of the classic novels.
18. Marion Shaw and Sabine Vanacker, *Reflecting on Miss Marple* (London: Routledge, 1991), p. 21.
19. Shaw and Vanacker, p. 15.
20. Christie, *Miss Marple: Complete Short Stories*, p. 16 (our emphasis).
21. Alison Light, *Forever England: Femininity, Literature and Conservatism between the Wars* (London: Routledge, 1991), esp. the chapter 'Agatha Christie and Conservative Modernity', 113–55.
22. This story was first published in *The Grand Magazine* in December 1925.
23. Agatha Christie, The Listerdale Mystery (Glasgow: Harper Collins, 2003). All quotations are taken from this edition.
24. 'Philomel Cottage' was one of Christie's early successes and has been widely adapted, first into play form, and thereafter into a film, retitled in both incarnations *Love from a Stranger*. One of the markers of the 'plot' form of fiction is its ready adaptation into other forms.
25. Light, p. 158.
26. Forster, pp. 12–14.
27. Forster, p. 30.
28. Avril Horner and Sue Zlosnik, *Daphne du Maurier: Writing, Identity and the Gothic Imagination* (Basingstoke: Macmillan, 1998), p. 24.
29. All these stories are collected in Daphne du Maurier, *The Rendezvous and Other Stories*, ed. and intro. Minette Walters (London: Virago, 2005). Du Maurier's stories are difficult to date precisely, but these are all early works from the period between around 1930 and the outbreak of the Second World War.
30. All quotations are taken from Daphne du Maurier, 'The Apple Tree', rpt. in *The Birds and Other Stories*, ed. and intro. David Thomson (London: Virago, 2004).
31. Nina Auerbach, *Daphne du Maurier, Haunted Heiress* (Philadelphia: University of Pennsylvania Press, 2000), p. 64.

10   Introducing the Post-War Short Story

1. Dennis Vannatta, *The English Short Story 1880–1945* (Boston: Twayne, 1985), p. 35.
2. Cited in J. Dutton, 'Why Magazines Die', *Guardian* (25 June 2005), p. 8.
3. V. S. Pritchett, 'The Short Story', *London Magazine* 6.6 (September 1966), 6–8, p. 6.
4. Francis King, 'The Short Story', *London Magazine* 6.6 (September 1966), 11–12.
5. Gill Plain, *Women's Fiction of the Second World War: Gender, Power and Resistance* (Edinburgh: Edinburgh University Press, 1996), p. 14.
6. Anne Boston, 'Introduction', in *Wave Me Goodbye: Stories of the Second World War* (London: Penguin, 1988), p. 12.
7. Elizaneth Bowen, 'The Short Story in England', *Britain To-Day* 109 (May 1945), 12–16, p. 15.
8. John Bars, 'The Initiation of Alan Sillitoe's Long Distance Runner', *Modern Fiction Studies* 22.4 (1976), 584–90, p. 585.
9. Cited in Dominic Sandbrook, *Never Had It So Good: A History of Britain from Suez to the Beatles* (London: Abacus, 2006), p. 80.
10. John Russell Taylor, *Anger and After* (London: Methuen, 1988), p. 41.
11. Kenneth Allsop, *The Angry Decade* (London: Peter Owen, 1958), p. 9.
12. All quotations are taken from Alan Sillitoe, *The Loneliness of the Long Distance Runner* (1959; London: Flamingo, 1993).
13. Cited in Clare Hanson, *Understanding Alan Sillitoe* (Columbia: University of South Carolina Press, 1999), p. 39.
14. Hanson, p. 44.
15. Bars, p. 586.
16. Alan Penner, *Alan Sillitoe* (New York: Twayne, 1972), p. 46.
17. Clare Hanson, *Re-Reading the Short Story* (London: Macmillan, 1989), p. 2.
18. Pam Morris, *Literature and Feminism* (Oxford: Blackwell, 1993), p. 64.
19. Cited in Allsop, p. 10.
20. Stephen Brooke has written of the 'celebration, particularly in fictional treatments of working-class life, of an aggressive masculinity, one which stressed misogyny'. Stephen Brooke, 'Gender and Working-Class Identity in Britain during the 1950s', *Journal of Social History* 34.4 (2001), 773–97, p. 775.
21. For more on these publications, see John J. Stinson, 'The English Short Story, 1945–1950', in *The English Short Story, 1945–1980*, ed. Dennis Vannatta (Boston: Twayne, 1985), 29–31.
22. C. L. Dallat, 'New Voices Abroad', *Guardian* (28 May 2005), p. 10.
23. Frank O'Connor, *The Lonely Voice: A Study of the Short Story* (New York: World, 1963), p. 20.
24. Julia Bell and Jackie Gay, eds., *England Calling* (London: Phoenix, 2001), p. xi.
25. Nicholas Blincoe and Matt Thorne, eds., *All Hail the New Puritans* (London: Fourth Estate, 2000).
26. Clare Hanson, *Short Stories and Short Fictions, 1880–1980* (London: Macmillan, 1985), p. 172

11   Women's Stories, 1940s to the Present

1. Simone de Beauvoir, *The Second Sex* (1949), cited in Ruth Robbins, ' "Snowed Up": Feminist Perspectives', in *Literary Theories*, ed. Julian Wolfreys and William Baker (London: Macmillan, 1996), p. 118.
2. Diana Wallace, ' "Writing as Re-Vision": Women's Writing in Britain, 1945 to the Present Day', in *An Introduction to Women's Writing: From the Middle Ages to the Present Day*, ed. Marion Shaw (Hemel Hempstead: Prentice Hall, 1998), pp. 236, 237.
3. Mary Joannou, *Contemporary Women's Writing: From The Golden Notebook to The Color Purple* (Manchester: Manchester University Press, 2000), p. 7.
4. Joannou, p. 9.
5. Hermione Lee, 'Introduction', in *The Secret Self: A Century of Short Stories by Women* (London: Phoenix Giants, 1995), pp. x, xi.
6. Mary Eagleton, 'Gender and Genre', in *Re-Reading the Short Story*, ed. Clare Hanson (London: Macmillan, 1989), pp. 64, 66.
7. Dean Baldwin, 'The English Short Story in the Fifties', in *The English Short Story: 1945–1980*, ed. Dennis Vannatta (Boston: Twayne, 1985), p. 74.
8. Anthea Trodd, *British Women's Writing, 1900–1945* (Harlow: Longman, 1998), p. 38.
9. Deborah L. Parsons, *Streetwalking the Metropolis: Women, the City and Modernity* (Oxford: Oxford University Press, 2000), p. 124.
10. Clare Hanson, 'Introduction', in *Re-Reading the Short Story*, p. 1.
11. Elizabeth Bowen, 'Preface' to the American edition of *The Demon Lover* (1950), p. 95, qtd. in Gill Plain, *Women's Fiction of the Second World War: Gender, Power and Resistance* (Edinburgh: Edinburgh University Press, 1996), p. 16.
12. Trodd, p. 203.
13. All quotations are taken from Elizabeth Bowen, *Collected Stories*, ed. Angus Wilson (London: Vintage, 1999).
14. John Bayley, *The Short Story: Henry James to Elizabeth Bowen* (Brighton: Harvester, 1988), p. 176.
15. Maud Ellmann, *Elizabeth Bowen: The Shadow across the Page* (Edinburgh: Edinburgh University Press, 2003), p. 171.
16. Plain, p. 181.
17. Parsons, p. 205.
18. Plain, p. 122.
19. Helen Carr, *Jean Rhys* (Plymouth: Northcote House, 1996), p. 29.
20. All quotations are taken from Jean Rhys, *Tigers Are Better-Looking, with a Selection from The Left Bank* (London: André Deutsch, 1968).
21. Coral Ann Howells, *Jean Rhys* (Brighton: Harvester Wheatsheaf, 1991), p. 141.
22. Parsons, p. 125.
23. Howells, p. 127.
24. Howells, p. 127.
25. Joannou, p. 7.
26. Wallace, p. 237.
27. Lynn Knight, *The Secret Woman: The Virago Book of Classic Short Stories* (London: Virago, 1993), p. ix.
28. Betty Friedan, *The Feminine Mystique* (Harmondsworth: Penguin, 1963), p. 1.

29. A. L. Barker, 'Introduction', in Elizabeth Taylor, *Hester Lilly and Other Stories* (1954; London: Virago, 1990), p. xiii. All quotations are taken from this edition.
30. Ellen Cronan Rose, 'Crystals, Fragments and Golden Wholes: Short Stories in *The Golden Notebook*', in Hanson, p. 126.
31. All quotations are taken from Doris Lessing, *To Room Nineteen: Collected Stories, Volume One* (London: Jonathan Cape, 1978).
32. Claire Sprague, 'Genre Reversals in Doris Lessing: Stories Like Novels and Novels Like Stories', in Hanson, p. 114.
33. Susan Watkins, *Twentieth-Century Women Novelists: Feminist Theory into Practice* (Basingstoke: Palgrave, 2001), pp. 25, 26.
34. Joannou, p. 16.
35. Friedan, p. 1.
36. Wallace, p. 250.
37. All quotations are taken from Fay Weldon, *Polaris and Other Stories* (London: Hodder & Stoughton, 1985). 'Weekend', from *Watching Me, Watching You* (1981), is reprinted in Lee's anthology.
38. Lee, pp. 372–3.
39. Qtd. in Weldon, *Polaris and Other Stories*, n.p.
40. Lee, p. x.
41. Emma Donoghue, 'The Tale of the Shoe' and 'The Tale of the Kiss', in *Kissing the Witch* (Harmondsworth: Penguin, 1997), pp. 7, 8, 209.
42. This article was reprinted in the introduction to Helen Simpson's edition of *The Bloody Chamber*, P. V. The full reference appears in the note 51.
43. Patricia Duncker, 'Re-Imagining the Fairy Tales: Angela Carter's Bloody Chambers', *Literature and History* 10.1 (1984), 3–14, pp. 6–7.
44. Susan Sellers, *Myth and Fairytale in Contemporary Women's Fiction* (Basingstoke: Palgrave, 2001), p. 24.
45. Joseph Bristow and Trev Lynn Broughton, *The Infernal Desires of Angela Carter: Fiction, Femininity, Feminism* (Harlow: Longman, 1997), p. 4.
46. Angela Carter, 'Introduction', in *The Virago Book of Fairy Tales* (London: Virago, 1990), p. xviii.
47. Carter, *Virago Book of Fairy Tales*, p. xiv.
48. Interview with Angela Carter in *Novelists in Interview*, ed. John Haffenden (London: Methuen, 1985), p. 84.
49. All quotations are taken from Angela Carter, *The Bloody Chamber and Other Stories*, ed. Helen Simpson (London: Vintage, 1998).
50. Qtd. on the back cover of *The Bloody Chamber*.
51. Judith Butler, *Gender Trouble: Feminism and the Subversion of Identity* (London: Routledge, 1990), pp. 140, 141 (emphasis in original).
52. Helen Simpson, 'Introduction', in Carter, *The Bloody Chamber*, p. vii.
53. Merja Makinen, 'Female Sexuality', in *Angela Carter*, ed. Alison Easton (Basingstoke: Macmillan, 2000), p. 34.
54. Richard Todd, *A.S. Byatt* (Plymouth: Northcote House, 1997), p. 41.
55. All quotations are taken from A. S. Byatt, *The Djinn in the Nightingale's Eye: Five Fairy Stories* (London: Vintage, 1995) and *Elementals: Stories of Fire and Ice* (London: Vintage, 1999).
56. Sellers, p. 38.
57. Qtd. on the back cover of *Elementals*.
58. Sellers, p. 30.

12   The British Short Story Today

1. Dominic Head, *The Cambridge Introduction to Modern British Fiction, 1950–2000* (Cambridge: Cambridge University Press, 2002), p. 156.
2. Head, p. 156.
3. Mark Stein, *Black British Literature: Novels of Transformation* (Columbus: Ohio University Press, 2004), p. 4.
4. Charles Taylor, 'The Politics of Recognition', in *Multiculturalism: Examing the Politics of Recognition*, ed. Amy Gutman (Princeton: Princeton University Press, 1994), p. 25.
5. Stuart Hall, 'New Ethnicities', in *Black Film, British Cinema*, ed. Kobena Mercer (London: Institute of Contemporary Arts, 1988), p. 29, qtd. and discussed in Stein, p. 13.
6. Dennis Vannatta, 'Introduction', in *The English Short Story, 1945–1980* (Boston: Twayne, 1985), p. xviii.
7. Susan Watkins, *Twentieth-Century Women Novelists: Feminist Theory into Practice* (Basingstoke: Palgrave, 2001), p. 16.
8. Aida Edemaniam, review of *Why Don't You Stop Talking?*, *Times Literary Supplement* (15 February 2002), p. 22.
9. Alex Clark, 'Speaking in Tongues', review of *Why Don't You Stop Talking?*, *Guardian* (2 February 2002), p. 10.
10. All quotations are taken from Jackie Kay, *Why Don't You Stop Talking?* (London: Picador, 2002) and *Wish I Were Here* (London: Picador, 2006).
11. Joanne Winning, 'Crossing the Borderline: Post-Devolution Scottish Lesbian and Gay Writing', in *The Edinburgh Companion to Contemporary Scottish Literature*, ed. Berthold Schoene (Edinburgh: Edinburgh University Press, 2007), pp. 288, 289.
12. Head, p. 223.
13. Stein, p. 8.
14. Hanif Kureishi, 'Turning *The Black Album* into a Stage Play', *Guardian* (29 June 2009), p. 21.
15. Susie Thomas, ed., *Hanif Kureishi: A Reader's Guide to Essential Criticism* (Basingstoke: Palgrave, 2005), p. 2.
16. All quotations are taken from Hanif Kureishi, *Love in a Blue Time* (London: Faber & Faber, 1997) and *Midnight All Day* (London: Faber & Faber, 1999).
17. Kureishi, 'Turning *The Black Album* into a Stage Play', p. 19.
18. Bradley Buchanan, *Hanif Kureishi* (Basingstoke: Palgrave, 2007), p. 91.
19. Thomas, p. 146.
20. Stein, p. 135.
21. Buchanan, p. 85.
22. A. S. Byatt, ed., *The Oxford Book of English Short Stories* (Oxford: Oxford University Press, 1998), p. 15.
23. See Tony Brown, 'The Ex-Centric Voice: The English Language Short Story in Wales', *North American Journal of Welsh Studies* 1.1 (2001), 25–41.
24. Neil Corcoran, *After Yeats and Joyce: Reading Modern Irish Literature* (Oxford: Oxford University Press, 2003), pp. 78–80.
25. Jurgen Neubauer, *Literature as Intervention: Struggles over Identity in Contemporary Scottish Fiction* (Marburg: Tectum, 1999), p. 9.

26. Ian Bell, 'Imagine Living There: Form and Ideology in Contemporary Scottish Fiction', in *Studies in Scottish Fiction, 1945 to the Present*, ed. Susanne Hagemann (Frankfurt: M. Lang, 1996), p. 219.
27. Berthold Schoene, 'Going Cosmopolitan: Reconstituting "Scottishness" in Post-Devolution Criticism', in Schoene, pp. 8, 10.
28. Jackie Kay in an interview (2001), qtd. in Matthew Brown, 'In/Outside Scotland: Race and Citizenship in the Work of Jackie Kay', in Schoene, p. 220.
29. Douglas Dunn, 'Introduction', in *The Oxford Book of Scottish Short Stories* (Oxford: Oxford University Press, 1995), p. xxv.
30. James Kelman, 'The Importance of Glasgow in My Work', in *Some Recent Attacks: Essays Cultural and Political* (Stirling: A.K. Press, 1992), p. 81.
31. Neubauer, p. 24.
32. Duncan Petrie, *Contemporary Scottish Fictions: Film, Television and the Novel* (Edinburgh: Edinburgh University Press, 2004), p. 46.
33. Dunn, p. xxi.
34. Petrie, pp. 59, 61.
35. Alison Lumsden, 'Scottish Women's Short Stories: "Repositories of Life Swiftly Apprehended"', in *Contemporary Scottish Women Writers*, ed. Aileen Christianson and Alison Lumsden (Edinburgh: Edinburgh University Press, 2000), p. 157.
36. Petrie, pp. 67, 66.
37. From 'Not Changing the World' (1995), a short autobiographical piece, qtd. in Kaye Mitchell, *A.L. Kennedy* (Basingstoke: Palgrave, 2008), p. 13.
38. Mitchell, p. 13.
39. All quotations are taken from A. L. Kennedy, *Night Geometry and the Garscadden Trains* (1990; London: Vintage, 2004) and *Indelible Acts* (London: Jonathan Cape, 2002).
40. Mitchell, pp. 56, 57.
41. Email interview with A. L. Kennedy by Kaye Mitchell (2006), in Mitchell, p. 127.
42. Lumsden, p. 162.
43. From a review in *List*, qtd. on the back cover of Ali Smith, *The Whole Story and Other Stories* (Harmondsworth: Penguin, 2003), from which all quotations are taken.
44. All quotations are taken from Ali Smith, *The First Person and Other Stories* (Harmondsworth: Penguin, 2008).
45. Katy Guest, review of *The First Person and Other Stories*, *Independent* (3 October 2008).

Further Reading

1 Introduction: What Is a Short Story?

Clare Hanson. *Short Stories and Short Fictions, 1880–1980* (London: Macmillan, 1985).

Paul March Russell. *The Short Story: An Introduction* (Edinburgh: Edinburgh University Press, 2009).

Thomas Gullason. 'The Short Story: An Underrated Art'. *Studies in Short Fiction* 2/1 (Fall, 1964), pp. 13–31.

Valerie Shaw. *The Short Story: A Critical Introduction* (London & New York: Longman, 1983).

2 Introducing the Victorian and Edwardian Short Story

Dean Baldwin. 'The Tardy Evolution of the British Short Story'. *Studies in Short Fiction* 30: 1 (1993), 1–10.

Harold Orel. *The Victorian Short Story: Development and Triumph of a Literary Genre* (Cambridge: Cambridge University Press, 1986).

Peter D. MacDonald. *British Culture and Publishing Practice 1880–1914* (Cambridge: Cambridge University Press, 1997).

Tim Killick. *British Short Fiction in the Early Nineteenth Century* (Aldershot: Ashgate, 2008).

Wendell Harris. 'Vision and Form: The English Novel and the Emergence of the Short Story'. *Victorian Newsletter* 47 (1975), 11–16.

Winnie Chan. *The Economy of the Short Story in British Periodicals of the 1890s* (London: Routledge, 2007).

3 Victorian Sensations: Supernatural and Weird Tales

Alison Milbank. *Daughters of the House: Modes of the Gothic in Victorian Fiction* (London: Macmillan, 1992).

Fred Botting. *Gothic* (London: Routledge, 1996).

Harold Orel. *The Victorian Short Story: Development and Triumph of a Literary Genre* (Cambridge: Cambridge University Press, 1986).

Kristin Brady. *The Short Stories of Thomas Hardy: Past and Present* (London: Macmillan, 1982).

Nicola Bown *et al.* eds. *The Victorian Supernatural* (Cambridge: Cambridge University Press, 2004).

Vanessa Dickerson. *Victorian Ghosts in the Noontide: Women Writers and the Supernatural* (Columbia: University of Missouri Press, 1996).

4   New Woman Short Stories

Clare Hanson. *Short Stories and Short Fictions, 1880–1980* (London: Macmillan, 1985).

Elaine Showalter, ed. *Daughters of Decadence: Women Writers of the Fin de Siecle* (London: Virago, 1992).

Jane Eldridge Miller. *Rebel Women: Feminism, Modernism and the Edwardian Novel* (London: Virago, 1994).

Marion Shaw and Lyssa Randolph. *New Woman Writers of the late Nineteenth Century* (Plymouth: Northcote House, 2004).

Sally Ledger. *The New Woman: Fiction and Feminism at the fin de siecle* (Manchester: Manchester University Press, 1997).

5   Imperial Adventures and Colonial Tales

Elleke Boehmer, ed. *Empire Writing: An Anthology of Colonial Literature 1870–1918* Oxford: Oxford University Press, 1998).

J. H. Stape, ed. *The Cambridge Companion to Joseph Conrad* (Cambridge: Cambridge University Press, 1996).

Owen Knowles and Gene M. Moore, eds. *The Oxford Reader's Companion to Conrad* (Oxford: Oxford University Press, 2000).

Patrick Brantlinger. *Rule of Darkness: British Literature and Imperialism 1830–1914* (New York: Cornell University Press, 1988).

Phillip Mallett. *Rudyard Kipling: A Literary Life* (London: PalgraveMacmillan, 2003).

6   Introducing the Twentieth-Century Short Story

George Moore. *The Collected Short Stories of George Moore.* 5 Vols. Ed. Ann Heilmann and Mark Llewellyn (London: Pickering and Chatto, 2011). See especially the introductions to the volumes for a very useful overview of Moore's work.

Margaret Drabble. *Arnold Bennett: A Biography* (London: Omega, 1974).

Paul Thompson. *The Edwardians: The Remaking of British Society* (1974; London: Routledge, 2005). A really useful historical and contextual overview of the period.

Ruth Robbins. *Pater to Forster, 1873–1924* (Basingstoke: Palgrave, 2003).

7   The Short Story and the Great War

Angela K. Smith, ed. *Women's Writing of the First World War: An Anthology* (Manchester: Manchester University Press, 2000).

Jane Potter. *Boys in Khaki, Girls in Print: Women's Literary Responses to the Great War, 1914–1918* (Oxford: Oxford University Press, 2005).

Paul Fussell. *The Great War and Modern Memory* (Oxford: Oxford University Press, 1977).

Samuel Hynes. *A War Imagined: The First World War and English Culture* (London: Bodley Head, 1990).
Trudi Tate, ed. *Women and Men of the Great War* (Manchester: Manchester University Press, 1995).

8   Experiment and Continuity: The Modernist Short Story

Andrew Thacker, ed. *James Joyce, Dubliners: Contemporary Critical Essays* (Basingstoke: Palgrave Macmillan, 2006).
Anne Fernihough, ed. *The Cambridge Companion to D.H.Lawrence* (Cambridge: Cambridge University Press, 2001).
Christine Reynier. *Virginia Woolf's Ethics of the Short Story* (Basingstoke: Palgrave Macmillan 2009).
Claire Tomalin. *Katherine Mansfield: A Secret Life* (Harmondsworth: Penguin, 2003).
Dominic Head. *The Modernist Short Story: A Study in Theory and Practice* (Cambridge: Cambridge University Press, 1992; 2009).

9   The Short Story and Genre Fiction: The Same Old Story?

Charles J. Rzepka and Lee Horsley, eds. *A Companion to Crime Fiction* (London: Basil Blackwell, 2010).
David Duff, ed. *Modern Genre Theory* (London: Longman, 2000).
Helen Taylor. *The Daphne du Maurier Companion* (London: Virago, 2007).
John Frow. *Genre*, The New Critical Idiom Series (London: Routledge, 2005).

10   Introducing the Post-War Short Story

Dennis Vannatta, ed. *The English Short Story, 1945–80* (Boston: Twayne, 1985).
Frank O'Connor. *The Lonely Voice: A Study of the Short Story* (London: Macmillan, 1963).
Ian Haywood. *Working-class Fiction: From Chartism to 'Trainspotting'* (Plymouth: Northcote House/British Council, 1998).
Malcolm Bradbury, ed. *Modern British Short Stories* (London: Penguin, 1988).

11   Women's Stories, 1940s to the Present

John Bayley. *The Short Story: From Henry James to Elizabeth Bowen* (Brighton: Harvester Press, 1988).
Clare Hanson, ed. *Re-reading the Short Story* (London: Macmillan, 1989).
Coral Ann Howells. *Jean Rhys* (Brighton: Harvester Wheatsheaf, 1991).
Gill Plain. *Women's Fiction of the Second World War: Gender, Power and Resistance* (Edinburgh: Edinburgh University Press, 1996).
Susan Sellers. *Myth and Fairytale in Contemporary Women's Fiction* (Basingstoke: Palgrave, 2001).

12   The British Short Story Today

Aileen Christianson and Alison Lumsden, eds. *Contemporary Scottish Women Writers* (Basingstoke: Palgrave, 2000).

Berthold Schoene, ed. *The Edinburgh Companion to Contemporary Scottish Literature* (Edinburgh: Edinburgh University Press, 2007).

Dominic Head. *The Cambridge Introduction to Modern British Fiction, 1950–2000* (Cambridge: Cambridge University Press, 2002).

Kaye Mitchell. *A.L. Kennedy* (Basingstoke: Palgrave, 2008).

Susie Thomas, ed. *Hanif Kureishi: A Reader's Guide to Essential Criticism* (Basingstoke: Palgrave, 2005).

Tony Brown. 'The Ex-centric Voice: The English-Language Short Story in Wales'. *North American Journal of Welsh Studies* 1.1 (Winter 2001): 25–41.

Bibliography

Short story collections and anthologies

Aldington, Richard. *Death of a Hero* (London: Hogarth Press, 1984).

Aldington, Richard. *Roads to Glory* (London: Imperial War Museum, 1992).

Baldwin, Dean, ed. *The Riverside Anthology of Short Fiction: Convention and Innovation* (Boston and New York: Houghton Mifflin, 1998).

Bennett, Arnold. *The Grim Smile of the Five Towns* (1907; Harmondsworth: Penguin, 1946).

Bennett, Arnold. *The Matador of the Five Towns* (1912; Stroud: Nonsuch Press, 2007).

Boston, Anne, ed. *Wave Me Goodbye: Stories of the Second World War* (London: Penguin, 1988).

Bowen, Elizabeth. *Collected Stories*. Ed. Angus Wilson (London: Vintage, 1999).

Byatt, A. S. *The Djinn in the Nightingale's Eye: Five Fairy Stories* (London: Vintage, 1995).

Byatt, A. S., ed. *The Oxford Book of English Short Stories* (Oxford: Oxford University Press, 1998).

Byatt, A. S. *Elementals: Stories of Fire and Ice* (London: Vintage, 1999).

Campbell, R. W. *The Kangaroo Marines* (London: Casell, 1915).

Carter, Angela, ed. *The Virago Book of Fairy Tales* (London: Virago, 1990).

Carter, Angela, ed. *Wayward Girls and Wicked Women* (London: Virago, 1991).

Carter, Angela. *The Bloody Chamber*. Ed. Helen Simpson (London: Vintage, 1998).

Christie, Agatha. *The Listerdale Mystery* (1934; London: HarperCollins, 1997).

Christie, Agatha. *Miss Marple: Complete Short Stories* (London: HarperCollins, 1997).

Collins, Wilkie. *The Dream-Woman and Other Stories*. Ed. Peter Miles (London: Orion, 1998).

Collins, Wilkie. *Miss or Mrs? The Haunted Hotel and The Guilty River*. Ed. Norman Page and Toru Sasaki (Oxford: Oxford University Press, 1999).

Conrad, Joseph. *The Complete Short Fiction* (London: Pickering & Chatto, 1992).

Conrad, Joseph. *The Nigger of Narcissus*. Ed. Jacques Berthoud (Oxford: Oxford University Press, 1984).

Conrad, Joseph. *Tales of Unrest*. Ed. Antony Fothergill (London: Everyman, 2000).

Conrad, Joseph. *Typhoon and Other Tales*. Ed. Cedric Watts (Oxford: Oxford University Press, 2002).

Cox, Michael and R. A. Gilbert, eds. *The Oxford Book of English Ghost Stories* (Oxford: Oxford University Press, 1986).

Dalby, Richard, ed. *The Virago Book of Victorian Ghost Stories*, with an introduction by Jennifer Uglow (London: Virago, 1988).

Denisoff, Dennis, ed. *The Broadview Anthology of Victorian Short Stories* (Peterborough: Broadview Press, 2004).

Dickens, Charles. *The Haunted House*. Ed. Peter Ackroyd (1859; London: Hesperus Press, 2002).

Dickens, Charles. *Mugby Junction*. Ed. Robert Macfarlane (1866; London: Hesperus Press, 2005).

Donoghue, Emma. *Kissing the Witch* (Harmondsworth: Penguin, 1997).

Donoghue, Emma, ed. *The Mammoth Book of Lesbian Short Stories* (London: Robinson, 1999).

Doyle, Arthur Conan. *His Last Bow*. Ed. Owen Dudley Edwards (Oxford: Oxford University Press, 1993).

Dunn, Douglas, ed. *The Oxford Book of Scottish Short Stories* (Oxford: Oxford University Press, 1995).

Egerton, George. *Keynotes & Discords*. Ed. Martha Vicinus (1893/4: London: Virago, 1983).

le Fanu, Sheridan. *In a Glass Darkly*. Ed. W. J. McCormack (1872; Gloucester: Alan Sutton, 1990).

Ford, Ford Madox. *War Prose*. Ed. Max Saunders (Manchester: Carcanet Press, 1999).

Galsworthy, John. *Tatterdemalion* (London: William Heinemann, 1920).

Galsworthy, John. *Caravan* (London: William Heinemann, 1925).

Gaskell, Elizabeth. *Gothic Tales*. Ed. Laura Kranzler (Harmondsworth: Penguin, 2000).

Hall, Radclyffe. *Miss Ogilvy Finds Herself* (London: William Heinemann, 1934).

Hardy, Thomas. *Outside the Gates of the World: Selected Short Stories*. Ed. Jan Jedrzejewski with an introduction by John Bayley (London: J.M. Dent, 1996).

Hayes, Michael, ed. *The Supernatural Short Stories of Charles Dickens* (London: John Calder, 1978).

Hudson, Derek, ed. *Modern English Short Stories, 1930–1955* (World's Classics, 1956; Oxford: Oxford University Press, 1985).

Hyne, Charles. *Atoms of Empire* (London: Macmillan, 1904).

James, Henry. *The Real Thing* (London: Macmillan, 1893).

James, Henry. *The Turn of the Screw and Other Stories*. Ed. T. J. Lustig (Oxford: Oxford University Press, 1992).

Joyce, James. *Stephen Hero* (London: Jonathan Cape, 1969).

Joyce, James. *Dubliners*. Ed. Terence Brown (Harmondsworth: Penguin, 1992).

Joyce, James. *Dubliners*. Ed. Margot Norris (Norton Critical Edition; New York: W.W. Norton, 2006).

Jump, Harriet Devine, ed. *Nineteenth-Century Short Stories by Women: A Routledge Anthology* (London and New York: Routledge, 1998).

Kay, Jackie. *Why Don't You Stop Talking?* (London: Picador, 2002).

Kay, Jackie. *Wish I Was Here* (London: Picador, 2006).

Kennedy, A. L. *Indelible Acts* (London: Jonathan Cape, 2002).

Kennedy, A. L. *Night Geometry and the Garscadden Trains* (1990; London: Vintage, 2004).

Kipling, Rudyard. *The Day's Work* (Leipzig: Tauchnitz, 1898).

Kipling, Rudyard. *Debits and Credits*. Ed. Sandra Kemp (London: Penguin, 1987).

Kipling, Rudyard. *A Diversity of Creatures*. Ed. Paul Driver (London: Penguin, 1987).

Kipling, Rudyard. *Life's Handicap*. Ed. A. O. J. Cockshutt (Oxford: Oxford University Press, 1987).

Kipling, Rudyard. *Plain Tales from the Hills.* Ed. Andrew Rutherford (Oxford: Oxford University Press, 1987).

Kipling, Rudyard. *Wee Willie Winkie, The Phantom Rickshaw and Other Stories.* (London: Macmillan, 1913) Vol. 3 of the Bombay Edition of the Works of Rudyard Kipling.

Knight, Lynn, ed. *The Secret Woman: The Virago Book of Classic Short Stories* (London: Virago, 1993).

Kureishi, Hanif. *Love in a Blue Time* (London: Faber & Faber, 1997).

Kureishi, Hanif. *Midnight All Day* (London: Faber & Faber, 1999).

Lawrence, D. H. *Selected Short Stories.* Ed. Brian Finney (Harmondsworth: Penguin, 1982).

Leavitt, David and Mark Mitchell, eds. *The Penguin Book of Gay Short Stories* (London: Penguin, 1991).

Lee, Hermione, ed. *The Secret Self: A Century of Short Stories by Women* (London: Phoenix Giants, 1995).

Lee, Vernon. *Hauntings and Other Fantastic Tales.* Ed. Catherine Maxwell and Patricia Pulham (Peterborough: Broadview Press, 2006).

Lessing, Doris. *To Room Nineteen: Collected Stories, Volume One* (London: Jonathan Cape, 1978).

Machen, Arthur. *The Bowmen and Other Legends of the War* (London: Simpkin Marshal, 1915).

Mansfield, Katherine. *Selected Stories.* Ed. Angela Smith (Oxford: Oxford World's Classics, 1999).

Mansfield, Katherine. *The Collected Stories.* Ed. and intro. Ali Smith (Harmondsworth: Penguin, 2007).

Mansfield, Katherine. *The Colleted Letters of Katherine Mansfield.* 5 Vols. Vincent O'Sullivan and Margaret Scott (eds.) (Oxford: Oxford University Press, 2008).

du Maurier, Daphne. *The Birds and Other Stories.* Ed. and intro. David Thomson (London: Virago, 2004).

du Maurier, Daphne. *The Rendezvous and Other Stories.* Ed. and intro. Minette Walters (London: Virago, 2005).

Moore, George. *The Untilled Field* (1903; No Place: Bibliobazaar, 2006).

Page, Ra, ed. *The City Life Book of Manchester Short Stories* (Harmondsworth: Penguin, 1999).

Poe, Edgar Allan. *The Collected Works of Edgar Allan Poe.* 3 Vols. Ed. Thomas Ollive Mabbott (Cambridge, Mass.: Harvard University Press, 1978).

Prescott, Lynda, ed. *A World of Difference: An Anthology of Short Stories from Five Continents* (Basingstoke: Palgrave Macmillan, 2008).

Reid, J. M., ed. *Classic Scottish Short Stories* (Oxford: Oxford University Press, 1989).

Richardson, Angelique, ed. *Women Who Did: Stories by Men and Women, 1890–1914* (Harmondsworth: Penguin, 2002).

Rhys, Jean. *Tigers Are Better-Looking, with a Selection from The Left Bank* (London: André Deutsch, 1968).

Saki [Hector Hugh Munro]. *The Penguin Complete Saki.* Intro. Noël Coward (Harmondsworth: Penguin, 1976).

Sapper. *Men, Women and Guns* (London: Hodder, 1916).

Sapper. *Sapper's War Stories* (London: Hodder, 1930).

Sapper. *The Best Short Stories* (London: Dent, 1984).

Sayers, Dorothy L. *Lord Peter Views the Body* (London: Hodder & Stoughton, 1930).
Sayers, Dorothy L. *Hangman's Holiday* (London: Victor Gollancz, 1933).
Sayers, Dorothy L. *In the Teeth of the Evidence* (London: Victor Gollancz, 1939).
Sharp, Evelyn. *Rebel Women* (London: London: A.C. Fyfield, 1910).
Shepherd, Leslie, ed. *The Book of Dracula* (New York: Wings Books, 1991).
Showalter, Elaine, ed. *Daughters of Decadence: Women Writers of the Fin de Siècle* (London: Virago, 1993).
Sillitoe, Alan. *The Loneliness of the Long Distance Runner* (1959; London: Flamingo, 1993).
Smith, Ali. *The Whole Story and Other Stories* (Harmondsworth: Penguin, 2003).
Smith, Ali. *The First Person and Other Stories* (Harmondsworth: Penguin, 2008).
Smith, Joan, ed. *Femmes de Siècle: Stories from the '90s: Women Writing at the End of Two Centuries* (London: Chatto & Windus, 1992).
Stevenson, Robert Louis. *The Works of Robert Louis Stevenson* (New York: Charles Scribner's Sons, 1922).
Tate, Trudi, ed. *Men, Women and the Great War* (Manchester: Manchester University Press, 1995).
Taylor, Elizabeth. *Hester Lilly and Other Stories*. Ed. A. L. Barker (1954; London: Virago, 1990).
Taylor, Elizabeth. *A Dedicated Man and Other Stories*. Ed. Joanna Kingham (1965; London: Virago, 1993).
Urquhart, Fred and Giles Gordon, eds. *Modern Scottish Short Stories* (London: Faber, 1978).
Weldon, Fay. *Polaris and Other Stories* (London: Hodder & Stoughton, 1985).
Wells, H. G. *The Country of the Blind and Other Stories* (London: Nelson, 1911).
Williams, A. Susan, ed. *The Penguin Book of Classic Fantasy by Women* (Harmondsworth: Penguin, 1992).
Woolf, Virginia. *The Mark on the Wall and Other Short Fiction*. Ed. David Bradshaw (Oxford: Oxford University Press, 2001).

Critical books and articles published after 1900

Note: This list does not include short review articles in magazines, journals or newspapers. For full references to these, please see the endnotes to individual chapters.

Adams, Jad. *Rudyard Kipling* (London: Haus, 2005).
Aldington, Richard. *Life for Life's Sake* (London: Viking, 1941).
Allsop, Kenneth. *The Angry Decade* (London: Peter Owen, 1958).
Ardis, Ann L. *New Women, New Novels: Feminism and Early Modernism* (New Brunswick and London: Rutgers University Press, 1990).
Armitt, Lucie. *Contemporary Women's Fiction and the Fantastic* (Basingstoke: Palgrave, 2000).
Armstrong, Tim. *Modernism: A Cultural History* (Cambridge: Polity, 2005).
Auerbach, Nina. *Daphne du Maurier: Haunted Heiress* (Philadelphia: University of Pennsylvania Press, 2000).
Baldwin, Dean. 'The Tardy Evolution of the British Short Story'. *Studies in Short Fiction* 30.1 (1993), 23–33.

Bars, John. 'The Initiation of Alan Sillitoe's Long Distance Runner'. *Modern Fiction Studies* 22.4 (1976), 584–90.

Basham, Diana. *The Trial of Woman: Feminism and the Occult Sciences in Victorian Literature and Society* (Basingstoke: Macmillan, 1998).

Bauer, Helen. *Rudyard Kipling: A Study of the Short Fiction* (New York: Twayne, 1994).

Bayley, John. *The Short Story: Henry James to Elizabeth Bowen* (Brighton: Harvester, 1988).

Beetham, Margaret. *A Magazine of Her Own? Domesticity and Desire in the Woman's Magazine, 1800–1914* (London and New York: Routledge, 1996).

Bell, Ian. *Peripheral Visions: Visions of Nationhood in Contemporary British Fiction* (Cardiff: University of Wales Press, 1995).

Bell, Julia and Jackie Gay, eds. *England Calling* (London: Phoenix, 2001).

Blincoe, Nicholas and Matt Thorne, eds. *All Hail the New Puritans* (London: Fourth Estate, 2000).

Booth, Bradford A., ed. *The Letters of Anthony Trollope* (Oxford: Oxford University Press, 1951).

Boston, Anne. 'Introduction'. *Wave Me Goodbye: Stories of the Second World War* (London: Penguin, 1988).

Botting, Fred. *Gothic* (London: Routledge, 1996).

Bowen, Elizabeth. 'The Short Story in England'. *Britain To-Day* 109 (May 1949), 12–16.

Bowlby, Rachel, ed. *Virginia Woolf: A Woman's Essays: Selected Essays*. Vol. 1 (Harmondsworth: Penguin, 1992).

Bown, Nicola, Carolyn Burdett and Pamela Thurschwell, eds. *The Victorian Supernatural* (Cambridge: Cambridge University Press, 2004).

Boyd, Kelly. *Manliness and the Boys' Story Paper in Britain: A Cultural History, 1855–1940* (New York: Palgrave Macmillan, 2003).

Brady, Kristin. *The Short Stories of Thomas Hardy: Tales of Past and Present* (London: Macmillan, 1982).

Brake, Laurel. *Print in Transition, 1850–1910: Studies in Media and Book History* (Basingstoke: Palgrave, 2001).

Brantlinger, Patrick. *Rule of Darkness: British Literature and Imperialism, 1830–1914* (New York: Cornell University Press, 1993).

Brantlinger, Patrick and William Thesing, eds. *A Companion to the Victorian Novel* (Oxford: Blackwell, 2002).

Briggs, Julia. *Night Visitors: The Rise and Fall of the English Ghost Story* (London: Faber, 1977).

Bristow, Joseph. *Empire Boys: Adventures in a Man's World* (London: HarperCollins, 1991).

Bristow, Joseph and Trev Lynn Broughton, eds. *The Infernal Desires of Angela Carter: Fiction, Femininity, Feminism* (Harlow: Longman, 1997).

Brittain, Vera. *Testament of Youth* (London: Fontana, 1979).

Brooker, Stephen. 'Gender and Working-Class Identity in Britain during the 1950s'. *Journal of Social History* 34.3 (2001), 775–95.

Brown, Julie, ed. *American Women Short Story Writers* (New York: Garland, 1995).

Brown, Tony. 'The Ex-centric Voice: The English Language Short Story in Wales'. *North American Journal of Welsh Studies* 1.1 (2001), 25–41.

Buchanan, Bradley. *Hanif Kureishi* (Basingstoke: Palgrave, 2007).

Buitenhuis, Peter. *The Great War of Words: British, American, Canadian Propaganda and Fiction 1914–1933* (Vancouver: University of British Columbia Press, 1987).

Burdett, Carolyn. *Olive Schreiner and the Progress of Feminism* (Basingstoke: Palgrave, 2001).

Butler, Judith. *Gender Trouble: Feminism and the Subversion of Identity* (London: Routledge, 1990).

Caballero, Carlo. ' "A Wicked Voice": On Vernon Lee, Wagner, and the Effects of Music'. *Victorian Studies* 35.4 (Summer 1992), 385–406.

Carabine, Keith, Owen Knowles and Wieslaw Krajia, eds. *Conrad's Literary Career*. 2 Vols. (New York: Columbia University Press, 1992).

Carabine, Keith, Owen Knowles and Wieslaw Krajia, eds. *Contexts for Conrad* (New York: Columbia University Press, 1993).

Carey, John. *The Intellectuals and the Masses* (London: Faber, 1992).

Carr, Helen. *Jean Rhys* (Plymouth: Northcote House, 1996).

Castle, Terry. *Noel Coward and Radclyffe Hall* (New York: Columbia University Press, 1996).

Cavaliero, Glen. *The Supernatural and English Fiction: From The Castle of Otranto to Hawksmoor* (Oxford: Oxford University Press, 1995).

Chan, Winnie. *The Economy of the Short Story in British Periodicals of the 1890s* (London: Routledge, 2007).

Childs, Peter. *Modernism* (London: Routledge, 2000).

Christianson, Aileen and Alison Lumsden, eds. *Contemporary Scottish Women Writers* (Edinburgh: Edinburgh University Press, 2000).

Christie, Agatha. *Autobiography* (London: HarperCollins, 1993).

Cline, Sally. *Radclyffe Hall: The Woman Who Was John* (London: John Murray, 1997).

Conrad, Joseph. *A Personal Record* (London: Dent, 1919).

Corcoran, Neil. *After Yeats and Joyce: Reading Modern Irish Literature* (Oxford: Oxford University Press, 2003).

Cornell, Louis. *Kipling in India* (New York: St. Martin's, 1966).

Cox, R., ed. *Thomas Hardy: The Critical Heritage* (London: Routledge & Kegan Paul, 1979).

Dallat, C. L. 'New Voices Abroad'. *Guardian* (28 May 2005), 'Review', 27–8.

Daly, Saralyn. *Katherine Mansfield* (New York: Twayne, 1994).

Davies, Laurence *et al.* eds. *The Collected Letters of Joseph Conrad*. 9 Vols. (Cambridge: Cambridge University Press, 1983–2008).

DiCenzo, Maria. 'Gutter Politics: Women Newsies and the Suffrage Press'. *Women's History Review* 12.1 (2003), 15–33.

Dickerson, Vanessa. *Victorian Ghosts in the Noontide: Women Writers and the Supernatural* (Columbia: University of Missouri Press, 1996).

Dillingham, William. *Rudyard Kipling: Hell and Heroism* (London: Palgrave, 2005).

Dixon, Rob. *Writing the Colonial Adventure* (Cambridge: Cambridge University Press, 1995).

Donovan, Stephen. *Joseph Conrad and Popular Culture* (Basingstoke: Palgrave, 2005)

Doyle, Charles. *Richard Aldington* (London: Macmillan, 1987).

Drew, John M. L. *Dickens the Journalist* (Basingstoke: Palgrave, 2003).

Dryden, Lynda. *Joseph Conrad and the Imperial Romance* (London: Palgrave, 2000).

Duncker, Patricia. 'Re-Imagining the Fairy Tales: Angela Carter's Bloody Chambers'. *Literature & History* 10.1 (1984), 3–14.

Dutton, J. 'Why Magazines Die'. *Guardian* (25 June 2005), 'Review', 8.

Easton, Alison. *Angela Carter* (Basingstoke: Macmillan, 2000).

Ellmann, Maud. *Elizabeth Bowen: The Shadow across the Page* (Edinburgh: Edinburgh University Press, 2003).

Fielding, Penny. *Writing and Orality: Nationality, Culture and Nineteenth-Century Scottish Fiction* (Oxford: Clarendon Press, 1996).

Fisher, Benjamin F. 'The American Reception of Ella D'Arcy'. *Victorian Periodicals Review* 28.3 (1995), 232–48.

Ford, Ford Madox. *A Personal Remembrance* (London: Duckworth 1924).

Ford, Ford Madox. *It Was the Nightingale* (London: William Heinemann, 1933).

Forster, E. M. *Aspects of the Novel* (Harmondsworth: Penguin, 1927).

Forster, Margaret. *Daphne du Maurier* (London: Arrow, 2007).

Franks, Claudia Stillman. *Beyond The Well of Loneliness: The Fiction of Radclyffe Hall* (Aldershot: Ashgate, 1982).

Friedan, Betty. *The Feminine Mystique* (Harmondsworth: Penguin, 1963).

Galsworthy, John. *Sheaf* (London: William Heinemann, 1916).

Gillies, Mary Ann and Aurelea Mahood. *Modernist Literature: An Introduction* (Edinburgh: Edinburgh University Press, 2007).

Gilvert, Stuart, ed. *Letters of James Joyce*. Vol. 1 (New York: Viking, 1957).

Glover, David. *Vampires, Mummies and Liberals: Bram Stoker and the Politics of Popular Fiction* (London: Duke University Press, 1996).

Goldie, David. *A Critical Difference: T.S. Eliot and John Middleton Murray in English Literary Criticism 1919–28* (Oxford: Clarendon Press, 1998).

Graver, Laurence. *Conrad's Short Fiction* (Berkeley: University of California Press, 1969).

Green, R. L., ed. *Kipling: The Critical Heritage* (London: Routledge, 1971).

Gutmann, Amy, ed. *Multiculturalism: Examining the Politics of Recognition* (Princeton: Princeton University Press, 1994).

Haffenden, John, ed. *Novelists in Interview* (London: Methuen, 1985).

Hagemann, Susanne, ed. *Studies in Scottish Fiction, 1945 to the Present* (Frankfurt: M. Lang, 1996).

Hamilton, Susan, ed. *Criminals, Idiots, Women and Minors: Nineteenth-Century Writing by Women on Women* (Peterborough: Broadview Press, 1995).

Hanson, Clare. *Short Stories and Short Fictions, 1880–1980* (London: Macmillan, 1985).

Hanson, Clare, ed. *Re-Reading the Short Story* (London: Macmillan, 1989).

Hanson, Clare. *Understanding Alan Sillitoe* (Columbia: University of South Carolina Press, 1999).

Harris, Wendell. 'Vision and Form: The English Novel and the Emergence of the Short Story'. *Victorian Newsletter* 47 (1975), 11–16.

Harris, Wendell. *British Short Fiction of the Nineteenth Century: A Literary and Bibliographic Guide* (Detroit: Wayne State University Press, 1979).

Head, Dominic. *The Modernist Short Story* (Cambridge: Cambridge University Press, 1992).

Head, Dominic. *The Cambridge Introduction to Modern British Fiction, 1950–2000* (Cambridge: Cambridge University Press, 2002).

Heilmann, Ann. *New Woman Fiction: Women Writing First-Wave Feminism* (Basingstoke: Macmillan, 2000).

Hoggart, Richard. *The Uses of Literacy: Aspects of Working-Class Life with Special Reference to Publications and Entertainments* (1957; Harmondsworth: Penguin, 1992).

Holden, Philip and Richard J. Ruppel, eds. *Imperial Desire: Dissident Sexualities and Colonial Literature* (London: University of Minnesota Press, 2003).

Horner, Avril and Sue Zlosnik. *Daphne du Maurier: Writing, Identity and the Gothic Imagination* (Basingstoke: Macmillan, 1998).

Howells, Coral Ann. *Jean Rhys* (Brighton: Harvester Wheatsheaf, 1991).

Hughes, Linda and Michael Lund. *Victorian Publishing and Mrs Gaskell's Work* (London: University Press of Virginia, 1999).

Hunter, Adrian. *The Cambridge Introduction to the Short Story in English* (Cambridge: Cambridge University Press, 2007).

Joannou, Mary. *Contemporary Women's Writing: From The Golden Notebook to The Color Purple* (Manchester: Manchester University Press, 2000).

John, Angela V. ' "Behind the Locked Door": Evelyn Sharp, Suffragette and Rebel Journalist', *Women's History Review* 12.1 (2003), 5–13.

Johnson, Paul. *Land Fit for Heroes: The Planning of British Reconstruction, 1916–1919* (Chicago: Chicago University Press, 1968).

Kelly, Lionel, ed. *Richard Aldington* (Reading: University of Reading, 1987).

Kelman, James. *Some Recent Attacks: Essays Cultural and Political* (Stirling: A.K. Press, 1992).

Kennelly, Brendan. 'George Moore's Lonely Voices: A Study of His Short Stories'. *George Moore's Mind and Art*. Ed. Graham Owens (Edinburgh: Oliver & Boyd, 1968), 146–59.

Kermode, Frank. *The Sense of an Ending: Studies in the Theory of Fiction* (Oxford: Oxford University Press, 1968).

Kersley, Gillian. *Darling Madame: Sarah Grand & Devoted Friend* (London: Virago, 1983).

Kestner, J. *Masculinities in Victorian Painting* (Aldershot: Ashgate, 1995).

Killick, Tim. *British Short Fiction in the Early Nineteenth Century* (Aldershot: Ashgate, 2008).

Kincaid, James. *The Novels of Anthony Trollope* (Oxford: Clarendon Press, 1977).

King, Francis. 'The Short Story'. *London Magazine* 6.6 (September 1966), 11–12.

Kipling, Rudyard. *Something of Myself: For Friends Known and Unknown* (London: Macmillan, 1981).

Knight, Stephen. *Form and Ideology in Crime Fiction* (London: Macmillan, 1980).

Lawrence, D. H. *A Selection from Phoenix*. Ed. A. A. H. Inglis (Harmondsworth: Penguin, 1979).

Lawrence, D. H. *Reflections on the Death of a Porcupine and Other Essays*. Ed. Michael Herbert (Cambridge: Cambridge University Press, 1988).

Leavis, F. R. *The Great Tradition: George Eliot, Henry James, Joseph Conrad* (Harmondsworth: Penguin, 1962).

Leavis, Q. D. *Fiction and the Reading Public* (1932; London: Bellow, 1978).

Ledger, Sally. *The New Woman: Fiction and Feminism at the Fin de Siècle* (Manchester: Manchester University Press, 1997).

Ledger, Sally and Roger Luckhurst, eds. *The Fin de Siècle: A Reader in Cultural History, c.1880–1900* (Oxford: Oxford University Press, 2000).

Ledger, Sally and Scott McCracken, eds. *Cultural Politics at the Fin de Siècle* (Cambridge: Cambridge University Press, 1995).

Lemon, Lee T. and M. J. Reis, eds. *Russian Formalist Criticism: Four Essays* (Lincoln: University of Nebraska Press, 1965).

Letley, Emma. *From Galt to Douglas Brown: Nineteenth-Century Fiction and Scots Language* (Edinburgh: Scottish Academic Press, 1988).

Levine, George. *Darwin and the Novelists: Patterns of Science in Victorian Fiction* (London: University of Chicago Press, 1988).

Levy, Andrew. *The Culture and Commerce of the American Short Story* (Cambridge: Cambridge University Press, 1993).

Light, Alison. *Forever England: Femininity, Literature and Conservatism between the Wars* (London: Routledge, 1991).

Luckhurst, Roger. *Science Fiction* (Cambridge: Polity, 2005).

Majumdar, Robin and Allen McLaurin, eds. *Virginia Woolf: The Critical Heritage* (London and Boston: Routledge & Kegan Paul, 1975).

Marcus, Laura. *Virginia Woolf* (Plymouth: Northcote House, 1997).

Matthews, Brander. *The Philosophy of the Short Story* (New York: Longmans, Green, 1901).

Matthiessen, F. O. and Kenneth Murdock, eds. *The Notebooks of Henry James* (New York: Oxford University Press, 1947).

Maunder, Andrew, ed. *A Companion to the British Short Story* (New York: Facts on File, 2007).

May, Charles E., ed. *The New Short Story Theories* (Athens: Ohio University Press, 1994).

May, Charles E. *The Short Story: The Reality of Artifice* (New York and London: Routledge, 2002).

McClure, John. *Kipling and Conrad: The Colonial Fiction* (London: Harvard University Press, 1981).

Milbank, Alison. *Daughters of the House: Modes of the Gothic in Victorian Fiction* (Basingstoke: Macmillan, 1992).

Miller, Jane Eldridge. *Rebel Women: Feminism, Modernism and the Edwardian Novel* (London: Virago, 1994).

Mitchell, David. *Women on the Warpath* (London: Jonathan Cape, 1966).

Mitchell, Kaye. *A.L. Kennedy* (Basingstoke: Palgrave, 2008).

Moore, Gene M., ed. *Joseph Conrad's Heart of Darkness: A Casebook* (Oxford: Oxford University Press, 2004).

Morris, Pam. *Literature and Feminism* (Oxford: Blackwell, 1993).

Najder, Zdzisaw, ed. *Conrad under Familial Eyes*. Trans. Halina Carroll Najder (Cambridge: Cambridge University Press, 1983).

Naufftus, William F., ed. *British Short Fiction Writers, 1880–1914: The Romantic Tradition* (Dictionary of Literary Biography, Vol. 156; New York: Gale, 1996).

Neubauer, Jurgen. *Literature as Intervention: Struggles over Identity in Contemporary Scottish Fiction* (Marburg: Tectum, 1999).

O'Connor, Frank. *The Lonely Voice: A Study of the Short Story* (New York: World, 1963).

Ong, Walter J. *Orality and Literacy: The Technologizing of the West* (London: Routledge, 1981).

Orel, Harold. *The Victorian Short Story: Development and Triumph of a Literary Genre* (Cambridge: Cambridge University Press, 1986).

Ostrom, John Ward, ed. *The Letters of Edgar Allan Poe*. 2 Vols. (New York: Gordian Press, 1966).

Ostry, Elaine. '"Social Wonders": Fancy, Science, and Technology in Dickens's Periodicals'. *Victorian Periodicals Review* 34.1 (2001), 54–78.

Owen, Alex. *The Darkened Room: Women, Power and Spiritualism in Late Victorian England* (Philadelphia: University of Pennsylvania Press, 1990).

Page, Norman. *A Conrad Companion* (London: Macmillan, 1986).

Pain, Barry. *The Short Story* (New York: Doran & Co., 1912).

Parfitt, George. *Fiction of the First World War* (London: Faber, 1988).

Parsons, Deborah L. *Streetwalking the Metropolis: Women, the City and Modernity* (Oxford: Oxford University Press, 2000).

Pater, Walter. *The Renaissance: The 1893 Text*. Ed. Donald L. Hill (Berkley and London: University of California Press, 1980).

Penner, Alan. *Alan Sillitoe* (New York: Twayne, 1972).

Petrie, Duncan. *Contemporary Scottish Fictions: Film, Television and the Novel* (Edinburgh: Edinburgh University Press, 2004).

Pinney, Thomas, ed. *The Letters of Rudyard Kipling*. 6 Vols. (London: Macmillan, 1990–2004).

Plain, Gill. *Women's Fiction of the Second World War: Gender, Power and Resistance* (Edinburgh: Edinburgh University Press, 1996).

Porter Abbott, H. *The Cambridge Introduction to Narrative* (Cambridge: Cambridge University Press, 2008).

Pound, Reginald. *Mirror of the Century: The Strand Magazine, 1891–1950* (New York: A.S. Barnes, 1966).

Priestley, J. B. *Margin Released* (London Methuen, 1962).

Pritchett, V. S. 'The Short Story'. *London Magazine* 6.6 (September 1966), 6–8.

Pykett, Lyn. *The Sensation Novel* (Plymouth: Northcote House, 1994).

Pykett, Lyn. *Charles Dickens* (Basingstoke: Palgrave, 2002).

Rae, Patricia. *Modernism and Mourning* (Lewisburg: Bucknell University Press, 2007).

Reid, Ian. *The Short Story* (London: Methuen, 1977).

Richards, Jeffrey, ed. *Imperialism and Juvenile Literature* (Manchester: Manchester University Press, 1989).

Richardson, Angelique and Chris Willis, eds. *The New Woman in Fiction and in Fact: Fin-de-Siècle Feminisms* (Basingstoke: Palgrave, 2001).

Ricketts, Harry. *The Unforgiving Minute: A Life of Rudyard Kipling* (London: Chatto & Windus, 1999).

Russell, Paul March. *The Short Story: An Introduction* (Edinburgh: Edinburgh University Press, 2009).

Rutherford, Andrew, ed. *Kipling's Mind and Art* (Stanford: Stanford University Press, 1964).

Sandbrook, Dominic. *Never Had It So Good: A History of Britain from Suez to the Beatles* (London: Abacus, 2006).

Sassoon, Siegfried. *Siegfried's Journeys 1916–1920* (London: Faber, 1945).

Sceats, Sarah and Gail Cunningham, eds. *Image and Power: Women in Fiction in the Twentieth Century* (London: Longman, 1996).

Schoene, Berthold, ed. *The Edinburgh Companion to Contemporary Scottish Literature* (Edinburgh: Edinburgh University Press, 2007).

Schwartz, D. R. *The Transformation of the English Novel, 1890–1930* (New York: St. Martin's, 1989).

Sellers, Susan. *Myth and Fairy Tale in Contemporary Women's Fiction* (Basingstoke: Palgrave, 2001).

Shaw, Marion, ed. *An Introduction to Women's Writing: From the Middle Ages to the Present Day* (Hemel Hempstead: Prentice Hall, 1998).

Shaw, Marion and Lyssa Randolph. *New Woman Writers of the Late Nineteenth Century* (Plymouth: Northcote House, 2007).

Shaw, Marion and Sabine Vanacker. *Reflecting on Miss Marple* (London: Routledge, 1991).

Shaw, Valerie. *The Short Story: A Critical Introduction* (London and New York: Longman, 1983).

Sherry, Norman. *Joseph Conrad: The Critical Heritage* (London: Routledge, 1973).

Showalter, Elaine. *The Female Malady: Women, Madness and English Culture 1830–1980*, (London: Virago, 1980).

Showalter, Elaine. *Sexual Anarchy* (London: Virago, 1992).

Sinha, M. *Colonial Masculinity: The Manly Englishman and the Effeminate Bengali in the Late Nineteenth Century* (Manchester: Manchester University Press, 1995).

Smith, Angela. *The Second Battlefield: Women, Modernism and the First World War* (Manchester: Manchester University Press, 2000).

Smith, Angela, ed. *Gender and Warfare* (Manchester: Manchester University Press, 2004).

Stape, J., ed. *The Cambridge Companion to Joseph Conrad* (Cambridge: Cambridge University Press, 1996).

Stein, Mark. *Black British Literature: Novels of Transformation* (Columbus: Ohio University Press, 2004).

Stewart, Clare. '"Weird Fascination": The Response to Victorian Women's Ghost Stories'. *Feminist Readings of Victorian Popular Texts*. Ed. Emma Liggins and Daniel Duffy (Aldershot: Ashgate, 2001), 112–23.

Sullivan, Zohreh T. *Narratives of Empire: The Fictions of Rudyard Kipling* (Cambridge: Cambridge University Press, 1993).

Taylor, John Russell. *Anger and After* (London: Methuen, 1988).

Thomas, Deborah. *Dickens and the Short Story* (Philadelphia: University of Pennsylvania Press, 1982).

Thomas, Susie, ed. *Hanif Kureishi: A Reader's Guide to Essential Criticism* (Basingstoke: Palgrave, 2005).

Todd, Richard. *A.S. Byatt* (Plymouth: Northcote House, 1997).

Trodd, Anthea. *Women's Writing in English, 1900–1945* (Harlow: Longman, 1998).

Trollope, Anthony. *An Autobiography*. Ed. David Skilton (London: Penguin, 1996).

Trotter, David. *The English Novel in History 1895–1920* (London: Routledge, 1993).

Tylee, Clare, ed. *War Plays by Women*. (London: Routledge, 1999).

Van Gunsteren, Julia. *Katherine Mansfield and Literary Impressionism* (Amsterdam:, Rodopi, 1990).

Vannatta, Dennis, ed. *The English Short Story, 1880–1945* (Boston: Twayne, 1985)

Vannatta, Dennis, ed. *The English Short Story, 1945–1980* (Boston: Twayne, 1985).

Walker, Mary. 'Between Fiction and Madness: The Relationship of Women to the Supernatural in Late Victorian Britain'. *That Gentle Strength: Historical Perspectives on Women in Christianity.* Ed. Lynda L. Coon, Katherine J. Haldane and Elisabeth W. Sommer (Charlottesville and London: University Press of Virginia, 1990), 230–42.

Watkins, Susan. *Twentieth-Century Women Novelists: Feminist Theory into Practice* (Basingstoke: Palgrave, 2001).

Watts, Cedric. *Joseph Conrad: A Literary Life* (London: Macmillan, 1989).

Watts, Cedric. *Joseph Conrad* (Plymouth: Northcote House, 1994).

Wedmore, Frederick. 'The Short Story'. *The Nineteenth Century* 43 (1898), 406–16.

Wells, C. T., ed. *Joseph Conrad's Letters to Cunninghame Graham* (Cambridge: Cambridge University Press, 1969).

West, Rebecca. *Ending in Earnest* (New York: Doubleday, 1971).

Williams, Raymond. *The English Novel from Dickens to Lawrence* (London: Hogarth Press, 1985).

Windholz, Anne M. 'The Woman Who Would Be Editor: Ella D'Arcy and the *Yellow Book*', *Victorian Periodicals Review* 29.2 (1996), 116–30.

Wolfreys, Julian and William Baker, eds. *Literary Theories* (London: Macmillan, 1996).

Wood, Jane. *Passion and Pathology in Victorian Fiction* (Oxford: Oxford University Press, 2001).

Woolf, Virginia. *The Letters of Virginia Woolf, 1912–1922*. Ed. Nigel Nicolson (London: Hogarth Press, 1966).

Woolf, Virginia. *A Room of One's Own* (London: Panther, 1984).

Wyatt, Woodrow. *English Story.* 4th series (London: Collins, 1943).

Zipes, Jack. *Fairy Tales and the Art of Subversion: The Classical Genre for Children and the Process of Civilization* (New York: Routledge, 1985).

See also the Story website at www.theshortstory.org.uk for information about and discussion of the contemporary short story.

Index